Out of Obscurity

Out of Obscurity

Mormonism since 1945

Edited by

PATRICK Q. MASON AND
JOHN G. TURNER

OXFORD
UNIVERSITY PRESS

OXFORD
UNIVERSITY PRESS

Oxford University Press is a department of the University of Oxford.
It furthers the University's objective of excellence in research, scholarship,
and education by publishing worldwide. Oxford is a registered trade mark of
Oxford University Press in the UK and certain other countries.

Published in the United States of America by Oxford University Press
198 Madison Avenue, New York, NY 10016, United States of America.

© Oxford University Press 2016

Library of Congress Cataloging-in-Publication Data
Names: Mason, Patrick Q., editor. | Turner, John G., editor.
Title: Out of obscurity : Mormonism since 1945 / edited by Patrick Q. Mason
and John G. Turner.
Description: New York : Oxford University Press, [2016] | ?2016 | Includes index.
Identifiers: LCCN 2016000073| ISBN 978-0-19-935821-2 (cloth : alk. paper) |
ISBN 978-0-1-9935822-9 (pbk. : alk. paper)
Subjects: LCSH: Church of Jesus Christ of Latter-day Saints-History-20th
century. | Church of Jesus Christ of Latter-day Saints-History-21st
century. | Mormon Church-History-20th century. | Mormon
Church-History-21st century. | Mormons-History-20th century. |
Mormons-History-21st century.
Classification: LCC BX8611 .O982 2016 | DDC 289.3/320904-dc23 LC record available at
http://lccn.loc.gov/2016000073

1 3 5 7 9 8 6 4 2
Paperback printed by Webcom, Inc., Canada
Hardback printed by Bridgeport National Bindery, Inc., United States of America

Contents

Contributor Biographies

Matthew Bowman is associate professor of history at Henderson State University. He is the author of *The Mormon People: The Making of an American Faith* (2012) and *The Urban Pulpit: New York City and the Fate of Liberal Evangelicalism* (2014).

Rebecca de Schweinitz is associate professor of history at Brigham Young University. She received her PhD from the University of Virginia and has been a fellow at Yale's Gilder Lehrman Center. A founding member of the Society for the History of Children and Youth, she is the author of *If We Could Change the World: Young People and America's Long Struggle for Racial Equality* (2009).

Kristine Haglund holds degrees in German studies and German literature from Harvard and the University of Michigan. Her research interests include gender and religion, Mormon women's and children's history, and religious publications in new media. She is the former editor of *Dialogue: A Journal of Mormon Thought*.

J. B. Haws is assistant professor of church history at Brigham Young University and is the author of *The Mormon Image in the American Mind: Fifty Years of Public Perception* (2013). He has a PhD in American history from the University of Utah, and he and his wife, Laura, live with their four children in Provo, Utah.

Amanda Hendrix-Komoto is assistant professor in the History and Philosophy Department at Montana State University. She has written articles on the intersections of colonialism, gender, and race in Mormon missionary work. She is currently revising her dissertation, "Imperial Zions: Mormons, Polygamy, and the Politics of Domesticity in the Nineteenth Century," into a book manuscript.

Kate Holbrook holds a PhD in religious studies from Boston University and is a specialist in women's history at the LDS Church History Department. She is coeditor of *The First Fifty Years of Relief Society: Key Documents in Latter-day Saint Women's History* (2016) and *Women and Mormonism: Historical and Contemporary Perspectives* (2016).

Caroline Kline is a PhD candidate in religion at Claremont Graduate University. Her areas of interest are Mormon women, gender theory, and theology. She is the coeditor of *Mormon Women Have Their Say: Essays from the Claremont Oral History Collection* (2013) and has been published in the journal *Feminist Theology*.

James Dennis LoRusso is a research fellow in the Center for the Study of Religion at Princeton University. He completed his PhD in American religious cultures at Emory University. His research examines how governments, markets, businesses, and workplaces are entangled with the history of religion in the United States.

Patrick Q. Mason is Howard W. Hunter Chair of Mormon Studies and associate professor of American religious history at Claremont Graduate University. He is the author of *The Mormon Menace: Violence and Anti-Mormonism in the Postbellum South* (2011), and editor of *Directions for Mormon Studies in the 21st Century* (2016).

Max Perry Mueller is an assistant professor of American religion in the Department of Classics and Religious Studies at the University of Nebraska–Lincoln. He holds a PhD in the study of religion from Harvard University. He is also cofounder and contributing editor of *Religion & Politics*, the online journal of the John C. Danforth Center on Religion & Politics at Washington University in St. Louis.

Nathan B. Oman is Tazewell Taylor Research Professor at William and Mary Law School. He earned his JD, *cum laude,* from Harvard Law School, where he served on the Articles Committee of the *Harvard Law Review* and as an editor of the *Harvard Journal of Law and Public Policy.* After law school, he clerked for the Honorable Morris Shepard Arnold of the US Court of Appeals for the Eighth Circuit and worked as a litigation associate in the Washington, DC office of Sidley Austin, LLP.

Sara M. Patterson teaches courses in theological studies, history of Christianity, and religion in the Americas at Hanover College. Patterson's research investigates the intersections of religious experience, place, and community. She is coeditor, with Fay Botham, of *Race, Religion, Region: Landscapes of Encounter in the American West* (2005). More recently, she is the author of *Middle of Nowhere: Religion, Art, and Pop Culture at Salvation Mountain* (2016).

Taunalyn F. Rutherford is a PhD candidate in religion at Claremont Graduate University, where she was the recipient of the Robert L. Millet Fellowship in

Mormon Studies as well as the CGU-Tanner Center Summer Dissertation Fellowship. She is currently an adjunct instructor in religious education at Brigham Young University.

John G. Turner teaches at George Mason University. He is the author most recently of *The Mormon Jesus: A Biography* (2016) and *Brigham Young: Pioneer Prophet* (2012).

Neil J. Young is an independent historian and the author of *We Gather Together: The Religious Right and the Problem of Interfaith Politics* (2016). He has taught at Princeton University and Columbia University. He is cohost of the history podcast *Past Present*.

Out of Obscurity

Introduction

Patrick Q. Mason

WE KNOW THE story. Joseph Smith has some visions and revelations. He translates the Book of Mormon from gold plates he found in a hill. Mormonism is born. Then: persecution, pioneers, polygamy. Polygamy ends (mostly), and Mormons become mainstream (mostly). Then: Mitt Romney, Prop 8, and *The Book of Mormon* musical. That, in a nutshell, is the story of Mormonism.

This narrative is not so much incorrect as incomplete. No religion's history, even if it is less than two hundred years old, can be neatly summarized in fifty words or less. Nevertheless, this skeletal outline probably reflects the outer limits of knowledge about Mormon history not only for the general public (if they even know that much) but also for many scholars, even scholars of religion. On some level this is to be expected, as asking most people (including scholars) to say everything they know about other significant modern religions such as Bahaism or Caodaism may yield even less than fifty words.

While religious illiteracy remains a problem not fully addressed by primary or secondary education, what is equally telling about the above encapsulation of Mormon history is that in caricatured fashion, it more or less reflects the state of Mormon studies scholarship. There has been an avalanche of quality academic publications about Mormonism in recent years, corresponding with the emergence of the Church of Jesus Christ of Latter-day Saints (LDS) as a subject of considerable cultural intrigue, political debate, and scholarly interest. The vast majority of those publications understandably deal with either Mormonism's nineteenth-century origins and early development or with the religion's intersections with contemporary politics and culture. As a result of decades of prodigious research, we know a great deal about the first seventy years of Mormon history (1820–1890), from the time that Joseph Smith had his first vision of God to the year that the LDS Church originally announced the end of plural marriage. Scholarship on Joseph Smith and early Mormonism has proliferated and matured, while the development of Mormon theology and ritual, anti-Mormonism, the early history of Mormon settlement in Utah, and polygamy have also received sustained and increasingly sophisticated scholarly attention.

While this scholarship has brought about a much richer appreciation of Mormonism's nineteenth-century history, comparably few resources exist to help readers understand the growth and evolution of Mormonism in recent decades. With the exception of a handful of excellent treatments of Mormonism's period of transition and assimilation in the late nineteenth and early twentieth centuries, scholars have spent comparatively little time examining what became of Mormonism once it moved, in sociological terms, from sect to church.[1] The most significant interpretation of twentieth-century Mormonism is sociologist Armand Mauss's 1994 book *The Angel and the Beehive: The Mormon Struggle with Assimilation*. Mauss traces the development of Mormonism from its highly assimilative phase in the early decades of the twentieth century to a postwar position he calls "retrenchment," which was characterized by increased centralization and bureaucratization, a renewed emphasis on obedience to priesthood authority, and a heightened effort at conservatively inflected religious indoctrination and proselytization.[2] Institutional developments in postwar Mormonism have been capably examined through the lens of biographies of two presidents of the LDS Church, David O. McKay and Spencer W. Kimball.[3] Taking somewhat more of a "lived religion" approach, Claudia Bushman helpfully introduces readers to the everyday lives and practices of contemporary Mormons, giving an overview of issues facing Mormons and Mormonism in the modern world.[4] Topical treatments, such as Martha Bradley's examination of Mormonism's complicated relationship with second-wave feminism and the women's rights movement, or J. B. Haws's history of the dramatic transformation in the American public's understanding of Mormons and Mormonism, are insightful but rare.[5]

---

1. The proceedings of a Brigham Young University symposium that sought to understand twentieth-century Mormonism from a distinctively LDS perspective were published as *Out of Obscurity : The Church in the Twentieth-Century* (Salt Lake City: Deseret Book, 2000). On Mormonism's transition period from 1890–1930, see Thomas G. Alexander, *Mormonism in Transition: A History of the Latter-day Saints, 1890–1930* (Urbana: University of Illinois Press, 1986); Ethan R. Yorgason, *Transformation of the Mormon Culture Region* (Urbana: University of Illinois Press, 2003); and Kathleen Flake, *The Politics of American Religious Identity: The Seating of Senator Reed Smoot, Mormon Apostle* (Chapel Hill: University of North Carolina Press, 2004).

2. Armand L. Mauss, *The Angel and the Beehive: The Mormon Struggle with Assimilation* (Urbana: University of Illinois Press, 1994). Mauss updated and reassessed his arguments in "Rethinking Retrenchment: Course Corrections in the Ongoing Campaign for Respectability," *Dialogue: A Journal of Mormon Thought* 44 (Winter 2011): 1–42.

3. Gregory Prince and Wm. Robert Wright, *David O. McKay and the Rise of Modern Mormonism* (Salt Lake City: University of Utah Press, 2005); and Edward Kimball, *Lengthen Your Stride: The Presidency of Spencer W. Kimball* (Salt Lake City: Deseret Book Company, 2005).

4. Claudia L. Bushman, *Contemporary Mormonism: Latter-day Saints in Modern America* (Lanham, MD: Rowman & Littlefield, 2008).

5. Martha S. Bradley, *Pedestals and Podiums: Utah Women, Religious Authority, and Equal Rights* (Salt Lake City: Signature Books, 2005); J. B. Haws, *The Mormon Image in the American Mind: Fifty Years of Public Perception* (New York: Oxford University Press, 2013).

These fine accounts notwithstanding, we need more robust, multifaceted, and analytical accounts of Mormonism in the period of its greatest growth, acceptance, and success as an increasingly global church. Though organized in 1830, the LDS Church did not reach the 1 million-member mark until after the end of World War II, in 1947. Mormonism then experienced a postwar boom, with membership growing exponentially. The church reached 2 million members in 1963, then 3 million in 1971, followed by a pattern of about a million new members added every three years or so, culminating in a claimed global membership of around 15 million in 2015.[6] There are many reasons for Mormon growth since the mid-twentieth century. One important factor is the Mormon birth rate, which has consistently remained higher than national averages and has ensured long-term growth and multigenerational stability.[7]

Natural growth has been only part of the equation, however, as the majority of expansion in the second half of the century came by way of new converts. A number of structural factors contributed to this proselytizing success. The LDS Church reversed its nineteenth-century policy of encouraging all converts to "gather to Zion," and now told people to "build Zion" where they lived, meaning that local members in wards and stakes around the globe took greater responsibility for and were more personally invested in local church growth. This was supplemented by a dramatic increase in the number of full-time proselytizing missionaries sent out by the church, spurred by prophetic proclamations that missionary work was every male priesthood holder's duty and oft-repeated slogans such as "every member a missionary." The establishment of Mormon centers of strength beyond the American Intermountain West meant that the church began investing in infrastructure in those areas, first by building chapels and then temples, thus meaning that members no longer had to travel to Utah to participate in the religion's most sacred rites, including marriage for all eternity.

The LDS Church also benefited, along with American evangelical foreign missions, from riding the wave of postwar American political, military,

---

6. "Growth of the Church," *Newsroom*, www.mormonnewsroom.org/topic/church-growth. Growth has lagged somewhat in recent years, and the number of people who self-identify as Mormon and actively attend church services is probably between a third to a half of the official membership total.

7. See Tim B. Heaton, "Vital Statistics," in James T. Duke, ed., *Latter-day Saint Social Life: Social Research on the LDS Church and its Members* (Provo: Religious Studies Center, 1998), 105–132; Tim B. Heaton, "Religious Influences on Mormon Fertility: Cross-National Comparisons," in James T. Duke, ed., *Latter-day Saint Social Life: Social Research on the LDS Church and its Members*, 425–440. A 2008 study by the US Census Bureau found that Utah had the highest birth rate in the nation, with 81 children born for every one thousand women, compared to the national average of fifty-eight. See "Utah Fertility Rate Tops the US Charts," *Deseret News*, November 7, 2010, www.deseretnews.com/article/700079435/Utah-fertility-rate-tops-the-US-charts.html.

and cultural influence. Just as Anglo-American Protestantism had expanded internationally in the wake of the British Empire in the eighteenth and nineteenth centuries, so did American religious groups, including Mormonism, in the twentieth. Indeed, many international branches of the church were established in order to service American Mormons stationed abroad with the military, foreign service, or international corporations, and then grew when those expatriates succeeded in meeting and converting locals. The church's close association with American power and identity proved to be a double-edged sword, particularly in the wake of decolonization and growing resentment of the United States' global hegemony. In recent decades, the church has had difficulty establishing itself in countries where the United States has poor diplomatic relations or where Americans are viewed with suspicion.[8]

While this steady and sometimes explosive growth thrilled many Latter-day Saints, it also reshaped the church and presented new institutional challenges. The majority of church members today are first-generation converts, and well over 90 percent of all Mormons in the entire history of the movement came into the church after World War II. Presuming the normativity of the nineteenth-century Mormon experience is parallel to reducing all Islam to seventh-century Arabia or Christianity to the eastern Mediterranean world of the first century. Mormonism can no more be understood in all its richness and complexity by an exclusive focus on its founding years than can any other religion; indeed, the theological, cultural, and political development of Mormonism did not stop when polygamy ended.

In its first century the LDS Church was concerned primarily with self-definition and survival. In its second century, however, it has faced a different set of challenges attendant to growth, internationalization, and modernization. While the church's internal discourse is often one of unity, harmony, and ahistorical steadiness, Mormonism is a diverse and dynamic tradition. Operating within history, Mormonism's development has been shaped by a variety of factors, including overarching religious structures, shifts in culture, and the decisions of leaders and members alike. This volume acknowledges the postwar period as the era of Mormonism's remarkable expansion without being held captive, as the church's official histories and some scholars' accounts have been, by a triumphant and teleological narrative of growth.[9] Rather, the religion's impressive emergence as a notable force in

---

8. For an encyclopedic overview of international Mormonism, see David G. Stewart Jr. and Matthew Martinich, *Reaching the Nations: International LDS Church Growth Almanac*, 2014 *Edition*, 2 vols. (Henderson, NV: Cumorah Foundation, 2013). See also Brandon S. Plewe, ed., *Mapping Mormonism: An Atlas of Latter-day Saint History*, 2nd ed. (Provo: BYU Studies, 2014).

9. The research of sociologist Rodney Stark, predicting that there may be as many as 265 million Mormons worldwide by the year 2080, has often by cited by Mormon scholars and leaders, no doubt to lend a sense of legitimacy and import to the movement. The orig-

American if not quite yet global culture becomes the canvas upon which the scholars in this volume conduct their studies, not the focus of analysis itself.

In short, post-1945 Mormonism has a history—a story with compelling characters, conflicts, and change. There was not a straight line, or a jump in time, from the achievement of Utah statehood to Mitt Romney's candidacy for the presidency. Twenty-first-century Mormonism cannot be fully explained, let alone reduced to, its nineteenth-century antecedents. Furthermore, just as scholars have gravitated to early Mormonism in large part because it provides such a rich proving ground for the study of nineteenth-century American religion, a closer examination of postwar Mormonism will help us better understand some of the unique aspects of religious history in the era of America's global ascendance. A study of Mormonism since 1945 gives insight into religion in a modern age of mass industrialization, near-universal literacy, urbanization and suburbanization, shifting norms of gender and sexuality, civil rights and youth movements, corporatization, globalization, Americanization, and technological revolutions.

Out of Obscurity is an attempt to shine a brighter light on Mormonism's modern period. Our goal is less to provide complete coverage of Mormonism since 1945—it would be impossible to do so in one volume—than to trace important developments and chart out fruitful lines of further inquiry. Indeed, one of the purposes of this book is to suggest broad narratives, historiographical trends, and conceptual frameworks within which to place recent and contemporary Mormonism. The authors also explore ways that modern Mormonism adds to or challenges our understandings of broader cultural and religious norms. In particular, this volume reflects on questions such as: How did an American-based religion seeking to present a standardized theology and experience export itself to other cultures, and to what extent has internationalization affected Mormonism in the United States? In what ways did Mormonism adopt new racial norms and codes as civil rights groups applied increasing pressure in the 1960s and 1970s, and as the religion expanded beyond the Intermountain West? How has the greater political prominence of Mormonism and its adherents affected the internal and external dynamics of the religion? In what ways have shifting discourses of gender and sexuality transformed LDS Church doctrine and culture and served to provide new boundaries of a distinctive, if sometimes contested, Mormon identity? How are boundaries maintained by a church that, especially in recent years, has prized cultural acceptance and international growth?

---

inal article was Rodney Stark, "The Rise of a New World Faith," *Review of Religious Research* 26, no. 1 (September 1984): 18–27; see also Rodney Stark, *The Rise of Mormonism,* ed. Reid L. Neilson (New York: Columbia University Press, 2005).

Because we wanted innovative inquiries into hitherto unexplored areas, as editors we assembled a team of authors who would contribute fresh, previously unpublished essays based upon original research. While also including some seasoned veterans, this collection deliberately features some of the brightest emerging scholars working in Mormon studies today. As a rule, Mormon studies has become increasingly interdisciplinary and consciously integrated in and influenced by broader fields of study, thus distinguishing its practitioners from a previous generation of scholars engaged in what was known as the "New Mormon History."[10] A historical approach remains dominant here, but the volume, and many of the individual chapters, reflects the heightened interdisciplinarity of both historical studies and Mormon studies. The essays herein draw on and contribute to fields, theories, and methods as diverse as American history, religious studies, legal studies, theology, gender studies, racial theory, postcolonialism, ethnography, and childhood studies.

The chapters here are arranged thematically, clustered in four general areas focusing on internationalization, political culture, gender, and religious culture. Several of the essays bridge these categories, demonstrating that most topics are too complex to be reduced to one single line of analysis. While the United States is the primary site of inquiry, several chapters understand the development of modern Mormonism within a broader, international context. Many churches trace their historical and theological lineage back to Joseph Smith, but our focus here is on the Church of Jesus Christ of Latter-day Saints, headquartered in Salt Lake City, Utah, which was by far the largest and most influential institutional manifestation of Mormonism throughout the twentieth century and into the twenty-first. For our purposes here, then, the term "Mormonism" is equated with the LDS Church and "Mormons" with that church's members, even while recognizing that we are excluding related groups such as the Community of Christ (formerly the Reorganized Church of Jesus Christ of Latter Day Saints) and the Fundamentalist Church of Jesus Christ of Latter-Day Saints (best known for its continued practice of polygamy). Though sharing common origins, these churches have followed unique paths

---

10. For an illustrative sampling of this previous generation of scholarship, much of which still holds up, see D. Michael Quinn, ed., *The New Mormon History: Revisionist Essays on the Past* (Salt Lake City: Signature Books, 1992). For an overview of developments within the writing of Mormon history, leading up to the emergence of Mormon studies, see Ronald Walker, David J. Whittaker, and James B. Allen, *Mormon History* (Urbana: University of Illinois Press, 2001). For an overview of and sampling of Mormon studies scholarship, see Blair Dee Hodges, "Mormon Studies: A Bibliographic Essay," *Mormon Studies Review* 1 (2014): 223–235; Quincy D. Newell and Eric F. Mason, eds., *New Perspectives in Mormon Studies: Creating and Crossing Boundaries* (Norman: University of Oklahoma Press, 2013); Stephen C. Taysom, ed., *Dimensions of Faith: A Mormon Studies Reader* (Salt Lake City: Signature Books, 2013); and Patrick Q. Mason, ed., *Directions for Mormon Studies in the Twenty-First Century* (Salt Lake City: University of Utah Press, 2016).

to the point that their differences substantially overshadow most similarities, thus rendering anything but an explicitly comparative study unwieldy.

With the majority of Latter-day Saints now living outside the United States (as of early 2015, some 8.7 million out of 15.1 million, or about 54 percent), *Out of Obscurity* begins with a consideration of what, exactly, this means—for Mormonism, and for the export of American religion into diverse national and regional cultures. Legal scholar Nathan Oman considers how Mormonism's international expansion has affected its own theology, in particular its theology of the state. He traces how nineteenth-century Mormon "theodemocracy," which was often one of the points of conflict between Latter-day Saints and the US government, has morphed into a nonconfrontational, quietist discourse emphasizing civic obedience and compliance with a wide range of political–legal systems, including those of nondemocratic states. Accommodations to a pluralistic international legal environment in countries from Nigeria to the Soviet Union to China has thus transformed Mormon political theology just as surely as did the church's confrontational relationship with the nineteenth-century American legal regime. Taunalyn Rutherford then follows with an analysis of Mormon internationalization on the ground, focusing her analysis on a case study of India. Employing oral history and ethnographic research, she offers insights on how LDS missiology responds to local context, the challenge of engaging with deep religious pluralism, the obstacles associated with operating in postcolonial settings, and the question of Mormonism's ability to translate and adapt to different cultures.

Even as the LDS Church was experiencing unprecedented international expansion in the decades since World War II, some of Mormonism's most important developments and conflicts came in the context of postwar American political culture. One of the fruits of Mormon assimilation into the American mainstream was greater representation and influence in the government, not just in local and state politics in the Intermountain West but at the federal level as well. We need look no further than the leadership of the 114th Congress, commencing in January 2015, in which Orrin Hatch, the senior Republican Senator, served as the President Pro Tempore of the Senate, and Hatch's fellow Mormon Harry Reid served as Senate Minority Leader and Democratic Caucus Chair. To date, the highest-ranking Mormon to serve in the federal government has been Ezra Taft Benson, who was Secretary of Agriculture for all eight years of the Eisenhower administration (1953–1961) while at the same time serving as a member of the LDS Church's Quorum of the Twelve Apostles. In my chapter I demonstrate that Benson, an ardent and outspoken political and economic conservative who would become LDS Church president and prophet in 1985, consistently deployed the Book of Mormon in speaking to Latter-day Saints about American exceptionalism, political freedom, and "secret combinations," which he typically identified with international communism. Used surprisingly lightly throughout most of Mormon history, the Book of Mormon became elevated to its current place of prominence due in large part to Benson's prophetic insistence. Though his particular interpretation of the Book of Mormon has undergone revisions, Benson was a key architect of modern Mormon conservatism.

Just as Benson's theology in many ways reflected American Cold War anxieties, the cases of two other prominent Mormon politicians, the father–son pair of George and Mitt Romney, similarly reflect developments in American religion and politics in their respective eras. J. B. Haws demonstrates that George Romney's religiosity was generally seen as an asset in his run for the presidency in 1964, betokening an era given to ecumenism and public piety. When Mitt Romney ran for the presidency in 2008 and 2012, on the other hand, he did so in the context of pronounced evangelical Protestant suspicion of Mormonism even as the two groups generally associated together in the conservative wing of the Republican Party, and in the wake of accusations that the LDS Church was racist and anti-feminist. The fact that evangelicals, despite much handwringing, voted for Mitt Romney at the same rate that they had for George W. Bush—as did Mormons—but nevertheless were unable to elect him president suggests not the strength but rather the weakening power of the Religious Right in the twenty-first-century electorate. Both Romneys, George and Mitt, originally rose to prominence as successful businessmen, providing evidence for many observers, both within and without the church, about Mormonism's particular friendliness toward capitalism. James Dennis LoRusso questions this assumption of innate affinity, arguing instead that the strong alliance between Mormonism and free enterprise developed in the mid-twentieth-century as the result of conscious decisions by church leaders in reaction to the expansion of the American welfare state beginning with the New Deal. Contrasting the cooperative economic values of nineteenth-century Mormonism with the wholehearted embrace of capitalism and business culture, LoRusso demonstrates that beginning in the mid-1930s LDS economic thought was both a reaction to an interventionist federal government, which the Mormons had good reason to be suspicious of given their own history, and part of the broader effort to assimilate mainstream American values and norms. Fully embracing free enterprise was both an ideological and pragmatic move that allowed Mormons to gain acceptance and maximize their chances at personal and proselytizing success in postwar American culture.

Nothing has shaped American politics since World War II more than the battles over equal rights for African Americans, women, and LGBT individuals. In all three cases the LDS Church found itself the subject of criticism from more progressive elements of the culture. Max Mueller rehearses how in the 1960s the NAACP and its allies targeted the church with protests and the threat of protests at Temple Square—not only the seat of LDS governance but the center of the Mormon imagination as well. While alternatingly resistant to and accommodating of civil rights' groups demands, the church developed a pattern of asserting its own constitutional rights of religious liberty and free speech, employing the rhetoric of religious intolerance and even persecution to describe those who complained of its unique theological views. Many of the rhetorical and strategic patterns established in the 1960s remain in effect today, as Neil Young reveals in his chapter tracing Mormon involvement in the politics of same-sex marriage from the 1970s onward. Carefully tracing both continuity and change in the church's theological, pastoral, and tactical positions over the course of four decades, Young also shows how the church's gradually softening stance toward gays and in favor of greater civil rights for the LGBT community differentiates it from some conservative religious allies.

Pressures related to changing discourses of gender and sexuality were not coming only from outside the church. Indeed, arguably no other issue has roiled Mormonism or provoked more internal discussion in recent decades. This has been reflected in everything from modesty standards to changing notions of women's and men's roles in the home to competing discourses by self-identifying feminist and nonfeminist Mormon women in blogs and other social media. Amanda Hendrix-Komoto reveals some of the stark tensions in Mormon discourses of gender and sexuality by tracing the conflict between LDS norms of modesty and the church's establishment of the Polynesian Cultural Center in Hawaii, where students were hired to entertain tourists in native costumes that would have been deemed unsuitable and even scandalous for white Mormon students or in other contexts. Charges of colonialism and hypocrisy were countered, however, by many of the local participants who saw the center as an invaluable means of retaining and reclaiming their ancient religious and cultural heritage, all with the blessing of the church. Kate Holbrook identifies another battlefront in the gender wars in the more prosaic world of women's housework. Examining LDS women's prescriptive literature and an analysis of the aesthetic and architecture of the Relief Society building, completed just as second-wave feminism was gaining momentum nationwide, she shows how Mormon leaders, female and male, defended separate spheres and critiqued modern feminism even before the divisive debates over the Equal Rights Amendment.

Increasingly sensitive in a feminist era to charges of patriarchy, LDS Church leaders have gradually softened language and imagery related to male headship within the family. As Caroline Kline shows, Mormon discourse has in recent decades evolved from a distinctly complementarian position, in which men were expected to provide leadership in the home by virtue of their ordination to the priesthood, to a more egalitarian position with both spouses supporting and helping one another as equal partners and coleaders. Mormon feminists have actively participated in and shaped this changing discourse, though they too range from more complementarian to critical positions. Kline suggests that increased male participation in the home means that Mormon gender norms will continue to evolve, with lived experience perhaps outpacing and thus conditioning formal theological articulations. The advent of the Internet has offered new venues and opportunities for Mormons to voice their deeply held convictions that previously were able to find expression only in their homes and local wards. The importance of online community for the development of a reenergized Mormon feminist community has been widely noted. But especially after the church leadership gave its blessing, more conservative Mormon women have also become active bloggers. Kristine Haglund particularly examines the genre of "Mormon mommy blogs," where traditionalist Mormon women reify their allegiance to the church, proudly display their orthodoxy and orthopraxis, and challenge liberal feminist values and assumptions. As shown in the often contentious divide between feminist and nonfeminist Mormon women's blogs, the Internet facilitates the self-selecting of community and thus challenges the traditional Mormon social cohesion developed through personal interactions in geographically defined wards.

Mormonism is, of course, more than a political or social movement—it is a religion, a church with distinctive doctrines, sacred spaces, rituals, and other practices. The final cluster of essays thus deal with developments in Mormon religious culture over the past seven decades. Although it can be overstated, one of the striking transformations in modern Mormonism has been its more intentional and explicit Christocentrism—evidenced no more clearly than by the fact that in 1982 the LDS Church officially added a subtitle to the Book of Mormon: "Another Testament of Jesus Christ." By the early twenty-first century, growing numbers of Latter-day Saints talked about their "relationship with Jesus" in ways as distinct from their predecessors as they were congruent with contemporary evangelicals—for whom this Mormon Christocentric turn proved simultaneously welcome and vexing. Ironically, as Matthew Bowman shows, at the very time that Mormons were becoming more Christocentric and certain LDS leaders were making theological arguments similar to evangelicalism, many evangelicals actively denounced Mormonism as a cult, and a particularly dangerous one at that precisely because of its increased public image otherwise. Despite their theological misgivings, evangelicals' embrace of Mitt Romney showed them coming back to the position taken by midcentury Protestant liberals, namely that civic cooperation was not predicated upon theological orthodoxy.

With religious identities destabilized across the country beginning with the cultural revolutions of the 1960s, Mormons have made herculean efforts to retain young people and forge a meaningful Mormon identity. In addressing the "youth crisis" of the 1960s and 1970s, Rebecca de Schweinitz shows, LDS leaders adopted the broader culture's language of freedom, choice, and authenticity, redeploying them to keep a hold of rather than lose Mormon youth while inculcating even stricter standards in response to the counterculture. Mormon youth were told they were part of a "chosen generation" with an essential role in the salvation of the world, at the same time that they were instructed to obey their parents and authorities and work within the framework of the church under adult direction. Especially since the 1997 sesquicentennial of the Mormon pioneers' entry into the Salt Lake Valley, one of the chief means used to forge a unique Mormon identity have been handcart reenactments performed by adults and youth alike, not just in the Intermountain West but in far-flung international locales as well. Sara Patterson considers the meaning of pioneer pilgrimages and reenactments in Mormon character development and the affirmation of prophetic authority. By spiritualizing and recreating the westward pioneer trek, Latter-day Saints ritually claimed the mythic virtues of the American West as an integral part of their religious heritage.

As much as the Latter-day Saints reenact their past and honor their ancestors, history also remains a vexing subject for the church. Beginning with the publication of Fawn Brodie's bestselling critical biography of Joseph Smith, and then accelerating when employees in the Church Historical Department began writing articles and books using modern historical methods, church leaders struggled to respond to scholarship that critically examined Mormon pieties about the church's nineteenth-century history. John Turner examines how the church has oscillated between defensive and more open postures toward the critical study of Mormon history, contending that Latter-day Saint conflicts over history resemble evangelical battles over scriptural inerrancy in their centrality for Mormon religious authority and in their resistance to easy or lasting resolution.

Even after the end of the Romney-fueled "Mormon moment," few religious organizations in the United States receive as much attention as the Church of Jesus Christ of Latter-day Saints—this despite the fact that it constitutes a mere 2 percent of the national population. It seems that hardly a week passes in which the *New York Times* or another major news outlet does not give space to a significant story on Mormonism: the church's treatment of theological and political dissidents, the place of women within the church, the church's stance toward homosexuality, or even church-owned Brigham Young University's policy regarding male grooming standards. If news headlines and Broadway musical tickets sold are any indication, Mormonism today is anything but obscure. The essays in this volume help us better understand how this came to pass.

PART I

Internationalization

1

International Legal Experience
and the Mormon Theology of
the State, 1945–2012

Nathan B. Oman

ON SEPTEMBER 2, 1945 the Empire of Japan formally surrendered to the United States, ending World War II. That same month, the First Presidency of the Church of Jesus Christ of Latter-day Saints began calling men to serve as mission presidents.[1] Beginning in 1939, the church shut down its overseas missions and recalled American Mormons serving as missionaries back to the United States. As war spread across the globe, the American government exercised extensive control over the US economy, imposing rationing and labor controls. Not surprisingly, religious proselytizing was far down on the wartime government's list of priorities, and the LDS Church ceased virtually all formal missionary work.[2] The mission presidents sent forth by the First Presidency in September 1945 helped create a very different kind of Mormonism than that which had existed before World War II. In 1945 there were roughly 980,000 Mormons, living mainly in the Intermountain West. Taking advantage of the Pax Americana wrought by the United States' victory and the tense stability of the Cold War, the LDS Church established itself as a global institution. By 2013, the church claimed more than 15 million baptized members, the majority living outside of the United States.

President George Albert Smith pointed toward the church's postwar emphasis on international growth in December 1947. In a front-page *Church News* editorial, he stated, "I assure every man and woman of the Church that you have a great obligation to spread the word of the Lord abroad and to carry the truth to every land and clime so that the power of the Priesthood will be made manifest among our Father's children in many places where it has

---

1. *Church Almanac 2013* (Salt Lake City: Deseret Book Company, 2012), 315.

2. James B. Allen and Glen M. Leonard, *The Story of the Latter-day Saints* (Salt Lake City: Deseret Book Company, 1992), 536–537.

never yet even been heard of."[3] In the succeeding decades Mormons would carry out this injunction by expanding the scope of missionary work, establishing the church in dozens of countries where it had never previously functioned. This expansion, however, transformed the LDS Church both institutionally and ideologically. Twenty years after Smith's 1947 editorial, Elder Franklin D. Richards remarked, "We are now twenty years into this new era of growth and development, and growth and development mean change. We must not resist change, as we believe that God 'will yet reveal many great and important things pertaining to the Kingdom of God.'"[4]

As the LDS Church expanded into new regions of the globe it confronted non-American legal systems. Some of these new legal environments were quite similar to the United States, while others were very different. All of them placed pressure on the church and affected the development of Mormon discourse in the last half of the twentieth century. In particular, international legal challenges created incentives that moderated Mormon theologies of the state. By the turn of the twenty-first century the dominant theology of the state in Mormon discourse was quietist and nonconfrontational, a marked contrast from the theodemocratic ambitions of the nineteenth century or the Cold War apocalypticism popular among many Mormons in the middle of the twentieth century. Just as law proved decisive in the development of Mormon belief and practice in the nineteenth century—particularly Mormon doctrines surrounding plural marriage—in the twentieth century law again exerted its influence on Mormon teachings.

International Legal Obstacles

As the Church of Jesus Christ of Latter-day Saints expanded beyond the United States it dealt with many legal challenges. Broadly speaking, these fell into four categories. First, it faced restrictions on missionaries' and general authorities' ability to enter countries, most commonly in the form of visa restrictions. Second, it faced laws limiting missionaries' ability to proselytize. Third, it faced laws restricting church members from meeting and worshiping together. Finally, it faced challenges in acquiring and owning property for church buildings.

Among the first steps in establishing the LDS Church in a new country was for missionaries and church leaders to enter the country. This was often preceded by the baptism of a national abroad who then assisted the church's initial access to a country or Latter-day Saint expatriates who introduced

---

3. George Albert Smith, "Looking Ahead: Into a New Century of Growth and Development," *The Church News*, December 20, 1947.

4. Franklin D. Richards, "Looking Ahead," *Conference Report*, October 1967, 146.

Mormonism to the country.[5] Governments, however, often restricted access by foreign missionaries. For example, in 1963 the church sought to establish a mission in Nigeria to serve self-proclaimed Mormon congregations that had formed after reading materials about the church and its doctrines. The effort was blocked, however, when the Nigerian government refused to issue visas to the assigned mission president.[6] During the Cold War the LDS Church was unable to send missionaries to most of the nations behind the Iron Curtain, although there were notable exceptions—Poland and the German Democratic Republic—as well as sporadic visits by church authorities.[7] Some governments only allowed missionaries to visit on short-term tourist visas or required local citizens to formally invite missionaries into the country. In the 1990s, for example, Russian converts frequently spent hours waiting in long lines to fill out the paperwork necessary to formally invite foreign missionaries into the country.[8]

In some instances governments expelled missionaries after previously allowing them. In 1946, the church sent missionaries into Czechoslovakia to reestablish missionary work in that country. After a communist coup in 1948, however, the secret police began monitoring missionaries, and in 1950 two missionaries were arrested and imprisoned for a month on suspicion of espionage. The government passed a law banning non-Czech pastors and all American missionaries were withdrawn after the release of the two imprisoned elders.[9] Similarly, Mormon missionaries were expelled from Ghana by the government in 1989, although foreign LDS missionaries were allowed back into the country

---

5. For example, the first missionaries to enter Slovenia, which declared independence from Yugoslavia in 1991, were aided by Albin Lotric, a Slovenian national who had joined the Church in Norway. Jeffery G. Moore oral history interview, interview by Jeff Anderson, November 22, 1991, transcript, Church History Library, Salt Lake City, Utah.

6. Gregory A. Prince and Wm. Robert Wright, *David O. McKay and the Rise of Modern Mormonism* (Salt Lake City: University of Utah Press, 2005), 81–94; James B. Allen, "Would-Be Saints: West Africa Before the 1978 Priesthood Revelation," *Journal of Mormon History* 17 (January 1991): 207–247. The Nigerian government's refusal came during the era when the LDS Church still banned black men from receiving priesthood ordination, and black men and women from entering its temples.

7. Raymond M. Kuehne, *Mormons as Citizens of a Communist State: A Documentary History of the Church of Jesus Christ of Latter-Day Saints in East Germany, 1945–1990* (Salt Lake City: University of Utah Press, 2010), 331–334; Kahlile Mehr, "An LDS International Trio, 1974–97," *Journal of Mormon History* 25 (October 1, 1999): 107, 112. In the 1978, the church also sent missionaries into Yugoslavia. They arrived on student visas and could answer questions but not openly proselytize. They wore ordinary clothes and grew their hair to shoulder length to avoid drawing undue attention.

8. Gary Browning, "Out of Obscurity: The Emergence of The Church of Jesus Christ of Latter-Day Saints in 'That Vast Empire' of Russia," *BYU Studies* 33, no. 4 (1993): 678.

9. Kahlile Mehr, "Enduring Believers: Czechoslovakia and the LDS Church, 1884–1990," *Journal of Mormon History* 18 (October 1, 1992): 140–141.

a year later.[10] In other cases, visas have been so difficult to obtain that the church has simply withdrawn non-native missionaries. This happened in 2005, for example, when the church withdrew over two hundred missionaries from Venezuela as a result of actions by the government of Hugo Chavez.[11]

Second, the LDS Church has faced restrictions on missionaries' ability to openly proselytize. For example, the church obtained permission to send missionaries to Poland and Yugoslavia in the 1970s, but the government would not allow them to proselytize.[12] More recently the church called missionaries to work among members in Israel, many of whom are Eastern European guest workers and European and North American expatriates, but the church does not allow them to proselytize.[13] The situation in Israel illustrates the complex relationship between legal and other pressures on the church. The Israeli Supreme Court has recognized a basic right to religious conversion, and religious proselytizing is legal under Israeli law, subject to various restrictions.[14] Beginning in 1979, however, Brigham Young University sought to build a study abroad center in Jerusalem. The building became controversial in Israel, with conservative groups opposing construction and claiming it was part of a broader effort to evangelize Jews to Mormonism. The Interior Committee of the Knesset, Israel's parliament, took up the issue and demanded a pledge from the church not to proselytize as a condition for being allowed to build the center. The Mormons agreed, and in 1985 Jeffrey R. Holland, then president of Brigham Young University, promised on behalf of the LDS Church that Mormons in Israel would refrain from proselytizing, regardless of Israeli law.[15]

---

10. Emmanuel A Kissi, *Walking in the Sand: A History of the Church of Jesus Christ of Latter-Day Saints in Ghana*, ed. Matthew K Heiss (Provo: Brigham Young University Press, 2004), 200.

11. United States Commission on International Religious Freedom, *Annual Report* 2009 (Washington, DC: US Department of State, 2009), 216.

12. Edward L Kimball, *Lengthen Your Stride: The Presidency of Spencer W. Kimball* (Salt Lake City: Deseret Book Company, 2005), 138; Mehr, "An LDS International Trio, 1974–97," 112.

13. Joseph Bentley, interview by Nathan B. Oman, June 2011. At the time of this conversation, Elder Bentley and his wife were serving as missionaries in Israel.

14. See HCJ 1031/93 *Passaro (Goldstein) v. Minister of the Interior* [1995] IsrSC 49(4) 661 (Isr.). For an English language summary of the case see Rahel Rimon, "Non-Orthodox Conversions in Israel," *Justice: The International Association of Jewish Lawyers and Jurists* 1 (December 1997): 43–48. A 1977 law prohibits inducing religious conversation by offering something of value. See Penal Law Amendment (Enticement to Change Religion Law), 5738/1977; Peter G. Danchin, "Of Prophets and Proselytes: Freedom of Religion and the Conflict of Rights in International Law," *Harvard International Law Journal* 49 (Summer 2008): 279, n. 114.

15. The details are recounted in Matthew L. Sandgren, "Extending Religious Freedoms Abroad: Difficulties Experienced by Minority Religions," *Tulsa Journal of Comparative and International Law* 9, no. 1 (2001): 268–272.

Third, the LDS Church has faced restrictions on the ability of Latter-day Saints to meet and worship together. In some cases restrictions on proselytizing have included restrictions on public meetings.[16] In other cases, church members were allowed to meet but subject to varying levels of harassment. During its history, for example, the German Democratic Republic generally allowed Latter-day Saints to meet for worship services. However, the police frequently monitored services, which scared away some members. In other cases, the police required onerous and detailed reports from church leaders on each meeting.[17] In 1989 the government in Ghana issued decrees prohibiting all church meetings, rescinding the decrees in 1990.[18] In Nicaragua, hostility toward the church spiked in the 1980s in response to the Reagan Administration's support for the right-wing Contra rebels that were battling the socialist Sandinista government. Anti-American hostility by local Sandinista leaders was directed against Nicaraguan Mormons, who lost control of their own meetinghouses. Thereafter, according to one Latter-day Saint, "we met in secret in the homes of some members.... We didn't meet very often."[19]

Finally, the LDS Church has faced restrictions on its ability to own and use property. As the church expanded beyond the United States it has had to fragment its legal personality in order to own property. Mexico, for example, has legal restrictions on the foreign ownership of land.[20] Furthermore, successive waves of Mexican reform in the nineteenth and early twentieth centuries directed at the land holdings of the Catholic Church resulted in laws complicating the ecclesiastical ownership of land.[21] Other jurisdictions often have legal prerequisites for church ownership of property. Accordingly, one of the first legal tasks for the church upon entering a new country was to incorporate or otherwise gain the ability to own land.[22] This often required a native member or

---

16. See, for example, Mehr, "Enduring Believers: Czechoslovakia and the LDS Church, 1884–1990," 134.

17. Kuehne, *Mormons as Citizens of a Communist State*, 69–70.

18. Kissi, *Walking in the Sand*, 200.

19. Quoted in Henri Gooren, "Latter-day Saints under Siege: The Unique Experience of Nicaraguan Mormons," *Dialogue: A Journal of Mormon Thought* 40 (Fall 2007): 145.

20. See Mexican Const. art. XXVII §I ("Foreigners may not acquire direct ownership of lands and water within a boundary of one hundred kilometers along the border and fifty along the beach").

21. William D. Signet, "Grading a Revolution: 100 Years of Mexican Land Reform," *Law & Business Review of the Americas* 16 (Summer 2010): 487–493.

22. For example, in Albania the church created an entity called the Liahona Foundation of the Church of Jesus Christ of Latter-day Saints, which gives the church a legal personality under Albanian law. David and Joan Haymond oral history, interview by Matthew K Heiss, March 12, 1996, 14–15, transcript, Church History Library, Salt Lake City, Utah.

group of members to be formal titleholders for church property. Furthermore, the process of registration has often been chaotic, with early missionaries and church leaders not fully understanding the legal status that they obtained.[23]

Individual Latter-day Saints have also faced legal problems not directly related to the institutional church but flowing out of their Mormon faith. For example, in 2008 the Court of Appeals (Civil Division) of the United Kingdom heard an appeal by a Muslim convert to Mormonism from Afghanistan who sought asylum in Britain, arguing that he would face religious persecution if forced to return to his homeland.[24] There are similar cases in other countries.[25] In Belgium, Mormons employed by Catholic schools lost their jobs because of their religion. In these cases the members found other employment rather than pursuing legal claims under Belgian law. Belgian Latter-day Saints have also found their religion used against them in divorce proceedings, where courts have awarded custody of children to non-Mormon parents to avoid religious indoctrination or placed restrictions on religious activities during child visits.[26] In these cases, Latter-day Saints receive no formal assistance from the church. Church attorneys represent the church as an institution, and church handbooks discourage local priesthood leaders from becoming involved in members' legal proceedings.[27] Furthermore, in some

---

23. As one long-time leader of the LDS Church in Belgium has noted, "Indeed the understanding behind 'recognition' can be bizarre. In Belgium an American mission president confirmed in a letter that the LDS Church was officially recognized as a church (copy in my possession). He based his claim on the fact that the church had registered as a nonprofit organization (something anyone can do) and the statutes had appeared in the State Paper. In the Netherlands I was shown the 'official document recognition': a perfunctory form letter from the Dutch Ministry acknowledging receipt of the church's request for recognition, sent shortly after the request has been submitted." Wilfried Decoo, "Issues in Writing European History and in Building the Church in Europe," *Journal of Mormon History* 23 (Spring 1997): 165, n.20.

24. See *MT (Afghanistan) v. The Secretary of State for the Home Department*, [2008] EWCA Civ 65. The convert in this case was successful in obtaining a rehearing before an immigration judge after his first, unsuccessful bid for asylum.

25. In New Zealand, a Russian covert sought asylum on the grounds that he would face persecution if returned to his home country. The New Zealand court found that while Mormons were subject to discrimination in Russia this harassment did not rise to the level of persecution. See IF, Refugee Appeal No. 70097/96, Refugee Status Appeals Authority, New Zealand, March 26, 1997.

26. Wilfried Decoo to Nathan B. Oman, "Legal Problems of Non-American Mormons," October 15, 2013.

27. "To avoid implicating the Church in legal matters to which it is not a party, leaders should avoid testifying in civil or criminal cases reviewing the conduct of members over whom they preside." *Handbook 1: Stake Presidents and Bishops* (Salt Lake City: The Church of Jesus Christ of Latter-day Saints, 2010), 66. This policy, however, does not always preclude members and church leaders from providing assistance in legal proceedings. For example, in the New Zealand case discussed in supra note 29, the Latter-day Saint asylum seeker was supported by testimony from a local Mormon.

contexts—such as discrimination by religious employers—the church's institutional interests are not necessarily aligned with the interest of members. So, for example, in *Obst v. Germany*, the LDS Church successfully defended its right to dismiss an employee for failing to comply with church standards before the European Court of Human Rights, arguing that religious discrimination was necessary to maintain its institutional integrity.[28]

Given the unique political and legal cultures of the various jurisdictions in which the LDS Church operated in the postwar era, it is difficult to generalize about the causes of the legal difficulties that Mormonism faced. There were, however, at least three recurring themes. The first was the difficulty of fitting the programs of the church into legal systems that have specific assumptions about how religions operate that are at odds with Latter-day Saint practice, which itself was shaped historically by the church's nineteenth-century battles within the American legal regime. This resulted in attempts to shove the square peg of Mormonism into the round hole of a foreign legal system. The second source of legal friction was the church's status as an American institution. Despite its efforts to internationalize, Mormonism was generally regarded as an American church. Accordingly, it was often a lightning rod for international resentments against American government policies and American cultural influence. Finally, the church found itself caught up in political and legal disputes internal to the societies where it has sought to expand. In many cases all three factors were present, reinforcing one another.

The 1964 decision of the House of Lords in *Church of Jesus Christ of Latter-day Saints v. Henning* illustrates the difficulty of fitting Latter-day Saint practices into legal systems with differing assumptions about how religions should behave. Beginning in the seventeenth century, the English government began assessing local property taxes to finance poor relief. Property belonging to the Church of England was exempt from this tax, but properties belonging to dissenting sects were assessed for the tax. In 1833, parliament eliminated the special treatment for the Church of England by exempting all "public places of worship" from assessment, and the exemption was codified in subsequent English revenue law. After the London Temple was dedicated in 1958, the local English taxing authority took the position that the temple did not qualify as a "public place of worship" because it was closed to everyone except members in good standing. The House of Lords rejected the LDS Church's argument that public worship meant corporate as opposed to private,

---

28. See *Obst v. Germany*, Application No. 425/03 (Dec. 23, 2010) (European Court of Human Rights). For an account of the historical and theological importance of institutional autonomy for the church see Cole Durham and Nathan B. Oman, "A Century of Mormon Theory and Practice in Church-State Relations: Constancy Amidst Change," November 7, 2006, http://papers.ssrn.com/sol3/papers.cfm?abstract_id=942567.

household worship and accepted the local taxing authority's interpretation of the law. As the church's barrister pointed out, this placed the London Temple in the odd position of being the only house of worship in the United Kingdom subject to taxation.

As an American-headquartered denomination, the Church of Jesus Christ of Latter-day Saints has often served as a target of convenience for those hostile to American policies and cultural influence. In the years immediately following World War II, the church enjoyed much of the international goodwill directed toward the United States. But as the Cold War continued, confrontation with the Soviets and other communist movements pushed the United States to take actions that ultimately dissipated much of this goodwill, particularly in the Third World countries where the church was expanding most rapidly.

Anti-American sentiment directed against the LDS Church has sometimes been violent. In 1977, there was an unsuccessful attempt to assassinate church president Spencer W. Kimball with a bomb during a visit to Santiago, Chile. Chilean officials foiled the plot, killing three of the plotters. In all likelihood the plotters were seeking to embarrass the Pinochet government by killing a prominent American leader.[29] More tragically, in the 1980s and early 1990s, leftist guerilla groups murdered both American and Latin American missionaries in Peru and Bolivia.[30] In addition, dozens of LDS Church buildings in Bolivia, Peru, Chile, and Colombia were bombed in the 1980s.[31] Although all of these groups had complex local ideologies, they were also driven by hostility toward American policies in Latin America and historical resentment against the *gringos* and *yanquis*.[32] Elsewhere, it was quite common for Mormon missionaries to be identified in the media or political debate as CIA agents. At times this diffuse association between espionage and Mormonism led to concrete action, as when Mormon missionaries were arrested as spies by the Czechoslovakian government in 1950. It has also led to overt symbolic actions against the church by politicians eager to exploit popular resentment against the United States. For example, in the early

---

29. The assassination attempt and its connection with Pinochet's government is discussed in Edward L Kimball, *Lengthen Your Stride: The Presidency of Spencer W. Kimball*, 16–17.

30. David Clark Knowlton, "Missionaries and Terror: The Assassination of Two Elders in Bolivia," *Sunstone*, August 1989.

31. David Clark Knowlton, "Mormonism in Latin America: Toward the Twenty-First Century," *Dialogue: A Journal of Mormon Thought* 29 (Spring 1992): 169; David Clark Knowlton, "Mormonism and Guerrillas in Bolivia," *Journal of Mormon History* 32 (Fall 2006): 180–208.

32. Knowlton, "Mormonism and Guerrillas in Bolivia."

1980s, leftist MPs made Mormonism the topic of questions in the Finnish parliament, and in 1970 when a coup d'état brought the populist general Juan Jose Torres to power in Bolivia, he threatened to ban Mormonism in the country, insisting that it was an agent for American imperialism. (A right-wing military putsch deposed Torres in 1971 before he could act on these threats.)[33]

Finally, the LDS Church was been subject to legal pressure because of internal political or social dynamics in the countries where it was sought to expand. For example, on December 8, 1989, the church sent the first full-time missionaries from Finland into Soviet Union. The Mormons were not the only group moving into the rapidly crumbling Soviet bloc in this era. Mikhail Gorbechev's policy of *glasnost*, which eased restrictions on religion, and the subsequent dissolution of the Soviet Union, led to a religious land rush in Central and Eastern Europe.[34] American churches were particularly aggressive in proselytizing the former communist world, with Baptists, Seventh Day Adventists, and Jehovah's Witnesses all sending missionaries into the former Soviet bloc.

This led to a backlash as the Russian Orthodox Church recovered from Soviet-era repression and the public odium of forced cooperation with the communist state.[35] In the 1990s, the Russian economy went into free fall and a mafia-infested economic oligarchy emerged, souring the optimism about Western-inspired reforms. The sense of social and cultural dissolution was exacerbated by Russia's two bloody wars (1994–1996 and 1999–2000) against the breakaway province of Chechnya and the resulting terrorist attacks in Moscow and elsewhere. This hostility often focused on western churches, including the LDS Church.[36] In 1996 Alexander Lebed, a former Soviet general, ran in the presidential elections on a nationalist and authoritarian platform. After finishing third, he was installed by his rival, President Boris

---

33. For a detailed analysis of the politics of Mormonism and espionage in Finland, see Kim B. Östman, "The Mormon Espionage Scare and Its Coverage in Finland, 1982–84," *Journal of Mormon History* 34 (Winter 2008): 82–117. On Torres's attempt to ban Mormonism in Bolivia, see Knowlton, "Mormonism and Guerrillas in Bolivia," 187.

34. Emily B. Baran, "Negotiating the Limits of Religious Pluralism in Post-Soviet Russia: The Anticult Movement in the Russian Orthodox Church, 1990–2004," *Russian Review* 65 (Fall 2006): 639–640.

35. See W. Cole Durham, Natalie J. Petersen, and Elizabeth A. Sewell, "Introduction: A Comparative Analysis of Religious Association Laws in Post-Communist Europe," in W. Cole Durham and Silvio Ferrari, eds., *Laws on Religion and the State in Post-Communist Europe* (Leuven: Peeters, 2004), xi.

36. For a summary of the attitudes of cultural hostility toward Mormon missionaries see Decoo, "Issues in Writing European History and in Building the Church in Europe," 154–157.

Yeltsin, as security chief. In a widely reported speech before a nationalist rally, he referred positively to Russia's "established traditional religions" including Russian Orthodoxy, Islam, and Buddhism, but then reviled against "all these Mormons, Aum Supreme Truth, all this is mold and scum that is artificially brought into our country with the purpose of perverting, corrupting and breaking up our state."[37] Lebed's grouping of Mormons with Aum Supreme Truth, a Japanese group associated with fatal gas attacks in a Tokyo subway, was telling. Beginning in the 1990s, Russian activists—many of them associated with the Russian Orthodox Church—began forming ties with American and Western European anti-cult activists. In the 1990s and 2000s, these ties generated a political movement within Russia directed against so-called totalitarian cults that allegedly corrupted the morals of their victims through brainwashing, thus undermining Russian society.[38]

In 1997, the Russian Duma passed a new law governing religious associations. It threatened to revoke the status of all religious groups that could not demonstrate a presence within the country for fifteen years, limiting their ability to hold property or publish their views. The law provoked widespread concern in the United States. Senator Gordon Smith, a Mormon representing Oregon, introduced a law making US foreign aid contingent on a finding that "the Russian Federation has enacted no statute or promulgated no executive order that would discriminate...against religious minorities...in violation of accepted international agreements on human rights and religious freedoms."[39] Acting independently of the church, another Mormon Senator, Utah's Robert Bennett, traveled to Russia on behalf of the US State Department, where he met with the chairman of the Duma committee on religious affairs, President Yeltsin's chief of staff, and lawyers from the Russian Ministry of Justice. These officials assured him that despite its language, the law would not be applied to Mormons and other new religions. In addition, officials from the LDS Church's Area Office in Frankfurt flew to Moscow to lobby members of the Duma.[40] Shortly after the law was passed,

---

37. Richard Boudreaux, "Yeltsin Aide Denounces Foreigners, Urges Curbs," *Los Angeles Times*, June 28, 1996.

38. See Baran, "Negotiating the Limits of Religious Pluralism in Post-Soviet Russia," 638.

39. See 143 *Cong. Rec.* S7518 (July 16, 1997). For a discussion of the Smith Amendment, see W. Cole Durham and Lauren B. Homer, "Russia's 1997 Law on Freedom of Conscience and Religious Associations: An Analytical Appraisal," *Emory International Law Review* 12, no. 1 (1998): 237–240.

40. Robert F. Bennett, interview by Nathan B. Oman, November 15, 2013. Bennett also met with an official he described as "the secretary of state for the Russian Orthodox Church," who claimed that that the law would exclude new religious groups but only for 15 years, enough time to give the Russian Orthodox Church "breathing space."

the LDS Church was recognized under an exemption in the law for "centralized religious organizations," a provision originally designed to exempt the Russian Orthodox Church from the law's restrictions on other religious groups.[41] Notwithstanding official recognition, however, the US State Department reported that after the passage of the 1997 law, the church routinely faced difficulties with officials in proselytizing and obtaining property.[42]

Toward an Apolitical Theology of the State

It is impossible to recount the development of Mormon theology in the nineteenth century without acknowledging the influence of the law on Latter-day Saint teachings. Most dramatically, the concerted effort of the federal government to suppress polygamy from 1862 to 1890 forced the LDS Church to abandon the practice of plural marriage and ultimately its teaching as well. The power of the law, however, was also deployed against other aspects of the

---

41. Mark Elliott and Sharyl Corrado, "The 1997 Russian Law on Religion: The Impact on Protestants," *Religion, State & Society* 27, no. 1 (1999): 111–112. Indeed, Elliott and Carrado concluded that "Mormons actually appear for the moment to be enjoying something of a privileged status, despite the minimal responses of the Russian people to their missionaries." For a summary of the treatment of religious minorities under the law during its first ten years, see Wallace L. Daniel and Christopher Marsh, "Russia's 1997 Law on Freedom of Conscience in Context and Retrospect," *Journal of Church and State* 49 (Winter 2007): 5–18.

42. The US Commission on International Religious Freedom has documented the following abuses in recent years: government officials obstruct efforts to rent or build property, see United States Commission on International Religious Freedom, *Annual Report* 2013 (Washington, DC: US Department of State, 2013), 256–257; renting and building places of worship difficult United States Commission on International Religious Freedom, *Annual Report* 2012 (Washington, DC: US Department of State, 2012), 318; government officials take an inordinate interest in fire and other safety regulations to assess fines and shut down services United States Commission on International Religious Freedom, *Annual Report* 2011 (Washington, DC: US Department of State, 2011), 293; difficulty in obtaining places of worship, restrictions on visas for missionaries, vandalism of a church building, and perception that law enforcement will not protect church services or property United States Commission on International Religious Freedom, *Annual Report* 2010 (Washington, DC: US Department of State, 2010), 279–281; difficulty obtaining worship space United States Commission on International Religious Freedom, *Annual Report* 2009 (Washington, DC: US Department of State, 2009), 183; pro-Kremlin demonstrations outside Mormon building in Saratov United States Commission on International Religious Freedom, *Annual Report* 2008 (Washington, DC: US Department of State, 2008), 254; chronic problems obtaining legal recognition United States Commission on International Religious Freedom, *Annual Report* 2007 (Washington, DC: US Department of State, 2007), 50; government officials warn that Mormons are a threat to "spiritual security" United States Commission on International Religious Freedom, *Annual Report* 2006 (Washington, DC: US Department of State, 2006), 155; Mormons and other minority religions must secure permission of local Russian Orthodox leaders before being allowed by the government to obtain places of worship United States Commission on International Religious Freedom, *Annual Report* 2005 (Washington, DC: US Department of State, 2005), 91.

nineteenth-century Mormon commonwealth. Forced to abandon theocratic ambitions, the church reinterpreted Zion in less literal terms and postponed its utopian hopes to an ever-receding millennium following the Second Coming of Christ. For the Latter-day Saints, the American ideal of a religiously neutral law and an autonomous religious sphere free of government coercion proved illusory. Law was a causal force in the development of Mormon practices and teachings.[43]

Law was also a powerful influence on Mormon teachings in the latter half of the twentieth century. As Mormonism achieved a grudging cultural acceptance in the United States after 1904, it could avail itself of the freedom of religion, speech, and association protected by the First Amendment of the US Constitution. At the same time, the Supreme Court steadily began expanding those freedoms. In 1938, the Court signaled the beginnings of its midcentury "rights revolution" with the famous footnote 4 of *United States v. Carolene Products*,[44] stating that the deferential attitude of the courts toward legislation entrenched by the constitutional settlement of the New Deal did not extend to laws aimed at "discrete and insular minorities."[45] By the late 1960s and 1970s this judicial attitude had produced decisions such as *Sherbert v. Verner*,[46] *Wisconsin v. Yoder*,[47] and *National Labor Relations Board v. Catholic Bishop of Chicago*,[48] all of which took a deferential stance toward individual and institutional religious practice. Indeed, the LDS Church was an important agent in creating post-rights-revolution religion clause jurisprudence, fighting the case of *Amos v. Presiding Bishop of the Church of Jesus Christ of Latter-day Saints* to the Supreme Court, establishing the legitimacy of statutory exemptions designed to accommodate religious practice and protect the independence of religious institutions.[49]

---

43. See Elizabeth Harmer-Dionne, "Once a Peculiar People: Cognitive Dissonance and the Suppression of Mormon Polygamy As a Case Study Negating the Belief-Action Distinction," *Stanford Law Review* 50.4 (Spring 1998): 1295–1347.

44. *United States v. Carolene Products Co.*, 304 US 144 (1938).

45. Ibid., 152–153, n. 4.

46. *Sherbert v. Verner*, 374 US 398 (1963) (holding that laws burdening the free exercise of religion—in this case a law requiring a Seventh Day Adventist to work on the Adventist Sabbath—were subject to strict scrutiny).

47. *Wisconsin v. Yoder*, 406 US 205 (1972) (holding that Old Order Amish could be excused from compulsory education laws on the basis of freedom of religion).

48. *NLRB v. Catholic Bishop of Chicago*, 440 US 490 (1979) (holding that religious institutions were constitutionally protected from invasive laws governing their administration).

49. *Corp. of Presiding Bishop v. Amos*, 483 US 327 (1987) (holding that the exemption of religious institutions from laws prohibiting discrimination on the basis of religion did not violate the Establishment Clause of the First Amendment). Compare *Obst v. Germany*, Application No. 425/03 (Dec. 23, 2010) (European Court of Human Rights).

It is one of the unappreciated ironies of Mormon history, however, that just at the moment when Mormonism had, after more than a century of struggle and accommodation, achieved maximal freedom and flexibility under American law, the LDS Church was increasingly constrained and influenced by non-American legal systems. In navigating this bewildering new legal environment, the church had to change. The changes, however, went beyond ecclesiastical structures or an increasingly professionalized apparatus of international lawyers. Interactions with non-American legal systems also had an influence on Mormon teachings. In particular, the necessity of accommodating Mormonism to a multiplicity of legal regimes required church leaders to articulate a largely apolitical Mormon theology of the state, one that emphasized the role of Latter-day Saints as good citizens and sought to reassure often skeptical government officials that the church was uninterested in operating as an agent of radical political or social change. This apolitical theology of the state triumphed over older, more apocalyptic political theologies.

During much of the nineteenth century the dominant Mormon theology of the state was theodemocratic.[50] Originally articulated by Joseph Smith during the Nauvoo period, it envisioned the Mormon community as the kingdom of God on earth, a government in waiting ready to step into the breach when the imminent end times destroyed all secular competitors. A regime of theodemocracy would be put in place to build Zion in the last days and redeem all human communities that survived the coming deluge. With fierce literalism and commitment to Joseph's vision, Brigham Young sought to realize the Mormon kingdom in the isolation of the Intermountain West. Mormon theodemocracy, however, was already declining in the decades after the Civil War and ended in the first decade of the twentieth century during the US Senate hearings regarding the seating of elected Senator Reed Smoot, a Mormon apostle. In his testimony before the Senate, LDS Church President Joseph F. Smith effectively committed the church to behaving largely like a Protestant denomination.[51] Theocratic ambitions were abandoned along with polygamy, the expansive jurisdiction of church courts over civil disputes, and the cooperative economic institutions of Brigham Young's Deseret.[52]

---

50. See Patrick Q. Mason, "God and the People: Theodemocracy in Nineteenth-Century Mormonism," *Journal of Church and State* 55 (Summer 2013): 1–27.

51. See Kathleen Flake, *The Politics of American Religious Identity: The Seating of Senator Reed Smoot, Mormon Apostle* (Chapel Hill: University of North Carolina Press, 2004).

52. On the rise and fall of civil disputes in Mormon courts see Nathan B. Oman, "Preaching to the Court House and Judging in the Temple," *Brigham Young University Law Review* (2009): 157–224.

For the decade or two following the Second World War, the main Mormon theology of the state could be called Cold War apocalypticism. The most articulate proponent of this view was Ezra Taft Benson, who leavened his Mormonism with the paranoid anti-communism of the John Birch Society.[53] Benson's output on the subject of communism and America was prodigious, but he was far from the only LDS Church leader who made anti-communism an important theme in his preaching.[54] The dominant church figures in the immediate postwar period, J. Reuben Clark and David O. McKay, were both staunch anti-communists.[55] In 1959, for example, McKay, speaking in the church's general conference, quoted from Salt Lake City's arch-anticommunist police chief W. Cleon Skousen's book *The Naked Communist*: "The conflict between communism and freedom is the problem of our time. It overshadows all other problems. This conflict mirrors our age, its toils, its tensions, its troubles, and its tasks. On the outcome of this conflict depends the future of mankind." McKay added, "I admonish everyone to read that excellent book of Chief Skousen's."[56] Other general authorities warned against communists who sought to "overthrow the government and forfeit all safeguards,"[57] insisted that "the spirit of communism is unquestionably wholly foreign to the spirit of true Americanism,"[58] and affirmed that "knowledge of the [communist] enemy teaches us wariness and caution."[59] The Manichean struggle between good and evil in the last days, which was a consistent theme of the early theodemocratic vision, was transposed to the midcentury struggle between the superpowers. In the nineteenth century American democracy had been identified with the degenerate end-times regimes. In the vision of Cold War apocalypticism, however, America became the primary agent of God's work in history. To be sure, it was an uncertain agent, in constant danger of moral and

---

53. See D. Michael Quinn, "Ezra Taft Benson and Mormon Political Conflicts," *Dialogue: A Journal of Mormon Thought* 26 (Summer 1993): 1–88.

54. Ezra Taft Benson, *The Red Carpet* (Salt Lake City: Bookcraft, 1962); *An Enemy Hath Done This* (Salt Lake City: Parliament Publishers, 1969); *The Constitution: A Heavenly Banner* (Salt Lake City: Deseret Book Company, 1986); *This Nation Shall Endure* (Salt Lake City: Deseret Book Company, 1977); *Stand Up for Freedom* (Belmont: American Opinion, 1966); *God Family Country: Our Three Great Loyalties* (Salt Lake City: Deseret Book Company, 1974); and *A Plea for America* (Salt Lake City: Deseret Book Company, 1975).

55. Prince and Wright, *David O. McKay and the Rise of Modern Mormonism*; D. Michael Quinn, *Elder Statesman: A Biography of J. Reuben Clark* (Salt Lake City: Signature Books, 2002).

56. David O. McKay, "Preach the Word," *Conference Report*, October 1959.

57. Stephen L. Richards, "The Wayward," *Conference Report*, April 1957.

58. Joseph F. Merrill, "The Gloomy Outlook and a Remedy," *Conference Report*, October 1946.

59. Ezra Taft Benson, "The Threat of Communism," *Conference Report*, April 1960.

political collapse from within.[60] Mormonism was cast as an agent of American righteousness in the global struggle against satanic communism. Even Mormon liberals who opposed Benson's politics, such as Hugh B. Brown of the First Presidency, sounded anti-communist themes in their sermons.

There are three things worth noting about Cold War apocalypticism. First, it was intensely political. It provided a tightly intertwined set of theological and political narratives in which Mormonism spoke to pressing current concerns. Second, it was intensely American. Indeed, at times it seemed to tie the destiny of the LDS Church to the destiny of the United States. Finally—and ironically—it was intensely local. Despite the international scope of the superpower struggle, Cold War apocalypticism ultimately spoke to American anxieties. In other words, it not only associated the church closely with America, it was almost exclusively directed toward an American audience.

As the LDS Church continued to expand, however, Cold War apocalypticism proved a theological luxury that Mormonism could not afford. Domestically, the fiery anti-communist rhetoric backfired. In July 1965, for example, the NAACP adopted a resolution at its national conference calling on all Third World nations "to refuse to grant visas to missionaries and representatives of The Church of Jesus Christ of Latter-day Saints...until such time as the doctrine of nonwhite inferiority is changed and rescinded by that church and a positive policy of support for civil rights is taken." Although the NAACP's was critical of the church's racial policies, the resolution itself was passed at the urging of the Utah chapter of the NAACP in response to Ezra Taft Benson accusing the civil rights movement of acting as a communist front.[61] As the Cold War and the era of anti-colonial struggles eroded the immediate postwar good will toward the United States abroad, any close association of the church with American policy became a liability. This was especially true as Mormonism moved into the Third World, a geopolitically liminal space between the superpowers. Mormon missionaries were seeking the same hearts and minds that American diplomats sought to win, but the church found it best to decouple its efforts from US policy. This was especially true as it began to deal with governments that might or might not be friendly to the United States or, perhaps worse, governments that oscillated back and forth depending on the last coup or election. The church's preferred strategy was to become as small a political and legal target as possible.

---

60. See Benson, *The Red Carpet*; and *An Enemy Hath Done This*.

61. Quinn, "Ezra Taft Benson and Mormon Political Conflicts," 35.

The LDS Church sought to limit its exposure to legal and political hostility abroad by adopting an apolitical theology of the state. At its center was the church's twelfth Article of Faith, penned in 1842 by Joseph Smith in a letter to Joseph Wentworth, editor of the *Chicago Democrat*. The penultimate article declared, "We believe in being subject to kings, presidents, rulers, and magistrates, in obeying, honoring, and sustaining the law." Written in Illinois amid Smith's increasingly desperate legal maneuverings to avoid extradition to Missouri and the rising chorus of complaints about Mormon political machinations in the state, the statement made good political sense. Smith was pouring oil on troubled political waters. In the mid-twentieth century this text was repurposed to suit the rhetorical needs of the internationally expanding church.

As early as 1950, LDS Church leaders cited the twelfth Article of Faith in response to the expulsion of missionaries from Czechoslovakia.[62] In 1956, the First Presidency invoked the same text to negotiate legal requirements abroad. Stephen L. Richards, first counselor in the First Presidency, told a general conference audience that year, "Within the past few weeks, in order to meet the requirements of a distant foreign country for the Church to hold property and otherwise carry forward its activities within that country, the First Presidency has caused to be prepared and submitted to the governing authority of the foreign country a statement of beliefs and objects of the Church."[63] After repeating the twelfth Article of Faith, the statement affirmed that "the Church of Jesus Christ of Latter-day Saints builds and maintains churches, temples, educational institutions for all ages.... It teaches loyalty to country and fosters good citizenship in all communities where it is established."[64] Tellingly, the twelfth Article of Faith was invoked in a context where the LDS Church was particularly vulnerable—the acquisition and use of real property. Hugh B. Brown, soon to be a counselor in the First Presidency, likewise told a general conference audience in the late 1950s that he had used the twelfth Article of Faith to answer questions about the church's beliefs posed to him during the dedication of the London Temple.[65]

By the 1970s, this apolitical message was the dominant Mormon theology of the state. To be sure, there were still sermons and articles that drew on the

---

62. Joseph F. Merrill, "Repentence ... or Slavery," *Conference Report*, April 1950.

63. Stephen L. Richards, "Our Message to the World," *Conference Report*, October 1956.

64. Ibid.

65. Hugh B. Brown, "We Affirm Our Faith," *Conference Report*, October 1958.

images of Cold War apocalypticism,[66] but increasingly the message to both insiders and outsiders was that above all, Mormons were law-abiding citizens uninterested in radical change.[67] The text of the twelfth Article of Faith was uniquely well suited for conveying this message for two reasons. First, the reference to "being subject to kings, presidents, rulers, and magistrates" is institutionally capacious. In contrast to philosophical liberalism, for example, it does not condition allegiance to the law on a particular institutional structure. If anything, the reference to "kings" and "rulers"—two models of authority that run counter to liberal ideas of legitimacy—suggests an almost unlimited allegiance to established authority. Second, the emphasis on law as the primary mediator of Latter-day Saint relationships to the state further suppresses any idea of political activism. Law has traditionally been presented as the antithesis of politics, a realm in which both obedience and authority are mediated through a system of impersonal principles that can be logically applied and obeyed without political judgment. To be sure, this ideal has always been something of an illusion, as critical theorists from Marx to realists of various stripes have been eager to point out. Still, as a rhetorical matter invoking law as a central trope tends to emphasize the apolitical character of the church.

Even at its most politically quietist, however, Mormon allegiance to established authority was not absolute. In the 1970s, Spencer W. Kimball called David Kennedy, a Latter-day Saint who served as US Secretary of the Treasury in the Nixon Administration, to serve as the First Presidency's personal representative in negotiations with foreign governments. Kennedy thus spent as much time thinking about these issues as any Mormon, and wrote:

> So long as the government permits me to attend church, so long as it permits me to get on my knees in prayer, so long as it permits me to baptize for the remission of sins, so long as it permits me to partake of the sacrament of the Lord's Supper, and to obey the commandments of the Lord, so long as the government does not force me to

---

66. It's worth noting that what I am calling Cold War apoclypticism went beyond Ezra Taft Benson's Mormonization of the paranoid visions of the John Birch Society. During the bicentennial celebrations of the United States in 1976, Spencer W. Kimball published a First Presidency message that was sharply critical of American materialism and castigated the United States and the Saints for being "a warlike people." See Spencer W. Kimball, "The False Gods We Worship," *Ensign*, June 1976.

67. This does not mean, of course, that this has always been an accurate description of the political beliefs of Latter-day Saints. Prior to the 1980s, for example, many Mormons in Nicaragua were supporters of the opposition Sandinistas, although many of these Latter-day Saints became disenchanted with the Sandinistas after they came to power and targeted the church. See Gooren, "Latter-day Saints under Siege."

commit crime, so long as I am not required to live separately from my wife and children, I can live as a Latter-day Saint within that political system.[68]

To be sure, the LDS Church has avoided states that cannot meet these minimal requirements, and thus avoided direct conflict.[69] Still, Kennedy's formulation provided a floor for the kinds of legal regimes within which the church was willing to exist. Ideally, this near complete abandonment of a critical stance toward constituted authority reduced the probability of hostile action by the state directed against Latter-day Saints. Mormons, according to this apolitical theology, posed no threat to the powers that be and those powers may safely ignore them.

As the legal experience of the LDS Church in the last half of the twentieth century shows, however, its apolitical theology of the state was never wholly successful. The church has been unable to shed its widespread association with America in general and, to a lesser extent, US policy. In large part, this was an inevitable result of the church's history and the geographic location of its administrative and demographic heartland in Utah. The American feel of the church was further reinforced in the late 1960s and early 1970s by a comprehensive effort to simplify church programs, known as correlation, which allowed the institution to concentrate its scarce resources but also homogenized Mormonism along lines that marked it as an American institution abroad.[70] In contrast to the international expansion and inculturation of

---

68. Quoted in Martin B Hickman, *David Matthew Kennedy: Banker, Statesman, Churchman* (Salt Lake City: Deseret Book Company, in cooperation with the David M. Kennedy Center for International Studies, 1987), 340–341.

69. For example, the church's presence in the Islamic countries of the Middle East is muted, as is its presence in China. However, even in the Middle East there are church units of expatriates and a smattering of local converts baptized abroad. In China, the population of native Latter-day Saints baptized abroad is sufficiently large that the church has begun producing Chinese language materials giving them guidance on how to operate as Latter-day Saints within China. The website affirms: "A basic tenet of The Church of Jesus Christ of Latter-day Saints is 'obeying, honoring, and sustaining' the law. In more that 160 countries around the world including in the People's Republic of China, The Church of Jesus Christ of Latter-day Saints and its members seek to obey, honor, and sustain the law. Everywhere, we teach members to be good citizens and good parents." It goes on to describe the restrictions under which native Chinese Latter-day Saints must function, including prohibitions on joint worship with expatriate Mormons in China, the distribution of church literature, blogging or microblogging on religious subjects, and baptizing friends or family members in China. See "Frequently Asked Questions by PRC Chinese Members Outside China," *The Church of Jesus Christ of Latter-day Saints*, www.mormonsandchina.org.

70. For a discussion of the history of the correlation movement, see Allen and Leonard, *The Story of the Latter-Day Saints*, 593–624.

other denominations, Mormonism has made very few concessions to local culture in terms of worship or ecclesiastical structure. Given these factors, the rhetorical weight placed on an apolitical Mormon theology of the state has not surprisingly proven too great at times. With a few exceptions, it protected Latter-day Saints from the kind violent persecution they suffered in the nineteenth century or that other religious groups have faced in the twentieth century. It did not, however, always shield the church from less dramatic forms of legal harassment.

A 1994 general conference address by Russell M. Nelson of the Quorum of the Twelve nicely illustrates this problem. As early as the 1970s, before being called as an apostle, Nelson negotiated with governments in Eastern and Central Europe on behalf of the church. Nelson reported:

> While in Moscow in June 1991, in that spirit of preparation and with the sincere respect for leaders of other religious denominations, Elder Dallin H. Oaks and I had the privilege of meeting with the presiding official of the Russian Orthodox Church. We were accompanied by Elder Hans B. Ringger and the mission president, Gary L. Browning. Patriarch Aleksei was most gracious in sharing a memorable hour with us. We perceived the great difficulties endured for so many years by this kind man and his fellow believers. We thanked him for his perseverance and for his faith. Then we assured him of our good intensions and of the importance of the message that missionaries of The Church of Jesus Christ of Latter-day Saints would be teaching among his countrymen. We affirmed that ours is a global church and that we honor and obey the laws of each land in which we labor.[71]

This was essentially the same message that Hugh B. Brown had reported giving during the London Temple dedication over thirty years earlier. Yet as the political situation in Russia soured in the 1990s and the Russian Orthodox Church reasserted some influence over the law, Mormon protestations of apolitical law-abidingness proved insufficient to counter religious hostility. Indeed, despite the 1991 meeting with Oaks, Nelson, and Ringger and the assurances that they offered, Patriarch Aleksei was one of the most ardent supporters of the Duma's unsuccessful 1997 attempt to suppress new religions in Russia.[72]

------

71. Russell M. Nelson, "Teach Us Tolerance and Love," *Ensign*, May 1994.

72. Daniel and Marsh, "Russia's 1997 Law on Freedom of Conscience in Context and Retrospect," 7.

Conclusion

After 1945, the Church of Jesus Christ of Latter-day Saints went through some of the most dramatic changes in its history. Over the course of two generations, it transformed itself from a community concentrated overwhelmingly within the confines of the Intermountain West into a global institution with ambitions to expand into every nation. This international expansion has created one of the unappreciated ironies of Mormon history. The postwar decades represent something of a high-water mark for the level of protection and autonomy enjoyed by the LDS Church within the American legal system. Yet at precisely the moment when the church successfully located itself within the legal culture of the United States, it found itself increasingly confronted by non-American legal systems. International expansion spawned a host of legal difficulties, and in trying to minimize itself as a target of potentially hostile governments, the church crafted an apolitical theology of the state that has largely come to dominate internal and external Mormon discourse on the relationship between Latter-day Saints and legal authority. This late-twentieth century approach, however, has never entirely minimized the church's exposure to legal hostility as it faces a diverse array of political arrangements in its attempt to expand its reach around the world.

2

The Internationalization of Mormonism

INDICATIONS FROM INDIA

Taunalyn F. Rutherford

*Religions are more like tents. No doubt they are the abodes
of divine stuff that matter. But analogous to tents, religions
are unlikely to be utterly sealed off; the fluidity of their
boundaries and substructures are inherent to their very
existence. Religions thus yield themselves to be discreetly and
deliberately dismantled, relocated and reassembled. Religions
are not finished products; they constantly hand themselves
over to their adherents.[1]*

THE TENT METAPHOR, borrowed from the literature on religious conversion in
India, has significant implications for the study of Mormonism's internationalization. It is particularly apt in reference to the Church of Jesus Christ of Latter-
day Saints, which explicitly invokes the tent imagery of the biblical prophet
Isaiah by naming its midlevel administrative units "stakes," all presumably radi-
ating out from and connected to the center pole in Salt Lake City while being
securely fastened in local ground.[2] The creation of stakes in various locales was
central to Joseph Smith's project of establishing Zion.[3] Two years after he established the first stakes in Ohio and Missouri, Smith prayed during the dedication

---

1. Sathianathan Clarke, "Section Three: Transformations of Caste and Tribe," in Rowena
Robinson and Sathianathan Clarke, eds., *Religious Conversion in India: Modes, Motivations,
and Meanings* (New Delhi: Oxford University Press, 2003), 217.

2. Isaiah 33:20.

3. As early as 1832, Joseph Smith envisioned the Latter-day Saint settlement in Kirtland,
Ohio, as a stake in relation to the center place in western Missouri; see *The Doctrine and
Covenants of the Church of Jesus Christ of Latter-day Saints* (Salt Lake City: The Church of Jesus
Christ of Latter-day Saints, 1981), 82:13–14.

of the Kirtland Temple that God would "appoint unto Zion other stakes besides this one which thou hast appointed, that the gathering of thy people may roll on in great power and majesty."[4] If Zion's tent truly were to cover the globe, then its stakes would need to be planted around the world. Smith's vision, however, would be delayed for more than a century after his death. While Mormon missionaries established church "branches" in many countries, the first LDS stake outside of North America was organized in New Zealand in 1958. Next came the Manchester England Stake in 1960, followed one year later by the first non-English speaking stake in The Hague, Netherlands.[5]

By the turn of the twentieth century, church leaders had begun de-emphasizing the principle of gathering to Utah.[6] When President David O. McKay began building international temples and stakes it was a clear indication of changes in the LDS conception of the gathering to and building of Zion. Rather than migrating to a centralized Zion, church members were told to remain in their native lands where stakes of Zion would be driven into foreign soil, thus strengthening the Saints in "distant" locations.[7] In spite of its worldwide expansion, the church has maintained its insistence on uniformity in administration, emphasizing that all of Zion is one tent. Mormon scripture affirms this idealized unity by declaring that the people of Zion must be "of one heart and one mind."[8] The emphasis of the LDS Church has been on maintaining a centralized and unified structure even when borders were enlarged, cords stretched, and stakes planted around the globe.

The logistics of stretching a metaphorical one-tent structure over vast distances, oceans, and borders has only increased in difficulty in the age of decolonization from the end of the Second World War to the present. While never relinquishing the "one heart and one mind" ideal, in this period the institutional church clearly saw the need for a simplified "tent" or message that

---

4. *Doctrine and Covenants* 109:59.

5. Brandon S. Plewe, "The Emergence of Modern Stakes and Wards 1834–1909," in Brandon Plewe, S. Kent Brown, Donald Q. Cannon, and Richard H. Jackson, eds., *Mapping Mormonism: An Atlas of Latter-day Saint History* (Provo: BYU Press, 2012), 128; see also Richard O. Cowan, "Stakes 1910–Present," in *Mapping Mormonism*, 184.

6. An official letter from the First Presidency in 1911 "urged converts to stay where they were and live according to the ideals of Zion in their own homelands." See Seth L. Bryant, Henri Gooren, Rick Phillips, and David G. Stewart Jr., "Conversion and Retention in Mormonism," in Lewis R. Rambo and Charles E. Farhadian, eds., *The Oxford Handbook of Religious Conversion* (New York: Oxford University Press, 2014), 762.

7. See Gregory A. Prince and Wm. Robert Wright, *David O. McKay and the Rise of Modern Mormonism* (Salt Lake City: University of Utah Press, 2005), 365–366.

8. Moses 7:18, in *The Pearl of Great Price* (Salt Lake City: The Church of Jesus Christ of Latter-day Saints, 1981).

could be dismantled, transported, and reassembled anywhere in the world. Part of the process of dismantling that the LDS Church undertook was known as correlation, referring to a process of consolidating the auxiliary programs of the church (Relief Society, Young Men's and Young Women's associations, Primary, and Sunday School) under central priesthood leadership. Historian Matthew Bowman has charted the origins, methods, and outcomes of the correlation process, which in many ways "wrought its own changes on the faith." Bowman argues that "correlation made it possible for Mormonism to become a global religion," as it simplified and streamlined what had been a "patchwork quilt of curriculum," enabling the religion's export overseas.[9] Other scholars have argued that the development and imposition of correlation's simplified and uniform structure reduced Mormonism's theological square footage, so to speak. Also, correlation limited local autonomy in a host of areas, such as architecture, artwork, and curricula.[10]

The creation of stakes out of branches and missions is a significant indicator of church growth and development in a given area, since a stake must not only meet certain numeric indicators but also must have local rather than imported leadership. Since 1945 the LDS Church has been slowly evolving from a US-centered church to a nascent global church through the process of stake building. In this essay, I will examine the dynamics of stake building and Mormon internationalization through a case study of the formation of the first LDS stake in India, located in Hyderabad. Analyzing the emergence of the LDS Church in India offers a unique vantage point to reflect on the theoretical question of whether Mormonism is now or might soon be considered a world religion or whether it is best understood as an American church with global outreach.

The Question of Mormonism as a World Religion

As the birthplace of Hinduism, Buddhism, Jainism, and Sikhism and a vibrant home for Christianity and Islam, India is an important location for the study of "world religions." Because Mormon Studies is a relatively new field, scholars grapple with the question of how to categorize Mormonism. Some predict it is just a mater of time before world religions status is conferred on Mormonism. Others relegate it to the status of an American religion that happens to be transported to other countries—a kind of caffeine-free

9. Matthew Bowman, *The Mormon People: The Making of an American Faith* (New York: Random House, 2012), 191, 194.

10. See Armand L. Mauss, "Refuge and Retrenchment," in Marie Cornwall, Tim B. Heaton, and Laurence A. Young, eds., *Contemporary Mormonism: Social Science Perspectives* (Urbana: University of Illinois Press, 2001), 30–31.

"Cocacolonization" of religion. For instance, Mormonism has been classified as "a new religious tradition,"[11] "America's fledgling contribution to the great world faiths,"[12] a "North American church with tendrils in other continents,"[13] and, as Rodney Stark predicted, "on the threshold of becoming the first major faith to appear on earth since the prophet Muhammed rode out of the desert."[14] David Knowlton emphasizes the problematic nature of arguments in favor of Mormonism as a world religion and yet suggests that such arguments require that we "look more deeply at the sociological issues that make world religions different from other religious forms, such as denominations or localized religions." I agree that the world religions question is problematic, and yet does add to the "precision in comprehending the place of religion generally and Mormonism specifically."[15] Mormon anthropologist Walter E.A. van Beek acknowledges the difficulty of outlining the criteria for identifying a world religion because the classification often operates more as a "public relations term" than an analytical category.[16] Religious studies scholars often see the category of world religions as helpful for an undergraduate survey course but too problematic for professional scholarly discourse.[17] Although defining precisely "what constitutes a world religion remains a vexed question,"[18] such arguments are indicative of the way Mormon studies scholars find it important to view Mormonism in relation to traditions that are considered world religions.

The trend in the academy is toward calling religions—even those in the traditional world religions canon—"global," referring to "the global transportation of peoples and the transnational acceptance of religious ideas," rather

---

11. Jan Shipps, *Mormonism: The Story of a New Religious Tradition* (Urbana: University of Illinois Press, 1987)

12. Eric A. Eliason, ed., *Mormons and Mormonism: An Introduction to an American World Religion* (Urbana: University of Illinois Press, 2001), 15.

13. Rick Phillips, "Rethinking the International Expansion of Mormonism," *Novo Religio: The Journal of Alternative and Emergent Religions* 10 (August 2006): 53–68.

14. Rodney Stark, *The Rise of Mormonism* (New York: Columbia University Press, 2005), 139.

15. David Clark Knowlton, "Mormonism as a World Religion," in W. Paul Reeve and Ardis E. Parshall, eds., *Mormonism: A Historical Encyclopedia* (Santa Barbara: ABC-CLIO, 2010), 359–365.

16. Walter E. A. Van Beek, "Mormonism, a Global Counter-Church?," *By Common Consent* blog, June 18, 2009, http://bycommonconsent.com/2009/06/18/mormonism-a-global-counter-church-i/.

17. Tomoko Masuzawa, *The Invention of World Religions* (Chicago: University of Chicago Press, 2005.), xi.

18. Jehu J. Hanciles, "'Would that All God's People Were Prophets': Mormonism and the New Shape of Global Christianity," *Journal of Mormon History* 41 (April 2015): 35–68.

than focusing on the traditional world religions taxonomy.[19] Jehu Hanciles, a scholar of world Christianity, applies the "rubric of cultural globalization" to the LDS Church. He clarifies that determining how or when a "movement becomes globalized requires attentiveness to complex questions pertaining to cultural adaptation, translatability of its core message and vision, diversity of forms, and the shaping of identity outside its original context, as well as the nature and inclusiveness of its outreach."[20] In short, according to Hanciles, "successful globalization requires at least two defining attributes: localization and multidirectional (reciprocal) transformation."[21] Based on this rubric, Hanciles perceives "that the global expansion of Mormonism is marked by major limitations that require serious attention."[22] Hanciles does acknowledge, however, that the 1978 lifting of the LDS priesthood ban was an example of multidirectional transformation. He argues that the revelation (and official pronouncement) bear "all the hallmarks of unidirectional change—it came from the top, literally!" At the same time, "it is also undeniable that particular developments and experiences outside the US context, specifically in Brazil and Africa, had a critical bearing on producing this outcome."[23] Additionally the reciprocity of the change, which can be seen as growing out of non-Western realities, is evident in that "the policy change in turn had profound effect on the growth of Mormonism in non-western contexts."[24]

Based on the critical analysis of the aforementioned scholars, one of the central questions that informs my study of Mormonism in India is the degree to which the LDS Church is able to adapt to local culture. I also look for any evidence of multidirectional transformation. I suggest that when stakes have been established in a country the process of globalization that Hanciles refers to is present, even if gradual. At the stake level local leaders have greater authority to take the principles of the church and, within doctrinal boundaries, make them their own. The church "tent" has been dismantled, relocated, and reassembled at the stake level. International stakes in turn help to secure the larger central structure and also contribute to its whole. Cultural adaptation of the stake is relatively slow, but it is eventually and increasingly a localized and a reciprocal process. In the week-to-week

---

19. Mark Juergensmeyer, ed., *Global Religions: An Introduction* (New York: Oxford University Press, 2003), 5.

20. Hanciles, "'Would that All God's People Were Prophets,'" 44.

21. Ibid., 43.

22. Ibid., 54.

23. Ibid., 59.

24. Ibid., 51.

activities of the church, it is the local leaders and members who teach, lead, plan, and implement the work of the church within their own unique culture.

The Hyderabad India Stake

In April 2014, I spent one month conducting ethnographic research on Mormonism in India, interviewing LDS Church members and attending various church meetings. The first meeting I attended was an adult-only session of district conference in Delhi. The president of the New Delhi Mission, a native of Canada, spoke about the need to help establish a stake in Delhi. As I sat with approximately 150 members in the rented chapel that had been converted from an old apartment building, the mission president outlined very clearly what was needed to reach this milestone. He explained that 1,900 total members were required for a district to become a stake, and that the Delhi district needed 383 more members to qualify. He clarified that before a stake is organized, there must be a sufficient number of local Melchizedek Priesthood holders prepared to take the lead.[25] To fully staff a stake it would take 130 active, tithe-paying priesthood holders—fifty-eight more than the Delhi district contained. The implicit message was that the creation of a stake was based as much or more on quantifiable metrics than on the spiritual maturity of the community. Furthermore, many of the metrics cited by the mission president focused exclusively on the religious commitment and activity of male priesthood holders, with women's involvement clearly a secondary concern in the determination of whether an area was prepared for the creation of a stake.

The following Sunday I attended stake conference in Hyderabad, which was held in a large LDS meetinghouse. The church architecture, art on the walls, and organ music was virtually identical to other LDS congregations around the world—clues that I was in a "correlated" building unique within the landscape of India, and also indicative of a more developed stage of church growth than I saw in Delhi. I noticed various other signs that I was in a stake rather than a district meeting. For instance, every speaker at the stake conference was a locally born Indian except for a visiting general authority from Singapore. The topics were more geared to an audience of second- and third-generation Latter-day Saints rather than new converts. All of the men on the program and almost all male members in attendance were wearing what

---

25. The Melchizedek Priesthood is the authority under which the church is governed. It is conferred on all worthy adult men, though only those men who are actively attending church, paying tithing (10 percent of one's income), and conforming to the church's other disciplines are considered active priesthood holders and therefore eligible for priesthood leadership positions.

Indian members call "priesthood attire"—a white shirt, dress slacks, and a tie. The women were dressed in colorful saris or salwar kameez (long tunics worn with pants). There were fewer full-time missionaries and more local families in attendance. The contrast between the congregations in Delhi and Hyderabad illustrated that LDS Church growth and development is taking place simultaneously but unevenly in different locales throughout the same country.

Modern LDS mission work began in Hyderabad in 1978, the same year that the church lifted its ban on black men holding the priesthood and all black Latter-day Saints entering temples. India witnessed very slow growth for many years, with a mission not even fully organized in the country until 1993. Not until 2012 did Hyderabad become the site of the first LDS stake in India. This stands as a stark contrast to other areas of the world, such as Latin America and the Philippines, where the LDS Church enjoyed far more rapid growth in the last quarter of the twentieth century. I suggest that the different trajectory of church development in India can best be understood by a consideration of four factors: the evolution of LDS missiology in response to local contexts; the challenge of engaging with startling religious pluralism, especially the prevalence of non-Christian religions; the obstacles associated with operating in India's unique context of caste, class, and (post)colonialism; and the question of Mormonism's ability to translate and adapt to different cultures. Although each of these categories is unique to the Indian situation, they also speak to broader trends, particularly in areas of the world in which the LDS Church has not enjoyed substantial growth. Operating in non-Western cultures will become increasingly important if the church seeks to become more fully global. Studying how these dynamics have played and continue to play out in India provides a window for better understanding the internationalization of Mormonism in the late twentieth and early twenty-first centuries.

LDS Missiology

Though we often speak of Mormonism's internationalization, the fact is that the LDS Church encounters not a single international culture when it goes beyond the United States but an infinitely diverse range of local contexts and histories.[26] Therefore, to fully appreciate the Mormon missionary encounter in India, we must understand the political discourse regarding the term "conversion" and how it has been central to historical events in modern India. Debates over religious conversion cannot be separated from India's

---

26. This observation holds true within the United States as well, as LDS missionaries have to navigate the particularities of local and regional culture.

colonial past; many scholars consider missionary work to have been a part of European colonizers' "apparatus of cultural coercion."[27] Members of the Indian independence movement promoted the integrity of indigenous Indian religions against the intrusions of perceived outsiders. Gandhi argued, "Every nation considers its own faith to be as good as that of any other. Certainly the great faiths held by the people of India are adequate for her people. India stands in no need of conversion from one faith to another."[28] Yet when an independent India adopted its constitution in 1949, liberal notions of a free religious market won out. The constitution declared: "All persons are equally entitled to freedom of conscience and the right freely to profess, practise [*sic*] and propagate religion."[29] India was conceived as a secular nation that would allow for the free exercise of any religion rather than the privileging of any particular form.

During the early years of independence, Christian missionaries were tolerated because of their contributions to education, medicine, and social work. An expanding postcolonial consciousness and the increasing numbers of foreign missionaries along with the mass conversion of *adivasis* (indigenous tribal peoples) and *dalits* (meaning "oppressed," formerly known as untouchables) expanded Christian influence in India. However, the Indian nationalist government grew anxious and even suspicious of Christian missions. Religion became increasingly politicized and tied to socioeconomic aims. Thus, during the early 1950s the Indian government began severely restricting visas for foreign missionaries.[30] It was in this period that the Church of Jesus Christ of Latter-day Saints reentered the scene of Christian mission in India. Mormon missionaries had been sent to India in the 1850s but were unsuccessful in creating a permanent presence for several reasons, not the least of which was the doctrine of gathering that took the British converts in India to Salt Lake and left the few indigenous members of the church, those without the resources to finance the transoceanic voyage, to flounder. There were various attempts to send missionaries back to India over the next hundred years but none resulted in a permanent presence for the church.

One of the first members of the LDS Church in modern India was S. Paul Thiruthuvadoss, a Christian in South India who in 1954 found an LDS missionary

---

27. Jean Comaroff and John Comaroff, *Of Revelation and Revolution: Christianity, Colonialism, and Consciousness in South Africa* (Chicago: University of Chicago Press, 1991), 250–251.

28. Mahatma Gandhi, *Young India*, April 23, 1931, quoted in Sebastian C.H. Kim, *In Search of Identity: Debates on Religious Conversion in India* (New Delhi: Oxford University Press, 2003), 12.

29. Article 25 of the Constitution of India, quoted in Kim, *In Search of Identity*, 37.

30. For a more detailed overview of this argument see Kim, *In Search of Identity*, 40–55.

tract tucked inside a book he bought at a secondhand bookstore. He recounted that he "read it two or three times and found it to be a revelation…the thing for which I had been searching over twenty-five years. A portion of it was the testimony of Prophet Smith." He noticed an address at the bottom of the tract and wrote to church headquarters that day for more information. He received missionary tracts and copies of the LDS scriptures and was told to contact the Hong Kong mission president. After reading the Book of Mormon five times over the next three years and becoming convinced of its truthfulness, he asked to be baptized but was told by his contacts in the church that he would need to wait because the Church was not yet officially recognized by the Indian government and a support structure was not in place to administer the church properly.[31]

Thiruthuvadoss began to teach people and hold an informal Sunday School program in the villages surrounding the city of Coimbatore. In 1962, church apostle Richard L. Evans was visiting India on a Rotary program and made the first official visit to Thiruthuvadoss. In December 1964 apostle Gordon B. Hinckley dedicated India for official evangelization and made a visit to see Thiruthuvadoss. After a full day of traveling to the congregations that Thiruthuvadoss was teaching, Hinckley wrote a journal entry that read in part,

> My thoughts are greatly troubled over what I have seen. I do not know what we should do. These are earnest people, but they have been schooled in the Pentecostal ways, which are not our ways. Furthermore, the task of working among the poor of India is so great that I do not know where we should start. We certainly need the inspiration of the Lord in whatever action we take here.[32]

Hinckley's concerns notwithstanding, on February 7, 1965, Thiruthuvadoss was finally baptized. The mission president in Singapore assigned two missionaries to continue the work in India on tourist visas for six months. During the 1960s tensions concerning freedom of religion and the right to proselytize in India heated up considerably. In 1967, Hindu nationalists succeeded in passing the Orissa Freedom of Religion Act, which stated, "No person shall convert or attempt to convert, either directly or otherwise, any person from

---

31. Jerry C. Garlock, "A History of the Church in India," 110–111, unpublished manuscript in author's possession. The title page says the manuscript was compiled by Elder Jerry C. Garlock in 1995 under the direction of John K. Carmack, Asia Area President, Gurcharan Singh Gill, India Bangalore Mission President, and "'Written' by the Labors of the Single Missionaries, the Couples, and the Saints Who Lived and Served in India."

32. From Gordon B. Hinckley diary, December 12, 1964, quoted in Garlock, "A History of the Church in India," 115.

one religious faith to another by the use of force or by inducement or by any fraudulent means."[33] Similar bills followed in other states. Many Christians and Muslims complained that the "Freedom of Religion" laws actually limited the freedoms granted to citizens by the Indian constitution. Individuals are required to gain government consent before undertaking rituals like baptism that signify conversion to a different religion. Furthermore, this legislation leaves the interpretation of the phrase "by the use of force or by inducement or by any fraudulent means" nebulous. As Eliza F. Kent has explained, the imprecision of interpretation "means that the laws regulating conversion primarily serve the interests of those who profit most from the status quo."[34]

The opening of the Indian mission field was particularly challenging for the LDS Church in the 1950s and 1960s due to visa limitations and the politically charged nature of religious switching. While other larger Christian denominations could point to educational and medical institutions to validate their presence, the LDS Church had no such justifications for its presence in India beyond pure proselytization. Additionally, as Gordon B. Hinckley's concerns revealed, church leaders worried that a too hasty indigenization of the church, without sufficient leadership and training from missionaries and other priesthood leaders sent from the United States who could teach them "our ways," would result in a religion that more closely resembled Pentecostalism than institutional Mormonism. Furthermore, as Hinckley's second concern reveals, the LDS Church was simply not prepared in the 1960s to take on the issues of poverty in India.

Thanks in large part to Thiruthuvadoss's efforts, the LDS Church took root in Coimbatore among a group of poor and lower caste people who spoke very little English. To this day, the village branches in the Coimbatore area are the only native language units in the country and are often administered by a leader from the city that serves as branch president. As historian Lanier Britsch explained, "Since about 1980, Church leaders in India have followed a general policy of teaching people who are literate, generally in English as well as in local languages, and who are capable of building the Church and not being dependent upon it for support."[35] This missiological approach has been termed "centers of strength" and is best explained by juxtaposing it with the opposite approach taken by the RLDS/Community of Christ in India. During

---

33. The Orissa Freedom of Religion Act, 1967, quoted in Kim, *In Search of Identity*, 59.

34. Eliza F. Kent, *Converting Women: Gender and Protestant Christianity in Colonial South India* (New York: Oxford University Press, 2004), 239.

35. R. Lanier Britsch, *From the East: The History of the Latter-day Saints in Asia, 1851–1996* (Salt Lake City: Deseret Book Company, 1998), 515.

the 1960s the Reorganized Church of Jesus Christ of Latter Day Saints baptized its first members in India. The RLDS Church grew among Sora tribal peoples in Orissa. Today the now-named Community of Christ congregations in this area report attendance at Sunday meetings of up to 15,000 people—more than the entire number of LDS Church members in all of India. David Howlett, who also conducted ethnographic research in India during 2014, interviewed the leader of a third "Mormonism" which broke off from RLDS growth and claims even higher numbers than the LDS and Community of Christ churches in India.[36]

The Community of Christ and the LDS Church both experienced organic growth during the 1960s, but as the Community of Christ charged toward full inculturation and evangelization among tribal peoples in their native tongues, the LDS Church deliberately limited growth, aside from the Coimbatore area, to English-speaking missions and building "centers of strength." This has created two very different outcomes. The Community of Christ congregations located mainly in poorer villages look more like the surrounding Pentecostal churches in India, and the challenge according to leaders is to help them embrace their Community of Christ identity.[37] Howlett has suggested that "affiliation" may be a more accurate word than "membership" to "describe the Soras' belonging within the Community of Christ."[38] On the other hand, LDS centers of strength are located in larger metropolitan areas where there is a growing middle-class population. LDS members clearly "belong" to the centralized correlated structure of the church in what might be seen as a neocolonial system of authority. The policy provides ease of administration but also has economic implications. When Hinckley visited India in 1964 and struggled to conceptualize how exactly to preach to the masses of India's poor, he wrote, "I would hope that a branch might be established here of people of what we might term the middle class and that as they become strong they can bring others into the church, including the poor."[39] The stake in Hyderabad resembles Hinckley's hope.

---

36. David Howlett in discussion with the author, September 2014.

37. See David J. Howlett, "'When I Became Christian . . . the Goddesses Left Me': Conversions, Ruptures, and Continuities among Community of Christ in Tribal India," paper presented at the Mormon History Association Conference, Provo, Utah, June 6, 2015; Steve Shields, oral history interview by author, August 2014.

38. Howlett, "'When I Became Christian," 7.

39. John Santosh Kumar Murala, "Kirtland, Nauvoo and Now Looking Towards Stakes of Zion in India," paper presented at the Mormon History Association, Provo, Utah, June, 5, 2015; see also Garlock, "A History of the Church in India," 11.

The history of the Hyderabad Stake starts with Edwin and Elsie Dharmaraju, Hyderabadians who joined the LDS Church in 1977 when they lived in Samoa. In 1978 they were sent on a short-term mission to teach the gospel to family members in Hyderabad. During their three-month mission Elsie and Edwin taught family members, twenty-two of which were baptized. John Murala, a nephew of Edwin's who at age eight was the youngest of these 1978 converts, was serving as a member of the Bangalore mission presidency at the time of my visit to Hyderabad. Murala is a pediatric heart surgeon by trade and an amateur historian. Not only does he represent Hinckley's desired middle class, but his historical efforts indicate that the "huge task of historical interpretation" will not always remain "firmly in Western hands" and the flow of discourse on the history of the church in India will be multidirectional.[40]

Murala compares the initial history of the church in Hyderabad with the Kirtland/Missouri period in early Mormon history. In his view, the first two years between the time of the baptisms and the arrival of the first missionary couple was "like the first saints in Kirtland after the missionaries left and before Joseph Smith arrived. We were trying to make sense of our new faith on our own."[41] During these years they had periodic visits from mission presidents usually based in Singapore and the first missionaries—senior couples who were called to serve in India starting in 1978, assigned to act as Church representatives and instructed to "refrain from active proselyting."[42] These visits were brief and sporadic; the longest was a month-long stay in September 1980 by a senior missionary couple assigned specifically to work with the relatives of Edwin Dharmaraju.

For several years, LDS missionaries in India were primarily senior couples, assisted by a limited number of young single "elders" from the Singapore Mission who were assigned to India for brief periods of time. The impact of these senior missionaries was substantial even if their visits were short. Without exception, each of the members I interviewed who joined the church during the first decade in Hyderabad, including some who have now disaffiliated from the church, talk about the work that was done by the senior missionary couples, mentioning many by name and recounting the things they learned from them. They spoke of a range of insights, from how to properly administer the church, to how to bake a cake, to how to have a successful

---

40. Hanciles, "'Would that All God's People Were Prophets,'" 66.

41. Murala, "Kirtland, Nauvoo and Now Looking Towards Stakes of Zion in India," 19.

42. Garlock, "A History of the Church in India," 55.

marriage.[43] One senior couple put up a volleyball net in the yard of the mission home/church building. Many converts, including John Gutty, the first and current president of the Hyderabad Stake, attributes the fellowship developed while playing volleyball as the reason they became or stayed active in the church.[44] A significant number of these senior missionaries were not Americans. Many were from British Commonwealth nations like Canada, Australia, England, New Zealand, and Scotland, who were able to obtain Indian visas more easily than US citizens.[45] The imposition of American culture observed in so many other mission fields was therefore attenuated in India, ironically enough, by those who were connected to the history and legacy of the British Empire.

Beginning in 1986, young native elders who could legally proselytize in their own country were assigned to full-time missionary service in India. This development led to steadier growth until the church finally established a mission in India in 1993. India followed the typical pattern of experiencing an upswing in membership following the permanent establishment of a mission in the country. However, compared to almost every other LDS mission field in the global south, membership growth in India has been considerably slower. The consensus among mission presidents who have served in India is that the greatest challenge to LDS Church growth is the lack of missionaries because of visa limitations, especially in light of the country's massive population.[46] A former mission president explained in 2013, "if we had the same number of missionaries in North America that the Church has in India—on a per capita basis—we'd have 35–40 missionaries in North America."[47] There is a sense of pride among members in India, particularly in Rajahmundry (which has been dubbed "the missionary factory"), because India has been able to supply a proportionately large number of native missionaries. The presence of a predominantly native missionary force has resulted in a missionary culture that is less Americanized than in other foreign missions where North American missionaries are a majority. This is especially true for sister missionaries since,

---

43. See oral history interviews by author, 2014: John Murala, Annapurna Murala, Pushpa Daniel, Alice Katighar, John Gutty, Victor Gutty, Madhura Gutty, Anishright Braganza, Zacharias Pulla, and Sujata Pulla, all recordings and transcripts in author's possession.

44. John Gutty, oral history interview by author, May 7, 2014 interview by author. See also Murala, "Kirtland, Nauvoo and Now Looking Towards Stakes of Zion in India," 31.

45. Garlock, "A History of the Church in India," 64.

46. Briana Stewart, "The LDS Church in India," *LDS Living*, April 23, 2013, 4, www.ldsliving.com/The-LDS-Church-in-India/s/72316.

47. Stewart, "The LDS Church in India," 5.

because of safety concerns, no young foreign (white) women are currently sent to India. The native Indian sister missionaries that I interviewed and accompanied on visits reflect the "new generation of experienced, independent, empowered, twenty-first century women" who "will be coming home after eighteen months of service transformed and eager to continue serving."[48]

A common theme in the oral history interviews I conducted was "when the Church is finally in the native languages it will explode with growth," or "I know of an entire congregation in a village that is ready to convert to the church if they were allowed."[49] These enthusiastic projections notwithstanding, the LDS Church has taken a decidedly cautious approach to growth in India partly in response to the vocal concerns of Hindu nationalists but perhaps also because of lessons learned in other countries. A prediction that I sometimes hear from returned missionaries is that "India will be the next Brazil," referring to the massive LDS Church growth that occurred in that nation after 1978. Considering the current 25 percent activity rates in Brazil, it's logical to surmise that senior church leaders are trying to ensure that India is *not* the next Brazil.[50] In 2002 the church consolidated stakes around the world, resulting in a net loss of the number of stakes. In the years since, "stake formation has been more cautious" and in most cases the church has not been "handed over" to local stake leadership as quickly.[51] New missionary standards and procedures introduced throughout the church in 2004 also emphasized the importance of not simply baptizing converts but retaining them, suggesting a more deliberate approach than had sometimes been taken previously.[52]

Church leaders' caution about explosive growth and evangelization in native languages in India may also have had its roots in similar lessons learned in the Philippines. LDS growth in the Philippines from the time the mission opened (1967) to first stake (1973) to first temple (1984) was relatively rapid. Today there are three temples, twenty-one missions, and forty-five stakes in the Philippines, but with an estimated 20 percent activity rate.[53] The

---

48. Courtney Rabada, "A Swelling Tide: Nineteen-Year-Old Sister Missionaries in the Twenty First Century," *Dialogue: A Journal of Mormon* Thought 47 (December 2014): 19–45.

49. See oral histories, India 2014, also comment from attendee at India Bangalore mission reunion, April 2014.

50. Statistical information in this essay is taken primarily from David G. Stewart Jr. and Matthew Martinich, *Reaching the Nations: International LDS Church Growth Almanac, Volume I: The Americas, Oceania, and Europe* (Henderson, NV: Cumorah Foundation, 2013), 335.

51. Cowan, "Stakes 1910–Present," in *Mapping Mormonism*, 185.

52. *Preach My Gospel: A Guide to Missionary Service* (Salt Lake City: The Church of Jesus Christ of Latter-day Saints, 2004).

53. Stewart and Martinich, *Reaching the Nations*, 806.

fact that a member of the Quorum of the Twelve Apostles, Dallin H. Oaks, was sent to serve as the area president in the Philippines from 2002–2004 evidenced the concern that leaders in Salt Lake felt over the issues resulting from rapid growth.

Engaging Religious Pluralism

The early members of the Hyderabad Stake all came from Christian backgrounds. Missionaries in India were initially only allowed to seek out Christians because of the political sensitivities of seeking to convert Hindus or Muslims. As a byproduct, those who had already made the change from Hinduism to Christianity had an easier time transitioning to membership in the LDS Church. This is indicative of a broader trend: the spread of the LDS Church, including its internationalization since 1945, has taken place predominantly in Christian majority cultures, with the vast majority of converts coming from Christian (mostly Protestant and Catholic) backgrounds. The Church does not record the previous religious background of members; however, I interviewed several members in Hyderabad and other areas who came from Hindu backgrounds.

The next major horizons of LDS Church growth will require greater understanding of and engagement with religious cultures outside of Western Christianity. There is still very little attention in LDS missionary training materials of how to adapt the gospel message to cultures that are predominantly Buddhist, Hindu, Animist, or Muslim, for instance. This makes India—a country of 1.2 billion people where an estimated 80 percent are Hindu, 14 percent are Muslim, and only 2 percent are Christian—a unique endeavor for the LDS Church. Engaging prospective converts who are not already familiar with the basic narratives, discourse, and cosmology of Christianity will require a more multidirectional missionary approach. Pioneering converts who hail from non-Christian traditions will act as important bridges and "translators" as the church builds institutional resources to operate in genuinely pluralistic environments. The prominence of these bridge figures, as well as the pure necessity of adapting to local contexts if substantial conversions are desired, will necessitate and facilitate localization and indigenization in the church.

One way that the LDS Church could engage global religious pluralism more robustly would be to develop an internal ethic and theology of pluralism. Diana Eck has suggested that "within each tradition there are particular religious resources" for pluralist engagement.[54] Inspired by the Book of Mormon,

---

54. Diana L. Eck, *Encountering God: A Spiritual Journey from Bozeman to Banaras* (Boston: Beacon Press, 2003), 189.

prominent twentieth-century Mormon essayist Eugene England proposed a richer LDS appreciation of the wisdom and inspiration in other world scriptures.[55] Mormons also have the internal resources to understand and value temples, revelations, dreams, and visions as well as the strong emphasis on families and ancestors that exist in other world religions.[56] Former church president Gordon B. Hinckley modeled a particular kind of pluralism in encouraging "people everywhere" to "bring with you all the good that you have, and let us add to it."[57] Yet when I tried to elicit responses from Hindu converts about what they brought from their Hinduism to inform their Mormonism, I was met with confusion or near horror. Most have been taught to view Hinduism as "idol worship" (a common Western Christian assumption) and thus cast away their supposedly benighted former traditions in order to fully embrace the light and truth that comes with being a Latter-day Saint. Developing an ethic of interreligious pluralism may therefore be a particularly tough sell for converts who have often made significant personal sacrifices and adjustments in leaving one religion to embrace another.

Moments of intercultural adaptation do appear, however. One woman, from a Brahmin Hindu background who joined the church in Hyderabad, talked about how as her community celebrated various Hindu festivals based on stories from the *Ramayana* she would bring gospel principles to light from the accompanying stories and customs, not unlike Christian/Latter-day Saint appropriations of the pagan customs associated with Christmas and Easter. The same woman, rather than discourage her sons' excitement for the great warriors of Hindu mythology, has learned to expand and direct their interest to appreciation for the great warriors in the Book of Mormon.[58] Another woman talked about how she continued the ritual of cleaning her home each Friday, no longer in anticipation for the worship of the goddess Durga but to create a better atmosphere for her family and because cleanliness is a gospel principle.[59] Additionally, one can readily conceive of the parallels between the LDS doctrine of a Mother in Heaven and Hindu goddesses and other female consorts to Hindu deities, but none of my interviewees from Hindu backgrounds made this connection.

---

55. Eugene England, "Becoming a World Religion: Blacks, the Poor—All of Us," *Sunstone*, June 1998, 49–60.

56. See Hanciles, "'Would that All God's People Were Prophets,'" 55–56.

57. "Words of the Living Prophet," *Liahona*, June 1997, www.lds.org/liahona/1997/06/words-of-the-living-prophet?lang=eng.

58. Annapurna Gutty, oral history interview by author, May 2014.

59. Alice Katighar, oral history interview by author, May 7, 2014.

Caste, Class, and Colonialism

Each of these three C's denote locations for important work to be done in the LDS Church in India. Caste in India is complicated and constantly evolving. Caste is much broader than the simple explanation we often get of four hierarchical divisions referring to a person's *varna* (a term that means color), with outsiders referred to as "untouchables" because of their impure status. In addition to *varna* people are also identified by their *jati*, or "birth group," of which there are thousands in India.[60] Reified both in the colonial system and by postcolonial efforts to abolish it, caste can encompass skin color, economic relationships, and power or social order, as well as purity. An increasing number of Indians, particularly in urban centers, reject "castism," and it is technically illegal to discriminate according to caste. Caste persists as a "symbol of collective identity and a basis for political organization,"[61] as well as in "affirmative-action-type programs (called 'reservations')" which are intended "to make-up for past discrimination in schooling and employment."[62] While caste also appears in religions outside of Hinduism, Christians are essentially outcastes and the choice to become a Christian and then openly declare it means losing privileges of reservations.

I asked my interviewees about their experiences with caste both in and out of the church. The results were mixed, though many portrayed themselves as oblivious to caste. Most said, "There is no caste in the church," a sincere sentiment which is only half true. Caste is never taught as a principle in Mormonism and is in fact clearly condemned. However, church members come from castes and live in a world with castes—for instance, marriage outside of one's caste is still frowned upon.[63] The caste system has been resilient in the face of numerous global, national, and socioeconomic challenges, from colonialism to democratization to market liberalism, and it persists through and in spite of Mormon egalitarian doctrines. Caste-like identities develop in Indian Mormonism corresponding to those who are endowed in the temple, BYU-educated, returned missionaries, fluent English speakers, and so forth. Yet the LDS Church does provide resources for resisting and transcending caste. For instance, church units are formed by geographic boundaries rather than by caste affiliation, as much of traditional Indian society is organized. The lay ministry of the church is also ideally structured to overcome caste

---

60. Diane P. Mines, *Caste in India* (Ann Arbor: Association for Asian Studies, Inc., 2009), 15.

61. Ibid., 76.

62. Ibid., 33.

63. Ibid., 34.

hierarchy, although it could also reify it if leadership positions are only granted to higher caste members. Even something as simple as the worldwide church policy of local members cleaning and caring for their church buildings has an anti-caste dimension in a country where Gandhi protested against the notion of untouchability through the revolutionary act of cleaning the latrines in his community, which is the "work of the untouchables."[64] I heard members in Hyderabad talk about a man who is a prominent figure in the community and of a high caste who makes it a point to take his turn to clean the church toilets.[65] Temple worship, administering of the sacrament, and women serving in leadership roles also serve to challenge caste norms and assumptions.

In looking at the complexity of caste we see that economic class is only one small aspect and often is own separate issue. Thanks to India's place in the globalizing economy, individuals from the "low class" can go on an English-speaking mission and gain valuable language and cultural skills that facilitate connections to international companies and higher paying jobs. An increase in wealth, however, does not change their caste.

The endemic social, economic, and political challenges faced in the global south are increasingly facing the LDS Church as it expands there. Mass poverty is deeply entrenched in India. One missionary couple who served in an emerging area of the church in India expressed concern that the church would never be able to really reach outside the middle class.[66] Indeed, basic economic concerns will become even more salient as Mormonism grows in India and other areas in the developing world.[67] If current trajectories hold steady and the LDS Church grows at a far more rapid pace in the global south than in more prosperous countries in North America and Western Europe, the church's ability to provide the same standard and quality of resources to all its members will be strained. Growth thus poses substantial challenges for Mormonism, especially if it seeks to maintain a consistent model of church buildings, for instance, predicated on North American standards. The church has pursued some variations in church architecture, but it raises questions of justice when Indian tithe payers receive fewer church resources than do American tithe payers, or when direct benefits from the church's significant expenditures to subsidize Brigham Young University are essentially out of

---

64. Eck, *Encountering God*, 207.

65. See field notes, Hyderabad.

66. Conversation with Stephen and Ilene Ferris, June 2015.

67. See Armand Mauss, "Mormonism Begins Its Third Century: Seven Predictions," *Patheos Public Square* blog, August 5, 2015, www.patheos.com/Topics/Future-of-Faith-in-America/Mormonism/Mormonism-Begins-Its-Third-Century-Armand-L-Mauss-08-05-2015.

reach for most international members. An unequal distribution of resources within the church that mirrors the global economy's inequities risks undermining Mormon theology's ideal of creating a Zion society in which all members of the church, regardless of geographic location, are "of one heart and one mind," with "no poor among them."[68] Furthermore, as the church expands in emerging economies it faces not only economic inequality but a whole host of social issues such as higher rates of corruption, addiction, illiteracy, and physical and sexual abuse. Government leaders who control the flow of missionaries into their nations often expect social contributions from churches, and tolerate proselytization efforts only insofar as churches provide tangible benefits to the society.[69] Although the LDS Church has become expert in providing humanitarian relief to disaster areas around the world, in recent decades it has eschewed institutional social service investments such as building and maintaining hospitals and schools.

Cultural Adaptation in Mormonism

Scholars have identified a "striking failure of inculturation" in the LDS Church internationally.[70] The single tent vision of the correlation-era church and the corresponding "centralized control of form and content that marks Mormonism means that the Church takes on a decidedly American image in non-Western contexts at the expense of local creativity and rootedness."[71] However, past shortcomings do not necessarily predict let alone predestine future failures. Hyderabad provides a vision of what the near-term future of Mormon inculturation and globalization might look like.

Descriptions of the culture of the stake in Hyderabad fall across the spectrum. Some complain of the Westernized handshakes or hugs offered so freely at church meetings, seeing them as signs that church culture promulgates American culture.[72] Others, including a member with roots in Hyderabad who has lived most of her life in Utah (and complains about some women in the church wearing the *bindi* on their foreheads), say the culture is "Indian, definitely Indian!" Others maintain that something is emerging that is outside

---

68. Moses 7:18.

69. Humanitarian missionaries in Delhi and Vikram Dutt in conversation with author.

70. Philip Jenkins, "Letting Go: Understanding Mormon Growth in Africa," *Journal of Mormon History* 35 (Spring 2009): 1–25; see also Hanciles, "'Would that All God's People Were Prophets,'" 56.

71. Hanciles, "'Would that All God's People Were Prophets,'" 57.

72. Samuel Babu Kakiletti, oral history interview by author, May 12, 2014.

of both American and India cultures. Many in this latter category have latched on to the notion of "gospel culture" promoted in recent years by church leaders such as Dallin H. Oaks.[73]

All of these articulations are at once valid and inadequate. Rather than pure Americanization, indigenization, or a vaguely defined and problematic notion of "gospel culture," my research shows signs of a hybridization of cultures in Hyderabad. The closest parallel to Mormon cultural development in India may be the case of New Zealand.[74] Grant Underwood and Marjorie Newton have illustrated the complicated relationship that has existed between Maori and Mormon culture in New Zealand from the first contact of Mormon missionaries in 1854 to today.[75] Grant Underwood has argued that the establishment of Mormonism among those of Maori cultural heritage offers "a compelling case study in how cultural conjunctures can yield an authentic hybrid."[76] Marjorie Newton cautions against inferring that "the Mormon Church ever formulated explicit, official Church policies of either biculturalism or assimilation for its Maori converts." She affirms that for the most part, Mormon mission presidents "administered the mission according to their own perceptions of the compatibility of Maori culture and Mormon doctrine."[77]

The fact that the negotiation of "dismantling and rebuilding the tent" in New Zealand occurred on a level below the centralized church is instructive to understanding the internationalization of the LDS Church. It is not exclusively a top-down process. True, the centralized authority in Mormonism is resilient and will always be a distinguishing characteristic of the LDS Church. However, I contend that scholars often underestimate the influence of local members in "peripheral" stakes who carry on the process of indigenization

---

73. See Dallin H. Oaks, "Repentance and Change," *Ensign*, October 2003 and Dallin H. Oaks, "The Gospel Culture," *Ensign*, March 2012. For a critique of this concept of gospel culture, see Walter E. A. van Beek, "Church Unity and the Challenge of Cultural Diversity: A View from across the Sahara," in Patrick Q. Mason, ed., *Directions for Mormon Studies in the Twenty-First Century* (Salt Lake City: University of Utah Press, forthcoming 2016).

74. India and New Zealand offer an interesting comparative study, since both countries boast activity rates around 40–45 percent, which is unusually high especially for congregations outside the Intermountain West. See Stewart and Martinich, *Reaching the Nations*, 1:525, 2:905.

75. See Grant Underwood, "Mormonism, the Maori and Cultural Authenticity," *Journal of Pacific History* 35 (September 2000): 133–146; Marjorie Newton, *Mormon and Maori* (Draper, UT: Greg Kofford Books, 2014), Kindle edition; Marjorie Newton, *Tiki and Temple: The Mormon Mission in New Zealand* (Draper, UT: Greg Kofford Books, 2012).

76. Underwood, "Mormonism, the Maori and Cultural Authenticity," 145.

77. Newton, *Mormon and Maori*, Kindle locations 4330–4334.

gradually but with results that can eventually influence the "center."[78] Though public statements by general authorities are significant, it is a mistake to confuse them as normative descriptions of what actually happens at the grassroots. Mormonism is lived at the local, not general, level. Especially once a stake is established, policies are interpreted and applied by local leaders who are products of their own culture and recognize the necessity of adapting general policies to local circumstances. Furthermore, the primacy of personal revelation in Mormonism means that individuals are often left to follow their own inspiration in negotiating culture and interpreting authoritative proclamations. The outcomes of this dynamic translation of the general to the local often surprise everyone.

One example of this process in India is in customs of dating and marriage. The most recent edition of the LDS Church's correlated handbook of moral standards for teenagers, *For the Strength of Youth*, says that "in cultures where dating is acceptable . . . you should not date until you are sixteen." Every Indian leader that I asked about the practice of dating called attention to the need for them to "interpret" this teaching for local members. An unwritten, universally agreed upon policy in India is that the age to begin dating is nineteen. Still the final interpretation is left to parents (or whoever is considered the patriarch of the family), and dating is still often not allowed or postponed until college degrees are completed.[79] It is more common for youth who are second- or third-generation Latter-day Saints or youth who have served missions to engage in dating activities. The majority of young women will only date when they feel certain that they are going to marry the young man, for fear of damage to their reputation and marriageability.

For their part, many Indian youth welcome the church's discussion of dating because they see it as enhancing their agency in selecting a marriage partner in a culture where arranged marriages are still quite common. Neither forbidden nor encouraged from the pulpit, arranged marriage still occurs among members of the church. The youth generally resist this model, however, and church leaders have realized that the youth program of the church was more popular when it allowed interaction between boys and

---

78. See Taunalyn Rutherford, "Shifting Focus to Global Mormonism: The LDS Church in India," in Michael A. Goodman and Mauro Properzi, eds., *The Worldwide Church: Mormonism as a Global Religion* (Provo: BYU Religious Studies Center, 2016), 71–94.

79. There is a wide spectrum of what constitutes a date in Indian Mormon culture from talking to a person of the opposite sex at a church activity to socializing in a group with both boys and girls to going on an exclusive activity with the person that you are quite sure you are going to marry.

girls and encouraged dating (at the appropriate age). The result has often been "love-cum-arranged" marriages. Youth find someone they are interested in and "propose" or declare their intention to "date." If things work out, they get their families to agree to a wedding. The interesting Mormon spin that I observed is what I would call a "Spirit-arranged marriage." I met several couples who had no prior experience socializing with each other but through their own process of what they defined as receiving personal revelation—which often included fasting, prayer, and reasoning, but not dating per se—were drawn to a partner. Submitting to what they considered to be the wisdom of the Holy Spirit, they would arrange a marriage or help their family to arrange the marriage. This evolving culture of dating and marriage among Indian Latter-day Saints shows a culture in flux, a dynamic negotiation between traditional Indian customs and correlated transnational Mormonism. What results is neither Americanization nor indigenization, but the creation of something that is unique and authentic—in other words, hybridization.

Conclusion

The aforementioned manifestations of hybridization in Hyderabad reveal an emerging—but not yet emergent—global LDS Church. The establishment of new stakes in India and other places around the world will be one of the best measures and platforms for a more dynamic interplay between localizing and generalizing tendencies. Furthermore, the presence of at least three varities of Mormonism on the subcontinent indicates signs of an emerging world religion. I anticipate that in time Mormonism will eventually become a world religion, though it will probably never claim the title as a result of massive numbers. Contrary to Rodney Stark's bullish predictions,[80] the size and influence of Mormonism will be less like Islam and historic Christianity and more akin to Sikhism or Judaism. As Patrick Mason suggests, "it is not inconceivable that the Mormons of twenty-first-century America might become like the Jews of twentieth-century America—concentrated in numbers but disproportionately influential because of a core set of values that fosters an ethic of serving and transforming not just their internal religious community but also the nation and the world."[81] It is important to observe in the internationaliza-

---

80. See Stark, *The Rise of Mormonism*.

81. Patrick Mason, "Mormonism Future: Influential Beyond Numbers," *Patheos Public Square* blog, August 5, 2015, www.patheos.com/Topics/Future-of-Faith-in-America/Mormonism/Mormonisms-Future-Patrick-Mason-08-05-2015.

tion of Mormonism, as Dieter F. Uchtdorf of the LDS First Presidency observed, "the restoration is an ongoing process."[82] In other words, even the LDS Church with its emphasis on correlation is not a finished product. As stakes are built and authority is handed over to adherents in locations all over the earth, international members and leaders will, along with their American counterparts, fashion and refashion new local expressions of the LDS Church.

---

82. Dieter F. Uchtdorf, "Are You Sleeping Through the Restoration?," *Ensign*, April 2014.

PART II

Political Culture

3

Ezra Taft Benson and Modern (Book of) Mormon Conservatism

Patrick Q. Mason

IN THE EARLY twenty-first century it has become axiomatic to refer to Mormons as one of the most solidly reliable voting blocs for the Republican Party. A 2012 study by the Pew Forum on Religion and Public Life revealed that fully two-thirds of American members of the Church of Jesus Christ of Latter-day Saints called their political ideology conservative, 22 percent moderate, and only 8 percent liberal. These findings were especially remarkable compared to the general US public, which in contemporaneous polls by Pew came in at 37 percent conservative, 37 percent moderate, and 22 percent liberal. The Pew study's findings on US Mormon party affiliation were even more striking: nearly three-quarters of Mormon respondents identified the Republican Party as their political party of choice, with only 17 percent opting for the Democrats; the split skewed even more heavily Republican among those reporting high religious commitment.[1] That preference for the GOP tracked with how Mormons voted in recent presidential elections, with 80 percent opting for George W. Bush in 2004, and 78 percent for Mitt Romney in 2012. Such a strong correlation between religious affiliation and voting behavior is hardly an anomaly in the contemporary United States. Indeed, similarly high correlations can be found between white evangelical Protestants and the Republican Party, and between the Democratic Party and both black Protestants and Jews.[2]

---

1. Pew Research Center, *Mormons in America: Certain in Their Beliefs, Uncertain of Their Place in Society* (Washington, DC: Pew Research Center's Forum on Religion and Public Life, 2012), 56–57. For the sake of convenience, in this chapter I will use the term "Mormon" to refer exclusively to the Church of Jesus Christ of Latter-day Saints and its members.

2. Pew Research Religion and Public Life Project, "How the Faithful Voted: 2012 Preliminary Analysis," *Pew Research Center*, November 7, 2012, www.pewforum.org/2012/11/07/how-the-faithful-voted-2012-preliminary-exit-poll-analysis. For insightful analysis on the intersections of religious affiliation and commitment with political ideology and behavior, see also Robert D. Putnam and David E. Campbell, *American Grace: How Religion Divides and Unites Us* (New York: Simon & Schuster, 2010), chapters 11 and 12.

The political preference of modern Latter-day Saints is matched, and in many ways driven, by a corresponding theological and cultural conservatism that serves as one of the distinguishing markers of contemporary Mormonism, particularly in the United States. With a few exceptions such as immigration policy, the political views of American Mormons line up fairly consistently, and strongly, with the Republican Party platform: most prefer smaller government, support the use of American military force abroad, and oppose gay marriage and abortion, for instance. Of course, with millions of adherents the Church of Jesus Christ of Latter-day Saints is hardly a monolith; even in its traditional center of strength in the American Intermountain West there is notable diversity among Mormons in their religious practice and social and political views. Nevertheless, given the solid majority of American Mormons that identify with conservative positions, it is appropriate to speak of early twenty-first-century American Mormonism as a politically and socially conservative religious tradition.

Many of the roots of contemporary Mormon conservatism found expression in the life and career of Ezra Taft Benson (1899–1994), who served as an apostle in the LDS Church for over five decades, including the final nine years of his life as president and prophet of the church. Benson's prominence was not purely ecclesiastical. Especially in the middle decades of the century, he was arguably the most famous Mormon in the country and perhaps the world. Born and raised in a Mormon village in southeastern Idaho, Benson spent most of the first half of his life as a farmer and then agricultural administrator at the county, state, and national level. His call as an apostle came in 1943, and one of his early assignments was to spend a yearlong mission in Europe immediately following the end of World War II. This mission, accomplished with considerable verve and often in the face of genuine privation, had two primary goals: to reorganize and reconstitute the European missions and branches of the church, and to coordinate and oversee the delivery of desperately needed aid to Latter-day Saints in communities devastated by the war. One could rightly say that Benson was the principal enactor of the Mormon precursor to the Marshall Plan.

Benson's emergence as a national figure of import beyond Mormonism came in late 1952 when the newly elected Dwight Eisenhower appointed him to serve in his cabinet as Secretary of Agriculture. Benson spent much of his eight years in the cabinet on the road. He traveled to dozens of countries promoting American agricultural interests, including widely reported visits to the Soviet Union and other communist nations. Back at home, he barnstormed the country promoting the administration's farm policy as well as politicking for Republican candidates. He held more press conferences than any of the other cabinet secretaries, was featured on the cover of *Time* magazine twice, and in general emerged as one of the most prominent—and controversial—faces of the administration and the Republican Party throughout the 1950s. Although always conservative in ideology, he was a loyal administrator in the centrist Eisenhower administration; ironically, the USDA actually grew in budget and staff during his tenure, despite his personal belief in shrinking government bureaucracies.[3]

Almost immediately upon leaving the cabinet in 1961, Benson's political ideology turned even more sharply to the right. He embraced the ideology and discourse of the rabidly anti-communist John Birch Society, and became one of its most outspoken proponents. Though he never officially joined, he repeatedly called the Birch Society "the most effective non-Church organization in our fight against creeping socialism and Godless communism."[4] In the 1960s, while serving full time as an apostle, he took every opportunity and accepted invitations around the country first to denounce communism and what he considered to be its softer forms of socialism and liberalism, and then to promote political, economic, and religious conservatism. He was dismayed at the elections and subsequent policies of John F. Kennedy and Lyndon B. Johnson, and he avidly supported Barry Goldwater's leadership of the conservative wing of the Republican Party in the mid-1960s. In 1967 a group of private businessmen recruited Benson to run for president on an independent ticket, with Strom Thurmond as his running mate. When that effort fizzled, George Wallace asked Benson to join his American Party ticket, an overture that ultimately was denied by LDS Church President David O. McKay.[5]

Of course, Benson was hardly the only conservative in the LDS Church's highest echelons of leadership during the late twentieth century, but he was the most vociferous, particularly on political and economic matters. He was as enthusiastic to combine church and politics in his public discourses and published writings, particularly in the 1960s and 1970s, as his ecclesiastical colleagues were reticent. If figures such as Bruce R. McConkie and Joseph

---

3. Ezra Taft Benson's own account of his cabinet years is *Cross Fire: The Eight Years with Eisenhower* (Garden City, NY: Doubleday & Company, 1962).

4. Ezra Taft Benson, "Stand Up for Freedom," 13, typescript of address given at the Utah Forum for the American Idea, Salt Lake City, Utah, February 11, 1966, L. Tom Perry Special Collections, Harold B. Lee Library, Brigham Young University, Provo, Utah.

5. See D. Michael Quinn, *The Mormon Hierarchy: Extensions of Power* (Salt Lake City: Signature Books in association with Smith Research Associates, 1997), 99. For more on Benson, McKay, and the John Birch Society, see Gregory A. Prince, "The Red Peril, the Candy Maker, and the Apostle: David O. McKay's Confrontation with Communism," *Dialogue: A Journal of Mormon Thought* 37 (Summer 2004): 37–94.

Fielding Smith played a more prominent role in formulating modern Mormonism's doctrinal and theological conservatism, Ezra Taft Benson was one of the primary shapers, if not the chief architect, of late twentieth-century Mormon political and economic conservatism. Benson's strident messages inspired many Latter-day Saints to consider liberalism in all its forms as not only politically dangerous, but as genuine opposition to God's kingdom. When asked by a newspaper reporter in 1974 about whether a good Mormon could be a "liberal Democrat," Benson replied, "I think it would be very hard if he was living the gospel and understood it."[6] For Benson, Mormonism and conservatism were one and the same. "I have always felt that the Church is essentially in its philosophy and its teachings conservative," he said in an interview. "It's difficult for me to understand how a real Latter-day Saint could become one of these far-out liberals, because their philosophy and the philosophy of the Church just don't coincide."[7]

While certainly remembered in Mormon circles for his conservatism, arguably Benson's most prominent achievement and legacy, in terms of influencing modern Mormon thought and culture, was the strong emphasis he placed on the Book of Mormon. Though revered from the beginnings of the church as tangible evidence of Joseph Smith's prophetic calling and the opening of the heavens in the last days, for most of Mormon history the Book of Mormon had been underutilized and even neglected by Latter-day Saints, both in terms of personal devotional reading and institutional usage. In his study of historical Book of Mormon usage, Noel Reynolds showed that LDS Church leaders cited the book a meager 12 percent of the time when they appealed to scriptural authority in General Conference addresses from 1942 to 1986.[8] In this respect, Benson represented the exception rather than the rule of mid-twentieth-century Mormonism. His love affair with the Book of Mormon long preceded his call to the apostleship. He preached from (not just about) the book on his mission, and continued to give it a central place in

6. "Support for Candidate Possible Some Day, LDS Apostle Says," *Salt Lake Tribune*, February 22, 1974.

7. Oral history of Ezra Taft Benson by James B. Allen, Salt Lake City, Utah, October 1974– May 1975, 89, Church History Library, Salt Lake City, Utah. Benson's views were not universally shared by senior church leadership. His chief foil throughout the 1960s was Hugh B. Brown, a member of the First Presidency widely known in the church for his liberal politics. For broader treatment of these conflicts, see Quinn, *The Mormon Hierarchy*, chapter 3; and Gregory A. Prince and Wm. Robert Wright, *David O. McKay and the Rise of Modern Mormonism* (Salt Lake City: University of Utah Press, 2005), chapter 12.

8. See Noel B. Reynolds, "The Coming Forth of the Book of Mormon in the Twentieth Century," *BYU Studies* 38, no. 2 (1999): 6–47.

his personal study as a stake president.[9] He frequently cited it in his General Conference talks, as will be seen below. He even quoted from the Book of Mormon in personal correspondence with President Eisenhower, offering its prophecies regarding America as a source of "assurance and support" to the commander in chief.[10]

It would be an overstatement to claim that Ezra Taft Benson was single-handedly responsible for the increased attention paid to the Book of Mormon by Latter-day Saints beginning in the late twentieth century. But a series of General Conference addresses he delivered in the 1980s, both as president of the Quorum of the Twelve Apostles and then, even more influentially, as president of the church, represented a watershed. In 1984 he told the Saints that he had received "the distinct impression that God is not pleased with our neglect of the Book of Mormon." Two years later, in one of his earliest addresses to the church as prophet and president, he highlighted Joseph Smith's claim that the Book of Mormon constituted the "keystone" of Mormonism in its witness of Christ, its doctrine, and its claims to truth. Having established the book's centrality, Benson urged the church to "flood the earth" with copies of the Book of Mormon, and promised that it would be the catalyst for a new wave of conversions. Latter-day Saints responded enthusiastically to their prophet's call, and for the three decades since Benson's seminal addresses the Book of Mormon has enjoyed a kind of "first among equals" status within the LDS scriptural corpus.[11] Historian Paul Gutjahr argues that Benson's importance was "as a kind of culminating catalyst whose presidency served as a tipping point within the Church that propelled the Book of Mormon to the forefront of LDS consciousness."[12] Terryl Givens similarly confirmed Benson's influence in situating the Book of Mormon squarely at the center of the

---

9. See Ezra Taft Benson Journal, 1921–1923, November 22, 1922, Church History Library; Ezra Taft Benson Journal, 1939, November 26, 1939, Church History Library.

10. Ezra Taft Benson to Dwight D. Eisenhower, November 26, 1957, in Benson-Eisenhower Correspondence, Church History Library, Salt Lake City, Utah.

11. Ezra Taft Benson, "A New Witness for Christ," *Ensign*, November 1984; Ezra Taft Benson, "The Book of Mormon—Keystone of Our Religion," *Ensign*, November 1986; Ezra Taft Benson, "Flooding the Earth with the Book of Mormon," *Ensign*, November 1988. One measure of the Book of Mormon's increased centrality in LDS discourse is the frequency with which it has been mentioned in addresses in the church's semiannual General Conferences. References to the book remained fairly steady for most of Mormon history until the 1980s, when the number shot up dramatically, and has remained high ever since. See "Corpus of LDS General Conference Talks," keyword search "Book of Mormon," http:// corpus.byu.edu/gc/.

12. Paul C. Gutjahr, *The Book of Mormon: A Biography* (Princeton, NJ: Princeton University Press, 2012), 108–109; italics removed.

teaching of LDS doctrine as well as personal and family devotion, a privileged place previously reserved for the Bible. In the aftermath of Benson's presidency, Givens observed, "the Book of Mormon is now absolutely central rather than peripheral"—a statement that could not be said for most earlier generations of Latter-day Saints.[13]

Elevating the Book of Mormon to its current position of prominence has had a profound impact on the theology and mental imagination of modern Mormonism. In this chapter I focus not so much on the fact of Benson's emphasis on the Book of Mormon, which is well established, but rather on the particular way he applied select aspects of the book's content in advancing his conservative political and economic worldview during the three decades of his greatest prominence and influence as a church leader, from the 1960s through the 1980s. Benson did not simply encourage Latter-day Saints to read the Book of Mormon and find whatever inspiration in it that they would. Rather, through his selective reading of the book he provided church members with a particular hermeneutical framework for understanding the scripture and applying its sacred imperatives. Benson's interpretive framework highlighted particular passages and privileged certain themes that resonated with his own American exceptionalism, anti-communism, and arch-conservatism. Late twentieth-century Mormons learned to read the Book of Mormon in no small part through Ezra Taft Benson's eyes. In so doing, they participated in cementing a conservative legacy in the LDS Church and culture that has far outlived its most prominent advocate—though, as I will conclude, they have not done so uniformly or uncritically.

Before proceeding, let me explain what I mean by saying that Benson offered a "selective reading" of the Book of Mormon. To be sure, he was intimately familiar with the entire book, having read it dozens if not hundreds of times throughout his life. By characterizing his reading as selective, I am not claiming it was ill-informed or wrong. Scripture is by definition multivalent and complex, allowing multiple and often competing interpretations, each of which is predicated on a reading that necessarily highlights certain passages, authors, or themes more than others. Indeed, there is no such thing as a non-selective, noninterpretive reading of scripture; even literalism is simply one interpretive choice and strategy among many. Benson consistently quoted certain scriptures from the Book of Mormon while ignoring most others, at least in his public preaching. Other LDS authorities, not to mention other individual readers, will gloss over or entirely skip Benson's favorite passages in

---

13. Terryl L. Givens, *By the Hand of Mormon: The American Scripture that Launched a New World Religion* (New York: Oxford University Press, 2002), 242.

selecting a different core of their own. Like other books, and especially scripture, the Book of Mormon opens itself up to these various readings, all of which are grounded in the text and thrive in the rich literary, moral, and cosmological universe revealed there. Thus all readers of scripture, including prophets and other ecclesiastical authorities, are selective readers. Benson himself admitted as much when he taught, "Not all truths are of equal value, nor are all scriptures of the same worth."[14] Ezra Taft Benson's selective reading becomes interesting and important because his position as apostle and then president of the LDS Church provided him with an authoritative pulpit from which to promote his particular interpretation of the text.

In the October 1963 General Conference of the church, Benson succinctly stated, "The Book of Mormon has a lot to say about America, freedom, and secret combinations."[15] These three themes—America, freedom, and secret combinations—would dominate Benson's reading of and public preaching regarding the Book of Mormon in the 1960s and beyond. Benson often intertwined the three themes, as he did in a talk he delivered in General Conference in September 1961, just months after he departed the cabinet, regarding "the American heritage of freedom." The establishment of the American nation was, according to Benson, the result of a "divine plan designed by the Lord to raise up the first free people in modern times." Benson's account of American origins is decidedly and providentially exceptionalist. It was God who kept the Americas hidden and preserved for centuries, inspired Columbus to "discover America" for Europe, led subsequent generations of European "gentiles" to "escape the persecution and tyranny of the Old World and flee to America," and ensured that the American colonists would be victorious in their war for independence against Great Britain. God kept his eye on America and worked specially on its behalf because America had a special mission in world history. Once established as an independent nation, the United States was "a land of liberty" free of the rule of kings. A divinely inspired constitution guaranteed America's freedom and provided a foundation whereby it would become "the richest and most powerful nation on the face of the earth"—even a nation "above all other nations," to cite the Book of Mormon prophet Nephi.[16]

---

14. Benson, "A New Witness for Christ," *Ensign*, November 1984.

15. Ezra Taft Benson, in *One Hundred Thirty-Third Semi-Annual Conference of The Church of Jesus Christ of Latter-day Saints, Held in the Tabernacle, Salt Lake City, Utah, October 4, 5, 6, 1963, with a Report of Discourses* (Salt Lake City: The Church of Jesus Christ of Latter-day Saints, 1964), 17. Subsequent references to General Conference addresses will refer simply to the *Conference Report* and provide the corresponding date.

16. Ezra Taft Benson, *Conference Report*, September–October 1961, 69–70. See also 1 Nephi 13:30.

God would preserve the freedom of the gentile citizens of America, but only conditional upon their collective righteousness. The greatest danger to their freedom and righteousness would be "a vast, worldwide 'secret combination' which would not only threaten the United States but also seek to 'overthrow the freedom of all lands, nations, and countries.'" Here Benson was quoting passages from the Book of Mormon that revealed the workings of a secret band that sought power and wealth and eventually accomplished the overthrow of the rightful government through a series of assassinations and other intrigue. Benson read the Book of Mormon's warnings about the dangers of "secret combinations" as a prophecy with direct application to the twentieth-century global struggle between democratic capitalism and communism. In modern times, Benson taught, "the whole program of socialistic-communism is essentially a war against God and the plan of salvation." Therefore, it was incumbent that "every American, and especially every member of the priesthood, become informed about the aims, tactics, and schemes of socialistic-communism." This was not simply a matter of political preference or recommended counsel; rather, "the fight against godless communism is a very real part of every man's duty who holds the priesthood."[17]

The Book of Mormon was therefore a clear guide for modern domestic and global politics. Apostle Benson echoed the ancient prophet Moroni's description of how a secret combination would "take over a country and then fight the work of God, persecute the righteous, and murder those who resisted." Benson found it to be no coincidence that "the exposed hard-core structure of modern communism is amazingly similar" to the secret societies described in the Book of Mormon. In fact, the entire account of the secret combination in the Book of Ether was deliberately inserted by the last keeper of the plates "so that modern man could recognize this great political conspiracy in the last days." Benson thus had a prophetic fellow traveler in Moroni, who "seemed greatly exercised" over the possibility that members of the church in the last days would not recognize the "criminal conspiracy" in their midst, which would if unabated decimate their civilization just as it had the Jaredites, Nephites, and Lamanites.[18] Though he was hardly alone in his anti-commu-

---

17. Benson, *Conference Report*, September–October 1961, 70–71. See also Ether 8:22–25. Though Benson's identification of fighting communism with priesthood duty did not necessarily exclude women from taking part in the struggle, it did reflect his traditional view of men as the primary actors in the public sphere. As a counterpoint, historians have recently emphasized the importance of women, including housewives, in grassroots anti-communism and conservative politics. See Lisa McGirr, *Suburban Warriors: The Origins of the New American Right* (Princeton, NJ: Princeton University Press, 2001); and Michelle M. Nickerson, *Mothers of Conservatism: Women and the Postwar Right* (Princeton, NJ: Princeton University Press, 2012).

18. Benson, *Conference Report*, September–October 1961, 70–72.

nist stance—plenty of other church leaders at the time, including President David O. McKay, preached against the evils of godless communism—Benson's rhetorical posture was one of a lonely voice in the wilderness. He not only quoted but seemed to take on the modern mantle of Moroni, who had raised a prophetic warning voice only to be tragically ignored by his own people. Benson knew that the Nephites' failure to heed Moroni's admonitions had led not simply to moral decay, but also to genuine civilizational collapse and holocaust in ancient times. Would things turn out any different in the civilizational struggle against the modern secret combination of international communism?

Benson expanded upon his themes of America, freedom, and secret combinations-cum-communism in the ensuing years. In 1962, a quarter century before his more famous addresses as church president in which he urged the membership to "flood the earth" with the Book of Mormon, he expressed his wish that "every American and every living soul would read the Book of Mormon." Why? To increase their faith in Jesus Christ? To receive a testimony of Joseph Smith's prophetic mission? To invite the Holy Spirit into their lives? No, the reason why Benson wanted everyone to read the Book of Mormon in 1962 was so they could learn about "the prophetic history and mission of America." The United States, he taught, "is not just another nation, not just a member of the family of nations. This is a great and glorious nation with a divine mission and a prophetic history and future." At the same time that American troop levels were annually tripling in Vietnam, Benson referred to the importance of America serving as the Lord's "base of operations" in the last days, both for the spread of the gospel and in the fight against communism. The frontlines may be elsewhere—in international mission fields or in Cuba and Vietnam—but the security and integrity of the operational headquarters must not be compromised.[19]

Benson gave mixed messages about the invincibility of this base of operations. On the one hand, he guaranteed that "this base will not be shifted out of its place—the land of America." In an era of mutually assured destruction and "duck and cover," and only months before the Cuban Missile Crisis threatened to start a nuclear World War III, Benson promised that God would protect righteous Americans even if it meant "send[ing] fire from heaven to destroy their enemies." On the other hand, he taught that divine protection would extend to America only so long as it served God and followed correct principles. Both personal and national righteousness were needed to preserve divine favor. The list of sins that would compromise the base of operations

---

19. Benson, in *Conference Report*, April 1962, 103–104.

was lengthy: desecrating the Sabbath day; breaking the law; parental neglect and juvenile delinquency; viewing sexually explicit or suggestive movies, television, magazines, and books; complacency; "idleness, subsidies, doles, and soft governmental paternalism"; and "unsound economic policies which encourage creeping socialism and its companion, insidious, atheistic communism," including an unbalanced national budget and a failure to fully engage world markets.[20] This dual emphasis on individual and national morality is deeply characteristic of the Book of Mormon prophets, for whom the personal and the political were never really separate categories.

Benson interpreted the Book of Mormon as a grand narrative about the "great and prolonged struggle for liberty" that was at the heart of not only the American experience, but the entirety of salvation history. One of the Book of Mormon's major characters is a military commander named Moroni, whose years-long war at the head of the Nephite armies against their Lamanite enemies occupies nearly two dozen chapters in the heart of the book. (This Moroni, often referred to as "Captain Moroni," is not to be confused with his namesake, the last author of the book and the angel who delivered the gold plates to Joseph Smith.) At the outset of the war, Captain Moroni rallies the people and his troops by tearing off a piece of his cloak and scrawling upon it a motto: "In memory of our God, our religion, and freedom, and our peace, our wives, and our children." He then fastens it upon a pole, which becomes known as the "title of liberty."[21]

Captain Moroni's fight against the Lamanites, and his use of the Title of Liberty to rally his people in defense of "our God, our religion, and freedom," became emblematic for Benson of the modern need "to plant the standard of liberty among our people throughout the Americas." This reference to "the Americas," rather than simply "America," was significant. In the early 1960s Benson became obsessed with the spread of communism not only in Europe, Asia, and Africa, but in the western hemisphere as well. The issue was more poignant than ever because of what Benson called "the Cuban menace": for the first time in the twentieth century, "a hostile foreign power," namely the Soviet Union, had "established a firm beachhead in the Americas."[22] Like many other Cold Warriors, Benson refused to admit that Fidel Castro or any other leader who flirted with or openly accepted communism could be anything but a dupe or a tool of the Soviet Union.[23]

---

20. Ibid., 104–106.

21. Alma 46:12–13.

22. Benson, *Conference Report*, October 1962, 14–16.

23. This was also the case, for instance, for Eisenhower's Secretary of State John Foster Dulles and CIA Director Allen Dulles. See Stephen Kinzer, *The Brothers: John Foster Dulles, Allen Dulles, and Their Secret World War* (New York: Times Books, 2013).

Benson had often extolled the divine virtues of the Constitution. Now, with a communist state established on America's doorstep, he added to that sacred and inviolable corpus of American scripture the Monroe Doctrine, or the principle of European noninterference in the affairs of independent republics in the western hemisphere. Benson drew on statements by LDS leaders such as Joseph Fielding Smith and J. Reuben Clark in establishing both the authority and divine inspiration behind the Monroe Doctrine. In a pattern he would increasingly follow throughout the decade, he also drew upon analysis published in *American Opinion*, the organ of the John Birch Society, in its admonition that if the American people were "too blind or too cowardly" to resist the spread of communism in the western hemisphere, then they must "suffer the doom that history mercilessly imposes on fools." Benson ominously warned that "our liberty is in danger." Quoting President David O. McKay, who was in turn quoting J. Edgar Hoover—a common rhetorical strategy employed by Benson in compounding the authority of his stated positions—he declared that lethargy and apathy would not suffice. "This godless, treacherous conspiracy" that had spread in dozens of nations around the world had to be vigorously resisted. This was a fight of cosmic proportions. Just as Captain Moroni had rallied his people against evil and in support of liberty, Benson called upon his listeners to join him in "our fight against the forces of anti-Christ."[24] Lest his listeners think that Benson was merely offering political counsel, he emphasized that "the cause of freedom is the most basic part of our religion."[25] Benson's modern-day application of the Book of Mormon made clear that fighting communism was literally an article of faith—and perhaps even the preeminent one.

If America and freedom were the twin pillars of Benson's political worldview, then the secret combination of communism constituted the constantly lurking menace that threatened to erode their foundations. Fortunately, in Benson's view, God had anticipated the challenges his Saints would face in the last days, and provided the Book of Mormon as "the greatest handbook for freedom in this fight against evil." Benson's reading of the Book of Mormon convinced him that the world's most dire threat was the presence of "secret conspiracies whose desire was to overthrow the freedom of the people." To his detractors who saw him as a Chicken Little, Benson appealed to the authority

---

24. Benson, *Conference Report*, October 1962, 16–17.

25. Ezra Taft Benson, "Our Immediate Responsibility," devotional address at Brigham Young University, October 25, 1966, www.latterdayconservative.com/ezra-taft-benson/our-immediate-responsibility/.

of the Book of Mormon: "There is no conspiracy theory in the Book of Mormon," he retorted, "it is a conspiracy fact."[26]

Particularly in the 1960s, Benson consistently documented in great detail the features of this international godless communist conspiracy during his General Conference and other official church addresses. In these speeches Benson read world events and the Book of Mormon intertextually—it is difficult to determine where one ends and the other begins, or which was the primary lens on the other. By the late 1960s, having spent nearly a decade honing his message in response to the series of epic domestic and international crises that had unfolded, and deeply influenced by the writings of the John Birch Society, Benson was prepared to provide an exhaustive list of all the manifestations of "the international, criminal, communist conspiracy." In a 1968 devotional address at Brigham Young University titled "The Book of Mormon Warns America," Benson outlined in precise detail what exactly the Book of Mormon warned America about. The list of perils was frighteningly expansive: the Supreme Court of the United States was leading the country "down the road to atheism...anarchy and atheistic communism"; communists were receiving help "from right within our own government"; the Constitution hung by a thread and could only be saved by "the elders of Israel"; the devolution of the civil rights movement, which had always been the puppet of the communist conspiracy, was now leading the country into civil war; communists had "penetrated every major segment of our society," including "the news media, the schools, the churches, the unions...[and the] government"; the US government was signing treaties and trade agreements with "criminals" and "butchers"; fervent American anti-communists were "passed over, smeared and silenced"; and the military was being "handcuff[ed]" in Vietnam and prevented from winning a war "against a third rate country." Just as Benson diagnosed the long list of America's maladies, he also provided a simple five-step cure: "repent prayerfully, study the Book of Mormon, follow the Prophet, do our homework, and wake up." In warning America of its potential self-destruction at the hands of modern secret combinations, the Book of Mormon would be vital in America's salvation, and thus the preservation of freedom and the salvation of the world.[27]

In the 1970s and 1980s, Benson steadily moved beyond his three themes of America, freedom, and secret combinations when he preached from or about the Book of Mormon. He increasingly emphasized that the Book of

---

26. Ezra Taft Benson, "Civic Standards for the Faithful Saints," *Ensign*, July 1972.

27. Benson, "The Book of Mormon Warns America," in Ezra Taft Benson, *An Enemy Hath Done This*, comp. Jerreld L. Newquist (Salt Lake City: Parliament Publishers, 1969), 328–342.

Mormon was first and foremost a testimony of Jesus Christ. This would constitute the core of his message, particularly in the 1980s. The "major purpose" of the Book of Mormon, he taught, was "to bring men [and women] to Christ and to be reconciled to Him, and then to join His church."[28] In a modern age of doubt, when even Christian churches were questioning traditional beliefs, the Book of Mormon was an anchor in testifying of the divinity of Christ, humanity's need for redemption, and the crucial need for individuals to become converted to Christ and his gospel. In contrast to the Bible, "which passed through generations of copyists, translators, and corrupt religionists who tampered with the text," the Book of Mormon's testimony of Christ was "clear, undiluted, and full of power."[29] More than anything else, for Benson the Book of Mormon established the Latter-day Saints' distinctive claims to be the true inheritors, custodians, and disciples of the gospel of Jesus Christ.

For Benson, the Book of Mormon's Christocentrism was not limited to a positive expression of the gospel. Part of the book's utility was that in addition to outlining the characteristics of the disciples of Christ, it simultaneously worked to expose "the enemies of Christ." Benson's list of enemies now reflected a somewhat less intense focus on international conspiracies and a greater emphasis on domestic troubles. It is not coincidental that this shift began in the 1970s, during the era of détente in which the Cold War saw something of a thaw, when at the same time the culture wars were heating up within the United States. Whereas Benson had previously focused on communism and its fruits, now he was concerned with a more expansive list of false ideologies, still including socialism but also encompassing "organic evolution, rationalism, [and] humanism."[30] In a controversial 1980 address delivered at Brigham Young University outlining "Fourteen Fundamentals in Following the Prophet," Benson cited the Book of Mormon prophet Jacob's warning against the "learned [who] think they are wise."[31] This came on the heels of an address to church educators in which he had cautioned his listeners that "disaffection from the gospel and the Lord's Church was brought about in the past by the attempts to reconcile the pure gospel with the secular

---

28. Benson, "A New Witness for Christ."

29. Benson, "The Book of Mormon—The Keystone of Our Religion," *Ensign*, November 1986.

30. Ezra Taft Benson, "The Book of Mormon Is the Word of God," *Ensign*, May 1975. This message was repeated, with some variation, when Benson was president of the church; see "The Book of Mormon Is the Word of God," *Ensign*, January 1988. See also Benson, "Jesus Christ—Gifts and Expectations," *New Era*, May 1975.

31. Ezra Taft Benson, "Fourteen Fundamentals in Following the Prophet," *Liahona*, June 1981. See also 2 Nephi 9:28–29.

philosophies of men."[32] Benson testified that God in his foreknowledge had specifically prepared the Book of Mormon to "combat false educational, political, religious, and philosophical concepts of our time."[33] If Christ's communist enemy had receded somewhat in its threat level, it had been joined by a host of devious allies, including secular humanism and intellectualism.

Even with this development in Benson's approach to the Book of Mormon and its use as a lens on modern history, the key themes of America, freedom, and secret combinations remained. In 1988, as his health was clearly declining, the eighty-nine-year-old Benson offered his "pure testimony and witness" of the things he knew were true. Much of this included core Mormon doctrine regarding the plan of salvation, the ministry and atonement of Christ, and the restoration of the gospel. He then testified, in quick succession, of the truth of the Book of Mormon as the word of God, that "America is a choice land...and is the base from which God will continue to direct the worldwide latter-day operations of His kingdom," and that "a secret combination that seeks to overthrow the freedom of all lands, nations, and countries is increasing its evil influence and control over America and the entire world." He abruptly, and without any further comment, moved on without naming this secret combination, which nevertheless retained a privileged place in his testimony.[34]

By October 1988, the Soviet Union was gasping its last breaths, and international communism was about to be dealt a series of deathblows that would leave many in the West declaring a final victory for liberal democracy, thus heralding what Francis Fukuyama (prematurely) called "the end of history."[35] The Soviet Union's loosened grip in Eastern Europe sparked a wave of democratic protest movements that culminated in the fall of the Berlin Wall in late 1989. Benson's reading of the Book of Mormon seemed to adapt to the changing tides of history. His April 1989 General Conference talk, read by his counselor Gordon B. Hinckley because of Benson's poor health, is perhaps his best remembered among Latter-day Saints. The Book of Mormon was once again Benson's central text, but there was no mention of external enemies threatening America and freedom. Now the enemy to beware of was entirely personal, namely "the sin of pride." In many of his previous

---

32. Ezra Taft Benson, "The Gospel Teacher and His Message," address to religious educators, Assembly Hall, Salt Lake City, Utah, September 17, 1976, 11, typescript in Leonard J. Arrington Papers, Special Collections, Merrill-Cazier Library, Utah State University, Logan, Utah.

33. Benson, "The Book of Mormon Is the Word of God," *Ensign*, January 1988.

34. Benson, "I Testify," *Ensign*, November 1988.

35. Francis Fukuyama, *The End of History and the Last Man* (New York: Free Press, 1992).

addresses, Benson's list of proof texts from the Book of Mormon had consisted of a handful of passages in only about a half dozen chapters: 1 Nephi 13, 2 Nephi 1 and 28, Alma 46, and Ether 2 and 8. However, in this one talk, Benson cited more than twenty different Book of Mormon chapters, dramatically expanding his own use of the scripture and implicitly inviting members of the church to do the same.[36] It was only in the previous year that Benson had warned of an unnamed global secret combination and testified that the Book of Mormon brought people to Christ in large part by "revealing His enemies."[37] Now, however, "the great stumbling block to Zion" was pride. The Book of Mormon continued to warn America, but now of the enemy within the human heart, not the international political-economic system.

This message was consistent with the last General Conference address Benson delivered before becoming president of the church in 1985. In that sermon he drew on various passages especially in the Book of Alma in describing the process of Christian conversion as having a "change of heart" and being "born of God." One of the talk's most widely quoted passages insisted on an individual rather than structural approach to reforming human hearts and behavior:

> The Lord works from the inside out. The world works from the outside in. The world would take people out of the slums. Christ takes the slums out of people, and then they take themselves out of the slums. The world would mold men by changing their environment. Christ changes men, who then change their environment. The world would shape human behavior, but Christ can change human nature.[38]

Benson's characterization of true conversion echoed what had become a pillar of modern American conservatism, namely a greater emphasis on the autonomous individual actor than on the systems or structures of society. Mid- to late-twentieth-century conservatism rejected what conservative political strategist Frank Meyer called the "aggrandizement of the power of the state over the lives of individual persons," and promoted instead the classical liberal principle of "individual liberty and the limitation of the state."[39] This philosophy was captured perhaps even more trenchantly by Senator Barry Goldwater

---

36. Benson, "Beware of Pride," *Ensign*, May 1989.

37. Benson, "I Testify"; Benson, "The Book of Mormon Is the Word of God."

38. Ezra Taft Benson, "Born of God," *Ensign*, November 1985.

39. Frank Meyer, "What Is Conservatism?" in Donald T. Critchlow and Nancy MacLean, eds., *Debating the American Conservative Movement, 1945 to the Present* (Lanham, MD: Rowman & Littlefield Publishers, 2009), 178.

in explaining why he voted against the 1964 Civil Rights Act. His opposition came not, he said, because of he supported racial segregation or discrimination—quite the opposite. Rather, he believed that the law was not only unconstitutional but also that it simply could not achieve what it set out to do. "The problems of discrimination can never be cured by laws alone," he stated, since the problem of racism "is fundamentally one of the heart," which cannot be changed merely by externally imposed constraints.[40]

His reading of the Book of Mormon led Benson to believe that conversion constituted the very essence of Christian experience, which was, to paraphrase Goldwater, fundamentally a matter of the heart. This understanding echoed the preaching of Billy Graham and other mid- to late-twentieth-century evangelicals for whom individual conversion constituted the theological bedrock of their social and political conservatism.[41] Benson's theory of Christian conversion, operating from the inside-out rather than the outside-in, thus would have resonated with a Mormon audience that increasingly identified themselves within the canopy of American conservatism. By making Christ himself the great champion of an individual approach to social change, Benson placed liberal advocates of structural solutions—such as government programs for poverty reduction—squarely on the defensive. Their support for government welfare put them on the wrong side of a contentious social and political issue, to be sure, but more significantly put them at odds with Christ.

Ezra Taft Benson never made a grand distinction between his religion and his politics. He "definitely" believed his selection as Secretary of Agriculture came as "a call" from God.[42] What seemed to others to be incessant political preaching from the pulpit he considered to be a bold declaration of core gospel principles. If he believed that Mormonism was essentially conservative, he was equally convicted that his conservatism was essentially Mormon. The Book of Mormon laid at the foundation of his religio-political philosophy, and the persistence and force of his public addresses elevated the book—and especially his reading of it—to a prominent place in the modern Mormon consciousness.

---

40. Barry Goldwater speech to Congress, June 1964, in Critchlow and MacLean, *Debating the American Conservative Movement*, 83–85.

41. The literature on postwar evangelicalism-fundamentalism and conservatism is now considerable. A few recent works include Grant Wacker, *America's Pastor: Billy Graham and the Shaping of a Nation* (Cambridge, MA: Belknap Press of Harvard University Press, 2014); Matthew Avery Sutton, *American Apocalypse: A History of Modern Evangelicalism* (Cambridge, MA: Belknap Press of Harvard University Press, 2014); Darren Dochuk, *From Bible Belt to Sunbelt: Plain-Folk Religion, Grassroots Politics, and the Rise of Evangelical Conservatism* (New York: Norton, 2012); Daniel K. Williams, *God's Own Party: The Making of the Christian Right* (New York: Oxford University Press, 2010); and Bethany Moreton, *To Serve God and Wal-Mart: The Making of Christian Free Enterprise* (Cambridge, MA: Harvard University Press, 2010).

42. Oral history of Ezra Taft Benson by James B. Allen, 55.

Indeed, perhaps more significant than any of the particularities within Benson's messages about the Book of Mormon was his ardent insistence on the scripture's centrality for the church and its members. Mormons picked up the Book of Mormon and started reading it regularly and seriously in large part because of Ezra Taft Benson. That has changed the face of modern Mormonism, most dramatically by helping usher in a new age of Mormon Christocentrism. Benson may originally have intended for readers to discover "America, freedom, and secret combinations" in their study of the Book of Mormon, but when they opened the book they found a lot more than those three themes. Empowering people to read scripture has always had unintended consequences. Texts can never be reduced to a single set of predetermined conclusions. Readers bringing their own independent perspectives, concerns, and judgments will find in the text aspects that were invisible to (or perhaps consciously repressed by) those who put the book in their hands.

Ezra Taft Benson was thus the crucial figure in making the Book of Mormon not only the "keystone," but also the foundation of modern Mormonism across the ideological spectrum. He would no doubt disagree with contemporary Mormon liberals who invoke the Book of Mormon for their own purposes, citing texts speaking to the construction of a Zion society predicated on economic redistribution, deliberative democracy, gender equality, pacifism, and the elimination of racial and national differences. For all his rhetorical and ecclesiastical influence, Benson never had the power to entirely determine how the Book of Mormon would be deployed by the faithful. Still, for the majority of contemporary Latter-day Saints, the superstructure that has risen from renewed attention to the Book of Mormon has in many ways followed the conservative blueprint Benson established. His political and economic philosophy, which both shaped and reflected twentieth-century Mormonism's significant departure from its communitarian and economically centralized roots, has significant resonance for LDS conservatives.[43] His focus on American exceptionalism, freedom, and conversionist theology remain core principles for most American Latter-day Saints, even if the altered geopolitical environment since the end of the Cold War means that his obsession with communism has largely been eclipsed by an emphasis on limited government, religious liberty, military interventionism, and a critique of secular humanism.

Mormon libertarians, whose numbers are difficult to quantify exactly but whose significance has been felt in the politics of the Mormon culture region in

---

43. On nineteenth-century Mormon economics, see Leonard J. Arrington, *Great Basin Kingdom: An Economic History of the Latter-day Saints, 1830–1900,* new ed. (Urbana: University of Illinois Press, 2004).

recent years, are particularly energetic—and explicit—in carrying on Benson's legacy. One indicator of this is the website "Latter-day Conservative," which provides educational resources to "promote Liberty based on the Gospel of Jesus Christ" and warn against the advances of socialism. "Latter-day Conservative" is distinctly Bensonian in both tone and content. It contains links to articles and speeches from several LDS prophets, apostles, and thinkers, but the list is most heavily populated by Benson, and quotes by him are highlighted on various pages throughout the site. His talks and writings also dominate the website's twelve-part "Course on Liberty," which includes segments on some of Benson's favorite themes: freedom, the proper role of government, the Constitution, free enterprise, and secret combinations.[44] Benson is also one of the most frequently cited authorities in published treatises by Mormon libertarians such as Connor Boyack, whose book *Latter-day Liberty* was blurbed by Ron Paul.[45] A volume called *The Teachings of Ezra Taft Benson* occupies a prominent place on the shelf at American Heritage School in American Fork, Utah, where the LDS-oriented curriculum seeks to instill children with the knowledge that "America is a chosen land, established and preserved by the hand of God."[46]

Ezra Taft Benson was not the first to champion ideas such as American exceptionalism and individual freedom as some of the core elements of Mormonism. Nor were his articulations of these ideas particularly original. But the steady drumbeat of his public speeches and published writings over the course of many decades, reinforced by his eventual status as president and prophet of the church, helped engrain his political and religious worldview into the church's collective psyche. Inasmuch as Mormons identify left-wing ideas and programs as "secret combinations" that are spiritually as well as politically and economically dangerous, we can see Benson's continuing influence. The Book of Mormon became his most powerful tool in communicating his message, because it enjoyed the twin virtues of being embraced by Mormons as the word of God while simultaneously having been relatively little studied within the church, thus making it something of a blank slate for Benson to work with. A variety of external and internal processes contributed to the cementing of a conservative sensibility among most contemporary American Mormons, but no one infused that conservatism as a scriptural mandate, and thus a high and holy calling for the Saints, more so than Ezra Taft Benson.

---

44. See Latter-day Conservative website, www.latterdayconservative.com.

45. Connor Boyack, *Latter-day Liberty: A Gospel Approach to Government and Politics* (Springville, UT: CFI, 2011).

46. Elizabeth Stuart, "Utah County School with Mormon Values Aims to Go Worldwide Online," *Deseret News*, September 24, 2010; "Our Mission," *American Heritage*, www.american-heritage.org/Home/Why.

4

The Romney Lens

A BIFOCAL APPROACH TO MORMONISM, AMERICAN
RELIGION, AND POLITICS IN THE PAST
HALF-CENTURY

J. B. Haws

OUR STORY BEGINS in an unexpected place: Hooper, Utah. Hooper is a part-farming, part-suburban town of a few thousand people forty miles north of Salt Lake City, best known locally for residents' stubborn insistence on a strange pronunciation of the town's name (more like "cooker" than "cooper") and for growing some modestly famous tomatoes. Hooper figures into the story at the heart of this chapter—the story of both the changing place of Mormonism in the landscape of American religions, and the changing place of American religion in the landscape of American politics—because of a visit President Ronald Reagan made to Hooper on September 10, 1982.

President Reagan spent that September morning touring a cannery operated by The Church of Jesus Christ of Latter-day Saints in nearby (and much larger) Ogden, Utah. His host was Gordon B. Hinckley, a counselor to church president Spencer W. Kimball in the church's governing First Presidency. The cannery was part of the Mormon welfare system that had gained renown since its inception during the Great Depression. At President Reagan's request, his day ended with a small-town rally. Hooper had a fully fenced town park that could enhance security, and thus earned the honor of the president's visit.

At the Hooper event, President Reagan resoundingly endorsed the Latter-day Saints' welfare efforts. He called the Mormon Welfare Plan "one of the great examples in America today of what people can do for themselves if they hadn't been dragooned into the government's doing it for them." He reasoned that "if more people had had this idea back when the Great Depression hit, there wouldn't be any government welfare today or any need for it."[1] Coming from the leader of the free world during a personal visit, this was a high compliment to

---

1. For President Reagan's comments about the Mormon welfare program at the rally, see "Reagan Declares He's 'Terribly Hurt' by Vote to Override," *Boston Globe*, September 11, 1982.

the Mormon ideal and practice of self-reliance. For those with even a general sense of the Latter-day Saints' nineteenth-century troubles with the US government, the visit illustrated Mormonism's greatly improved public reputation.

President Reagan seemed to esteem Mormons—he appointed several to positions within his administration. Pundits recognized that Reagan perceived an affinity between the practices of the LDS Church and his own economic policies and philosophies.[2] Yet it was precisely this evidence of growing public acceptance of Mormonism that deeply troubled a constituency that felt itself largely responsible for Reagan's election: a coalition being dubbed the Christian Right or the new Religious Right.[3]

Jerry Falwell and his group, the Moral Majority, stood at the center of this coalition. In a move to expand the Moral Majority's influence and relevance beyond its mostly fundamentalist Christian core, Falwell often cast his group in as broad-based terms as possible. He repeatedly mentioned that his organization included Catholics and Jews—and Mormons. Researchers have suggested that the Mormon numbers in the Moral Majority were in reality quite small, and they represented a far-right fringe within the Latter-day Saint tradition.[4] Yet Falwell's very mention of Mormons caused discomfort in the

---

2. For a list of Latter-day Saint appointees in President Reagan's administration, including Secretary of Education Bell, Treasurer Angela Buchanan, and Solicitor General Rex Lee, see Michael K. Winder, *Presidents and Prophets: The Story of America's Presidents and the LDS Church* (American Fork, UT: Covenant Communications, 2007), 351–352. See also William V. Shannon, "The President Paints a Distorted Picture of Welfare," *Boston Globe*, September 15, 1982, for criticism of President Reagan's economic policies on display in his praise of Mormon Welfare. Several writers also saw evidence of President Reagan's esteem for Mormons when, in 1981, his administration dropped plans to station MX missiles in Utah after the LDS First Presidency protested the nuclear proliferation plan. See, for example, Robert Gottlieb and Peter Wiley, *America's Saints: The Rise of Mormon Power* (New York: Harcourt, Brace, Jovanovich Publishers, 1986), 2, 4; also John Heineman and Anson Shupe, *The Mormon Corporate Empire* (Boston: Beacon Press, 1985), 28, 176.

3. For discussion of the rise of the Religious Right—and especially correctives of misconceptions about pre-1970s Christian political activism—see William Martin, *With God on Our Side: The Rise of the Religious Right in America* (New York: Broadway Books, 1996); Daniel K. Williams, *God's Own Party: The Making of the Christian Right* (New York: Oxford University Press, 2010); Molly Worthen, *Apostles of Reason: The Crisis of Authority in American Evangelicalism* (New York: Oxford University Press, 2013); and Darren Dochuk, *From Bible Belt to Sunbelt: Plain-Folk Religion, Grassroots Politics, and the Rise of Evangelical Conservatism* (New York: Norton, 2011).

4. See, for example, Jerry Falwell, "Maligned Moral Majority," as a "My Turn" feature in *Newsweek*, September 21, 1981, 17. On Mormons in the Moral Majority, see Merlin B. Brinkerhoff, Jeffrey C. Jacob, and Marlene M. Mackie, "Mormonism and the Moral Majority Make Strange Bedfellows?: An Exploratory Critique," *Review of Religious Research* 28 (March 1987): 236–251. Their article came in response to Anson Shupe and John Heinerman, "Mormonism and the New Christian Right: An Emerging Coalition?," *Review of Religious Research* 27 (December 1985): 146–157. Compare also Peter Bart, "The Mormon Nation," *New York Times*, July 3, 1981, A19, and Kenneth L. Woodward, "A Distorted View of Mormonism," *New York Times*, July 23, 1981, A22.

evangelical world. A *Christianity Today* interviewer, for example, asked Reverend Falwell in 1981 if he would ever preach on his television program against "the deceptive advertising in the *Reader's Digest* by the Mormons." (The LDS Church was, at the time, offering information about the faith in inserts in the *Reader's Digest* magazine.) Judiciously, Falwell said that he would not attack Mormon members of his political coalition. The interviewer countered with what evangelicals certainly knew was the critical issue: "Say that in Salt Lake City they took the Moral Majority position right down the line, but because of false doctrine, they would not ultimately go to heaven....I'm concerned that we could get the country morally straight and people would still go to hell." Falwell answered that "if a nation or a society lives by divine principles, even though the people personally don't know the One who taught and lived those principles, that society will be blessed. An unsaved person will be blessed by tithing to the work of God. He'll still go to hell a tither, but God blesses the principle."[5]

That deep concern about the state of Mormon souls came to the fore again during Mitt Romney's presidential campaigns in 2008 and 2012. Evangelicals associated with the Religious Right worried that Romney's election would bring legitimacy to his Mormon faith and would boost his church's missionary efforts. Behind such anxiety were evangelical Christian concerns that Mormons were not simply idiosyncratic Christians, but *non*-Christians. Evangelicals worried that Mormonism was counterfeit Christianity, a wolf-in-sheep's-clothing deception that undermined efforts to bring people to the throne of grace. Thus in a 2007 email sent to hundreds of thousands of Christians, televangelist Bill Keller's ministry told his constituents that a vote for Mitt Romney would be a vote for Satan.[6]

Given the longstanding antagonism between Mormons and evangelical Christians, such a reaction is perhaps not overly surprising. What may be more surprising is that this was not the narrative when Mitt Romney's father ran for president forty years earlier. George Romney was called a kind of "political Billy Graham," and *The Nation* magazine deemed George Romney's Mormon faith one of his political "assets."[7]

What explains this Billy Graham-to-Satan trajectory? What changed from 1968 to 2008? This essay will employ a "Romney lens" as a kind of historical

---

5. "An Interview with the Lone Ranger of American Fundamentalism," *Christianity Today*, September 4, 1981, 23–24.

6. Bill Keller, "Daily Devotional," May 11, 2007, votingforsatan.com.

7. B. J. Widick, "Romney: New Hope for the G.O.P.?" *The Nation*, February 3, 1962, 96–97; "Holy George," *The New Republic*, December 3, 1966, 4.

bifocal approach to these questions. A retrospective look at the campaign of the elder Romney gives clarity to some things in the distance, the campaigns of the younger Romney to things that are more proximate. In moving from the micro (Mormonism specifically, in this case) to the macro (American religion and politics), the answer proposed here to that "what happened?" question follows these lines: When George Romney ran for president in 1967–1968, his Mormonism was almost a nonissue, a reality that was part John F. Kennedy, part pre-Religious Right, and part "golden era of Mormonism." Mormons in George Romney's day were riding a wave of positive press that carried them to national prominence as the face of family friendliness, well into the 1970s—and George Romney fit that face well.

When Mitt Romney ran for president in 2008 and 2012, Mormons were better known than ever before, and many Latter-day Saints had achieved remarkable prominence in every arena of American life. But that level of achievement produced added scrutiny and a sense of wariness that Mormonism, perhaps, was not what it appeared to be. History, it seemed, was repeating itself: to some observers, this twenty-first century angst partook of nineteenth-century accusations about Mormon theocratic ambitions. As in that earlier era, this reincarnation was, at least in part, the product of Latter-day Saint political involvement. But it was also the product of renewed religious opposition to Mormons—and of attention to historical controversies that dogged the LDS Church in the 1980s and early 1990s. If Mormonism's face was really a façade, critics charged, then Mitt Romney's character and candidacy should come into question, too.

With these issues in mind, this "Romney lens" will be turned here, first, on the biographies of father and son, with an eye on representativeness, on those biographical details that speak to larger trends and changes over time within Mormonism. Next, because both Romneys were, in their respective eras, probably better known than any of their coreligionists, this bifocal also offers insight into the public reputation of their minority faith. Finally, this lens has some utility when making observations about the role of religion, generally, in American politics and American public opinion.

A Bifocal Look at Biographies

George Romney's family history reads in most respects like that of so many of his Mormon contemporaries. His was a multigenerational, pioneer-stock Mormon family, and some of his progenitors were among Joseph Smith's close associates. But in one respect his story was unusual—Romney was born in northern Chihuahua, Mexico. A number of Latter-day Saint families, including Romney's grandparents, had established a handful of Mormon colonies in Mexico during the 1880s height of US federal prosecution of polygamy. George Romney, born in 1907, was the son of monogamists, but the grandson of polygamists.[8]

George Romney's time in Mexico was cut short in 1912 by the Mexican Revolution, when nearly all of the expatriate American Mormons left behind their Chihuahua homes and farms and moved back to the United States under the threat of violence from the warring factions. This forced exodus from one locale to another was reminiscent of much of Mormonism's nineteenth-century history. But it was also symbolic of changes in Mormonism as a whole at the time—this exodus from being polygamist pariahs to all-American patri-ots, from "satyr to Saint," as Jan Shipps puts it.[9] George Romney started life just as US Senator (and LDS apostle) Reed Smoot finally secured his seat in the Senate after years of protests and congressional hearings.[10]

The property and prosperity that George Romney's parents were forced to leave behind in Mexico meant that the family moved several times over the next decade in search of stability. George's father farmed in Oakley, Idaho, and did construction work in Los Angeles, Rexburg, Idaho, and finally Salt Lake City. From a young age, George and his brothers were involved in every family enterprise. In line with the traditional missionary thrust of his church, George Romney spent two years preaching the faith in England and Scotland. (That image of an enthusiastic evangelist would be one of the press's favorite ways of describing George Romney the businessman and political leader.) His missionary service was financed largely by the money he earned from a summer of dawn-to-dusk lathing and plastering.[11]

Upon returning from his missionary years abroad, Romney set his sights on Washington, DC. Although he would be drawn into politics later, it was Lenore LaFount that drew him east in 1929. George and Lenore had been high school sweethearts in Salt Lake, but her father's appointment to the Federal Radio Commission while George was in England took the LaFount

---

8. For George Romney's biography, see Clark R. Mollenhoff, *George Romney: Mormon in Politics* (New York: Meredith Press, 1968); also D. Duane Angel, *Romney: A Political Biography* (New York: Exposition Press, 1967). One of George Romney's great-grandfathers was Parley P. Pratt, a member of the LDS Church's first Quorum of the Twelve Apostles, appointed in 1835.

9. Jan Shipps, "From Satyr to Saint: American Perceptions of the Mormons, 1860–1960," in *Sojourner in the Promised Land: Forty Years among the Mormons* (Urbana: University of Illinois Press, 2000), 51–97.

10. On the implications of Reed Smoot's Senate hearings for Mormonism and for American religion, see Kathleen Flake, *The Politics of American Religious Identity: The Seating of Senator Reed Smoot, Mormon Apostle* (Chapel Hill: University of North Carolina Press, 2004).

11. See Mollenhoff, *George Romney*, 37–38.

family to Washington. George Romney was determined to follow. He attended some college in Utah and at George Washington University, but a budding career and his pursuit of Lenore interrupted his studies at first periodically—and then for good. When he arrived in Washington, on his personality and determination alone, he landed a job first with Senator David I. Walsh of Massachusetts, and then, because of contacts through the senator's office, with the Aluminum Company of America (ALCOA). When Lenore, who was achieving success as an actress, moved to Los Angeles to pursue a career with MGM, George arranged for a transfer to ALCOA's California office. It was there that he finally persuaded Lenore to marry him. They were married in the Salt Lake LDS Temple and then started their lives together in California.[12]

Before long, the Romneys were back in Washington. George was carving out a reputation as a well-respected lobbyist for ALCOA. A professional pattern was taking shape. Groups and individuals with whom he associated wanted him to work for them. That was true in the Senator's office, with ALCOA, and then with the Automobile Manufacturers Association. The AMA drew George away from ALCOA and Washington. He and his young family moved to Detroit, where he would make his mark in the car industry as president of American Motors, then in state politics after being elected governor in 1962, 1964, and 1966.

George Romney's case illustrates important trends within mid-twentieth-century Mormonism. Romney's family was a prominent example of what researchers have deemed the post-World War II Mormon "outmigration." Young Mormons deployed for military assignments across the United States and those who sought wider employment and educational opportunities set in motion a shift in American Mormon demographics, and the Romneys were in the thick of this change.[13] George Romney was appointed president of the Detroit LDS stake (a geographical unit of the church, akin to a diocese), in which capacity he oversaw Mormon congregations in Michigan and parts of Ohio and Canada.[14] The steady growth of stakes outside the Intermountain West reflected both the extent of Mormon outmigration and the success of the church's missionary efforts. "By 1960," Jan Shipps observes, "only Kentucky, Tennessee, and the Dakotas could not claim at least a thousand members of the LDS Church."[15]

---

12. See ibid., 40–46.

13. See G. Wesley Johnson and Marian Ashby Johnson, "On the Trail of the Twentieth Century Mormon Outmigration," *BYU Studies* 46, no. 1 (2007): 41–83. See also Richard O. Cowan, *The Latter-day Saint Century* (Salt Lake City: Bookcraft, 1999), 72.

14. See Deseret News, 2013 *Church Almanac: The Church of Jesus Christ of Latter-day Saints* (Salt Lake City: Deseret News, 2013), 213, 368.

15. Shipps, *Sojourner in the Promised Land*, 262–263.

One other note about Romney's representativeness deserves mention. George Romney had already been a key figure in the rewriting of Michigan's state constitution when he put his name forward as a candidate for governor in 1962. One account has it that George Romney "came down the stairs [of the family home], entered the dining room, and asked Mitt and the rest of the family a question: 'You know, I think I'm going to run for governor. Should I run as a Republican or a Democrat?'"[16] While this moment of political party ambivalence certainly reflected Romney's own moderate views and presaged his later position as the flag-bearer of a moderate wing of the Republican Party, it also seems indicative of an era before the so-called culture wars when Mormon voters had not yet so fully located themselves in the ranks of the GOP.[17]

Self-made man, devoted to family, celebrated for his integrity—this was the picture of Governor George Romney in the 1960s. Similar things could be said—and were said—about fellow standout Saints, like President Eisenhower's Secretary of Agriculture Ezra Taft Benson, or restaurant and hotel owner J. Willard Marriott. These were the respected faces of Mormonism, and none was better known nationally than George Romney.

George's youngest son Mitt grew up in circumstances much different than those of his father, but the parallels with his father's personal history are striking nonetheless. Furthermore, his biography shared in common many things with his generation of coreligionists.[18] Mitt was a child of the Mormon diaspora, growing up away from the Mormon cultural center in the West. While his Mormonism was always in the distinct minority in school and social settings, friends remember that he was nevertheless true to his religious standards.[19] Where his father knew the challenges of a family struggling to make

---

16. Michael Kranish and Scott Helman, *The Real Romney* (New York: HarperCollins, 2012), 23.

17. On twentieth-century political party trends in Mormonism, see Matthew Bowman, *The Mormon People: The Making of an American Faith* (New York: Random House, 2012), 208; David Magleby, "Contemporary American Politics," and Wm. Clayton Kimball "Political Culture," in Daniel H. Ludlow et al., eds., *Encyclopedia of Mormonism* (New York: Macmillan Publishing Company, 1992). The *Encyclopedia* is also accessible online; the two entries referenced here at http://eom.byu.edu/index.php/Politics. Mormon Republican leanings were confirmed in a January 2012 Pew Research study, "Mormons in America," which found that 74 percent of "Mormon registered voters are Republican or lean toward the Republican Party," as compared to 45 percent of the US general public. Sixty-six of the Mormons surveyed "call themselves conservatives," compared to 37 percent of the American public generally (www.pewforum.org/2012/01/12/mormons-in-america-executive-summary/#ideology). For recent data and analysis, see David E. Campbell, John C. Green, and J. Quin Monson's detailed study, *Seeking the Promised Land: Mormons and American Politics* (New York: Cambridge University Press, 2014).

18. See "Prologue" to Kranish and Hamel, *The Real Romney*, especially 3–5.

19. See, for example, Kranish and Hamel, *The Real Romney*, 54.

ends meet, Mitt Romney experienced life as the scion of the first family of Michigan. He attended a private prep school and then enrolled at Stanford University—the turbulent Stanford of the 1960s—as a freshman. Jan Shipps argues that the contrast between patriotic, family-centered, "clean-cut" Latter-day Saints and "counterculture," war-protesting "hippies" solidified in American consciousness the Mormon image of wholesomeness—and this could just as well have described Mitt Romney's early college experience.[20] In fact, a *Palo Alto Times* photographer captured Mitt Romney, dressed in a suit coat, holding a sign that read "Speak Out, Don't Sit In," arguing to convince protesters to give up their hold on the school's administration building and let classes continue.[21]

Stanford proved challenging to Mitt Romney in another way—his heart was still in Michigan, still with his high school girlfriend, Ann Davies. Like his father before him, when it came to love and romance, Mitt Romney made his choice early and tenaciously stuck to it. One college friend even remembered Mitt Romney auctioning off some of his clothes to pay for an airline ticket to visit Ann for a weekend. Ann wasn't a Latter-day Saint at the time, but she was interested in what she saw in the Romney family. When Mitt Romney put his studies on hold and left for a two-and-a-half-year church mission in France, Ann investigated the faith seriously. When Mitt returned from his mission, both Ann and her brother had been baptized into the LDS Church—by George Romney. The two converts were part of the 130,000 that joined the LDS Church in 1967, in a decade that saw LDS membership rolls grow by almost 75 percent, from 1.7 million to almost 3 million.[22]

Mitt and Ann were married in March 1969—like his parents, in the Salt Lake Temple. Mitt decided not to return to Stanford, enrolling instead at Brigham Young University. While a desire to attend a university with students who shared his beliefs must have been part of that decision—and Ann had already been attending BYU while Mitt was in France—it is also important to note that BYU was an institution on the rise. Mitt Romney enrolled at the tail end of a campus building boom. During the two-decade tenure of BYU President Ernest L. Wilkinson (1951–1971), "the student body increased six-

---

20. Shipps, *Sojourner in the Promised Land*, 100: "I am convinced that it was the dramatic discrepancy between clean-cut Mormons and scruffy hippies that completed the transformation of the Mormon image from the quasi-foreign, somewhat alien likeness that it had in the nineteenth century to the more that 100 percent super-American portrait of the late sixties and early seventies."

21. Kranish and Hamel, *The Real Romney*, 60–61; the photo is included in the photo section of the book after page 210.

22. See Kranish and Hamel, *The Real Romney*, 58, 70–72. For LDS membership numbers, see Deseret News, 2013 *Church Almanac*, 213.

fold to more than 25,000, the size of the faculty quadrupled, the number of faculty holding PhDs rose 18 percent, the number of departments doubled, the first of some twenty doctoral programs were authorized, library holdings rose nearly 500 percent, and the number of permanent buildings jumped more than twenty-fold."[23] Church support for that kind of growth at its flagship university spoke to the importance of education, both theologically and socially, in the LDS community. It is not insignificant to note that Mitt Romney graduated from college while his father did not. While this mirrored generational and societal changes at large in twentieth-century America, it also seemed representative of a strong trend in Mormonism. After 1945, Latter-day Saints increasingly attained higher educational degrees; social scientists in the closing decades of the twentieth century found a positive correlation between higher education and religiosity among Mormons.[24] Mitt Romney fit that pattern of religious activity: he would be appointed a bishop of a ward (akin to a Catholic or Anglican parish), and then—like his father—president of a stake in Boston.

Mitt's undergraduate success had launched him into graduate programs in law and business at Harvard. When he finished graduate school there, he and Ann put down roots in Boston. As with his father, job offers and opportunities seemed to crop up for Mitt from people who were impressed with an energetic and capable young man who rose quickly to the top of his field. In Mitt Romney's case, that was the world of investment at Bain Capital. Romney was a shining star in a constellation of young Mormons who found upward mobility in business and the law.[25] The tug of public service ultimately pulled on the younger Romney, too, and in 1994 he challenged Ted Kennedy for his seat in the

---

23. Gary James Bergera and Ronald Priddis, *Brigham Young University: A House of Faith* (Salt Lake City: Signature Books, 1985), 26. For a more detailed summary of the statistics related to BYU's growth during Ernest Wilkinson's presidency, see Ernest L. Wilkinson and W. Cleon Skousen, *Brigham Young University: A School of Destiny* (Provo: Brigham Young University Press, 1976), 745–749.

24. On American educational attainment, see the graph published from US Census Bureau data in Camille L. Ryan and Julie Siebens, "Education Attainment in the United States: 2009," www.census.gov/prod/2012pubs/p20-566.pdf, 3–4, which shows that in 1940, only "5 percent of the population aged 25 and older held at least a bachelor's degree." That number had doubled by the time Mitt Romney graduated from college. On studies of Mormon levels of education and religiosity in the late twentieth century, see Stan L. Albrecht and Tim B. Heaton, "Secularization, Higher Education, and Religiosity," in James T. Duke, ed., *Latter-day Saint Social Life: Social Research on the LDS Church and Its Members* (Provo: Brigham Young University Religious Studies Center, 1998), 293–314.

25. For an example of attention paid to Mitt Romney and other prominent Mormon business leaders, see "Schumpeter: The Mormon Way of Business," *The Economist*, May 5, 2012, www.economist.com/node/21554173.

Senate. In contrast with George Romney's initial indecision over political party fit, Mitt's Republican affiliation was never in doubt. Romney biographers called his campaign the "strongest challenge Ted Kennedy had ever faced," yet the incumbent ultimately put away the upstart Republican at the polls.[26]

National attention to Mitt Romney came again a few years later in the form of a different public role—that of chairman of the Salt Lake Olympic Committee. Utah Governor Mike Leavitt and others in the state recruited Romney to rescue a Games in chaos. A bribery scandal had discredited the previous committee leaders, and public distaste for the whole affair threatened community support for the Olympics. As it would become repeatedly reported in the media, the celebrated success of the Salt Lake 2002 Winter Olympics became a monument to the tenacity, optimism, and frugality of Mitt Romney and his team. "Turnaround" was the watchword—it even became the title of a memoir Romney wrote about the experience.[27] And the Games became a significant springboard for Romney when, later in 2002, he entered a wide-open race for governor of Massachusetts and won. He turned Republican heads nationwide with that victory.

Even this cursory overview of these father–son biographies can give a sense of why backers of both Romneys saw White House potential in the two men. Their personal histories also speak to why many observers saw them as exemplars of American Mormonism, characterized by a strong work ethic, moral rectitude, family devotion, and optimism. Their respective presidential campaign seasons thus offer insight into national perceptions about this key component of their respective biographies: their religion.

A Bifocal Look at Mormonism's Reputation

Bruce Olsen, who retired as managing director of the LDS Church's Public Affairs Department in 2008, memorably called the years of church president David O. McKay's administration—1951 to 1970—the "Golden Era of Mormonism."[28] The Church was riding a crest of unprecedented favorable publicity precisely at the time George Romney was on the national stage. This

---

26. Kranish and Hamel, *The Real Romney*, caption to a photo on the fifth page of the book's photo insert.

27. Mitt Romney, *Turnaround: Crisis, Leadership, and the Olympic Games* (Washington, DC: Regnery Publishing, 2004).

28. Bruce L. Olsen, Interview with Jonice Hubbard, September 8, 2006, transcript included in Hubbard "Pioneers in Twentieth Century Mormon Media: Oral Histories of Latter-day Saint Electronic and Public Relations Professionals" (Master's thesis, Brigham Young University, 2007), 121; http://scholarsarchive.byu.edu/etd/1256.

golden era was an alloy of several converging factors. As Jan Shipps's sampling of a century's worth (1860–1960) of national magazine coverage of Mormons showed, reporting on Mormons first tended on the positive side of the scale in the 1930s, and then kept rising from there.[29] The 1930s saw the aforementioned launch of the church's Welfare Plan, a response to the Great Depression that won wide acclaim for its emphasis on removing church members from the federal dole. Mormon resourcefulness was heralded as a model for the country.

These images of a well-ordered, self-sufficient people prospering in modern America contrasted favorably with all that had seemed threatening about Mormons in the nineteenth century, when the group had been depicted in terms of isolation, theocracy, and marital debauchery. In fact, in the late 1950s, sociologist Thomas O'Dea noted that some observers wondered if the Mormons' very success at conquering the desert meant that the church was headed toward obsolescence, now that the hard work of pioneering had been done. At the very least, contemporaries said, Mormonism was now simply one of America's religious denominations, notable for its adherents' remarkable commitment to a lifestyle of sobriety and activity and to a cheerful outlook on the future.[30]

Both that lifestyle and that outlook seemed stable—and that was widely appreciated. When contemporaries juxtaposed George Romney and President Lyndon Johnson, for example, it was Romney's religiously based lifestyle and outlook that came to the fore. Romney's business success represented the "clean money" of hard work, rather than the "family fortune" of LBJ that came from "wheeling and dealing" and questionable government contacts.[31] Where Johnson was well known for colorful language and backroom political wrangling, Romney was the straight-talking former missionary who prayed before entering a political race. Throughout 1967, Romney consistently led Johnson in hypothetical head-to-head presidential polls. Romney was the "antithesis" to Johnson, just as Mormon steadiness seemed the antithesis to the social upheaval of the sixties.[32]

---

29. Shipps, *Sojourner in a Promised Land*, 68.

30. See Thomas F. O'Dea, *The Mormons* (Chicago: University of Chicago Press, 1957), 259; Ferenc Morton Szasz, *Religion in the Modern American West* (Tucson: The University of Arizona Press, 2000), 156.

31. Mollenhoff, *George Romney*, 8.

32. See the important thesis by a former worker on the Romney campaign, Richard Melvin Eyre, "George Romney in 1968: From Front-Runner to Drop-Out: An Analysis of Cause" (Master's thesis, Brigham Young University, 1969), especially pages 66–73, for Eyre's detailed list of reasons for Romney's failure to secure the Republican nomination. Mormonism did not figure into Eyre's list, although he did list it as a principal factor in Romney's initial popularity, since Romney's image of honesty and morality stood as the "antithesis" to Lyndon Johnson that many Republicans sought.

This was behind *The Nation*'s estimation that Romney's religious commitment would be one of his political assets. Not everyone shared that sentiment; some commentators and political opponents were put off by Romney's piety, complaining that it was like "running against God" to face him in a contest, or suggesting that his praying for guidance was somehow manipulative or indicative of a messiah complex. But it seems telling that these complaints dealt with public display of religiosity in general, and not Mormonism specifically. There simply was not any kind of public groundswell against George Romney because he was a Mormon. Mormonism just did not seem troubling at the time.[33]

More than Mormonism's rising public reputation was at work here, though. John F. Kennedy's breakthrough as a Roman Catholic presidential candidate seemed to make any semblance of religiously motivated political prejudice distasteful, or, as *Time* noted during George Romney's first campaign, "irrelevant."[34] The religious mood in much of American Christianity was one of reunion, ecumenism, cooperation, and tolerance. This is not to say that there were no Americans who worried about Mormon influence. Baptist minister and prolific author Walter Martin first published *The Maze of Mormonism* in 1962 and *The Kingdom of the Cults* in 1965. Both books became countercult bestsellers. But in this pre-Religious Right era, evangelical and fundamentalist Christian concerns about Mormon heterodoxy did not register on the national political radar.[35] This says perhaps as much about the state of religion and politics in America of the 1960s as it does about Mormonism's reputation at the time. Historian Randall Balmer holds up George Romney as prime evidence of the general public's "dis-

---

33. See Stewart Alsop, "It's Like Running Against God," *Saturday Evening Post*, October 22, 1966, 20; the comment came from Zoltan Ferency, Romney's opponent in the 1966 Michigan gubernatorial race. Compare also this contemporary assessment from a Mormon image watcher, Dennis L. Lythgoe, "The 1968 Presidential Decline of George Romney: Mormonism or Politics?" *BYU Studies* 11 (Spring 1971): 240, for this telling summary of the place of religion, as Lythgoe read it, in the contemporary political climate: "The reaction of the public clearly suggested that any candidate relying heavily on piety, *be it Mormon or any other faith*, could have serious credibility problems. Perhaps Romney's major liability was not necessarily Mormonism, but *rather religious dedication*. Conceivably, a candidate of another faith could be faced with a similar problem; or a Mormon better able to compartmentalize his faith and his politics might erase that problem" (italics added).

34. "Michigan: The Mormon Issue," *Time*, March 2, 1962, 21. Randall Balmer offers insightful analysis about the impact that the presidencies of John F. Kennedy and Richard Nixon had on public perception of George and Mitt Romney in "Like Father, Unlike Son: The Governors Romney, the Kennedy Paradigm, and the Mormon Question," in Randall Balmer and Jana Riess, eds., *Mormonism and American Politics* (New York: Columbia University Press, 2016), 115–130.

35. There was also an important partisan element to the Religious Right's rise in prominence in the late 1970s and early 1980s that was not yet in full play in George Romney's day. See Williams, *God's Own Party*, 2, for his argument that "Evangelicals gained prominence during Ronald Reagan's campaign not because they were speaking out on political issues—they had been doing this for decades—but because they were taking over the Republican Party."

regard for candidates' religion" prior to 1976. Balmer seems right that Romney's "religion simply did not enter into the political calculus"—at least not beyond what his religion said about his personal morality.[36] That assertion is borne out by exploratory interviews the Romney team conducted nationwide in late 1966. In the notes of over a hundred of those interviews with local party officials from Oregon to Georgia, only three mention Mormonism as a potential negative factor; indeed, Mormonism was only mentioned five times in total.[37] Instead, an apparent lack of foreign policy experience—particularly his "brainwashed" comment about his changing stance on the Vietnam War—sank Romney's standing in the polls, and he withdrew from the race in early 1968. There simply is no compelling evidence that belonging to the Church of Jesus Christ of Latter-day Saints hurt George Romney's chance at the presidency.

As "super-American" as Mormonism seemed in George Romney's heyday, on one issue the LDS Church seemed less benign as the 1960s closed—and to a large degree, George Romney's candidacy drew the spotlight to this issue.[38] Black members of the LDS Church could not participate in the church's highest temple rites, and black men could not be ordained to the church's priesthood. That priesthood policy was a change from the church's earliest days under founder Joseph Smith, but by the 1960s the prohibition had been firmly in place for a century. Many LDS leaders and members expressed the hope that the policy would be changed, but church leaders felt a divine revelation was needed to alter course. The church did make some statements in favor of civil rights in the 1960s, but as the decade wore on, the church's position on priesthood ordination drew more and more well-publicized outcries.[39]

---

36. Randall Balmer, *God in the White House: How Faith Shaped the Presidency from John F. Kennedy to George W. Bush* (New York: HarperOne, 2008), 156.

37. See "Political Records: George Romney—Poll Data," box 167, folders 11–13, J. Willard Marriott Papers, special collections, Marriott Library, University of Utah. The states for which reports are available are Alabama, Arkansas, California, Colorado, Georgia, Florida, Kansas, Louisiana, Maine, Massachusetts, Mississippi, Missouri, Nebraska, New Hampshire, New Jersey, New Mexico, New York, North Carolina, Ohio, Oregon, Pennsylvania, South Carolina, Texas, Utah, Virginia, and Washington.

38. Martin E. Marty, "Foreword," in Klaus J. Hansen, *Mormonism and the American Experience* (Chicago: University of Chicago Press, 1981), xiii.

39. For nineteenth-century developments related to this policy, see W. Paul Reeve, *Religion of a Different Color: Race and the Mormon Struggle for Whiteness* (New York: Oxford University Press, 2015); see also "Race and the Priesthood," an essay published on the LDS Church's official website, under its "Gospel Topics" section, www.lds.org/topics/race-and-the-priesthood?lang=eng. For LDS Church leaders' twentieth-century deliberations surrounding this policy, including the related questions of civil rights legislation and public protests against Brigham Young University sports teams, see Edward L. Kimball, "Spencer W. Kimball and the Revelation on Priesthood," *BYU Studies* 47, no. 2 (2008): 4–78; Gregory A. Prince and Wm. Robert Wright, *David O. McKay and the Rise of Modern Mormonism* (Salt

Yet even on this issue George Romney's religion did not seem a political liability. At the same time that press attention was devoted to the priesthood and temple prohibition, Romney's record as an active civil rights supporter became a fixed feature of his campaign profile. In each of his three races for governor he had gained larger and larger percentages of the black vote. He himself had joined in a civil rights march for fair housing. In a nation where attitudes toward race and integration were still ambivalent, George Romney's personal civil rights activism complicated perceptions of Mormon racism.

One important case in point was the *New York Times'* Wallace Turner, who published *The Mormon Establishment* in 1966. He was highly critical of what he called "the anti-Negro Doctrine" of the LDS Church. But two excerpts from his book were emblematic of so much contemporaneous discussion of George Romney and the Mormons. In his chapter on George Romney, Turner wrote:

> After the interview there was no question in my mind that Governor Romney deeply regrets his church's position on Negroes. He never said this, or hinted it with words. But the impression was inescapable as he talked of the problem.... Certainly George Romney is not going to lead an apostasy movement on the Negro question, and he is not going to criticize publicly the church leadership for the position which it—and he— inherited from men long dead. He will go along and attempt to let people know that he stands four-square for civil rights for all races and religions. He also will work carefully within the LDS Church for some solution to the deadlock. Romney's influence already has been felt on this question.

Turner closed this chapter by saying that he left his interview "reassured about George Romney."[40]

His criticisms notwithstanding, Turner concluded his book with an overall favorable impression of Mormons: "The Mormons are a fine people. Their contribution to American life has been considerable. With a few exceptions, which are very plainly set out in these covers, I find their doctrine to be humane, productive of progress, patriotic, wholesome and praiseworthy.... There are weaknesses in that pattern of life; but there are strengths that far out-balance the defects." And then these final lines: "The Mormons

---

Lake City: University of Utah Press, 2005), 60–105; and J. B. Haws, *The Mormon Image in the American Mind: Fifty Years of Public Perception* (New York and Oxford: Oxford University Press, 2013), 47–73. See also Matthew L. Harris and Newell G. Bringhurst, *The Mormon Church and Blacks: A Documentary History* (Urbana: University of Illinois Press, 2015).

40. Wallace Turner, *The Mormon Establishment* (Boston: Houghton Mifflin Company, 1966), 307–308, 310.

have contributed much to the modern United States. They will contribute more. After all, God has told them to progress."[41]

This sense of Mormonism's strengths outbalancing its defects captured well much of the public sentiment about the religion in the 1960s. Even before LDS Church president Spencer W. Kimball announced the revelation that ended the racially based priesthood and temple restriction in 1978, Mormons had become best known for their family-centered theology. The Church's public relations team launched a hugely successful public service announcement campaign in 1972, termed *Homefront*, to encourage family solidarity. The commercials were sometimes sentimental, sometimes comical, and always about prioritizing the family. Along with these television and radio ads, the church used Mormon celebrities like the Osmonds, golfer Johnny Miller, and George and Lenore Romney in "Meet the Mormons" events and TV specials. Thanks at least in part to these campaigns and these prominent LDS faces, Mormons reached what probably was a favorability high point in 1977 in the Gallup poll—one year before the priesthood revelation—when 54 percent of Americans saw Mormons favorably.[42] By then, however, the "golden era" that George Romney in many ways personified was already fading.

Fast forward to the fall of 1994. Mitt Romney's promising bid for a Massachusetts Senate seat was suddenly looking less promising. Ted Kennedy and his nephew had questioned the fitness of Mitt Romney to serve if he belonged to a church that seemed to them to have a racist and anti-feminist past. The insinuations about Mitt Romney's Mormonism, by all accounts, were effective. In the thick of all of this, at a campaign event for his son, George Romney took the microphone and asked in frustration why religion was even part of this election. The moment was telling. Mormonism's public reputation had changed, and so had the role of religion in American politics.[43] In 1991, the Barna group conducted a national poll with a question about Mormonism similar to the one in Gallup's 1977 survey. Only this time around, just 27 percent of respondents gave Mormons a favorable rating. Even after ac-

---

41. Turner, *The Mormon Establishment*, 331.

42. See Question qn19k, The Gallup Poll #978, June 14, 1977, accessed at Gallup Brain database. The 1977 poll used a numerical scale to gauge opinion, from +5 (for a very favorable opinion) to -5 (for a very unfavorable opinion); 9.88 percent answered "+5," and 7.92 percent "+4," and 36 percent of respondents gave Mormons a "+1, +2, or +3" rating, meaning that 54 percent of those surveyed ranked Mormons on the positive side of the scale.

43. See Jonathan Darman, "Mitt's Mission," *Newsweek* October 1, 2007, www.newsweek.com/mitts-mission-103243.

counting for any difference in reporting or questioning criteria, the precipitous drop, with Mormon favorability slashed in half, was dramatic.[44]

The 1980s presented some steep public perception challenges for Mormons. Some press outlets battered LDS authorities for opposing the Equal Rights Amendment, and pro-ERA activists raised alarms about the church's economic and organizational might.[45] Then a young Mormon college student named Mark Hofmann repeatedly grabbed headlines over the course of five years with monumental document "finds" that seemed to shake the historical foundations of Mormonism by questioning Joseph Smith's accounts of the visionary origins of the faith. Tragically, it took Hofmann's murdering of two people before authorities determined that his finds were in fact forgeries—but by then the public opinion damage was already done. A concurrent surge in fundamentalist polygamist infighting among sects led by former Mormons seemed to mark Mormonism as deviant, ominous, mysterious, fanatical, and powerful.[46]

One group in particular seemed to care more than others about the public reputation of Mormons, and this is where religion and politics met in the new landscape of the 1980s. Evangelical and fundamentalist Christians had become a political force in the late 1970s in a way that they had not been for decades. Christian organizers successfully registered millions of new voters in the 1970s as they made an explicit and conscientious rhetorical turn to ask their congregants to get involved in national politics in the face of perceived social upheaval. *Newsweek* dubbed 1976 "The Year of the Evangelical."[47] But

---

44. Compare Barna Research Group, "Americans' Impressions of Various Church Denominations," September 18, 1991, copy in the author's possession, 1: "How favorably do you consider the Mormon denomination? Very favorably—6 percent"; only 21 percent felt "somewhat favorable" about Latter-day Saints, meaning that 27 percent chose a "very" or "somewhat" favorable response in 1991.

45. For a few examples, see Lisa Cronin Wahl, "A Mormon Connection?: The Defeat of the ERA in Nevada," *Ms.*, July 1977, 68; Judy Foreman, "It's New Do or Die for the ERA—Mormon Power is the Key," *Boston Globe*, June 30, 1981, 1. Also see D. Michael Quinn, "A National Force, 1970s–1990s," chapter 10 of *Mormon Hierarchy: Extensions of Power* (Salt Lake City: Signature Books, 1997).

46. See two examples of popular bestsellers that situated these tragic and violent episodes in the forefront of their narratives: Deborah Laake, *Secret Ceremonies: A Mormon Woman's Intimate Diary of Marriage and Beyond* (New York: William Morrow and Company, Inc., 1993); and Jon Krakauer, *Under the Banner of Heaven: A Story of Violent Faith* (New York: Doubleday, 2003). On Hofmann, see Richard E. Turley, *Victims: The LDS Church and the Mark Hofmann Case* (Urbana: University of Illinois Press, 1992).

47. For the voting numbers, see Adam Clymer, "Bush Says No Single Group Gave Reagan His Victory," *New York Times*, November 18, 1980, B10; for the "Year of the Evangelical," see Kenneth L. Woodward, John Barnes, and Laurie Lisle, "Born Again," *Newsweek*, October 25, 1976, 69; their article was the issue's cover story.

for most Christians, Mormons did not figure into these coalitions, even though there was plenty of overlap on social policy concerns. Christians who worried about the forces taking America from its Christian moorings identified Mormonism as one of those threatening forces. New political and cultural clout meant that Christian concerns over Mormonism also reached wider audiences—just at the time that other constituencies like ERA activists, historians, and investigative journalists had their own concerns about the faith.

All of this was in the background when George Romney reacted to the Kennedy barrage against his son in 1994. This was only a foretaste of what would come in 2008 and 2012. In the meantime, however, Mitt Romney benefited from the success of the 2002 Olympics. Probably no event did more to rehabilitate the Mormon public image from the pummeling it took in the 1980s than did the Salt Lake Winter Games. Although initial fears about overbearing Mormon proselytizing at every Olympic venue colored previews of the so-called Mo-lympics, what actually transpired was dramatically different. LDS Church President Gordon B. Hinckley announced that the church would not proselytize during the Games. Instead, the church opened its doors to the thousands of journalists whose curiosity about the place and its people generated human-interest stories by the hundreds. Plus the thousands of Utah volunteers who spoke any number of languages, thanks to their foreign Mormon missionary service, astounded appreciative visitors. "The subtle approach, in the end, was a brilliant move by the church," one columnist wrote. "The only religious shenanigans and Bible-thumping at the Winter Games came courtesy of angry other denominations, whose members circled Temple Square with anti-Mormon signs and pamphlets and posters." The irony was that in the end, "everyone looked nutty except the Mormons, who looked golden."[48]

Both Mitt Romney and his church shared in the glow of Olympic success. Romney emerged as a hometown hero, a man who saved the Games thanks to the qualities he had internalized as a lifelong Latter-day Saint. It was this "Olympics image" of Mormonism that led many Latter-day Saints to feel that their faith enjoyed broad public acceptance.[49] Hence the surprise for many of those same Latter-day Saints when Mitt Romney's first bid for the presidency demonstrated that the country did not feel as warmly about them and their religion as they had assumed. Public opinion polls about Mormons at the time were all over the map,

---

48. Hank Stuever, "Unmentionable No Longer: What do Mormons Wear? A Polite Smile, If Asked About 'the Garment,'" *Washington Post*, February 26, 2002, C1.

49. "Olympics image" was Jan Shipps's phrase, in Howard Berkes, "Mormons Confront Negative Ideas About Their Faith," *National Public Radio*, February 12, 2008, www.npr.org/templates/story/story.php?storyId=18905399.

depending on how questions were phrased, but repeatedly a quarter to a half of Americans expressed strong reservations to supporting a Mormon candidate for president. From the left and from the right, the concerns mounted.

For some, Mitt Romney was the quintessential flip-flopper, willing to change his political views depending on his audience and context. Some made out this shape-shifting to be endemic to Mormonism: behind the attractive Mormon façade, the argument went, lay sinister motivations for social control or financial gain, beginning with a founding prophet who was a religious charlatan.[50] Others, especially evangelical Christians, saw Mitt Romney's potential prominence as problematic for the way it could normalize Mormonism, which would make countercult inoculation against the religion that much harder. In either case, the question seemed to be about legitimacy. Could Mormons be trusted?

If George Romney's public portrait was painted in the hues of the Mormon reputation of the 1960s, Mitt Romney's profile was shaded by the Mormon reputation of the 1980s. In the late 1990s and early 2000s, significant moments of human interest—Mormon wagon train reenactments in 1997, the Olympics in 2002, disaster responses to Hurricane Katrina in 2005—played louder than did Mormon controversies. Yet fundamental worries about Mormons seemed to have been only latent or dormant, rather than resolved, during those years. Those fears surged during Romney's 2008 presidential run—and Mitt Romney's 2012 campaign appeared to bring more of the same, especially early on. Dallas Pastor Robert Jeffress famously told CNN in October 2011 that because Mitt Romney belonged to a "cult," committed "born-again followers of Jesus Christ should always prefer a competent Christian to a competent non-Christian" (in Jeffress's case, he was endorsing Texas Governor Rick Perry).[51]

But the 2012 campaign developed along a different trajectory than did the 2008 campaign, in terms of attention to Mormonism, for a number of reasons. Importantly, Mitt Romney was clearly the frontrunner for the Republican nomination in the 2012 election cycle. As his nomination seemed more and more likely, the volume of dissenting voices from the Religious Right diminished. Calls for party loyalty and united conservative opposition to Barack

---

50. See, for example, Jacob Weisberg, "Romney's Religion: A Mormon President? No Way," *Slate*, December 20, 2006, www.slate.com/id/2155902.

51. For Jeffress's comments, see Weiner, "Mormonism Takes Center Stage at Conservative Event" and the CNN clip with Anderson Cooper at Frances Martel, "Anti-Mormon Pastor To Anderson Cooper: Romney May Belong To A 'Cult,' But He Is Better Than Obama," *Mediaite. com*, October 8, 2011, www.mediaite.com/tv/anti-mormon-pastor-to-anderson-cooper-romney-may-belong-to-a-cult-but-he-is-better-than-obama/. Martel said Jeffress "stole the Friday news cycle."

Obama trumped religious differences. But this change in tone also reflected more than merely an alliance of necessity. A number of leading evangelical thinkers expressed new views on the persistent question of Mormonism's cult status, resultant in large part from a years-long series of Mormon-evangelical dialogues and other interfaith initiatives. Richard Mouw, president of Fuller Seminary, was a prime example of this move. For more than a decade Mouw had led (with BYU's Robert Millet) a biannual Mormon-evangelical dialogue, and when Pastor Jeffress made news with the "cult" comments, Mouw wrote a piece for CNN the very next week proclaiming, "This evangelical says Mormonism isn't a cult." At the same time, Biola University's John Mark Reynolds called for evangelicals "to stand up to anti-Mormon bigotry." The discourse was taking some new directions.[52]

Part of the 2012 story, too, was that the national media did not seem interested in rehashing all of the same controversies about Mormon history and practice that had come to the fore in the 2008 campaign; as one pollster put it, the press does not like "old news."[53] In a search for "new news," the media devoted more attention to aspects of lived Mormonism: Mormon family life, the church's lay ministry, humanitarian enterprises. The Mormon-related biographical vignettes from Mitt Romney's past that were on display at the Republican national convention followed in this vein. CNN's David Gergen observed that "for the convention as a whole, its biggest success may have been to warm up Mitt Romney," in that the "emotionally charged testimonials" of Romney's fellow Mormons "seemingly did well in erasing the impressions created by the barrage of negative advertising he's sustained." Even Democratic pundit and lobbyist Hilary Rosen agreed that Romney "decently" conveyed "who he is as a person of empathy and good intent"; she said that if she were a Romney supporter, "all I would talk about" were the "personal stories of Romney's speech." Columnist Ruben Navarette asked, "Where have the Republicans been hiding this guy?" He liked "the kinder, gentler, more emotive Mitt Romney" so much that he felt, going into the home stretch of the election season, "We got ourselves a ball game."[54]

---

52. Richard J. Mouw, "My Take: This Evangelical Says Mormonism Isn't a Cult," *CNN Belief Blog*, October 9, 2011, http://religion.blogs.cnn.com/2011/10/09/my-take-this-evangelical-says-mormonism-isnt-a-cult/; John Mark Reynolds, "Why Evangelicals Must Stand Up to Anti-Mormon Bigotry," *Washington Post* blog *On Faith*, October 10 2011, www.washingtonpost.com/blogs/on-faith/post/why-evangelicals-must-stand-up-to-anti-mormon-bigotry/2011/10/10/gIQAo6PqZL_blog.html.

53 Gary Lawrence, interview by author, October 11, 2011, transcript in author's possession, 5.

54. "Did Mitt Romney Gain Ground?," *CNN.com*, August 31, 2012, www.cnn.com/2012/08/31/opinion/opinion-roundup-romney/index.html.

If national notice of George Romney's campaign drew increased attention to the Mormon priesthood policy in the late 1960s, national notice of Mitt Romney's campaigns drew increased attention to Mormon diversity—racial, political, and geographical. This attention was at least one factor that figured into the Associated Press's unexpected headline in the days following Mitt Romney's November 2012 defeat: "And the Winner Is…the Mormon Church."[55] If Mormons came away from the campaign with a sense of cautious optimism about the direction that the public's perception of their faith was heading, that hopefulness seemed borne out by a Pew study released in December 2012. The public favorability temperature seemed to be rising, even if only moderately so. By six points, a greater share of Americans used positive terms such as "good people," "dedicated," and "honest" when asked for one-word impressions of Mormons than had been the case the previous year. Pew reported an overall four-point decrease from 2011 in the number of Americans who saw Mormonism as "very different" from their own religious beliefs. Forty-two percent of respondents in that Protestant group said that Mormonism had "a lot in common" with their own religious beliefs, up from only 28 percent just one year earlier. Even among evangelical Protestants, a four-point boost on that same question was noteworthy.[56]

A Bifocal Look at Religion in American Politics

If George Romney's frustration at the Kennedy tactics in 1994 revealed that the worlds of Mormonism and American politics had both turned since 1968, the 2012 election showed signs of yet another turn. Mitt Romney's second presidential run thus becomes an important lens on religion in the public square in modern America. Exit polling showed that in the end, evangelical voters supported Mitt Romney in greater percentages than they did John McCain four years earlier. While it is possible that some conservative Christians simply sat

---

55. Rachel Zoll, "And the Winner Is…the Mormon Church," *Athens (Georgia) Banner-Herald*, November 22, 2012, http://onlineathens.com/faith/2012-11-22/and-winner-mormon-church; Rachel Zoll's Associated Press story appeared under a slightly different headline in the *Deseret News*: "And the Winner in the 2012 Presidential Election Is…the Mormon Church," *Deseret News*, November 15, 2012, www.deseretnews.com/article/765615656/And-the-winner-is--the-Mormon-church.html. Historian Matthew Bowman told National Public Radio that, in his view, Mitt Romney's run had "done a fair amount to refute the great myth of Mormonism: that it's a monolith"; in Liz Halloran, "What Romney's Run Means for Mormonism," *National Public Radio*, November 1, 2012, www.npr.org/blogs/itsallpolitics/2012/11/01/164101548/what-romneys-run-means-for-mormonism.

56. "Americans Learned Little About the Mormon Faith, But Some Attitudes Have Softened," *Pew Forum on Religion and Public Life*, December 14, 2012, www.pewforum.org/Christian/Mormon/attitudes-toward-mormon-faith.aspx.

out the election when faced with what they saw as untenable options from either party, the 2012 numbers for Mitt Romney matched the level of evangelical voter support for George W. Bush in 2004. Significantly, of course, Mitt Romney still lost the general election, even with that evangelical support. What some observers saw as a 2012 takeaway was that the conservative Christian bloc had lost its "king-making" status. In the aftermath of the 2012 campaign, the loudest calls were for the Republican Party to do some soul-searching, since the white evangelical vote now appeared to carry less clout than it had for three decades.[57]

But that level of evangelical voter support for a Mormon candidate also seemed to be one indication that there would continue to be greater space for Mormon cooperation on social policy with evangelicals and other religious conservatives. Opposition to same-sex marriage made for a prominent opportunity for coalition building—the 2008 campaign for Proposition 8 in California provided both an opening and evidence for that. But as the American judicial and cultural ground shifted on this issue in the years after 2012, the LDS Church sought to carve something of a middle path in its support of anti-discrimination legislation and LGBT rights on the one hand, while advocating strongly, as one journalist put it, for protections "for religions that stand against homosexuality" on the other.[58] Ultimately—and most recently—this shared concern over religious liberty has united Latter-day Saints with evangelicals and other religious conservatives.[59] The degree of acceptance granted—however grudgingly—by many conservatives to a Mormon presidential

---

57. Jonathan Merritt, "Election 2012 Marks the End of Evangelical Dominance in Politics," *The Atlantic*, November 13, 2012, www.theatlantic.com/politics/archive/2012/11/election-2012-marks-the-end-of-evangelical-dominance-in-politics/265139/. Merritt noted that "the evangelical vote was 27 percent of the overall electorate—the highest it's ever been for an election." See also "The Media, Religion and the 2012 Campaign for President," Pew Research Center's Project for Excellence in Journalism, December 14, 2012, which calculated 79 percent of white evangelicals voted for George W. Bush in 2004 and Mitt Romney in 2012, while 73 percent of evangelicals voted for John McCain in 2008, based on exit polling; www.journalism.org/2012/12/14/media-religion-and-2012-campaign-president. In fact, evangelicals voted for Romney at a rate one percentage point higher than even Mormons did. For Pew's estimate that 79 percent of evangelicals and 78 percent of Mormons voted for Romney, see "How the Faithful Voted: 2012 Preliminary Analysis," November 7, 2012, www.pewforum.org/2012/11/07/how-the-faithful-voted-2012-preliminary-exit-poll-analysis/.

58. Lindsey Bever, "Utah—Yes, Utah—Passes Landmark LGBT Rights Bill," March 12, 2015, *Washington Post*, www.washingtonpost.com/news/morning-mix/wp/2015/03/12/utah-legislature-passes-landmark-lgbt-anti-discrimination-bill-backed-by-mormon-church/.

59. For recent examples of this, see these reports on the LDS Church's official "Newsroom" blog: David Porter, "Religious Leaders Consider Vital Need for Religious Freedom," *The Newsroom Blog*, May 29, 2012, www.mormonnewsroom.org/article/religious-leaders-consider-vital-need-for-religious-freedom; Samuel B. Hislop, "Mormon Apostle Joins Faith Leaders to Honor Rabbi Sacks," *The Newsroom Blog*, May 16, 2014, www.mormonnewsroom.org/article/mormon-apostle-honors-rabbi-sacks; also see Michael Otterson (managing

candidate made this kind of engagement more possible. On that front, Mitt Romney's candidacy opened doors for new alliances.[60]

Historian Daniel Williams's observation about evangelicals and Catholics' pragmatic rapprochement has a Mormon analog. Williams suggested that "conservative Protestants" in the 1960s "were alarmed by Kennedy's election, but shortly thereafter, they decided that secularism, rather than Catholicism, posed a greater threat to the country." This meant that "evangelicals—and eventually many fundamentalists, as well—decided it was imperative to unite with socially conservative allies, even if they happened to be Catholic." There are, of course, some larger doctrinal impediments to a similar reframing of Mormon–evangelical (or even Mormon–Catholic) partnerships because of Mormonism's non-Trinitarian theology, its expanded canon, and its temple-centered religious rites that still generate suspicion. The strong outcry that followed the Billy Graham Evangelical Association's decision, in the weeks before the 2012 election, to remove from its website references to Mormonism as a cult certainly spoke to those deep-seated anxieties about Mormonism's acceptability. Yet Franklin Graham's open letter at the time argued that Mormons and Catholics and Jews shared with evangelical Christians values that were "biblically based"; perhaps this will be the next chapter in the story that Daniel Williams saw opening in the 1970s, when "conservative Protestants" began "redefining their vision of a Christian nation as anti-secular, rather than explicitly Protestant."[61]

These are the possibilities that start to come into focus with the Romney lens. With George Romney, there exists a correlation (if not causation) between his campaign and widespread attention to racial issues within Mormonism—and hence the public relations response that came in the form of the *Homefront* ads, which in turn secured Mormonism's family-first reputation. With Mitt Romney, there exists a correlation (if not causation) between

---

director of LDS Church Public Affairs), interview by author, October 25, 2013, transcript in author's possession, 8.

60. For examples of this, see Robert Jeffress, "Romney and the Disappearing Evangelical Dilemma," FoxNews.com, September 19, 2012, www.foxnews.com/opinion/2012/09/19/mitt-romney-and-disappearing-evangelical-dilemma; also Richard Mouw, quoted in Zoll, "And the Winner Is ... the Mormon Church." See also Neil J. Young, *We Gather Together: The Religious Right and the Problem of Interfaith Politics* (New York: Oxford University Press, 2016), 287–297, where Young describes "evangelical institutions—*Christianity Today*, the Southern Baptist Convention, the Billy Graham Evangelistic Associations, and others" as "supporting Romney's candidacy and remaking their own positions on Mormonism" (290).

61. Williams, *God's Own Party*, 5; Franklin Graham, "Can An Evangelical Christian Vote for a Mormon?" *Decision Magazine*, October 22, 2012, http://billygraham.org/decision-magazine/october-2012/can-an-evangelical-christian-vote-for-a-mormon/; Daniel Burke, "Billy Graham Faces Backlash Over Mormon 'Cult' Removal," *Washington Post*, October 24, 2012, http://articles.washingtonpost.com/2012-10-24/national/35501066_1_mormonism-evangelicals-christians.

his campaign and widespread attention to other famous Mormons, to Mormon scholarship, to Mormon humanitarian work, to everyday Latter-day Saints, and to growing Mormon diversity.

What should not be ignored in this is the impact of personal interactions— a natural byproduct of the more diffuse geographical distribution of the LDS Church's membership and, significantly, its cultural visibility. Political scientists David Campbell, Quin Monson, and Jay Green found in a 2008 study that individuals who showed familiarity with Mormonism "were much less likely to be bothered by the claim that Mormons are not Christians." "When people understood [Romney's] Mormon faith," they wrote, "the bias melted away." And in the summer of 2014, Pew released a nationwide poll showing that while Mormons had made modest overall gains in terms of public favorability since the 1990s, there was a detectable trend that those who personally knew a Mormon held measurably more favorable opinions of the faith than did those who did not know a Mormon. In fact, Mormon gains in favorability since the 1990s seemed to mirror concurrent rises in more widespread personal acquaintance with Mormons.[62]

For these reasons, the Romneys' respective campaigns deserve something of the much-trumpeted "Mormon moment" superlative with which they have been tagged. It is almost certain that their campaigns will still reverberate, both within and without the faith, when the next Mormon moment comes along.

---

62. David E. Campbell, John C. Green, and J. Quin Monson, "Tolerance? We Have a Ways to Go," *USA Today*, November 30, 2009, 21A. Pew Research Religion and Public Life Project, "How Americans Feel About Religious Groups," *Pew Research Center*, July 16, 2014, www.pewforum.org/2014/07/16/how-americans-feel-about-religious-groups/. In 1998 and 2002, LDS Church-commissioned studies found that respondents ranked Latter-day Saints at 40.3 and 45.3, respectively, on a 1-to-100 favorability thermometer scale; Pew reported that ranking at 48 in 2014. In 1994, a church study found that 36 percent of Americans reported having Mormon family or friends. See Deseret News, *Church Almanac* (Salt Lake City: Deseret News, 2004), 544. In 2014, 44 percent of respondents to the Pew study reported knowing a Mormon personally. While the metrics and methodology of these surveys might not line up perfectly, the comparison does seem to bear out the correlation between acquaintance and favorable feelings suggested in other studies.

5

"The Puritan Ethic on High"

LDS MEDIA AND THE MORMON EMBRACE OF FREE ENTERPRISE IN THE TWENTIETH CENTURY

James Dennis LoRusso

THE 2012 PRESIDENTIAL campaign season was, according to many in the media, the definitive "Mormon moment." Besides two candidates, Jon Huntsman and Mitt Romney, running for the Republican nomination, the Latter-day Saints seemed to be everywhere in American life. Libertarian talk show host Glenn Beck, a convert to the Mormon faith, was a leading critic of the Obama administration and a darling of the Tea Party movement. In popular culture, the cable television series *Big Love* had enjoyed a successful run on HBO, and fans purchased tickets months in advance for the chance to see a performance of *The Book of Mormon* on Broadway. Readers, particularly adolescents, reveled in Mormon author Stephanie Meyer's tales of chaste vampires in her bestselling *Twilight* series.

Much of the media coverage fixated on the idea that, somehow, a more thorough understanding of Latter-day Saint scripture and doctrine could explain Mormonism's political culture. For instance, the author of one article in *Newsweek* attributed the strong political conservatism of Mormons to particular doctrinal commitments. "According to Mormon tradition, God and Satan fought a 'war in heaven,'" he wrote, "with God on the side of personal liberty and Satan seeking to enslave mankind," a story that lends itself to government minimalism and robust individualism.[1]

This idea that the Mormon faith was inherently supportive of free enterprise and prepared believers for professional success became a signature trope in the press. *The Economist* featured an article discussing the "The Mormon Way of Business," stating that "had Max Weber lived a century later, he might have made sweeping generalizations about the 'Mormon work ethic.'"[2] Caroline Winter, writing for *Businessweek,* claimed that while

---

1. Walter Kirn, "The Mormon Moment," *Newsweek,* June 5, 2011.

2. "The Mormon Way of Business," *The Economist,* May 5, 2012.

Latter-day Saints comprise only a fraction of the population, they "hold, or have held, a seemingly disproportionate number of top jobs."[3] One blogger even nominated Mormonism as "the world's most capitalist religion."[4]

Mormon writers and scholars seemed to echo such sentiments, such as Jeff Benedict's biopic of nine Mormon businessmen, *The Mormon Way of Doing Business* (2012). In the *Harvard Business Review*, Greg McKeown, a prominent Mormon business consultant, argued that "many Mormons have played an active role in shaping modern management theory,"[5] and Harvard Business Professor Clay Christensen declared, "if Harvard Business School were a religion, it could be Mormonism." Writing in *The Washington Post*, Christensen suggested a symbiosis between business and his faith: "There is something about the LDS Church that is helping these people become even more influential executives in business and leaders in society. And, in turn, the approach to management and leadership at HBS is strengthening their faith rather than eroding it."[6] Mormonism is, according to one business professor at BYU, "the Puritan Ethic on high…there's a total emphasis on self-sufficiency, on working hard."[7]

Amidst this chorus, however, others questioned the veracity of these assertions. To be sure, from hotel magnate J. Willard Marriott to leadership guru Stephen Covey, individual Saints have left an indelible mark on corporate America, but the degree to which Mormons as a whole achieve business success remains obscure. Lane Williams, teacher of Journalism at Brigham Young University–Idaho, states unequivocally that "yes, Latter-day Saints are successful in business. Yes, they are successful in sports and in other pursuits, but I see no reason to think unusually so until more detailed studies emerge."[8] Moreover, while aspects of church doctrine might promote the virtues of

---

3. Caroline Winter, "God's MBAs: Why Mormon Missions Produce Leaders," *Businessweek*, June 9, 2011

4. Hamish McKenzie, "The Book of Mormon—Why the World's Most Capitalist Religion Breeds So Many Entrepreneurs," *Pando*, July 31, 2013, https://pando.com/2013/07/31/the-book-of-mormon-why-the-worlds-most-capitalist-religion-breeds-so-many-entrepreneurs.

5. Greg McKeown, "How Mormons Have Shaped Modern Management," *Harvard Business Review*, October 17, 2012.

6. Clay M. Christensen, "If Harvard Business School Were a Religion, It Could Be Mormonism," *The Washington Post*, May 14, 2012.

7. Nathan Farr, assistant professor of entrepreneurship at Brigham Young University, quoted in Caroline Winter, "God's MBAs: Why Mormon Missions Produce Leaders," *Businessweek*, June 9, 2011.

8. Lane Williams, "Are Mormons Really More Successful in Business?," *Deseret News*, May 21, 2012.

self-reliance and hard work, to suggest that such values render Mormonism *essentially* capitalistic is problematic at best. The problem, I contend, stems from the particular way in which popular discourse typically frames discussions about "faith," as a fundamentally stable set of shared beliefs out of which adherents act in the world. Because this assumption positions religion as an irreducible *causal* agent, we fail to properly discern how norms, values, and doctrine are themselves *effects* of social relations. In short, to assert that there is such a thing as a "Mormon work ethic" or to declare Mormonism as inherently "capitalistic" overlooks the complex historical processes out of which these concepts emerge. This fresh perspective enables us to jettison altogether the task of accurately describing the "capitalistic dimensions" of Mormonism, and instead to account for how and why popular discourse frequently associates one with the other.

While other scholars have outlined the shifting image of Mormonism in the American public, this chapter focuses on Mormon self-understanding.[9] In particular, a content analysis of the LDS monthly periodical *The Improvement Era* between 1930 and 1970 undermines claims of Mormonism as inherently capitalistic and demonstrates how these notions emerge out of particular historical experience of the LDS Church during these decades. Contributors to *The Improvement Era* mobilized pro-capitalist rhetoric to further its interests and in the process cultivated a mode of Mormon self-understanding that valorized free enterprise and recast Mormon life through the language of business. The pro-capitalist stance of the church resulted not from some innate "Mormon affinity" for free enterprise, but from strategies aimed at both protecting and extending the power of the church. The 1930s saw a dramatic expansion of federal authority under FDR's New Deal policies, a development quite unwelcome in a church whose historical relationship with the US government was anything but congenial. Under these conditions, church leaders used mass media to propagate a sustained critique of the welfare state by celebrating economic liberty and industriousness while condemning dependence and idleness. As postwar hopes gave way to Cold War antagonisms, the church employed anti-communist rhetoric to perpetuate this resistance to the New Deal, which in the process presented an image of Mormonism as necessarily capitalistic. The mid-twentieth century was also a period of rapid expansion, and the church found pro-business rhetoric a useful tool to manage its mushrooming membership LDS leaders adopted the language of business to bolster to support for its global missions, and subsequently produced a kind

---

9. See J. B. Haws, *The Mormon Image in the American Mind: 50 Years of Public Perception* (New York: Oxford University Press, 2013).

of "business-minded" Mormonism that continues to shape Mormon self-understanding to this day.

Church Welfare: Crafting the Mormon Work Ethic

Since the Great Accommodation of 1890, when the LDS Church agreed to ban polygamy in return for statehood, the church had maintained a quiet uneasy truce with Washington. It had relinquished its vision of an independent Mormon kingdom and sought instead to "accommodate" itself to the broader American society. As historian Matthew Bowman writes, the Mormons' "task became assimilation, finding ways to translate the things America demanded from them into the language and imperatives of their own faith."[10] Having ceded political authority to the state, the church found other ways to sustain its power, particularly through its vast economic interests. Until statehood the church had forcefully resisted the expanding national economy, perceiving it as a threat to Mormon social and political experiment. Consequently, church authorities established numerous LDS-operated enterprises aimed at maintaining a wholly independent economic order. These companies continued to operate and grow following Utah statehood. For the typical church member living in the Salt Lake Basin at the turn of the twentieth century, hardly any aspect of life would have been untouched by this broad complex of Mormon enterprise, from life insurance companies, banks, shipping, and utilities.[11]

Although the Republican Party had led the national effort to extirpate Mormon polygamy, after 1890 church leaders with a stake in such enterprises gradually formed an alliance with the business-friendly GOP. While the Utah electorate-at-large preferred progressive anti-monopolistic politics, writes Bowman, "many Mormon elites had entered the demographic of Republican supporters across the nation: middle-class, well-to-do, educated, and urban, interested in business."[12] This class-based partisan divide among Mormons, nonetheless, posed no substantial threat to the integrity of the church until the fragile post-World War I economic order began to unravel. As in virtually all domains of American society, the stock market crash in the fall of 1929 greatly disturbed the LDS Church and its constituents. The ensuing hardship

---

10. Matthew Bowman, *The Mormon People: The Making of American Faith* (New York: Random House, 2012), 153.

11. See D. Michael Quinn, *The Mormon Hierarchy: Extensions of Power* (Salt Lake City: Signature Books, 1997), 214–215. Quinn offers a fictitious account of a hypothetical Mormon in order to demonstrate the pervasiveness of this array of LDS-owned businesses during the early years of the twentieth century.

12. Bowman, *The Mormon People*, 153.

experienced by ordinary Mormons demanded a vigorous response from church authorities, a response that would pit them against their old adversary: the federal government. In 1932, Franklin Roosevelt rode a wave of popular reaction against the ineffective policies of the Hoover administration to the presidency. Indeed, despite Church President Heber J. Grant's opposition, Utah voters overwhelmingly supported Roosevelt and would do so three more times.[13]

To church authorities, Roosevelt's New Deal represented a dual threat. On the surface, it dealt a blow to the commercial empire of the LDS Church, foisting unwanted restrictions on LDS-run businesses in which the church and its leaders were heavily invested. More deeply, however, the New Deal reignited fears of encroaching federal power that had lain dormant since the struggle over plural marriage and statehood. After all, it had been the "stick" of government political and economic intervention, more than the "carrot" of statehood, that ultimately helped to decide the fate of plural marriage. Frustrated in its attempts to reign in polygamy, Congress passed the 1887 Edmunds-Tucker Act, which revoked incorporation of the church and transferred its property to the federal government. Shortly after the Supreme Court upheld Edmunds-Tucker in 1890, the church formally abolished the practice of plural marriage.[14] Now, four decades later, the meddling of the federal government in economic affairs seemed to once again threaten the authority of the church.

The church responded to this threat by embarking on an elaborate public relations campaign to undermine Mormon support for the expanding welfare state. Church authorities mobilized particular Mormon scriptural and doctrinal resources to portray the faith as inherently incompatible with the interventionist policies of Washington. Instead, they envisaged Mormonism as sympathetic to classic economic liberalism, anti-communist, and a religious tradition founded on the virtues of hard work and self-reliance.

The passage of the Social Security Act in 1935 appears to mark the turning point for the church hierarchy, when LDS leaders began to take a more active role in steering Mormon self-understanding toward pro-capitalist views. By the following year, they had initiated an all-out effort to turn Mormons against the New Deal. In *The Improvement Era,* LDS authorities employed two overlapping rhetorical strategies of resistance. First, they rolled out the Church Welfare Plan, a bold initiative to combat the effect of the Depression on the faithful. Second, the church hierarchy began to stoke fears that the New Deal represented the first stage in a communist takeover of the United States,

---

13. Ibid, 157. In 1932, Utah gave 56.52 percent of the popular vote to FDR. Source: US Election Atlas, http://uselectionatlas.org/RESULTS/state.php?f=0&fips=49&year=1932.

14. Bowman, *The Mormon People,* 147–149.

threatening not only free enterprise but the very fabric of Mormon life itself. Over the next few decades, these two rhetorical strategies became routine means by which LDS media effectively rendered Mormonism and capitalism as natural companions.

The Church Welfare Program: A Mormon Ethic of Work

Introduced in 1936, the Church Welfare Plan established storehouses for surplus goods, a nonprofit chain of thrift stores named *Deseret Industries*, and numerous employment projects throughout its stakes in the western United States. While it mirrored several New Deal initiatives, the church programs were, from their inception, positioned in opposition to public welfare. The Social Security Act (SSA) of 1935, which introduced old-age subsidies, unemployment insurance, and means-tested public relief, levied substantial tax burdens on not only employees but employers as well, including the extensive commercial interests of the church and its leaders. The Church Welfare Plan (originally referred to as "Church Security") would rely solely on voluntary contributions of time, money, and goods. According to Robert Gottlieb and Peter Wiley, "it was the [Mormons'] first effort since the Great Accommodation to reassert their independence of the federal government...directed at their own members in an effort to weaken the growing support for the New Deal."[15] Thus, the Plan represented a zealous countermeasure against what church leaders likely saw as a direct intrusion of the state into their economic affairs.

While the Welfare Plan provided material assistance to Mormons in need, it was the church's accompanying public relations campaign, which touted the virtues of self-reliance, charity, and hard work, that left a lasting imprint on the Mormon faith. On the one-year anniversary of the Plan, Church President Heber J. Grant reminded *Improvement Era* readers that the "primary purpose of the Church Security plan was to set up, in so far as it might be possible, a system under which the curse of idleness would be done away with, the evils of the dole abolished, and independence, thrift and self-respect be once more established among our people."[16] Furthermore, he wished "work" to be "reenthroned as a ruling principle of the lives of our Church membership," situating an ethic of work at the moral center of Mormonism.[17] Grant bragged that "everything that has been done has been accomplished by the purely voluntary gift or labor of

---

15. Robert Gottlieb and Peter Wiley, *America's Saints: The Rise of Mormon Power* (New York: G. P. Putnam's Sons, 1984), 71.

16. Heber J. Grant, "The President on Church Security," *The Improvement Era*, March 1937, 131.

17. Ibid.

members of the Church as well as the gifts of many non-members who have contributed most generously of their substance to aid the Church in its efforts."[18] While the New Deal utilized the coercive power of the state to redistribute resources, the Church Welfare Plan relied on the goodwill of individuals to fuel its activities, which according to Grant illustrates its moral superiority.

Church leaders declared "hard work" and "self-reliance" as the central theological underpinnings of Mormon belief and practice. "The divine injunction to labor," LDS Apostle Richard L. Evans declared, "is obligatory upon all men regardless of their need for daily bread."[19] Federal welfare initiatives, conversely, undermined this essential Mormon principle. Public relief programs, as he made clear in a 1936 opinion piece from *The Improvement Era*, though beneficial for the unemployed, "will not insure any man against moral, spiritual, and intellectual deterioration."[20] The practice of labor, nor merely its fruits, he suggested, "is fundamental to the Gospel," "inseparable from the doctrine of salvation," and "an integral part of the fabric of 'Mormonism.'"[21] Throughout the first years of the Church Welfare Plan, contributors routinely highlighted the central role that hard work played in Mormon life and condemned idleness as a dire threat to the moral order.[22]

If work was a Mormon virtue, idleness represented an absolute evil to both individual and society alike. "Work occupies the mind," one article from 1941 notes, "allowing no time for dangerous thoughts. The busy mind is the healthy mind. People who have all sorts of imaginary ills are those who do not have enough to do."[23] If Marx decried "religion" as the opiate of the working classes, for the leaders of the Church of Jesus Christ of Latter-day Saints during the Depression, it was virtuous "labor" itself that upheld religion for the Mormon masses.

In addition to valorizing "work" in the abstract, *The Improvement Era* offered instruction for putting the bourgeois values of thrift and industry into practice. For example, Ira J. Markham, a faculty member of Utah's Weber College, wrote a series of articles advising readers on personal finance: getting

---

18. Ibid.

19. Richard L. Evans, "The Right to Labor," *The Improvement Era*, September 1936, 552.

20. Richard L. Evans, "Faith, Work, and Security," *The Improvement Era*, December 1936, 768.

21. Ibid.

22. In no less than ten issues between August 1936 and December 1937, at least one article, editorial, or republished speech dealt considerably with Church Welfare, work ethic, or some aspect of Mormon economic life.

23. Henry H. Graham, "The Glory of Honest Work," *The Improvement Era*, September 1941, 519.

out of debt, thrift, and rational financial planning.[24] He recast the typical Mormon family as a business unit, relying on a strict division of labor in which the father serves as breadwinner, and the wife manages the household. Under such conditions, the family "will be a truly fifty-fifty partnership" where "the chances for a successful and happy home are greatly increased."[25]

While Markham's counsel for thrift only endorsed capitalism implicitly, others more overtly linked this Mormon work ethic to the system of free enterprise. Stephen L. Richards, a member of the Quorum of the Twelve Apostles, aptly summarized how the overall rhetorical strategy of the LDS Church to resist the New Deal had developed by 1940 in a tract from *The Improvement Era* titled "The Gospel of Work." "Work and faith," he wrote, "is a cardinal point of our theological doctrine and our future state—envisioned in terms of eternal progression through constant labor...This doctrine of work lies at the very foundation of the capitalistic system."[26] He then criticized public welfare initiatives, stating that the government "does not create wealth and prosperity" but can only "take from one and give to another."[27] And for Richards, "the Church of Christ will lead the way" to a restoration of the proper moral economic order for America.[28] Resisting the welfare state, therefore, was an act at once patriotic and pious.

This ethic of work stemming from the campaign against the New Deal would continue to shape how Americans understood the Mormon faith in the decades to come. When Mormon historian Leonard Arrington, for instance, published his seminal economic history of the LDS in 1959, he understood the Mormon work ethic as essential to the church's survival.[29] Similarly, Ronald Reagan later remembered the Church Welfare Plan as "one of the

---

24. For example, see Ira J. Markham, "Personal Progress Through Wise Money Management," *The Improvement Era*, January 1940; "Getting Out of Debt," *The Improvement Era*, February 1940; "Keeping Out of Debt," *The Improvement Era*, October 1940; "Gaining Economic Security Through the Payment of Tithing," *The Improvement Era*, March 1942; and "Developing Economic Security in a Changing World," *The Improvement Era*, October 1942.

25. Ira J. Markham, "Personal Progress Through Wise Money Management," *The Improvement Era*, January 1940, 52.

26. Stephen L. Richards, "The Gospel of Work," *The Improvement Era*, January 1940, 10–11.

27. Ibid, 63.

28. Ibid.

29. Arrington argued that "those habits of mind and patterns of collective behavior to which early capitalism owed so much were carried over into Mormonism and proved to be invaluable in meeting the problems encountered in settling the arid West." Leonard J. Arrington, *Great Basin Kingdom: An Economic History of the Latter-day Saints, 1830–1900* (Urbana: University of Illinois Press, 2005), 4.

great examples in America today of what people can do for themselves if they hadn't been dragooned into the government's doing it for them."[30] For Reagan, the Church Welfare program epitomized the moral supremacy of limited government, of minimally regulated markets, and demonstrated the vital role that religious communities play in sustaining social life. For the leaders of the LDS Church, however, the Welfare program represented an effective strategy of resistance against the expanding federal bureaucracy. The language of economic liberty allowed the Church to stand against its historic enemy, the government, while simultaneously branding itself as thoroughly American, as a community of hard working, God-fearing, rugged individuals who cleave together during times of duress.

Anti-Communism and a Mormon Doctrine of Free Enterprise

In 1966, Church President David O. McKay declared to a General Priesthood session that "communism debases the individual and makes him the enslaved tool of the state, to which he must look for sustenance and religion."[31] McKay understood Mormon belief and leftist political philosophy as utterly irreconcilable. "No member of this Church," he continued, "can be true to his faith, nor can any American be loyal to his trust, while lending aid, encouragement, or sympathy to any of these false prophecies."[32] Active church members could not accept or sympathize with communism. Moreover, McKay emphasized that "the position of the church had never changed" on this matter and that communism represents "the greatest satanical threat to peace, prosperity, and the spread of God's work."[33]

Despite these strong remarks, however, a closer examination of LDS media reveals suggests that this position emerged only gradually, displacing earlier more varied assessments of communism or state-sponsored socialism. In fact, the church only began to rally around free enterprise and oppose communism consistently after 1936 when its leaders were fighting against the New Deal. In the wake of the stock market collapse of 1929, some leading Mormons expressed indifference and at times even sympathy toward the

---

30. Quoted in John Heinerman and Anson Schupe, *The Mormon Corporate Empire: The Eye Opening Report on the Church and its Political and Financial Agenda* (Boston: Beacon Press, 1988), 180.

31. David O. McKay, "Statement on Communism," *The Improvement Era*, June 1966, 580.

32. Ibid.

33. Ibid, 477.

Soviet Union. After a visit to Moscow in 1930, for instance, BYU President Franklin Harris praised the Soviet system as morally astute and one from which the church might learn. Public ownership and the removal of the profit incentive seemed to prevent some of the worst practices of capitalist society. At a public event, Harris observed that "there is no overcharging, no tipping, and none of the petty gambling and questionable amusements such as we find so conspicuous at our own state fairs."[34] Other Mormon visitors at this time celebrated the Bolshevik commitment to ending unemployment and eliminating homelessness.[35] Milton Bennion, the Dean of the School of Education at the University of Utah, even advocated openly for socialist reform, linking "the domination of capitalist power" to the social strife of the early 1930s in the United States.[36]

While such sympathetic voices may have been rare, outright opposition to communism appears wholly absent from *The Improvement Era* during these years. One possible explanation for this ambivalence lies in an earlier period of Mormon history. For much of the nineteenth century, the LDS Church remained hostile to the expanding capitalist marketplace. In seeking an independent kingdom, far from the persecutions of mainstream America, the church stressed cooperation, not competition. "Cooperation meant," Leonard Arrington notes, "everyman's labor was subject to call by church authority to work under supervised direction in a cause deemed essential to the prosperity of the Kingdom."[37] After the Great Accommodation, Utah became integrated economically and politically with the national society, but the vestiges of this cooperative ethic nonetheless remained important to the church. For many educated Mormons in the early twentieth century, socialism, with its emphasis on public ownership and solidarity, seemed better suited to the historical Mormon social vision of a "United Order" than did capitalist notions of individual self-interest.

It was not until 1936 when the church began its vigorous campaign to resist the New Deal that leaders began to earnestly oppose communism. In the August issue of *The Improvement Era*, Church President Heber J. Grant, along with future president David O. McKay and others, penned "A Warning to Church Members," which characterized communism as incompatible with

---

34. Franklin S. Harris, "A Demonstration of Leisure-Time Activities in Russia," *The Improvement Era*, January 1930, 185.

35. Thomas L. Martin, "What of Russia?," *The Improvement Era*, April 1931, 392.

36. Milton Bennion, "A Spiritual Philosophy of Life: The Ethical Functions of the State," *The Improvement Era*, December 1930, 801.

37. Arrington, *Great Basin Kingdom*, 17.

the Mormon faith. It ruled through "intolerance and force" rather than "voluntary consecration and sacrifice," they said, and threatened "the sanctity of the family circle...in a manner unsanctioned under the Constitutional guarantees under which we in America live."[38]

In the years to come, church leaders crafted a narrative of Mormon history that characterized the faith as essentially capitalistic, differentiating the Mormon vision of a "United Order" from communism as the former required freedom of conscience and action while the latter demanded surrender to the overriding will of the state. Church leaders rejected the concept of public ownership as antithetical to Mormon life. "It was not contemplated that the church should own everything or that we should become in the Church, with reference to our property and otherwise, the same kind of automaton, manikin, that communism makes out of the individual," declared J. Reuben Clark of the First Presidency.[39]

This rhetoric of free agency, in turn, served as a vital tool in the church's struggle against the welfare initiatives of the New Deal. According to David O. McKay, "unwise legislation, too often prompted by political expediency, is periodically being enacted that seductively undermines man's right to free agency, robs him of his rightful liberties, and makes him a cog in the crushing wheel of regimentation."[40] Through LDS media, leaders argued that human freedom sought through Mormon life could only flourish under the conditions of American-style laissez faire capitalism. As Mark Peterson, general manager of *Deseret News*, wrote in 1946:

> Remember that you cannot preach that gospel without freedom of speech, and you cannot publish that gospel without freedom of the press, and you cannot gather together in congregation without freedom of assembly, and you cannot worship the Lord your God according to the dictates of your own conscience without freedom of religion. And remember that every time you give up any of your freedom, whether it be to some economic or political group, or to any group, you jeopardize these four freedoms of which I have spoken.[41]

---

38. Heber J. Grant, J. Reuben Clark, and David O. McKay, "A Warning to Church Members," *The Improvement Era*, August 1936, 488.

39. J. Reuben Clark, "Private Ownership under the United Order and the Guarantees of the Constitution," *The Improvement Era*, November 1942, 687.

40. David O. McKay, "Free Agency as a Divine Gift," *The Improvement Era*, May 1950, 366.

41. Mark E. Peterson, "In Defense of Liberty," *The Improvement Era*, May 1946, 288.

Here, Peterson claims that the other First Amendment freedoms buttress religious liberty, and although he does not name those "political or economic groups" who might threaten these freedoms, the language of "four freedoms" tacitly attacks FDR's famous "Four Freedoms" address in which he laid out the principle vision of the American welfare state. Such arguments, which positioned religious liberty in opposition to economic security, became effective rhetorical strategies through which church leaders mounted assaults on the New Deal. While they only rarely condemned the welfare state directly, authorities almost invariably depicted government as the enemy of liberty, and by extension of Mormon free agency.

As David O. McKay assumed the Presidency in 1951, the anti-communist stance of the church only became more pronounced. Under his leadership, other prominent anti-communist voices achieved influence within and without the church, individuals like Ezra Taft Benson, who also served as Eisenhower's Secretary of Agriculture. For Benson, capitalism was coterminous with the "American Way of Life," and best fostered the self-reliance and the liberty dear to "true Americans."[42] The expansion of federal power into the economic domain and the international spread of communism were dire trends for the future of America and the church.

Benson professed that the welfare state had already brought the United States across a critical threshold, which was tearing Mormons away from what he saw as their historical foundation in self-reliance. "For a generation now," he declared, "we have been teaching our people to depend on government instead of relying upon their own initiative as our pioneer forefathers. Our freedom to work out our individual destinies has already been abridged. We have been looking upon government as something apart from us and have failed to realize that we, the people, are the government."[43]

The exercise of state power, with few exceptions, represented for Benson a transgression of both temporal and spiritual truths. For Benson, the welfare state diminished individual autonomy just as it constrained the ability of business owners to decide for themselves how to operate, Supreme Court decisions such as *Engel v. Vitale* (1962)—which prohibited public school-sponsored prayers—restricted religious liberty, and federal education aid attached conditions on how local communities could raise their youth. Communism simply represented the most egregious example of this overreach, and for Benson, it

---

42. Ezra Taft Benson, "The Survival of the American Way of Life," *The Improvement Era*, June 1948, 404.

43. Ibid.

was the place toward which the "anti-Christ" was pulling his nation and, more importantly, the Saints.

In broad perspective, then, the church's antagonism toward communism reflects the deeper suspicions among a certain segment of LDS leadership regarding the power of the federal government. The Great Accommodation, which effectively ended plural marriage and brought statehood to the Utah territory, had been, in some sense, a marked defeat for the church, leaving its authorities wary of the state. When economic disaster led to the rapid extension of government activities, therefore, these church leaders dug in to defend their interests, leveraging LDS media to garner support from members. New Deal policies, they maintained, were moving the United States toward communism, which they saw as violation of a freedom essential to both America and the Mormon faith. As World War II gave way to the Cold War, these voices had effectively made their views the formal position of the LDS Church. For them, to be a Mormon was to be a capitalist.

Mormon Faith, Mormon Business

The church may have used anti-communist rhetoric to resist the New Deal, but the language of business also became part of its more general repertoire during the mid-twentieth century. At this time, the increasing dominance of LDS leadership by Mormon businessmen obfuscated the line between spiritual and temporal affairs. Scholars such as Robert Gottlieb and Peter Wiley have pointed out that during the Presidency of David O. McKay (1951–1970) LDS activities became increasingly entangled with business interests.[44] Moreover, a deeper examination of *The Improvement Era* of this period reveals multiple strategies, overlapping discourses that, when taken in concert, give an impression of mid-twentieth-century Mormon life intimately bound to the interests of commerce.

Like the vast majority of periodicals during this time, Mormon publications increasingly relied on selling advertising space for funding, particularly from LDS-affiliated companies. These advertisements positioned Mormon-owned brands as friends of the faith, its history and its leaders. For instance, the magazine began to collaborate with advertisers to celebrate the birthdays of church presidents. In the April 1950 issue, Union Pacific Railroad, a company with

---

44. Gottlieb and Wiley, *America's Saints*, 118–119. Although Gottlieb and Wiley note that a number of Mormon businessmen achieved prominence and that "church publications in this same period gave increasing attention to the success stories of Mormon businessmen and to the financial achievements of the members in general," they only mention this in passing without any substantiating evidence.

close ties to the church, took out a full-page for Church President George Albert Smith's eightieth birthday, referring to Smith as "churchman, businessman, friend."[45] In fact the entire issue was peppered with full-page accolades for Smith, from such firms as Utah Oil Refining Company (UTOCO), Utah Copper Division, Deseret News, and Utah-Idaho Sugar Company. The centerpiece of the issue was an article by LDS author and educator Bryant S. Hinckley titled "Service Through Industry...George Albert Smith as a Businessman."[46] The piece foregrounded Smith's less-known but nonetheless "bright record as a man of business" before embarking on a life of leadership in the church. Such praise anchored Mormon leadership to the world of business. In the pages of this issue, readers encountered a chorus of advertisements, in which Mormon companies sang in unison their praises of Smith, establishing an image of Mormon life bound up with the marketplace. Three years later, similar business-focused tributes celebrated the eightieth birthday of Smith's successor David O. McKay.

Even absent the advancement of church presidents to octogenarian status, advertisers frequently linked Mormon identity to business. Consider the text from a full-page ad for Zions National Bank in 1961:

> No subsidies? No guaranteed prices for buffalo hides? No pension for pioneering? No. All those pioneers had to go on was faith and character. They traveled two thousand miles for the opportunity to reap the benefits of their own hard work. They would have been ashamed to ask for something for nothing; they would have scorned those who demand pay for no work. The leader of these pioneers founded an organization which is now known as Zions First National Bank. His belief in preserving man's individual independence and dignity is still part of the principles for which this bank stands.[47]

The advertisement portrays Mormonism as inseparable from capitalism. It extols the virtues of hard work and self-reliance, while shunning subsidies, price controls, and pensions, all of which represent policies associated with the welfare state. Appealing to a romanticized account of the Mormon westward migration, it positions Zions Bank as the progeny of the "original" Saints and as carrier for the "individual independence and dignity" for which they

---

45. *The Improvement Era*, April 1950, 246.

46. Bryant S. Hinckley, "Service Through Industry...George Albert Smith as a Businessman," *The Improvement Era*, April 1950, 282–283.

47. *The Improvement Era*, December 1961, 893.

and their faith stood. Together, these rhetorical moves present rugged individualism as both inherently Mormon and capitalist, incompatible with the post-New Deal welfare state of the mid-twentieth century.

LDS Global Expansion: Toward a "Businessminded" Mormonism

Advertisements represented only one means by which the business world made its presence felt. Between 1957 and 1961, *The Improvement Era* featured a monthly series titled "Leadership Development," written by the former chairman of the Utah Board of Regents, Sterling W. Sill. His articles seem primarily concerned with outlining the skills and practices necessary to achieving personal success. These were neither moralizing tracts discussing some divinely ordained liberty nor anti-statist jeremiads. Rather, Sill wrote in a language that more closely resembled popular management literature than philosophy of religion. He drew upon Mormon scripture to describe "7 Success Ideas," discussed how to integrate one's faith into leadership, and declared that "our greatest contribution to the work of the Lord can only be made as we develop our abilities to their highest possible point."[48]

Columns like these, which employed the language of business, became increasingly prevalent in LDS media at the turn of the 1960s. These articles advocated not self-reliance but self-improvement. Instead of preaching traditional bourgeois thriftiness, they promoted wise money management. Rather than vouching for the inherent worthiness of all labor, they encouraged readers to seek out meaningful careers. While these differences might appear subtle, they are significant for two reasons. First, this semantic shift reflects pronounced changes across American society. The postwar economic boom led to historic levels of employment, which afforded many individuals (particularly the burgeoning middle class) the luxury of "choosing" a vocation. As production moved from wartime to peacetime a consumer culture, which rewarded spending over saving, took shape. "Self-help" and related therapeutic disciplines such as twelve-step groups and minister and bestselling author Norman Vincent Peale's "positive thinking" enjoyed popular appeal. In some sense, then, the church was simply swept up in these changes.

Yet from another perspective, the managerial turn can also be understood in light of challenges specific to the LDS Church during this time. The postwar years began a period of unprecedented growth for the church in both size and scope. Between 1947 and 1963, as missionary efforts began to win

---

48. Sterling W. Sill, "The Executive," *The Improvement Era*, September 1957, 665.

new converts across the globe, membership jumped from 1 to 2 million and the number of church stakes outside North America grew rapidly.

To meet the demands of an expanding membership base, LDS leadership instituted an ambitious set of reforms, which streamlined operations and restructured missions along corporate lines. Because expansion demanded a large, professional missionary force, McKay and other authorities stressed missions as an obligation, aspiring to make "Every Man a Missionary." In 1959, he fixed the age of missionaries at nineteen and introduced the characteristic dark suit and tie as standard appearance, a dress code reminiscent of the "organization men" of IBM. The church overhauled its missionary training, offering the youth brief but intensive preparation in languages, cultural literacy, and proselytizing before sending into the mission fields. All in all, the fleet of missionaries was beginning to resemble a corporate sales force.

One reason for this transition to a more businesslike model for missions was simple: many of the leaders called to lead these efforts were prominent Mormons with extensive experience in the private sector. Sterling W. Sill, for instance, began his career as an insurance salesman for New York Life, eventually heading the company's intermountain region. When called as an Assistant to the Quorum of the Twelve Apostles in 1954, therefore, he relied on his business acumen to inform his service to the church. Because business was the landscape with which he and other authorities were most familiar, the vision of Mormon life that they crafted for readers of *The Improvement Era* remained steeped in its logic.

Authorities represented the "businessman" as the exemplary Mormon, declaring that business enabled one to cultivate those values most dear to the faith. It was "by divine revelation that the industries among the Latter-day Saints have been developed, and their leading men have set before them this example," wrote Joseph Fielding Smith in *The Improvement Era*.[49] While other Christian denominations paid their clergy, LDS leaders "labored with their hands for a living" just as "the young men and women who are distributed over the face of the earth as missionaries of the Church pay their own way, or their parents do."[50]

To fund these ventures, parents were encouraged to think like investors and practice sound financial planning. Quinn G. McKay, Dean of the School of Economics at Weber State College in Utah, contributed a column during

---

49. Joseph Fielding Smith, "Why Do the Authorities of the Church Engage in Business?," *The Improvement Era*, July 1960, 496.

50. Ibid, 496, 497.

the late 1960s dedicated to helping families save for their child's future. Investments, he professed, are "particularly helpful to have for the retirement years or for missions or education."[51] McKay's column prompted families to budget, take second jobs if necessary, and to choose lucrative career paths in order to yield the greatest return.[52]

Of course, preparing youth as missionaries demanded more than solid financial planning. It required of the whole community a commitment to teaching young Mormons the proper values and skills they would need in adult life, and church leaders conveyed this through the language of business. One writer in *The Improvement Era* even cast salesmanship as "useful in child training," as "necessary to convince the child that goodness, that honesty is the best policy, that the Golden Rule is a profitable one by which to live."[53] Missionary training also incorporated sales techniques for speaking with potential converts. Sterling Sill, for instance, challenged missionaries to practice surface acting. "If you want to be friendly, act 'As If' you are already friendly … It is the axiom of the theater that each actor should live his part," he stressed.

Moreover, the primary purpose of the Mormon family unit was to prepare children for future careers in business. *The Improvement Era* told parents "to inform themselves on career openings in industry, analyze them in terms of [their child's] personality and talent, and suggest to him where he might start his ascent up the ladder of success: in accounting, administration, marketing… or in one of the dozen other arms of business."[54] Articles like these actively mapped the needs of business onto the stages of Mormon life, presenting childhood and adolescence as training for missions and subsequent careers in business.

Church leaders increasingly understood themselves as officials overseeing a growing (increasingly global) empire of employees for whom they assumed responsibility. In the words of Harvey L. Taylor, Vice President of BYU,

> It is now the executive's or leader's job to keep the worker encouraged
> and to make him feel that his job is important. If he needs special

---

51. Quinn G. McKay, "How to Make Money While you Sleep," *The Improvement Era*, March 1968, 34.

52. See Quinn G. McKay, "Where Does All the Money Go?," *The Improvement Era*, February 1968, "How to Earn up to $557 a Day," *The Improvement Era*, April 1968, and "Extra Salaries," *The Improvement Era*, May 1968.

53. Mabel Otis Robinson, "Use Salesmanship On Your Children," *The Improvement Era*, April 1965, 300.

54. Edmund C. Hasse, "Help Your Child Choose the Right Career," *The Improvement Era*, May 1961, 302.

training for the job, arrangements must be made for this. See that he is properly introduced to his fellow workers within the organization and to the class or group to which he has been assigned.

The Church of Jesus Christ of Latter-day Saints is a church of activity. It is said, "By their fruits ye shall know them." Executives therefore are charged with the responsibility of calling into some kind of service as many of the membership as possible.[55]

By embracing the language of corporate America, LDS leaders like Taylor believed that the church could sustain and control its unprecedented growth. They could use managerial strategies to motivate the faithful in the same way that CEOs might inspire their laborers.

Success in business, unsurprisingly, translated easily into spiritual status among one's peers. As stated earlier, leaders were selected on the basis of their business savvy. "These leaders," suggested Taylor, "should be students of human relations so that they can, when necessary, 'pour oil on troubled waters' and keep a smooth-working organization."[56] Lower in the hierarchy are the "assistants," who is "willing to co-operate" and "demonstrate loyalty to presiding officers."[57] Finally, Taylor recommended that the "record-keepers" should exhibit "dependability, neatness, orderliness, exceptional accuracy," all qualities of importance in the expanding white-collar world of mid-twentieth-century America.

Conclusion

By the end of the 1960s (when *The Improvement Era* ended its seven-decade run as the church's official periodical for adult members), the language of business saturated Mormon self-understanding. When Mormons like Clay Christensen credit their faith as the reason for their business success, they are drawing upon a conceptual world that was crafted by LDS leaders in response to particular challenges the church faced in the mid-twentieth century. In *The Seven Habits of Highly Effective People*, perhaps the bestselling popular business book of all time, leadership guru and Latter-day Saint Stephen Covey expresses that "correct principles are natural laws, and that God, the Creator

---

55. <IBT>Harvey L. Taylor, "Matching Men and Jobs," *The Improvement Era*, October 1964</IBT> 850.

56. Ibid, 848.

57. Ibid.

and Father of us all, is the source of them."[58] For Covey, the principles outlined in the Mormon belief facilitate individual success. Yet as much as Covey might locate the source of his success in the eternal truths of his faith, his views reflect the discursive world in which he was immersed as a young Mormon coming of age in the mid-twentieth century.

Prominent Mormons like Covey and Christensen appeal to their beliefs because they constitute a conceptual world with which they are quite comfortable, one that emphasizes the virtue of hard work, self-reliance, and a favorable view toward business and management. Certainly, many of these values were manifest even in the formative years of the LDS Church, but their extraordinary importance to Mormon self-understanding only emerged later. Although Momonism might very well be "the world's most capitalist religion," these values did not emerge fully formed from Mormon scriptures or from the church's earliest history. Rather, as LDS media reveals, the Mormon embrace of capitalism took place because, at least in part, it proved an effective strategy for serving the interests of the church. It justified resistance to the expanding welfare state under the New Deal; it sustained the business interests of church leaders; and it provided a useful set of tools for managing an ever-expanding global mission.

Pro-business rhetoric gave the church a means to sustain its distinctiveness for its members while simultaneously endearing itself to the broader American public. On the one hand, believers could witness their church taking a stand against its historical adversary, the federal government. On the other hand, business was and continues to be the *lingua franca* of American life. By the late twentieth century, that language—of business and capitalism—came so naturally to Latter-day Saints that church members understood it as part and parcel of their own distinctive religious ethic and heritage.

---

58. Stephen Covey, *The Seven Habits of Highly Effective People: Powerful Lessons in Personal Change, Deluxe Edition* (New York: Simon and Schuster, 2013), 308.

6

The Pageantry of Protest in Temple Square

Max Perry Mueller

ANY VISITOR TO Temple Square during the Church of Jesus Christ of Latter-day Saints' semiannual General Conference witnesses tens of thousands of Mormons filing in and out of the church's massive conference center. The quartz-monzonite edifice, adorned with its suspended waterfalls and garden terraces, seats 21,000 persons. Dressed in dark suits and long dresses, Mormons from as far as the Philippines and Ghana, and from as near as Salt Lake City's leafy avenues, come to hear their living prophets speak on matters of faith and family.

It is a pilgrimage and pageant to Mormonism's holiest site. What was once a patch of scratchy, high-plains desert, the long-persecuted but ever-industrious Mormon people transformed into Salt Lake City's showcase city blocks: at once cosmopolitan and insular, open to the public and highly regulated.[1] It is the international headquarters of a church with more than 15 million members worldwide, and the home to a religion whose diverse business interests and political clout dominate every aspect of the area's culture.

These city blocks now extend south of Temple Square to the LDS-owned upscale mall, City Creek Center. A visit to the Tabernacle during General Conference can include a quick trip to Prada, a prayer at the Handcart Memorial, followed by lunch at the Cheesecake Factory. A cup of coffee, however, is hard to come by, and a cocktail even harder.[2]

---

1. In this chapter, by "Temple Square" I do not mean simply the walled-off city block where the Salt Lake Temple itself, as well as the Tabernacle, the two Temple Square visitors' centers, and Assembly Hall, are located. Taking my cues from the church, in this essay Temple Square serves as shorthand for the entire ten-acre campus of the LDS Church's headquarters as well as the city streets and sidewalks that run through and around this area. See "Salt Lake City Temple Square," *LDS.org*, www.lds.org/locations/salt-lake-city-temple-square#d.

2. Scholars of sacred space will surely find City Creek Center (opened in 2012), and its relationship to Temple Square, fodder for new theorizing around American religion, pilgrimage, and consumerism. For a starting point, see Hillary Kaell, "Of Gifts and Grandchildren: American Holy Land Souvenirs," *Journal of Material Culture* 17 (July 2012): 133–151; Jon Pahl, *Shopping Malls and Other Sacred Spaces: Putting God in Place* (Eugene, OR: Wipf & Stock Publishers, 2008).

A key part of conference pageantry is passing by anti-Mormon protesters, often found gathered on both sides of North Temple Street. According to Salt Lake City ordinances, after registering at least thirty days in advance with the city, and paying five dollars to obtain a permit, protesters can participate in what the city calls "free expression activities" on the public sidewalks bordering church property. It is against the law to block the Saints from passing by, or "intentionally cause [them] inconvenience, annoyance, or alarm." But the law does permit protesters to stand in their cordoned-off swaths of sidewalk from which they can yell their version of the Christian Bible, as well as more than a little vitriol. [3] In the shadows of the Salt Lake Temple, protesters damn the LDS Church as a cult and conference attendees as heretics and religious dupes. At the same time, any number of LDS security detail, Salt Lake Police, and civil and religious liberties advocates also play close attention.[4] It is a carefully choreographed pageant: one part First Amendment free exercise of religion, one part free speech, and one part public safety. Benches full of lawyers are also on standby ready to litigate any real or perceived First Amendment (as well as private property) violations.

And yet the fact that Temple Square is a particularly charged place for the performance of America's most cherished and fought-over constitutional amendment is nothing new. Though for the most part neglected in the scholarship of the civil rights era, in the 1960s Temple Square became a First Amendment battleground where freedom of expression—in the dual form of protest for greater civil rights *and* religious freedom—was contested regularly in and around the city's central blocks, with their evolving amalgam of city-owned public spaces and LDS Church-owned private property. To be sure, Temple Square is not the only religious space in which Americans have asserted that God's law, and not the law of the state, reigns supreme. During the 1980s "Sanctuary Movement," dozens of Jewish and Christian congregations across the country provided aide and shelter to refugees fleeing the violent civil wars in Central America. Despite their First Amendment free exercise claims, notably that they had the right to practice the millennia-old concept of Sanctuary—the tradition of allowing some criminals and political dissenters to find asylum inside places of worship—a handful of Sanctuary Movement

3. See the ACLU of Utah's helpful guideline to the laws governing public protests in Salt Lake City: "Your Right to Protest in Salt Lake City," *American Civil Liberties Union of Utah*, www.acluutah.org/images/SLCprotest.pdf.

4. For a history of the ACLU in Utah, see Linda Sillitoe, *Friendly Fire: The ACLU in Utah* (Salt Lake City: Signature Books, 1996), 13–38.

activists were tried and convicted of "alien smuggling."[5] And yet what makes Temple Square distinctive is how the space has become a geographically defined synecdoche for the entire LDS Church—from which church projects its religion *and* politics outward and, in turn, to which opponents of the church can gather to contest its religion and politics.

While giving some attention to recent demonstrations for the ordination of women, as well as protests against the LDS Church's political actions opposing the legalization of same-sex marriage, the main focus of this essay is an examination of how the National Association for the Advancement of Colored People (NAACP) and its allies used protests and the threat of protests at Temple Square during the 1960s to move the LDS Church to publicly support civil rights. These public acts of free expression pressured the church to publicly back civil rights, and relatedly, pressured many church members in state government to back civil rights legislation aimed at ending the widespread discriminatory codes and practices in the state. And yet at least in the short term, the protesters failed to force the LDS Church to end its policy of excluding people of African descent from full church membership, a policy that ended more than a decade later in 1978, and only after church leaders announced that they had received a divine revelation.

These civil rights-era protests against the LDS Church's exclusionary practices and racist theologies effected change in Utah's public spaces and laws. At the same time, by asserting its own constitutional rights, the LDS Church successfully resisted changes to what takes place within private spaces, including what takes place within the walls of its temples. In the 1960s and 1970s, the LDS Church's insistence that it would only end its policies of racial exclusion on its own terms—or as church leaders would claim, on God's time—was an exercise of the church's constitutionally guaranteed religious liberty.

Temple Square as Town Square

In this essay, with debates over the proper place of African Americans, gays, and women in both American and Mormon culture serving as case studies, I propose that we think about Temple Square not only as Mormonism's sacred "square," but one that sometimes doubles as the region's own secular "town square." Rooted in the New England tradition of a

---

5. Amanda Rose, *Showdown in the Desert: Religion, Law, and the Immigration Controversy* (New York: Oxford University Press, 2012), 17–46.

central public space located at the heart of a Puritan village, I understand the American town square—what Richard J. Neuhaus called the "public square"—as the civic space where Americans practice, perform, and contest their constitutional rights.[6] Because it is the literal and symbolic focal point for the region's most powerful cultural and political institution, Temple Square—rather than the grounds of the Utah State Capitol or those of Salt Lake's City-County Building—has been the most popular place to carry out protests, even protests in which religion is not directly implicated.[7] This is the case because boundaries between religion and politics in Temple Square (and in Utah more generally) blur to a degree that is unique in American culture.

The blurring of boundaries is not mere metaphor. Since the late 1990s, questions about whether certain streets and sidewalks in Temple Square belong to Salt Lake City or to the LDS Church have been fiercely debated and fiercely litigated. Yet the results of these court battles only partially settle the question of whether Temple Square is a public space where citizens are free to exercise First Amendment-protected speech, or whether it is a private space where the LDS Church is free to exercise First Amendment religious liberty (along with private property ownership rights guaranteed in the Fourth and Fifth Amendments) and thus able to exclude protesters and anyone else it chooses.

The particularities of place play an essential role in this history. To claim that the LDS Church dominates the politics, economics, and culture of what demographers call the "Mormon culture Region" in the Intermountain West

---

6. See the early plat of New Haven, Connecticut, reprinted in Mark A. Noll, *A History of Christianity in the United States and Canada* (Grand Rapids, MI: Wm B. Eardmans Publishing, 1992), 41. My understanding of Temple Square as a town square, and as such, the location of protests against LDS Church policies and theologies, moves in the same direction as Neuhaus's public square, away from what we both perceive as cultural hegemonies. But the cultural hegemonies we name—for Neuhaus "secular America" and for my study here, the LDS Church—are certainly different in form and ideology. Richard J. Neuhaus, *The Naked Public Square: Religion and Democracy in America* (Grand Rapids, MI: Wm B. Eardmans Publishing, 1986), 78. Also see Noah Feldman, *Divided by God: America's Church-State Problem—and What We Should Do About It* (New York: FSG, 2006).

7. Most recently, supporters and opponents of gay marriage have rallied at the State Capitol and the City and County Building following the December 2013 ruling by the US District Court for Utah striking down Utah's ban on same-sex marriage. Richard Piatt and McKenzie Romero, "Groups Rally for, against Same-sex Marriage at Utah Capitol," *KSL.com*, January, 28, 2014, www.ksl.com/?sid=28528877; Michael Winter, "US Court: Utah Gay Marriages Can Continue," *USA Today*, December 24, 2013, www.usatoday.com/story/news/nation/2013/12/24/utah-gay-marriage/4187111/.

is to state the obvious.[8] In the summer of 1847, when Brigham Young and the vanguard company of Mormon pioneers arrived in the Salt Lake Basin, they designed their new capital city based on Joseph Smith Jr.'s 1830s City of Zion plat. City streets were laid out on a grid pattern with Temple Square as the geographical center of orientation.[9] Over the last century and a half, the city expanded with every city block and with every building's address oriented in relation to its distance from Temple Square. One might say that street signs serve as a sort of secular *qiblas*, pointing all of Salt Lake toward the Mormons' Mecca built just below the Salt Lake Basin's northern foothills.[10]

To borrow from Antonio Gramsci, as the seat of "cultural hegemony" in the Beehive State, Temple Square exerts a centripetal pull drawing inward critics of the LDS Church as well as pilgrims and tourists.[11] From the 1960s to the late 2000s, protesters targeting the LDS Church's resistance to racial and marriage equality have marched on the streets in and around Temple Square. More recently, Mormons calling for the ordination of women have brought their calls for change inside the walls of Temple Square itself. The protesters' goal is to bring critical attention to the beliefs that, through the force of its prophetic and institutional authority, the LDS hierarchy has made "common

---

8. For Donald Meinig's classic discussion of what he called the "Mormon Culture Region," see D. W. Meinig, "The Mormon Culture Region: Strategies and Patterns in the Geography of the American West, 1847–1964," *Annals of the Association of American Geographers* 55 (1965): 191–219. In Ethan Yorgason's recent expansion and correction of Meinig's original conception of a Mormon cultural region, which Yorgason described as "focused less on the content and derivations of cultural values than on identifying where Mormon power was most prevalent," see Ethan R. Yorgason, *Transformation of the Mormon Culture Region* (Urbana: University of Illinois Press, 2003), 2.

9. Benjamin E. Park, "To Fill the World: Joseph Smith as Urban Planner," *Mormon Historical Studies* 14 no. 1 (March 2013): 1–27; Craig D. Galli, "Building Zion: The Latter-day Saint Legacy of Urban Planning," *BYU Studies* 44, no. 1 (2005): 111–136.

10. Even the most virulent anti-Mormons are, in a sense, built into Salt Lake City's temple-centric grid. Take for example, Jerald and Sandra Tanner and their Utah Lighthouse Ministry. The Tanners' family home serves as their ministry's bookstore from which during the last half century these self-described "apostates"—Sandra Tanner claims to be a direct descendant of Brigham Young—have sold and given away thousands of copies of their anti-Mormon pamphlets and books, which chronicle the church's supposed sins of blasphemy, sexual deviancy, and racism (along with scores of others). The potency of the Tanners' fanatic anti-Mormonism draws its own power from its location, at 1358 S. West Temple, just fourteen blocks due south of the Temple. Sandra Tanner, "Reflections on 42 Years of Apostasy," Eighth Annual Ex-Mormon Conference, October 5, 2002, Salt Lake City, Utah; Laurence Foster, "Career Apostates: Reflections on the Works of Jerald and Sandra Tanner," *Dialogue: A Journal of Mormon Thought* 17 (Summer 1984): 35–64.

11. See Jennifer Huss Basquiat's powerful application of Gramsci's notions of cultural hegemony (along with those of Raymond Williams), in "Reproducing Patriarchy and Erasing Feminism: The Selective Construction of History within Mormon Community," *Journal of Feminist Studies in Religion* 17 (Fall 2002): 11–13.

sense" in Mormon culture. For example, protesters challenged the so-called common sense that blacks were unworthy of full American citizenship and equality within the church and questioned the church hierarchy's insistence that gay marriage threatens traditional, heterosexual, procreative marriage.[12] And yet because of its cultural hegemony within the region—though less so in increasingly liberal Salt Lake City itself——the LDS Church is able to reframe these protests to serve its own purposes. As Jennifer Huss Basquiat has written regarding the LDS Church hierarchy's relationship to feminist challenges to the Mormon patriarchy, "when the dominant culture has a significant stake in what is being challenged, it makes a move either to incorporate or appropriate these alternative or oppositional practices with the lexicon of acceptable everyday practice."[13]

I argue that we can find examples of this incorporation and appropriation in the LDS Church's reaction to protests for racial, and more recently, marriage equality. As critics of the church assert their First Amendment rights to protest discriminatory political and religious practices, the LDS Church defends itself by also asserting First Amendment protections of religious liberty. René Girard might call this move "mimetic rivalry." Both the church and its critics assert claims to the same space.[14]

Protest, Persecuted, and Persecutors

The long history of the Latter-day Saints as the targets of unconstitutional religious persecution has informed the LDS Church's relationship with the national politics of race and marriage. Although he had previously—if not consistently—defended slavery as a biblically sanctioned institution, in 1844 Joseph Smith Jr. ran for president of the United States as a gradual abolitionist. In the late 1830s, based in part on accusations that the Mormons were meddling with slaves and Indians, mobs and state militias in Missouri had run the Mormons out of that state to find safety—but only for a brief time—in

---

12. As Steven Jones warns, "We should not confuse Gramsci's notion of 'common sense' with its normal use in English. Gramsci emphatically does not conceive of common sense as practical wisdom that contradicts theorizing or dogma. Instead it is literally thought that is common—common to a social group, or common to a society as a whole." Steven Jones, *Routledge Critical Thinkers: Antonio Gramsci* (New York: Routledge, 2006), 54. Common sense, writes Gramsci, is "continually transforming itself, enriching itself with scientific ideas and with philosophical opinions, which have entered ordinary life." Antonio Gramsci, *Selections from the Prison Notebooks* (New York: International Publishers, 1971), 326.

13. Basquiat, "Reproducing Patriarchy and Erasing Feminism," 13.

14. See René Girard, *Violence and the Sacred*, trans. Patrick Gregory (Baltimore: Johns Hopkins University Press, 1979), especially chapter 6.

Illinois. Smith launched his unlikely bid for the White House after the five leading candidates to that office failed to promise him that they would use their powers to protect the Saints' constitutional rights to freely practice their religion.[15] In his presidential platform, Smith claimed that the laws of the Constitution as well as the ideals of the Declaration of Independence of "life, liberty and the pursuit of happiness" for "all men" had not protected the Saints from abuse, unlawful imprisonment, and religiously based assassinations. Yet Smith also pointed out that Mormons were not the only victims of unconstitutional persecution. In the opening paragraphs of the platform, Smith connected the plight of his people with the "some two or three millions of people [who] are held as slaves for life, because the spirit in them is covered with a darker skin than ours."[16]

In 1852, under Joseph Smith's successor, Brigham Young, the exclusively Mormon Utah legislature legalized slavery in the newly formed territory. The LDS Church also implemented restrictions on church membership for people of African descent, based on the belief that blacks were divinely cursed and destined to be the spiritual and political underclass of humanity.[17] However, the history of Mormonism and race is not simply one of declension away from more racially tolerant roots to racist policies, politics, and theologies. In the first decades of the twentieth century, for example, leading Mormons participated in what might be described as a mutual admiration society with Booker T. Washington and his Tuskegee Institute. The LDS-owned *Deseret News* frequently printed glowing reports on the progress at Tuskegee—6,000 bushels of sweet potatoes harvested, 250 suits tailored, 25 full harnesses constructed—reports that would have been familiar to the industrious Mormons. They saw in Washington and in his self-sufficient, quasi-utopian agricultural and industrial community in Alabama something that resembled the Saints' own success in Utah. Perhaps as the Mormons in Utah had done for them-

---

15. In his reply to Smith's letter requesting such protections, John C. Calhoun gave a states' rights response: "the case does not come within the Jurisdiction of the Federal Government." John C. Calhoun to Joseph Smith Jr., December 2, 1843, reprinted in *Niles' Register*, February 3, 1844, 357.

16. Joseph Smith Jr., "Gen. Smith's Views on the Government and Policy of the US," *Times & Seasons* 5 (May 15, 1844): 528. Samuel Brown has recently written about W. W. Phelps's work as Smith's "ghostwriter," including of his presidential platform. Samuel Brown, "The Translator and the Ghostwriter: Joseph Smith and W.W. Phelps," *Journal of Mormon History* 34, no. 1 (Winter 2008): 26–62.

17. Lester E. Bush, "Mormonism's Negro Doctrine: An Historical Overview," *Dialogue: A Journal of Mormon Thought* 8 (Spring 1973): 11–68; Newell G. Bringhurst, *Saints, Slaves, and Blacks: The Changing Place of Black People Within Mormonism* (Westport, CT: Greenwood Press, 1981); Armand L. Mauss, *All Abraham's Children: Changing Mormon Conceptions of Race and Lineage* (Urbana: University of Illinois Press, 2003).

selves, Tuskegee could serve as a model for how African Americans could learn to live independently of the white, "Gentile" world that persecuted them. "The institute is doing a good work for the moral and intellectual emancipation of the colored race," read one November 1905 report, "and it deserves all encouragement."[18]

Knowing something about the practice themselves, the Mormons also sided with Washington when it came to the return of "judge lynch" to the post-Reconstruction South. On August 28, 1900, the *Deseret News* printed an editorial praising the state of Texas for convicting members of a lynch mob to life in prison. The editors of the *Deseret News* noted that they agreed with Booker T. Washington that the practice of lynching threatened the moral and legal advancement of the nation.[19] "Washington is undoubtedly correct in his assumption that the race problem will be solved by means of education," continued the editorial. "Only the white people need some education too. They need to learn that American law protects life, and that all citizens have certain rights which should be respected." Whether the victims are black or white, asserted the *Deseret News*, "when mob turn assassins, they should be met by the full force of the law."[20]

The mutual admiration culminated in Washington's March 1913 visit to Salt Lake City, where the city's political and educational elite fêted him. Weeks later, in *The New Age*, Washington published glowing reports about his visit. "I have never been among a more intelligent, healthy, clean, progressive, moral set of people than these people are."[21] When Washington died two years later, the *Deseret News* eulogized him as a "great black man" and predicted, "it will be difficult to find a successor to step worthily into his place."[22]

What the Mormons liked about Washington was that he emphasized education instead of political agitation (or so they thought) as the most efficient means to "emancipate the race." What they feared about his successors, like

---

18. "Tuskegee Institute," *Deseret News*, November 7, 1905, 4.

19. Robert J. Norrell, *Up from History: The Life of Booker T. Washington* (Cambridge, MA: Belknap Press of Harvard University, 2009), 111–113, 172–173.

20. "Lynches Sentenced," *Deseret News*, August 29, 1900, 4. Such discourse was part of a long-established LDS critique of southern vigilantism in the postbellum South. Patrick Q. Mason, *The Mormon Menace: Violence and Anti-Mormonism in the Postbellum South* (New York: Oxford University Press, 2010), 29–34, 160–167.

21. Booker T. Washington, *New York Age*, April 17, 1913, in Louis R. Harlan and Raymond Smock, eds., *The Booker T. Washington Paper, Volume 12: 1912–1914* (Urbana: University of Illinois Press, 1982), 149.

22. "A Great Black Man," *Deseret News*, November 15, 1915.

W. E. B. Du Bois and the NAACP, was that they would push for immediate political and social equality. In 1928, William Pickens, the Yale-educated director of branches for the NAACP, made his own pilgrimage to Salt Lake City. And like Washington, Pickens printed his findings in a leading East Coast African American newspaper, this time in the *Amsterdam News*. Yet unlike Washington, who ignored the status of African Americans within the LDS Church, Pickens focused the majority of his article on the ban against full black membership. Pickens explained that this ban meant that not only were blacks forbidden from entering the Mormon temple, which he explained approximates heaven on earth for Mormons, but that they were also forbidden from entering heaven itself. Mormons believed that there was only one "Negro" in heaven, "the 'Body Servant' of Brigham Young." "You see this negro was a 'good servant,'" Pickens explained, "and Brigham Young, like all 'good white folks,' was somewhat partial to 'his negro,' and influenced God to let him in."[23]

Utah's relative isolation, as well as the LDS Church's anti-black theologies, kept many blacks from settling in Salt Lake City until the 1920s and 1930s, when many came to work in the railroads, mines, and the region's growing tourist industry. Yet in Utah, blacks encountered limitations in employment, housing, and access to restaurants and hotels similar to those many had left behind in the South. The Hotel Utah, now the Joseph Smith Memorial Building in Temple Square, gave Opera Star Marian Anderson lodging when she came to Salt Lake City in 1948 to perform at the Mormon Tabernacle. However, she was not allowed to use the hotel's grand entrance on South Temple Street, and had to agree to ride in the freight elevator.[24] That same year, Utah's chapter of the NAACP, which was formed in 1919 in response to discrimination in public schools, won its first major victory when it successfully pressured the Salt Lake City-County Building to end its policy of refusing blacks service at its lunch counter.[25]

---

23. In his reference to Young's "Body Servant," Pickens might be referring to the well-known early black Mormon convert, missionary, and priesthood holder, Elijah Abel. William Pickens, "Even the Mormons," *The New York Amsterdam News*, February 29, 1928.

24. Ronald G. Coleman, "Blacks in Utah History," in Helen Z. Papanikolas, ed., *The Peoples of Utah* (Salt Lake City: Utah State Historical Society, 1976), 137; "'Ave Maria' Will Be an Encore," *Salt Lake Tribune*, March 19, 1948. "Famous Contralto Had to Use Freight Lift in Hotel Utah," *Salt Lake Tribune*, April 1993, 9; Interview with Elva Plummer, widow of Gail Plummer, manager of Kingsbury Hall, Everett L. Cooler Oral History Project, box 36, folder 296, Special Collections, Marriott Library, University of Utah, Salt lake City, Utah.

25. Sillitoe, *Friendly Fire*, 17.

The legal and social exclusion of blacks in Utah first gained national attention in the early years of the civil rights movement. Our entry point to this period is the 1958 report issued by the Utah Advisory Committee on Civil Rights, the state chapter of the US Commission on Civil Rights, which was established as part of the Civil Rights Act of 1957. Chaired by Adam M. Duncan, an attorney, Utah state legislator, and founder of the Utah chapter of the ACLU—and an active Mormon—the committee found that for the "Jew," "Utah [was] a second Promised Land in the wilderness." Yet according to the report, the "Negro" faced employment discrimination and social segregation that rivaled southern Jim Crow. However, the biggest concern was housing: "[The Negro] is confined by 'gentlemen's agreements' to substandard dwellings in less desirable areas of Salt Lake City and Ogden." The committee found that city and state leaders tacitly supported this discrimination, forcing blacks into small, ghettoized enclaves.[26]

What was unique about the Utah report—one of many reports in which state committees found that racial discrimination was rampant—was that the Utah committee explicitly singled out one religious institution as the source of discrimination: the LDS Church. The committee even cited the Mormon view that birth in "any race other than the white race" was the result of "inferior performance in a pre-earth life." The committee did allow that nonwhites could, "by righteous living," become "white and delightsome." The Utah report did not go unnoticed. *Time* magazine excerpted its findings, including the Mormon theological justification for both civil and religious discrimination.[27]

Because it was "common sense" within Mormon culture that blacks were spiritually inferior, the authors of the Utah report assumed it to be common sense that the cultural hegemony of the LDS Church in the region played a central role in creating the social and political environment in which civil discrimination of African Americans in Utah occurred.[28] As such the streets and sidewalks around the church's Temple Square became the "town square"

---

26. "Utah Advisory Committee," *The National Conference and the Reports of the State Advisory Committees to the US Commission on Civil Rights,* 1959 (Washington, DC: US Government Printting Press, 1960), 379–380, www.law.umaryland.edu/marshall/usccr/documents/cr12st2959.pdf. The practice of redlining was not unique to Utah. For a history of redlining in Chicago, see Beryl Satter, *Family Properties: Race, Real Estate, and the Exploitation of Black Urban America* (New York: Macmillan, 2009).

27. "Mormons & Civil Rights," *Time,* April 13, 1959.

28. Since the 1960s, Armand Mauss has studied and challenged this common-sense connection between racial prejudice and discrimination. Mauss, *All Abraham's Children: Changing Mormon Conceptions of Race and Lineage,* 221–230.

where protests for civil rights were staged, protests whose purpose was to challenge the common sense of black inferiority and anti-black discrimination. After all, if Marian Anderson's experience at the Hotel Utah is any indication, such discrimination took place in church-owned buildings around Temple Square itself. In the 1960s, the NAACP joined liberal Christian leaders who brought national attention to the LDS Church's policies of religious exclusion as well as its support for legal and social discrimination in Utah.[29] The NAACP understood the power of protesting outside Mormonism's most sacred space. As such, throughout the decade, the NAACP organized a series of protests and marches around Temple Square, beginning with a planned protest in October 1963 that was called off thanks to the mediation of University of Utah philosophy professor Sterling McMurrin.

McMurrin was not a novice when it came to the politics of race, discrimination, and the LDS Church. In fact, in 1961, during McMurrin's confirmation hearing to become US Commissioner of Education in the Kennedy Administration, the lifelong but heterodox Mormon made a point of distancing himself from the racial views and practices of his church. "I do not agree with the policies of the Mormon church with respect to Negroes," McMurrin told the US Senate committee considering his nomination, "and I have made my position very clear to the leadership of the Mormon church." During his two-year term as commissioner, McMurrin was a champion of federal efforts to desegregate public schools and increase federal aid to public schools.[30]

McMurrin received word that the NAACP planned to march on the streets in front of the Mormon Tabernacle in October 1963 while General Conference took place inside. In the days prior to the scheduled protests, McMurrin arranged a meeting between First Presidency Counselor Hugh B. Brown, Apostle Nathan Eldon Tanner, and Salt Lake City NAACP chapter President Albert Fritz, which took place in Brown's Temple Square offices.

---

29. In 1966, Donald L. Foster, a pastor at Congregational Church in Orem, Utah, published an article in *The Christian Century* titled "A Unique Gospel in Utah" in which he insinuated that the Mormons' barriers to full black membership, "sets [the] Church apart from" other Christian communities: "The Church requires the Negro to accept subordination as a means of bearing that curse." Foster concluded his editorial with this prediction: "All in all, we can expect the Church of Jesus Christ of Latter-day Saints to continue to resist such social change and ecumenical developments as have been firing the imaginations and engaging the energies of many other American churchmen." Donald L. Foster, "Unique Gospel in Utah," *Christian Century*, July 14, 1965.

30. Sterling M. McMurrin and L. Jackson Newell, *Matters of Conscience: Conversations with Sterling M. McMurrin on Philosophy, Education, and Religion* (Salt Lake City: Signature Books, 1996) xxv–xxvi.

As a result of the meeting, during General Conference Brown delivered a statement, endorsed by Church President David O. McKay, which read in part:

> Be it known that there is in the church no doctrine, belief, or practice that is intended to deny the enjoyment of full civil rights by any person regardless of race, color, creed.... We have consistently and persistently upheld the Constitution of the United States, and as far as we are concerned that means upholding the constitutional rights of every citizen of the United States.[31]

During his own General Conference address, Brown went off script to call on members of the church "to commit themselves to the establishment of civil equality for all God's children."[32]

Impressed by Brown's forceful support for civil rights, Fritz not only called off the planned protest on the streets in front of Salt Lake's Temple Square, but also urged "all NAACP people in Utah and throughout the country" to cancel the pending protests in front of other LDS Church buildings. Yet the détente between the NAACP and the LDS Church did not last long. In March 1965, as fair employment and housing legislation was stalled in the Utah State legislature, 90 percent of which was made up of members of the LDS Church, the NAACP picketed in front of the Church Office Building. University of Utah football star and future NFL Pro-Bowler Roy Jefferson participated in the three-day long protest. He also told national media outlets like the *New York Times* and the Associated Press about his troubles securing housing in Salt Lake for himself and his family. The NAACP blamed the LDS Church's "official silence" on the subject for impeding the progress of civil rights legislation.[33] The protests and the national attention they garnered seemed to have worked. The *Deseret News*, which had previously refused to endorse the legislation, published an editorial titled "A Clear Civil Rights Stand," which recapitulated much of the statement Hugh B. Brown delivered at the October 1963 General Conference. By year's end, equal employment and housing protections were signed into state law.[34]

---

31. Bringhurst, *Saints, Slaves and Blacks*, 181.

32. "Mormon Leader Asserts Equality," *Utah Daily Chronicle*, October 10, 1963, 1. See Position of the LDS Church on Civil Rights, October 6, 1963, reprinted in Bringhurst, *Saints, Slaves, and Blacks*, 231. See also Sterling M. McMurrin, "A Note on the 1963 Civil Rights Statements," *Dialogue: A Journal of Mormon Thought* 12 (Summer 1978): 60–63.

33. "N.A.A.C.P. Presses Protests in Utah," *New York Times*, March 10, 1965; Bringhurst, *Saints, Slaves, and Blacks*, 181.

34. *Deseret News*, March 9, 1965; Bringhurst, *Saints, Slaves, and Blacks*, 181.

Yet at the highest level, the church hierarchy remained divided over the politics and morality of the civil rights movement. And the General Conference pulpit reflected this division. While in 1963 Hugh B. Brown declared support of civil rights a moral imperative, in his own 1967 General Conference address the stridently anti-communist Ezra Taft Benson described civil rights as merely a front for an insidious communist revolution, with blacks as the communists' unwitting puppets. Benson asserted that earlier in the century, as part of their plan for the "internal conquest of America," the communists proposed "splitting away the 'black belt,' those southern states in which the Negro held a majority, and calling them a Negro Soviet Republic." But with the great migration of blacks out of South, Benson said that the communists had moved the sites of the anti-American riots masquerading as protests to northern and western cities, including Salt Lake. "Just take a good look at what has been going on around us for the past few years," Benson exclaimed. "It is happening here!"[35] By "around us," Benson may have had in mind the local conflicts over civil rights, perhaps even the protests outside the Mormon Tabernacle in which he spoke.

This divide could also be seen among the Mormon intellectual elite. While condemning black nationalism and violent protests as counterproductive, in a 1968 statement published by the Salt Lake City Chapter of the NAACP, Sterling McMurrin did not stop supporting nonviolent protests protected by the First Amendment. He also described as justified the "mild demonstrations" of law-breaking "civil disobedience," like the "restaurant sit-ins in Atlanta or the bus boycott in Montgomery," because these acts were undertaken "in the interest of a higher moral principle." McMurrin did not go so far as to call for similar acts against his own church. Yet McMurrin also refused to hide his frustration that the LDS Church continued to adhere to "crude superstitions" about black inferiority, which he believed undergirded racial persecution in the civil sphere. McMurrin declared it a "tragedy" and "reprehensible" that the church failed "to use its considerable influence and economic and political power, in the State of Utah, its overwhelming political influence and power, to further the cause of civic justice for Negroes and other minorities." He asserted his belief "that the destruction of injustice and the establishment of justice are a primary moral responsibility of any church."[36]

However, sociologist Armand Mauss questioned the assertion made by McMurrin, other liberal Mormons, and the NAACP that the LDS Church's

---

35. Ezra Taft Benson, "Trust Not in the Arm of Flesh," *Conference Report*, September 29, 1967.

36. Sterling M. McMurrin, "The Negroes Among the Mormons," the Salt Lake City Chapter of the NAACP, June 21, 1968, Special Collections, Marriott Library, University of Utah, Salt lake City, Utah.

policy of racial exclusion contributed in any way to the discrimination and persecution of blacks in Utah. In 1967, Mauss wrote that in his own research he found "no evidence of a carry-over of the Mormon doctrine on the Negro into secular civil life; in fact there is evidence to the contrary." In his own fit of frustration, Mauss exclaimed, "My plea, then to the civil rights organizations and to all the critics of the Mormon Church is: get off our backs!" According to Mauss, continued protest against the Mormon Church was itself a form of "religious persecution.... Until it can be shown that the Mormon 'Negro doctrine' has behavioral consequences in the civil world, it is just as much a form of bigotry and persecution to picket the Church Office Building as it would be, say, to picket an Orthodox Jewish synagogue because of pique at the traditional doctrine that Jews are God's chosen people!"[37] For Mauss, "Get off our backs!" also meant "Get off our front lawn."

At least in terms of motivating the church to publicly back civil rights for African Americans, by the end of the 1960s, Brown and McMurrin's faction won. In 1969, the First Presidency released an official statement titled, "On [the] Position of Blacks with The Church and Civil Rights," in which the LDS Church declared its unequivocal support for the Constitution and the "equal opportunities and protection" of every citizens' civil rights. In doing so, the church also empathized with the denial of African Americans' civil rights, as it had done at the beginning of the century with Booker T. Washington: "May we say that we know something of the sufferings of those who are discriminated against in a denial of their civil rights and Constitutional privileges.... We as a people have experienced the bitter fruits of persecution." After directly citing the First Amendment, the First Presidency continued, "Matters of faith, conscience, and theology are not within the purview of the civil law."

By the end of the most turbulent decade of twentieth-century American race relations, in its attempt to explain its position on the "Negro race" within its membership the LDS Church made efforts to tone down its rhetoric. Yet it also remained defiant in upholding a practice it understood as scripturally and historically justified. The 1969 statement specified that the LDS Church and its prophets have always "taught that Negroes, while spirit children of a common Father, and the progeny of our earthly parents Adam and Eve, were not to receive the priesthood, for reasons which we believe are known to God, but which He has not made fully known to men." No longer did the First Presidency contend, as it had in its 1949 statement, "On the Question of Blacks within the Church," that the ban was an unequivocal "commandment from the Lord" established by Joseph Smith "from the days of [the Church's] organization."

---

37. Armand L. Mauss, "Mormonism and the Negro: Faith, Folklore, and Civil Rights," *Dialogue: A Journal of Mormon Thought* 2 (Winter 1967): 38, 34–38.

Instead at the end of the 1960s, a period when battles over African Americans' constitutional rights were fought almost literally on their doorstep, the LDS Church's highest officials taught that the restriction against full black membership should be understood as a mysterious matter of faith. They also taught that within the walls of Temple Square—as well as throughout the entire church—it was a religious restriction protected by the First Amendment.[38]

(Public) Main Street to "Private Property"

During the half-century since the end of the civil rights era, Temple Square has continued to function as Salt Lake's "town square, " the most important site of religious and political protest in the city. For example, in 1973 members of the American Indian Movement (AIM) protested General Conference, demanding that the LDS Church pay reparations for its role in Indian removal and persecution. The following year, Wallace "Mad Bear" Anderson added to AIM's demands, calling on the church to return Indian skulls housed in the Church History Museum so that these skulls could have a "proper burial."[39]

Some thirty years later as Salt Lake prepared to host the Winter Olympics, Temple Square became the venue for what was then a small group of activists who, not unlike the anti-black theologies, believed the church's anti-gay stance created a culture in Utah in which gay teens were bullied and harassed, leading to high rates of suicide.[40] And in November 2008, Temple Square became the site for a much larger protest against the LDS Church's support of California's successful anti-gay marriage ballot initiative, Proposition 8. The Friday after Election Day 2008, more than 3,000 people, including Utah's three-person delegation of gay state legislators, crowded the streets around Temple Square. Some protesters carried signs pointing out what many saw as the hypocrisy of a church whose members were once imprisoned for their "nontraditional" marriages was now supporting political efforts to outlaw gay

---

38. See "Appendix D" in Bringhurst, *Saints, Slaves, and Blacks* to read all the pre-1978 official church statements on blacks, the priesthood, and civil rights. Bringhurst, *Saints, Slaves, and Blacks*, 229–235.

39. Quoted in Amanda Hendrix-Komoto, "Boycotting General Conference 40 Years Ago: The Lamanite Generation, the American Indian Movement, and Temple Square," *Juvenile Instructor* blog, April 12, 2013, www.juvenileinstructor.org/boycotting-general-conference-50-years-ago-the-lamanite-generation-the-american-indian-movement-and-temple-square/. To protest the church's opposition to the Equal Rights Amendment, in 1980 Sonia Johnson chained herself to a gate at the entrance to the temple in Bellvue, Washington. Neil J. Young, "Equal Rights, Gay Rights and the Mormon Church," *New York Times*, June 13, 2012.

40. Michael Hiestand, "One Year to Go...Olympic Games Provide Opportunity for Mormons," *USA Today*, February 8, 2001.

marriage. "I didn't vote on your marriage," one side read. "Mormons once persecuted... Now persecutors," read another.[41]

As some prominent leaders had done during the civil rights-era protests, the LDS Church responded by insinuating that the church was in fact the target of persecution. LDS spokesman Scott Trotter said Mormons joined "millions" of people of other religions to support Proposition 8. Yet Trotter noted that LDS Church officials were "disturbed" that the church "was singled out for speaking up as part of its democratic right in a free election." "While those who disagree with our position on Proposition 8 have the right to make their feelings known," Trotter continued, "it is wrong to target the church and its sacred places of worship for being part of the democratic process." Attending a wedding at the Salt Lake Temple during the protests, one Latter-day Saint went even farther in her criticism, calling the gay rights actions un-American. Another wedding attendee said that it is "the gays" who are persecuting Mormons. "They're intolerant of me, of my beliefs and my way of life."[42]

For the last few decades, the LDS Church has employed more than rhetoric to respond to the protesters/persecutors who have marched on the streets around Temple Square. The church has literally taken control of a portion of these streets. In March 1999, the Salt Lake City Planning Commission recommended that the city go ahead with a proposed sale to the LDS Church of the portion of Main Street that runs adjacent to the Salt Lake Temple. The church's plan was to convert this space into a pedestrian plaza and create underground parking for Temple Square visitors and church employees. The city's planning commission did include the condition that the church allow for twenty-four-hour public access and that "there be no restrictions on the use of this space"—including protests—"that are more restrictive than is currently permitted at a public park." Yet after this condition was removed from the final agreement, the ACLU, joined by the century-old anti-Mormon group, Utah Gospel Mission, as well as the First Unitarian Church of Salt Lake, and the National Organization of Woman, among others, filed a lawsuit against the city opposing its forfeiture of ownership of Main Street to the church. The suit alleged that the church would impose free-speech restrictions on a public space. In October 2002, the US Tenth Circuit Court of Appeals ruled in the plaintiffs' favor, declaring it unconstitutional to curtail in public spaces like pedestrian walkways the "expressive conduct by the public," even if it would "interfere" or "inconvenience" the landowners abutting the walkways.[43]

---

41. Peggy Fletcher Stack, "Thousands in Salt Lake City Protest LDS Stance on Same-sex Marriage," *Salt Lake Tribune*, November 8, 2008, www.sltrib.com/ci_10929992.

42. Guy Adams, "Mormons Under Siege," *The Independent*, November 15, 2008.

43. *First Unitarian Church of Salt Lake v. Salt Lake*, No.01–4111, United States Court of Appeals (10th Cir. October 9, 2002).

Yet in 2005, after five years of continued legal battles and bitter public disputes, which often pitted Salt Lake's non-Mormon and Mormon residents against each other, the Tenth Circuit reversed its previous position. Because the Main Street Plaza now legally belongs to the LDS Church, it is no longer a "public forum," ruled the court. As such, the church has the right to control the behavior that occurs in the now privately held space. Citizens should still be permitted to use the walkway between South and North Temple Streets. Yet because the church has converted the space to, in the words of the court, "an ecclesiastical park," and marked off the space by "signs posted at all entrances to the Plaza, and its differentiation from the surrounding sidewalks, the objective, physical characteristics demonstrate that the Plaza is privately owned."[44]

By transforming this section of Main Street from a "public forum" to "an ecclesiastical park, " the LDS Church legally increased how much of the area around Temple Square it owns and controls. Yet the question remains, does this acquisition mean that Salt Lake City's "town square"—a space where the lines between secular and sacred, public and private intersect and often cross over—has become simply "Temple Square, " the unique purview and property of the LDS Church? Nevertheless, recent history indicates that Temple Square's blend of public and private space continues to serve as the region's town square and the backdrop for debates about citizenship, rights, and religion.

Though rumors of a large-scale gay rights protest during the first General Conference after the passage of 2008's Proposition 8 did not materialize, Temple Square became the center of controversy in 2009. In July of that year, while walking through Main Street Plaza after a concert at Salt Lake City's Gallivan Center, two gay men, Matt Aune and Derek Jones, stopped for a kiss in an area they believed was public property. LDS security intervened and handcuffed the couple for what the church later described as "passionate kissing, groping, profane and lewd language, and [the men] had obviously been drinking alcohol." After the Salt Lake police were called to the scene, the two men were ticketed for trespassing. Aune and Jones rejected the accusation that their behavior was inappropriate. They described their embrace as a "modest" display of affection. The charges were soon dropped. Though Jones suffered some bruises on his arms, ironically it seems that the LDS Church fared worse, as the story of the couple arrested for a kiss on Temple Square confirmed the post-Prop 8 media narrative that the LDS Church sought to police Americans' public and private acts of love.[45]

---

44. *Utah Gospel Mission v. Salt Lake City Corporation*, No. 04–4113, United States Court of Appeals (10th Cir. October 3, 2005).

45. Lindsay Whitehurst, "Tresspassing Case? Gay Couple Detained after Kiss Near LDS Temple," *Salt Lake Tribune*, July 10, 2009; Max Perry Mueller, "Undie Running on the Line between Church and State," *Dialogue: A Journal of Mormon Thought* 45 (Summer 2012): 101–102.

A week after Aune and Jones's kiss in Main Street Plaza, a few dozen gay and straight protesters participated in what they called a "kiss-in" on the plaza's sidewalk. After some of protesters moved their kisses from the (public) sidewalk into the (private) Main Street Plaza, the LDS security detail called the police. However, this act of civil disobedience was brief and did not lead to any trespassing tickets as the protesters eventually complied with Salt Lake police officers' instructions to move the protest back to the public sidewalks.[46] Not coincidentally, a few months after the kiss-in, and just days before the October 2009 General Conference, the church posted more conspicuous signs at the entrance to the plaza, which stated explicitly that the plaza was "private property," and "the [LDS] Church reserves the right to refuse access to any person for any reason." In less than ten years, a prominent portion of Main Street Salt Lake City had gone from a public forum, where First Amendment rights could be practiced without state or church interference, to the private property of a church, which did not hesitate to regulate behavior it deemed unfitting of its Temple Square. Even the promise of a public right-of-way disappeared into the expanding reach—metaphorical and literal—of Temple Square. And with opening of the church-owned City Creek Center across the street, which has also come under fire for policing outward expressions of homosexual affection, this reach has expanded into the commercial center of Salt Lake.[47]

When protesters came to Temple Square during the 2009 General Conference, they found a more circumscribed town square. However, in both April and October, conference-goers passed by the typical crowd of a few dozen anti-Mormons protesters, holding signs containing Bible verses and disparaging comments about Joseph Smith. However, the relationship between protesters and Mormonism was not always one of simple hostility. One protester held up a large sign thanking the LDS Church for its support of Proposition 8. And he did so while also wearing a placard that read, "Jesus said, 'You Must Be Born Again.'"[48]

To be sure, during General Conference, multiple versions of American Christianity continue to vie for space and attention in Temple Square. While theologically speaking Mormonism remains at arms length from evangelical

---

46. Arthur Raymond, "Couples Pucker up to Make Positive Point," *Deseret News*, July 13, 2009.

47. Rosemary Winters, "LDS Posts Tougher Signs on Plaza," *Salt Lake Tribune*, September 28, 2009; "City Creek Facing Discrimination Claims," *fox13now.com*, April 26, 2012, http://fox13now.com/2012/04/26/city-creek-center-facing-allegations-of-discrimination/.

48. Steve Evans, "General Conference Protesters," *By Common Consent* blog, April 9, 2009, https://bycommonconsent.com/2009/04/05/general-conference-the-protesters.

America, it also finds itself increasingly folded into American political and moral conservative culture, as the reluctant Republican embrace of Mitt Romney in 2012 highlighted. As Mormonism's cultural acceptability has increased, the protests outside Temple Square seem to have lost much of their bite and visibility. After the December 2013 ruling by the US District Court for Utah striking down Utah's ban on same-sex marriage, supporters and opponents of gay marriage have rallied not at Temple Square, but at the State Capitol and the City and County Building.[49] Following the Supreme Court decision on June 26, 2015, that made marriage equality the law of the land, hundreds of gay marriage supporters walked along North Temple Street, many carrying rainbow flags and wearing t-shirts declaring "love wins." Yet they celebrated the historic ruling in City Creek Park, which, while located cater-corner to Temple Square, was all-but out of view—obscured by the rich, green foliage of early summer—and, without the use of load speakers, would have been out of earshot of the people working and worshiping in Temple Square.[50]

Certainly the intersection of First Amendment freedom of speech and free exercise of religion that occurs in Temple Square can be contentious. Yet for today's LDS General Conference goers, the sight and sounds of anti-Mormon protesters—sequestered and monitored on the sidewalks of North Temple— often produce looks of bemusement, instead of fear or anger.[51] As such, perhaps we can think of the protesters as an integral part of the pageantry of Temple Square during General Conference. They are reminders of the long history of Mormon persecution, but a history that is now made sanitized, even safe.

When (Ordain) Women Entered the Gates and Crossed the Line

The bigger Mormon fights now occur *within* the walled-off section of Temple Square itself. On April 5, 2014, Kate Kelly, the founder of Ordain Women, accompanied by more than two hundred other Mormon women, entered the wrought iron gates of Temple Square. Dressed in their Sunday best and carrying umbrellas to shield themselves from the early spring rains, these

---

49. Piatt and Romero, "Groups Rally for, against Sam-sex Marriage at Utah Capitol"; McCombs and Foy, "Federal Court: No Halt to Gay Marriages in Utah."

50. "Love Wins Rally," *krcl.org*, June 29, 2015, www.krcl.org/blog/vox-pop-love-wins-rally/.

51. A few days before the October 2013 General Conference, *LDS Living* published Bryan Hall's story about how even befriended one regular "Anti-Mormon" General Conference protester. Bryan Hall, "How I Became Friends with a Conference Protester," *LDS Living*, October 1, 2013, http://ldsliving.com/story/73834-how-i-became-friends-with-a-conference-protester.

advocates for the ordination of women to the priesthood walked quietly to the entrance of the Tabernacle where they politely asked for, and were politely denied, entrance to the General Conference priesthood session.

Despite her professed optimism that she would be welcomed into the gathering—she even had procured tickets from sympathetic Mormon men—Kate Kelly likely anticipated this result. After all, Kelly and her group had tried to gain access to the priesthood session during the previous General Conference six months before. Even before the start of conference, church hierarchs communicated through their public relations staff that protesters were not welcome at the priesthood session, and the church asked Ordain Women not to make Temple Square a place of protest. Instead, the church told Ordain Women to go stand with the usual crowd of anti-Mormon protesters in the "free-speech zones adjacent to Temple Square, which have long been established for those wishing to voice differing viewpoints."[52]

Kate Kelly also likely anticipated the public upbraiding from the church that she received after the demonstration. LDS spokesman Cody Craynor called Ordain Women's decision to enter Temple Square and ask for admission into the priesthood session "divisive . . . [and] not the kind of behavior that is expected from Latter-day Saints and will be as disappointing to our members as it is to church leaders."[53] But before she was informed in June 2014 that she had been charged with "apostasy," Kelly did not expect that her actions would result in disciplinary actions, let alone her excommunication.[54]

In retrospect perhaps she should have. Kate Kelly, herself a civil rights attorney, attempted to leverage the First Amendment right to petition for redress of grievances in calling for changes to the LDS Church's position on female ordination. Yet such constitutional protections do not extend past the gates that separate the church's property in Temple Square and the sidewalks surrounding it. In the letter that Kelly's bishop wrote to her explaining how the (all-male) disciplinary council arrived at its decision to excommunicate her, among the list of her actions that the council found were "contrary to the laws of the Church" included Kelly's decision to proceed "with your protest on Temple Square

---

52. Peggy Fletcher Stack, "Mormon Women Seeking Priesthood to Be Shut Out of Temple Square," *Religious News Service*, March 18, 2014, www.religionnews.com/2014/03/18/mormon-women-seeking-priesthood-shut-temple-square/.

53. Whitney Evans, "Women Seeking Priesthood March Again to Temple Square," *Deseret News*, April 5, 2014, www.deseretnews.com/article/865600318/Women-seeking-admission-to-priesthood-meeting-march-again-to-Temple-Square.html?pg=all.

54. Kate Kelly, "Excommunication," *Ordain Women*, June 8, 2014, http://ordain%20women.org/excommunication/.

during General Conference despite the request of Church leaders that you not do so."[55]

Kate Kelly advocated for reforming the LDS Church from within the institution.[56] Yet when she brought her grievances—she insisted on calling them "questions"—inside Temple Square, she crossed a line that, at least for some LDS leaders, put her beyond the pale of acceptance within the (Mormon) body of Christ.[57] Temple Square was the center of Salt Lake City and the LDS Church, but for church leaders it was private, sacred space, off limits not only to non-Mormon protesters but also to church members such as Kelly who lacked the ecclesiastical sanction to broach the all-male priesthood meeting at the tabernacle. The protests of Ordain Women, like those of civil rights advocates and supporters of gay rights, illustrate the ongoing significance of Temple Square as contested space, claimed by the LDS Church and its critics for distinct private and public purposes.

---

55. Kelly has challenged the church's description of Ordain Women's request for admission to the priesthood session at Temple Square as a "protest." Kate Kelly to Scott M. Wheatley, Oakton Stake President, July 23, 2014, *Ordain Women*, http://ordain%20women.org/wp-content/uploads/2014/07/Kate-Kelly-Letter-of-Appeal.pdf.

56. Within hours of receiving word that she had been excommunicated, Kate Kelly told her supporters, "I love the gospel and the courage of its people. Don't leave [the church]. Stay, and make things better." "Reaction to Kate Kelly's Excommunication," *Ordain Women*, June 23, 2014, 2014, http://ordainwomen.org/reaction-to-kate-kellys-excommunication/.

57. Kelly, "Excommunication."

7

Mormons and Same-Sex Marriage

FROM ERA TO PROP 8

Neil J. Young

ON JUNE 26, 2013, the Church of Jesus Christ of Latter-day Saints used its Facebook and Twitter accounts to direct followers to an important announcement on its website.[1] There, a short statement defended "traditional marriage between a man and a woman, which for thousands of years has proven to be the best environment for nurturing children."[2] Earlier that day, the Supreme Court had issued two 5–4 rulings, *United States v. Windsor* and *Hollingsworth v. Perry*, which collectively struck a major blow to same-sex marriage opponents, including the LDS Church. In *Windsor*, the court found unconstitutional the Defense of Marriage Act (DOMA) which had defined marriage at the federal level to mean only the union of one man and one woman.[3] The court's other decision, in *Perry*, upheld a lower court's ruling overturning Proposition 8, a 2008 ballot proposition in California that had amended the state constitution to declare "only marriage between a man and a woman is valid or recognized in California."[4] While the LDS Church's announcement that day ostensibly concerned both court decisions, the statement concentrated on the blow to Prop 8. "Many Californians will wonder," the church declared, "if there is something fundamentally wrong when their government will not defend or protect a popular vote that reflects the views of a majority of their citizens."[5]

---

1. The Church of Jesus Christ of Latter-day Saints, Twitter post, June 26, 2013, 10:30am, https://twitter.com/LDSchurch; The Church of Jesus Christ of Latter-day Saints' Facebook page, June 26, 2013, www.facebook.com/LDS (posts since removed).

2. "Church Responds to Supreme Court Marriage Rulings," *Mormon Newsroom*, June 26, 2013, www.mormonnewsroom.org/article/church-responds-supreme-court-marriage-rulings.

3. *United States v. Windsor*, 570 US (2013).

4. *Hollingsworth v. Perry*, 570 US (2013).

5. "Church Responds to Supreme Court Marriage Rulings."

The focus on Prop 8 in its comments was hardly surprising given the LDS Church's prominence in supporting the ballot initiative in 2008. Despite its visibility in that fight, the Church of Jesus Christ of Latter-day Saints' longer history of anti-gay-marriage activism has gone largely unnoticed by scholarship. The historiography of modern conservatism has noted the religious right's influence in the nation's rightward political and cultural shift since the 1970s and the central role that the politics of gender and sexuality, including anti-gay efforts, played in that development. However, Mormon involvement in the rise of the religious right has remained curiously unexamined in light of far greater attention paid to evangelical and Catholic efforts.[6] The literature on anti-gay politics and the history of same-sex marriage has also concentrated on religious conservatives' objections to homosexuality and their work against gay rights. But Mormon political efforts in that story have largely been relegated, if noted at all, to small anecdotes in a larger narrative of evangelical and Catholic anti-gay activism.[7]

For nearly forty years, the LDS Church has focused on preventing the legalization of same-sex marriage. That work began in the church's involvement against the Equal Rights Amendment in the 1970s, an amendment the church believed would radically alter traditional heterosexual marriage. In fighting the ERA, the church established the political tactics, including covert grassroots activism, and the theological justifications that would aid its efforts against same-sex marriage in the years that followed. The ERA posed a particular challenge to the highly gendered and patriarchal conception of marriage that Mormons revered, and the LDS Church justified its work against the amendment as a "moral" defense of traditional marriage that necessitated political involvement. That same justification has accompanied LDS efforts to prevent the legalization of same-sex marriage. Yet even as the LDS Church has maintained a consistent fight against gay marriage, it has adopted an evolving position on questions of homosexuality

---

6. See Kenneth J. Heineman, *God is a Conservative: Religion, Politics, and Morality in Contemporary America* (New York: New York University Press, 1998); William Martin, *With God on Our Side: The Rise of the Religious Right in America* (New York: Broadway Books, 1996); and Daniel K. Williams, *God's Own Party: The Making of the Christian Right* (New York: Oxford University Press, 2010). I have argued for centralizing Mormons in the rise of the religious right and the story of modern conservatism. See Neil J. Young, *We Gather Together: The Religious Right and the Problem of Interfaith Politics* (New York: Oxford University Press, 2016).

7. George Chauncey, *Why Marriage? The History Shaping Today's Debate* (New York: Basic Books, 2004); Fred Fejes, *Gay Rights and Moral Panic: The Origins of America's Debate on Homosexuality* (New York: Palgrave Macmillan, 2008); and Craig A. Rimmerman and Clyde Wilcox, eds., *The Politics of Same-Sex Marriage* (Chicago: University of Chicago Press, 2007).

and gay rights—a transformation that tracks with the nation's shifting perspective on these matters. While the LDS Church has found itself a sympathetic ally with other same-sex marriage opponents, including conservative Catholics and evangelicals, the church's softening beliefs on homosexuality and its supportive positions for expanded civil rights for homosexuals outside of the issue of marriage have distanced it from those allies who have maintained a generally across-the-board opposition to gay rights as well as a consistent anti-gay theology. From the ERA to Prop 8, the church has opposed what it sees as changes to the institution of marriage whether proposed by feminists or gay activists. In examining its persistent work against same-sex marriage legalization we see the central place of the LDS Church in one of the religious right's most important political contests, even as the church's shifting stances on homosexuality and gay rights complicates our understanding of Mormonism's relationship to modern American conservatism.

From "Relative Tolerance" to a "Crime Against Nature"

Some Mormons may believe their church has maintained a consistent position on homosexuality. Writing in an LDS psychotherapy publication in the early 1990s two Mormon scholars contended that "Church leaders have consistently denounced homosexuality as a *sin*."[8] But Joseph Smith never mentioned homosexuality, and Mormon scriptures including the Book of Mormon contain no references to it either.[9] The historian D. Michael Quinn has demonstrated that throughout the nineteenth and early twentieth century Mormons engaged in "a range of same-sex dynamics" with little interference from their church.[10]

Despite this history, what Quinn calls Mormonism's "relative tolerance" gave way to a concerted church emphasis against homosexuality in the 1950s that laid the groundwork for later political campaigns against gay rights. In the midst of Cold War paranoia about a "Lavender Scare" sweeping the nation, the LDS Church began to directly address homosexuality for the first time and crack down on gays and lesbians in the church. In 1952, J. Reuben

---

8. Ronald D. Bingham and Richard W. Potts, "Homosexuality: An LDS Perspective," *AMCAP: Journal of the Association of Mormon Counselors and Psychotherapists* 19, no. 1 (1993): 3.

9. Robert J. Morris, "'What Though Our Rights Have Been Assailed?' Mormons, Politics, Same-Sex Marriage, and Cultural Abuse in the Sandwich Islands (Hawai'i)," *Women's Rights Law Reporter* 18 (Winter 1997): 145–146.

10. D. Michael Quinn, *Same-Sex Dynamics among Nineteenth-Century Americans: A Mormon Example* (Urbana: University of Illinois Press, 1996), 2.

Clark, counselor in the First Presidency, delivered the first public statement on homosexuality from LDS officials, listing homosexuality along with masturbation and bestiality as "abominations" and worrying that "homosexuals are today exercising great influence."[11] In the following years, the 1958 publication of Bruce R. McConkie's *Mormon Doctrine* included homosexuality as a sin; the Salt Lake City police began targeting men for same-sex activities; the church established an "aversion therapy" program at Brigham Young University in 1959; and BYU announced in 1962 it would not admit known homosexuals.[12] These developments resembled American Protestant responses, especially from conservative evangelicals, that identified homosexuality as a sin and supported criminal crackdowns on homosexual behavior.[13]

Mormon prohibitions and penalties regarding homosexuality only increased over time. Appointed in 1959 with the task of helping Mormons surmount their "homosexual problems," apostles Spencer W. Kimball and Mark E. Petersen oversaw the church's efforts and were instrumental in developing harsher punishments for Mormons accused of homosexuality.[14] As Kimball told a group of LDS psychiatrists in 1963, "God's Church must curb sin and eliminate it so far as possible."[15] By 1968, "homo-sexual acts" became grounds for excommunication as outlined in the church's *General Handbook of Instructions*.[16] A year later, Kimball authored *The Miracle of Forgiveness*, a book that quickly became a foundational text for Mormon teachings regarding homosexuality, arguing that masturbation led to homosexuality and homosexuality sometimes gave way to bestiality. Kimball noted the Old Testament had once required the death penalty for homosexual acts, but the "law is less severe

---

11. Ibid., 391 n. 45, 373.

12. Ibid., 375–379.

13. Didi Herman, *The Antigay Agenda: Orthodox Vision and the Christian Right* (Chicago: University of Chicago Press, 1997), 25–59; David. K. Johnson, *The Lavender Scare: The Cold War Persecution of Gays and Lesbians in the Federal Government* (Chicago: University of Chicago Press, 2006).

14. Rocky O'Donovan, "'The Abominable and Detestable Crime Against Nature': A Brief History of Homosexuality and Mormonism, 1840–1980," in Brent Corcoran, ed., *Multiply and Replenish: Mormon Essays on Sex and Family* (Salt Lake City: Signature Books, 1994), 147; Rick Phillips, *Conservative Christian Identity and Same-Sex Orientation: The Case of Gay Mormons* (New York: Peter Lang, 2005), 30.

15. Spencer W. Kimball, "Address of Elder Spencer W. Kimball to a Group of L.D.S. Psychiatrists," 1963, published in Research and Discussion Papers, Brigham Young University Counseling Center, vol. II, no. 2, 1964, 50, Americana Collection, L. Tom Perry Special Collections, Harold B. Lee Library, Brigham Young University, Provo, Utah (hereafter BYU).

16. Quinn, *Same-Sex Dynamics*, 380.

now, and so regrettably is the community's attitude to these grave sins."[17] Kimball argued homosexuality was "curable" for those who repented, and he advocated that the homosexual "force himself" into relationships with the opposite sex, including marriage.[18] Such advice resembled aspects of both conservative and mainline Protestant attitudes about homosexuality that deemed it a sin and a psychological disorder, respectively, that could be overcome.[19]

Recommending marriage as a pathway out of homosexuality may have not been surprising for the time, but Mormonism's theology of marriage-based salvation shaped LDS beliefs on homosexuality in a way that other objecting religious communities lacked. Linking salvation to marriage, Mormon theology not only sanctifies heterosexual marriage but also amplifies the danger of all extramarital sexual activity, including homosexuality, to one's eternal state. While sexual sins are all forgivable through repentance, heterosexual marriage is required in order to enter the celestial kingdom (the goal of Mormon soteriology), so homosexuality strikes at the heart of this aim.[20] Therefore, the legalization of same-sex marriage presumably poses a greater threat to Mormon beliefs than to those of other religious objectors. Religious conservatives, particularly Catholics and evangelicals, have opposed same-sex marriage as both unbiblical and harmful to the traditional heterosexual family unit. Mormons share those objections, but they also perceive that same-sex marriage would weaken foundational Mormon teachings about the patriarchal family structure, the religious obligation of reproduction, and "the eternal nature of gender and the family."[21] As Mormon theology and church teachings increasingly stressed the divinely ordained roles of men and women in the 1960s and 1970s, Mormonism's interlocking nexus of gender, sexuality, and salvation grew all the more powerful as both an ecclesiastical emphasis and a political

---

17. Spencer W. Kimball, *The Miracle of Forgiveness* (Salt Lake City: Bookcraft, 1969), 79.

18. Ibid., 82, 86.

19. Rebecca L. Davis, "'My Homosexuality Is Getting Worse Every Day': Norman Vincent Peale, Psychiatry, and the Liberal Protestant Response to Same-Sex Desires in Mid-Twentieth Century America," in Catherine A. Brekus and W. Clark Gilpin, eds., *American Christianities: A History of Dominance and Diversity* (Chapel Hill: University of North Carolina Press, 2011), 347–365; Heather Rachelle White, "Homosexuality, Gay Communities, and American Churches: A History of a Changing Religious Ethic, 1944–1977" (PhD diss., Princeton University, 2007).

20. Douglas J. Davies, *The Mormon Culture of Salvation: Force, Grace and Glory* (Aldershot: Ashgate Publishing Limited, 2000), 154–155, and passim. See also Phillips, *Conservative Christian Identity and Same-Sex Orientation*, 17–29.

21. Elizabeth Ellen Gordon and William L. Gillespie, "The Culture of Obedience and the Politics of Stealth: Mormon Mobilization Against ERA and Same-Sex Marriage," *Politics and Religion* 5 (August 2012): 347.

force. Stepping into the Equal Rights Amendment battle of the 1970s, the LDS Church argued the proposed constitutional protection for equality of the sexes would erase gender distinctions, undermine patriarchal authority, and destroy traditional marriage. It also routinely charged that the ERA would promote gay rights and ultimately legalize same-sex marriage. In fighting against the ERA, the LDS Church not only helped defeat the measure but also laid the groundwork for nearly forty years of Mormon activism against same-sex marriage.

Laying the Groundwork: The Equal Rights Amendment and Anti-Gay Initiatives

At first, the LDS Church offered no response to the Equal Rights Amendment that Congress sent to the states for ratification in 1972. Spencer W. Kimball's ascension to the LDS presidency in 1973 changed the church's relationship to national politics and moved the issues of ERA and homosexuality to the front of LDS concerns. Kimball had led the church's efforts against homosexuality since the 1950s, and he frequently targeted it during his presidency, speaking out against homosexuality so often as church president that he quickly attracted national attention.[22] With the ERA, Kimball saw the ratification fight as an opportunity to undermine feminism, weaken the movement for gay rights, and defend traditional marriage. Though thirty-three states had quickly approved the amendment, Kimball believed the church could prevent ratification in Utah and other Mormon-heavy states; after successes there he also directed the church toward a national campaign.[23]

Although the LDS Church waited nearly three years to speak out against the ERA, the church had been far less silent on homosexuality in the early 1970s and those views shaped LDS attitudes and arguments against the ERA. Kimball published *New Hope for Transgressors* (1970), revised and retitled *New Horizons for Homosexuals* (1971), warning against the degradation of society, the eradication of gender differences, and the earth's ultimate depopulation if homosexuality grew unchecked. A First Presidency statement in 1973 broadcasted a more official church teaching, charging homosexuality "runs counter to…divine objectives."[24] Similarly, the church argued the ERA would damage

---

22. Quinn, *Same-Sex Dynamics*, 382, 397 n. 90; "Mormon Church Elder Calls Homosexuality an Addiction," *New York Times*, April 5, 1981.

23. Neil J. Young, "'The ERA Is a Moral Issue': The Mormon Church, LDS Women, and the Defeat of the Equal Rights Amendment," *American Quarterly* 59 (September 2007): 626–627.

24. "Statement on Homosexuality," *The Priesthood Bulletin*, February 1973 vol. 9, no. 1, 3, Public Communications Department, July 1977, Church History Library, The Church of Jesus Christ of Latter-day Saints, Salt Lake City, Utah (hereafter Church History Library).

divinely ordained gender roles and encourage homosexuality. In its anti-ERA arguments, the LDS Church imagined a unisex society stripped of gender differences and vulnerable to homosexuality's advance.

Throughout the 1970s church officials increasingly discussed homosexuality in church documents, at the church's semiannual General Conference, and in church publications.[25] Mormon teachings on homosexuality, largely shaped by Kimball, stressed the mutability of sexuality. This was both the danger and the remedy for sexual sin: for just as one might fall into the trap of homosexuality after a morally degenerate path through masturbation and pornography, one could also, through repentance and moral fortitude, restore oneself to proper heterosexuality. Because homosexuality was a deviant choice rather than an inborn biological trait, LDS teachings worried about both the personal and cultural conditions that promoted homosexuality. Mormons could guard against homosexuality, LDS leaders argued, by cultivating the masculine and feminine traits God had granted them, and LDS teachings throughout the 1970s stressed the importance of fulfilling and enhancing their divinely created roles as men and women. For men, this meant embracing their patriarchal authority and obligations as provider while serving as a masculine role model for their sons; women were to remain in the home, submit to their husband's leadership, and develop their spiritual and physical beauty. The ERA, LDS officials argued, threatened all this. While the ERA's backers argued the amendment would merely grant equality of the sexes under the law, Mormon leaders (and other opponents) countered the amendment assumed and advocated for a sameness of function of men and women. If men and women were made the same under the law, they contended, then gender roles, traditional marriage, and even heterosexuality would lose their meanings. "We fear [the ERA] will even stifle many God-given feminine instincts," the church warned in 1976, demonstrating the Mormon logic that both heterosexual and homosexual inclinations could be enhanced or diminished.[26]

As the LDS Church became more active against the ERA, worries about the connection between the amendment and homosexuality increased in Mormon literature. In the church's monthly magazine, *Ensign*, in 1978, the First Presidency warned ratification would result in the "encouragement of those who seek a unisex society, an increase in the practice of homosexual and lesbian activities, and other concepts which could alter the natural,

---

25. Phillips, *Conservative Christian Identity and Same-Sex Orientation*, 20.

26. "LDS Leaders Oppose ERA," *Church News* supplement of the *Deseret News*, October 22, 1976.

God-given relationship of men and women."[27] Two years later, the church published a twenty-three-page booklet about the ERA attached within the *Ensign*'s March 1980 edition.[28] The pamphlet mentioned homosexuality nearly a dozen times, but now the church argued the ERA would not only increase homosexual practices but might also lead to the legalization of homosexual marriages. "The argument," the document explained, "of a homosexual male, for example, would be: 'If a woman can legally marry a man, then equal treatment demands that I be allowed to do the same.'"[29] This position was not unique to Mormon anti-ERA arguments, of course. Gillian Frank has noted that as early as 1973 anti-ERA literature was suggesting the amendment would lead to the legalization of gay marriage, and Phyllis Schlafly made the threat of same-sex marriage a prominent issue in her opposition to the ERA.[30] But the centrality of homosexuality and the specter of same-sex marriage in LDS anti-ERA arguments revealed Mormonism's particular concern with preventing gay marriages before many other political allies imagined such a threat.

Though late to the anti-ERA battle, the LDS Church organized quickly and efficiently to defeat the amendment. Apostle Gordon Hinckley, head of the Special Affairs Committee, the church's political arm, coordinated most of these efforts.[31] After victories in Mormon-heavy states like Utah, Idaho, and Nevada, the LDS Church organized its members in states that had yet to ratify the amendment. In these states with small Mormon populations, the LDS Church hid its involvement by creating grassroots organizations with names that lacked any Mormon reference, like the Virginia Citizens Council and the Illinois Citizens for Family Life.[32] LDS women, who spearheaded the church's efforts against the amendment through public rallies, door-to-door canvassing, and letters to state legislators, were instructed by the church to avoid mentioning their religious affiliation and instead introduce themselves as concerned citizens and homemakers. The church also raised funds through

---

27. "First Presidency Reaffirms Opposition to ERA," *Ensign*, October 1978, 63.

28. "The Church and the Proposed Equal Rights Amendment: A Moral Issue," *Ensign*, March 1980, 1–23.

29. Ibid., 9.

30. Gillian Frank, "'The Civil Rights of Parents': Race and Conservative Politics in Anita Bryant's Campaign against Gay Rights in 1970s Florida," *Journal of the History of Sexuality* 22 (January 2013): 136.

31. O. Kendall White Jr., "A Feminist Challenge: 'Mormons for ERA' as an Internal Social Movement," *Journal of Ethnic Studies* 13, no. 1 (Spring 1985): 34–35.

32. D. Michael Quinn, "The LDS Church's Campaign against the Equal Rights Amendment," *Journal of Mormon History* 20 (Fall 1994): 127.

its members and funneled the money through its network, directing collections from Utah and California to important battleground states that had a small but active LDS presence, like Florida.[33] All of these strategies would be deployed in the LDS Church's activities against same-sex marriage in the decades ahead. The LDS Church's success in helping defeat the ERA not only accomplished a political objective against a specified target, but, more importantly, it established a system and procedure for attacking issues at the local and state level. As gay rights advocates sought to advance civil liberties through legislation and court action, the LDS Church's grassroots network established in the ERA battle was ready to fight back in a citizens' campaign through ballot initiatives, referenda, state propositions, and other available options at the local and state level.

The 1970s offered plenty of opportunities to begin the fight against gay rights and same-sex marriage, but the LDS Church focused primarily on stopping the ERA. Still, church leaders closely watched the battle over gay rights in dozens of the nation's cities. At first the tide favored gay rights advocates: nearly thirty cities passed gay rights ordinances between 1972 and 1977.[34] That progress stopped when the Baptist gospel singer Anita Bryant organized her "Save Our Children" campaign to overturn a gay rights ordinance in Dade County, Florida, in 1977.[35] Emboldened by Bryant's victory, voters in more than half a dozen other cities overturned or defeated gay rights ordinances in the next three years.[36] The LDS Church encouraged these efforts. A church newspaper editorial in 1978 contended that "the persistent drive to make homosexuality an 'accepted' and legal way of life should disgust every thinking person." "In self-defense," it concluded, "America must launch a major offensive for virtue."[37] But the LDS Church stayed out of that offensive because the city ordinances concerned basic extensions of civil rights and anti-discrimination laws to gays and lesbians, not specifically the church's cherished issue of marriage.

In California, the church considered working against the Consenting Adult Sex Bill, which overturned the state's sodomy law and decriminalized gay sex in 1975, but decided against heavy involvement in an issue that didn't concern

---

33. Young, "'The ERA Is a Moral Issue.'"

34. Chauncey, *Why Marriage?*, 38.

35. Patrick McCreery, "Miami Vice: Anita Bryant, Gay Rights, and Child Protectionism" (PhD diss., New York University, 2009).

36. Fejes, *Gay Rights and Moral Panic*, 153–212; Chauncey, *Why Marriage?*, 39.

37. "Is it a Menace?," *Church News* supplement of the *Deseret News*, July 29, 1978.

marriage.[38] The church did direct California stake presidents to "give every support to the referendum regarding the 'homosexual' bill," but there was no coordinated campaign.[39] Three years later, State Senator John Briggs proposed a ballot initiative permitting school boards to fire or refuse to hire anyone who engaged in or even publicly supported homosexuality. Briggs, a Catholic, reached out to fundamentalist and Mormon congregations for backing, but LDS support never materialized.[40] In the more than 500,000 signatures collected to place Proposition 6 on the ballot, Briggs estimated Mormons provided less than three thousand. "If the church really wanted to," a Los Angeles LDS leader explained, "it could in eight days get 500,000 signatures." (400,000 Saints resided in California at the time.) But LDS officials claimed they were reluctant to tackle another ballot initiative after their involvement in a 1972 California anti-obscenity proposition failed to win.[41] More likely, the church stayed out of California because the Briggs Initiative didn't concern marriage but instead attacked the basic civil rights and employment protections of the state's teachers. Briggs understandably believed Mormons' sexual conservatism and prohibitions against homosexuality made the LDS Church a likely ally for his cause, but he did not understand that the church would only extend its political muscle to questions directly involving marriage. While this represented a shrewd political calculation on the part of the church, it also established a precedent that distinguished the question of same-sex marriage from other aspects of gay rights. Although the LDS Church often lamented the extension of those other rights in the 1970s and 1980s, it did not actively work against them. And in the decades following, the LDS Church would support various legal reforms that granted further civil rights to gay and lesbian Americans. This development happened not in spite of the LDS Church's increased involvement fighting same-sex marriage legalization, but because of it.

The Defense of Marriage Act State Battles

Bruised by scathing public responses to its anti-ERA efforts, the LDS Church largely abandoned national politics in the 1980s. The fight over same-sex

---

38. Gordon B. Hinckley to Wendell J. Ashton, September 24, 1975, Salt Lake Public Communications Council Files, 1976–1977, Church History Library.

39. The First Presidency to All Stake Presidents in California, July 3, 1975, Salt Lake Public Communications Council Files, 1976–1977, Church History Library.

40. Michael War and Mark Freeman, "Defending Gay Rights: The Campaign Against the Briggs Amendment in California," *Radical America* 13 (July–August 1979): 14.

41. John Dart, "Mormons Hold Back on Election Stands," *Los Angeles Times*, May 27, 1978.

marriage, however, prompted the church's return in the 1990s, although, as in the case of the ERA, it sought to hide its involvement. In May 1993, LDS apostle Boyd K. Packer cited the gay rights movement, along with feminism and the "ever-present challenge from so-called scholars or intellectuals," as the three greatest threats to the faith of Mormons.[42] Just two weeks earlier, the Hawaii Supreme Court declared the state had to provide a compelling interest in banning same-sex marriage, and many observers felt that Hawaii and other states would soon find unconstitutional any marriage prohibitions against gays and lesbians.

In response, the LDS Church launched a full-scale political fight against same-sex marriage. Substantive revisions to Mormon theology on homosexuality in the 1990s accompanied these political efforts. LDS leaders rebranded homosexuality as "same-gender attraction," a "condition" they now admitted could be "inborn" or "acquired from a complex interaction of 'nature and nurture,'" but one that must be resisted nonetheless.[43] Mormons were encouraged to extend compassion to those suffering from same-gender attraction, especially fellow Saints battling the temptation. The emphasis on compassion marked a turn in Mormon teachings about homosexuality—a departure from the more severe attitudes countenanced in earlier decades. But the movement to a compassionate stance on homosexuality worked hand-in-hand with the church's increasing work against same-sex marriage. Recognizing they could be branded as homophobic and hateful, Mormon officials sought to decouple the question of gay marriage from the issue of homosexuals. In other words, the church would demonstrate its compassion to homosexuals by acknowledging their existence and supporting them in resisting their legitimate, if sinful, temptations. At the same time, the church would characterize its efforts against same-sex marriage as a defense of marriage rather than an attack on homosexuals.

On the front against same-sex marriage, the First Presidency issued a 1994 statement opposing same-sex marriage, followed the next year with "The Family: A Proclamation to the World," both describing heterosexual marriage as God's "eternal" plan for humankind.[44] "The Family" also reaffirmed the "divine design" of gender roles, a crucial component of Mormon theological objections to gay marriage. Men were to "preside over their families," ensuring

---

42. Boyd K. Packer, "Talk to the All-Church Coordinating Council," May 18, 1993, www.zionsbest.com/face.html.

43. Dallin H. Oaks, "Same-Gender Attraction," *Ensign*, October 1995, 9.

44. The First Presidency and Council of the Twelve Apostles of the Church of Jesus Christ of Latter-day Saints, "The Family: A Proclamation to the World," September 23, 1995, www.lds.org/topics/family-proclamation.

both their necessities and protection; women were "primarily responsible for the nurture of their children."[45] These were hardly new ideas for Mormonism, but their reaffirmation undergirded and rationalized the church's entrance into the same-sex marriage state battles of the 1990s. Both documents implored Mormons to engage politically in defense of traditional marriage. As the LDS Church looked to its members to lead its efforts against same-sex marriage's legalization, this connection between Mormon theology of the gendered heterosexual family and the issue of same-sex marriage proved instrumental for Mormon grassroots mobilization because it imbued a political cause with moral and even sacred obligation, just as the church had done for the ERA.

By 2003, thirty-seven states had adopted Defense of Marriage Act (DOMA) bans against same-sex marriage.[46] The LDS Church actively worked for their passage in several states, beginning in Hawaii where Mormons represented approximately 5 percent of the population.[47] Church officials in Utah created a covert ground game for Hawaii. A church memo explained Mormon involvement needed to appear as "Hawaiian's [*sic*] worrying about Hawaii."[48] In part, this meant hiding the church's involvement by creating Hawaii's Future Today (HFT), a grassroots organization of "a coalition of Hawaii citizens" the church directed at every turn.[49] Almost all members were Mormons, though some conservative Catholics belonged as encouraged by Honolulu's bishop, Francis X. DiLorenzo.[50] Father Marc Alexander, a priest in Honolulu, served as the coalition's co-vice chairman, further obscuring the organization's Mormon origins and leadership, a plan coming from the church's highest office.[51] "President Hinckley wanted it that way," one LDS official wrote to another. "A coalition is hard to attack," and a "young mother...a popular

---

45. Ibid.

46. Barry D. Adam, "The Defense of Marriage Act and American Exceptionalism: The 'Gay Marriage' Panic in the United States," *Journal of the History of Sexuality* 12 (April 2003): 259–276.

47. D. Michael Quinn, "Prelude to the National 'Defense of Marriage' Campaign: Civil Discrimination Against Feared or Despised Minorities," *Dialogue: A Journal of Mormon Thought* 33 (Fall 2000): 10.

48. Loren C. Dunn to Elder M. Russell Ballard, "Re: H.L.M. Strategy for California and Hawaii," March 4, 1997, www.echols.info/Mormon%20Anti-Gay%20Game%20Plan%20 1997-2008.pdf.

49. Hawaii's Future Today, "Mission Statement," located at *Rights Equal Rights*, www. rightsequalrights.com/mormongate/church-documents.

50. Dunn to Ballard, "Re: H.L.M. Strategy for California and Hawaii."

51. Loren C. Dunn, "Report to the Public Affairs Committee on Same-Gender Marriage Issue in Hawaii," located at *Rights Equal Rights*, November 21, 1995, www.rightsequalrights. com/mormongate/church-documents/.

Catholic Priest…and a businessman"—the public faces of the coalition—
were particularly immune, the official reasoned.[52]

The LDS Church's involvement in Hawaii became more visible, however, as
the issue moved forward. Early in 1996, President Hinckley, who had sharp-
ened his political skills by spearheading the church's anti-ERA efforts, met
with Bishop DiLorenzo and Father Alexander in Honolulu about the prospects
for a constitutional amendment against same-sex marriage in the state.[53] In
church services, Hawaiian Saints heard a First Presidency letter urging their
support for HFT. Seven thousand Mormons responded by rallying before the
state legislature; thousands more wrote their legislators demanding support
for the amendment.[54] The LDS Church provided $50,000 for the amendment's
media campaign as the state senate considered a vote in 1996.[55] After the a-
mendment reserving marriage "to opposite sex couples" passed, the church
donated $600,000 to support voter turnout efforts before the November 1998
election, as Hawaiians were to decide whether or not to ratify the amendment.[56]
Those investments paid off; nearly 70 percent of Hawaiians voted to add the
amendment banning same-sex marriage to the state constitution.[57]

The Bellwether State: California, Proposition 22, and Proposition 8

The LDS Church had kept a close watch on same-sex marriage developments
in California since at least 1997.[58] As in Hawaii, LDS leaders planned to link
with Catholic officials to support any legislation against marriage equality, a

52. Loren C. Dunn to Elder Neal A. Maxwell, located at *Rights Equal Rights*, March 6, 1996,
www.rightsequalrights.com/mormongate/church-documents/.

53. Mike Cannon, "LDS and Catholic Coalition Opposes Hawaii Legislation," *Deseret News*,
February 21, 1996.

54. Dunn to Ballard, "Re: H.L.M. Strategy for California and Hawaii."

55. See Loren C. Dunn to Elder Neal A. Maxwell, March 21, 1996; and F. Michael Watson to
Elder Neal A. Maxwell, Public Affairs Committee, "Hawaii Same Gender Marriage Issue,"
April 1, 1996, both at *Rights Equal Rights*, www.rightsequalrights.com/mormongate/
church-documents/.

56. Richley H. Crapo, "Chronology of Mormon/LDS Involvement in Same-Sex Marriage
Politics," http://www.mormonsocialscience.org/wp-content/uploads/2009/11/Crapo-
R1997-Chronology-of-LDS-Involvement-In-Same-Sex-Marriage-Politics.pdf/;Jean
Christiansen and William Kresnak, "Mormons Give Big to Fight Same-Sex," *Honolulu
Advertiser*, October 24, 1998.

57. State of Hawaii Office of Elections, "General Election," November 3, 1998, http://elec-
tions.hawaii.gov/election-results/.

58. Dunn to Ballard, "Re: H.L.M. Strategy for California and Hawaii."

decision made since the Catholic Church was already leading efforts against same-sex marriage there, but also because a private church survey had found that the Catholic Church enjoyed a much better public image in California than the LDS Church. "In other words," a church memo explained, "if we get into this, they are the ones with which to join."[59]

An opportunity for deeper engagement emerged when State Senator Pete Knight proposed a Defense of Marriage Act for California. From the start, Sen. Knight's offices kept the LDS Church updated on Proposition 22, calling LDS headquarters in 1998 to let church officials know their plans to have the initiative on the 2000 election ballot.[60] Immediately, the LDS Church began organizing its 740,000 California members to ensure Prop 22's passage.[61] In May 1999, LDS officials sent a letter to be read in all California church services, reminding the state's Saints that the following spring Californians would vote on Proposition 22. "We ask you to do all you can by donating your means and time to assure a successful vote," the letter implored. "Marriage between a man and a woman is ordained of God, and is essential to His eternal plan," the letter continued. "It is imperative for us to give our best effort to preserve what our Father in Heaven has put in place."[62] A follow-up letter to California stake presidents outlined instructions for raising money, recommending California leaders start with their "more affluent members, suggesting an appropriate contribution and thereafter extend the invitation to those of lesser means." No church buildings or letterhead could be used for the fundraising efforts, the letter insisted. Money was to be donated via personal checks to Defense of Marriage Committee, the grassroots organization the church had established in California to hide its involvement. While the LDS Church could have no public connection to these fundraising efforts, church officials planned to closely monitor all the donations. "We will keep appropriate accounting records and make these available to you for your individual stake," the letter informed California Mormon leaders.[63]

---

59. Ibid.

60. "SGM Advisory Committee Meeting," March 12, 1998, https://archive.org/stream/811352-lds-church-gay-marriage-lobbying-reports/811352-lds-church-gay-marriage-lobbying-reports_djvu.txt.

61. Robert Salladay, "Mormons Now Target California," *San Francisco Chronicle*, July 4, 1999.

62. North America West Area Presidency to California Latter-day Saints, May 11, 1999, reprinted in full in "Proposition 22 Dominates California Wards' Attention, Divides Members," *Sunstone*, April 2001, 88.

63. Elder Douglas L. Callister to Stake Presidents in California, May 20, 1999, reprinted in full in "Proposition 22 Dominates California Wards' Attention, Divides Members," 88.

Once again, Mormons were to understand their efforts for Prop 22 as "voluntary" and in their "capacity as a private citizen," the position established during the ERA battle and repeated throughout the state DOMA campaigns, but the fact of a church-organized, church-administered political strategy strained the plausibility of such assertions.[64] Repeating patterns developed in the ERA fight, some church members received callings from their bishop or stake president to take grassroots leadership roles, and LDS officials tasked certain wards with providing fifty volunteers each for the cause. Some individual Mormons reported that they had been asked to donate specific financial contributions, while other Mormons indicated that their ward had received prescribed "assessments" to meet. One fundraising letter distributed to Mormons in Long Beach revealed that the church intended to raise 4 million dollars from California Saints with $30,000 coming from the Long Beach stake, and $5,000 from each ward.[65] "This is beyond the bounds of anything I've been asked to do," one Mormon admitted to a reporter.[66]

As with the ERA, Mormons were repeatedly told their political work was a moral matter. When some secular critics criticized religious groups for "interfering" in the political question of same-sex marriage, Mormon leaders responded that they only engaged in issues of morality. In his address at the October 1999 General Conference, LDS president Gordon Hinckley defended the church's political involvement on these grounds and scoffed at the prevailing characterization of same-sex marriage. "This is not a matter of civil rights; it is a matter of morality," Hinckley countered.[67] For LDS officials, this was a critical distinction that justified the church's engagement while maintaining its insistence of political neutrality. Furthermore, it provided grassroots Mormons with a sense of religious obligation, only deepened by the fact that the message came straight from the church president whom they considered to be a modern-day prophet of God. Mormons were not partisans working for political objectives, church leaders argued, but instead were concerned citizens moved to support the moral principles at the core of their faith.

As the election neared, California Mormons were urged "to redouble their efforts in this noble cause."[68] Those efforts escalated in the final weeks before

---

64. Ibid.

65. "Proposition 22 Dominates California Wards' Attention, Divides Members," 89–90.

66. Devin Gordon, Dara Horn, and Carrie Cooper, "Mormon Money," *Newsweek*, August 9, 1999, 6.

67. Gordon B. Hinckley, "Why We Do Some of the Things We Do," *Ensign*, November 1999, www.lds.org/ensign/1999/11/why-we-do-some-of-the-things-we-do.

68. North America West Area Presidency to All Stake Presidents and Bishops in California, January 11, 2000, reprinted in full in "Proposition 22 Dominates California Wards' Attention, Divides Members," 92.

the voting, with Mormons blanketing the state with "Yes on 22" signs, canvassing neighborhoods to encourage voters, and distributing petitions in favor of the initiative. Although no church buildings or services were supposed to be used for political purposes, discussions of Prop 22 became a frequent topic in Sunday meetings and organizing sessions often followed Sunday services in LDS wards across California.[69] Church members also donated generously to the $10 million raised to back the initiative. When the votes were counted, Californians had delivered a landslide win for Prop 22 with 61 percent voting in favor.[70]

The victory against same-sex marriage in the nation's most populous state had been a decisive one, but it was not definitive. Eight years later, the California Supreme Court overturned Proposition 22 and a related 1977 law as unconstitutional, thus opening the way for gay marriage in the state. In the months after that May 2008 ruling, thousands of same-sex couples legalized their relationships. While commentators cited the California decision as a harbinger for marriage equality across the nation, same-sex marriage opponents refused to accept the California ruling as settled law. Even before the court had issued its decision, pro-family activists had already collected far more than the 700,000 signatures needed to guarantee the California Marriage Protection Act, a state ballot proposition defining marriage as between a man and a woman in California's constitution, would be up for a vote that fall.[71]

A broad anti-gay-marriage coalition of religious activists, pro-family political groups, and churches mobilized support for Proposition 8, but the LDS Church quickly emerged as the leading organizer.[72] In June, the church's First Presidency sent a letter to all California wards. Citing the church's "unequivocal" teachings on marriage and the family, LDS leaders again implored Mormons to "do all you can to support the proposed constitutional amendment by donating of your means and time."[73] By September, LDS members had given nearly $5 million to the cause.[74] By Election Day, Protect Marriage,

---

69. "Proposition 22 Dominates California Wards' Attention, Divides Members," 90–91.

70. Elaine Herscher, "Gay Marriage Ban Pleases Leader of Mormon Church," *San Francisco Chronicle*, March 9, 2000.

71. Alexander J. Sheffrin, "Pro-Family Group Says Effort to Ban Calif. Gay 'Marriage' Looks 'Strong'," *Christian Post*, April 5, 2008, www.christianpost.com/news/pro-family-group-says-effort-to-ban-calif-gay-marriage-looks-strong-31814/.

72. The following section appears in Young, *We Gather Together*, 279-81.

73. "California and Same-Sex Marriage," Mormon Newsroom, June 30, 2008, www.mormonnewsroom.org/article/california-and-same-sex-marriage. Copy of letter at http://messengerandadvocate.files.wordpress.com/2008/06/fp-letter.pdf.

74. Joe Pyrah, "LDS Donate Millions to Fight Gay Marriage," *Daily Herald*, September 15, 2008, www.heraldextra.com/news/local/lds-donate-millions-to-fight-gay-marriage/article_%20 84a8a9bf-6851-56a1-8c36-f170e8cd9f13.html.

the leading pro-Prop 8 organization, estimated Mormons had contributed at least half of the more than $40 million raised by their side.[75] With Mormons making up approximately 2 percent of California's population, much of that LDS money turned out later to have come from elsewhere, particularly from members in Utah.[76] Yet despite their relatively small numbers in California, Mormons dominated the door-to-door canvassing, the phone banks, and other volunteer efforts on behalf of Prop 8 just as they had eight years earlier for Prop 22. One report claimed Mormons made up 80 to 90 percent of the volunteers canvassing California homes.[77]

All along the way, the LDS Church encouraged its members across the nation to work for Prop 8's passage. Similar constitutional amendments in Arizona and Florida also received the church's attention—LDS members there were urged to assist the battles in their home states—but the focus remained on California since LDS leaders and others saw it as the bellwether scenario for the nation's marriage equality question. The church created a website, PreservingMarriage.org, to educate Mormons on church positions regarding marriage and Proposition 8.[78] In August, LDS leaders released "The Divine Institution of Marriage," a robust elaboration of marriage's sanctity and its essential role in "the plan of salvation." The document also warned against the "harmful consequences" that would arise from the legalization of gay marriage, including requiring public schools to instruct students about marriage and sexuality in ways that contradicted conservative parents' beliefs, diminishing further the family unit in American society and culture, and eroding the "social identity, gender development, and moral character of children."[79] The document stopped short at claiming the legalization of same-sex marriage would force churches to change their beliefs or practices, but Prop 8 advertisements and materials frequently suggested churches might lose their tax exempt status

---

75. Jessie McKinley and Kirk Johnson, "Mormons Tipped Scale in Ban on Gay Marriage," *New York Times*, November 14, 2008, www.nytimes.com/2008/11/15/us/politics/15marriage. html?pagewanted=all&_r=0. Another estimate made by an anti-Prop 8 activist, pegged Mormon contributions as closer to $30 million. Stephanie Mencimer, "Of Mormons and (Gay) Marriage," *Mother Jones*, March/April 2010, www.motherjones.com/politics/2010/02/ fred-karger-save-gay-marriage.

76. James Kirchick, "The New Religious Right," *The Advocate*, December 3, 2008, www. advocate.com/news/2008/12/03/new-religious-right?page=full.

77. McKinley and Johnson, "Mormons Tipped Scale in Ban on Gay Marriage."

78. "Same-Sex Marriage and Proposition 8," *Mormon Newsroom*, October 16, 2008, www. mormonnewsroom.org/article/same-sex-marriage-and-proposition-8.

79. "The Divine Institution of Marriage," *Mormon Newsroom*, August 13, 2008, www. mormonnewsroom.org/article/the-divine-institution-of-marriage.

or face other punishments if they refused to accept the legal change.[80] One Mormon woman at a Prop 8 rally in Oakland told a reporter that without the a-mendment "there will be gay marriage in my church."[81]

In the final weeks, the LDS Church spearheaded vigorous efforts for Prop 8 that reenacted the tactics it had employed for more than thirty years since the ERA battle and through the state DOMA fights. Church officials traveled frequently to California to oversee the groundwork. Additional volunteers were bused in from Utah to aid California Mormons in their door-to-door canvassing. Direct mail sponsored by the church flooded Californians' mail-boxes.[82] The church asked California-born Saints living outside of the state to call friends and family back home urging their support for Prop 8.[83] Saying that only California citizens living outside of the state should make those calls, church leaders were probably hoping to ensure that all their actions looked aboveboard. But a reporter in heavily LDS Rexburg, Idaho, found a health products company's call center packed with Mormons phoning Californian voters. Across the nation, Mormons staffed similar phone banks, usually lo-cated in Mormon-owned business.[84]

Going into Election Day, most polling suggested Californians would defeat Prop 8, but when voting ended the amendment had won with more than 52 per-cent support.[85] (The anti-gay marriage bills in Florida and Arizona passed with even greater support.) In light of Barack Obama's historic victory in the presi-dential election that same night, many noted the irony of an election that had cracked the racial barrier to the nation's highest office while also rolling back the civil rights of thousands of Californians. In the following days, gay marriage

---

80. McKinley and Johnson, "Mormons Tipped Scale in Ban on Gay Marriage."

81. Elizabeth Gettelman, "Mormon Church GOTV for Prop 8: 'Do All You Can,'" *Mother Jones*, October 22, 2008, www.motherjones.com/mojo/2008/10/mormon-church-gotv-prop-8-do-all-you-can.

82. Arleen Garcia-Herbst, "California Ethics Commission Finds Mormons Guilty on 13 Counts of Late Prop 8 Campaign Reporting," *Examiner.com*, June 15, 2010, www.examiner.com/article/california-ethics-commission-finds-mormons-guilty-on-13-counts-of-late-prop-8-campaign-reporting.

83. "Church Readies Members on Proposition 8," *Mormon Newsroom*, October 8, 2008, www.mormonnewsroom.org/article/church-readies-members-on-proposition-8; Peggy Fletcher Stack, "Church: Utah Mormons Will No Longer Aid Prop 8," *Salt Lake Tribune*, October 24, 2008.

84. Ray Ring, "Prophets and Politics," *High Country News*, October 27, 2008, www.hcn.org/issues/40.19/prophets-and-politics.

85. Jessie McKinley and Laurie Goodstein, "Bans in 3 States on Gay Marriage," *New York Times*, November 5, 2008, www.nytimes.com/2008/11/06/us/politics/06marriage.html?ref=%20californiaproposition8samesexmarriage.

supporters organized anti-Prop 8 rallies in various American cities, several staged outside LDS temples as protesters focused their rage on the institution they believed had mobilized Californians to pass the amendment.[86]

After Prop 8

While thousands gathered outside their temples—an estimated ten thousand protested in New York—LDS leaders tried to shift attention away from the church. Noting that a majority of Californians had voted for Prop 8, LDS Church spokesman Michael Otterson also pointed to the "very broad-based coalition" of faiths that had worked on behalf of the amendment. "It's a little disturbing to see these protestors singling out the Mormon Church. What exactly are they protesting?" Otterson asked.[87] Amidst the protests, evangelicals and Catholics offered support. The US Conference of Catholic Bishops thanked the LDS Church's new president, Thomas S. Monson, for the church's work and offered "prayerful support and solidarity."[88] That same day, the National Organization for Marriage (NOM), a lobbying group that supported legislation against same-sex marriage across the country, sent a letter to Monson, signed by dozens of prominent Catholic and evangelical activists.[89] The NOM letter expressed "outrage at the vile and indecent attacks directed specifically and uniquely" at the LDS Church for its "courage in standing up for marriage."[90] More than four thousand supporters signed on to the letter at the website abovethehate.com.[91] A few days later, a *New York Times* advertisement purchased by a diverse group, including leaders of the National Association of Evangelicals, the Catholic League for Religious and Civil Rights, and Chuck Colson, acknowledged the "fundamental disagreements" between them and the LDS Church, referring to

---

86. "Proposition 8 Passes, Triggers Massive Protests Against LDS Church," *Sunstone*, December 2008, 76–79.

87. "New Yorkers Protest Gay Marriage Ban Outside Mormon Church," *Fox News*, November 13, 2008, www.foxnews.com/story/0,2933,451446,00.html.

88. USCCB News Release, "US Bishops Offer Support to Mormons Targeted for Defending Marriage, Backing California's Proposition Eight," *United States Conference of Catholic Bishops*, November 25, 2008, www.usccb.org/news/2008/08-187.cfm.

89. Peggy Fletcher Stack, "Online Petition Thanks LDS Church for Prop. 8 Support," *Salt Lake Tribune*, November 25, 2008, www.sltrib.com/ci_11071617.

90. Letter quoted in Kyle Mantyla, "Anti-Gay Forces Pretend to Rise 'Above the Hate,'" *Right Wing Watch*, November 25, 2008, www.rightwingwatch.org/content/anti-gay-forces-pretend-rise-above-hate.

91. Sarah Pulliam, "A Latter-day Alliance," *Christianity Today*, December 2, 2008, www.christianitytoday.com/ct/2008/decemberweb-only/149-22.0.html.

their theological differences, but deplored the "anti-religious bigotry" Mormons and other defenders of traditional marriage faced.[92]

The ecumenical defense of the LDS Church reflected Prop 8's base of conservative denominations, but it also obscured the interdenominational tensions that had sometimes arisen during the campaign, especially among evangelicals. Jim Garlow, the prominent pastor of San Diego's evangelical Skyline Church and leading figure for Prop 8, confessed about his Mormon allies, "I would not, in all candor, have been meeting them or talking with them had it not been for" Prop 8. Many other evangelicals similarly seemed to need to clarify their political versus theological positions vis-à-vis Mormonism during the campaign.[93] "Our theological differences with Mormonism are, frankly, unbridgeable," Rev. Garlow emailed 7,200 evangelical pastors after Prop 8's victory, "but these are our friends and neighbors and attacks on them are unacceptable." Still, Garlow imagined that same-sex marriage might draw evangelicals and Mormons closer just as the abortion issue had for evangelicals and Catholics.[94]

Catholics, on the other hand, expressed no such hesitations about working with Mormons. San Francisco's Archbishop George H. Niederauer, who previously had served as Salt Lake City's bishop, had first asked the LDS Church to enter the Prop 8 fight and join the Protect Marriage Coalition, the ecumenical organization that Mormons quickly came to dominate. Having worked closely in Hawaii and during California's Prop 22 battle in 2000, both Catholic and Mormon officials saw their latest alliance as a sensible political tactic that affirmed a general religious conservatism rather than raising pesky theological issues.[95]

Political observers agreed that a political alliance of conservative Mormons, evangelicals, and Catholics would likely only strengthen as the nation became more tolerant of homosexual rights. Yet Mormonism's evolving relationship to homosexuality and gay rights has limited a full partnership with other

---

92. "Full-Page Ad Calls Gay Rallies 'Mob Veto'," *Gay Salt Lake*, December 5, 2008, http://gaysaltlake.com/news/2008/12/05/full-page-ad-calls-gay-rallies-qmob-vetoq/. Link to advertisement at http://gaysaltlake.com/wp-content/uploads/2008/12/nytimes-no_mob_veto1.jpg.

93. Mark Schoofs, "Mormons Boost Antigay Marriage Effort," *Wall Street Journal*, September 20, 2008.

94. Peggy Fletcher Stack, "Prop 8 Involvement a P.R. Fiasco for LDS Church," *Salt Lake Tribune*, November 22, 2008.

95. Joseph L. Conn, "Uncivil Union: Catholic Prelate Says He Wooed Mormons for California Marriage Battle," *Americans United for Separation of Church and State*, December 4, 2008, www.au.org/blogs/wall-of-separation/uncivil-union-catholic-prelate-says-he-wooed-mormons-for-california.

opponents of gay marriage, especially evangelicals, who have not generally altered their views on homosexuality nor lessened their opposition to various protections for gays and lesbians. The LDS Church's particular balance between staunch opposition to same-sex marriage and generally increasing tolerance toward gays and lesbians and even support for gay civil rights emerged during Prop 8 when Mormon leaders insisted that their efforts were not part of a larger assault on individuals or their civil rights. In 2008's "The Divine Institution of Marriage," the LDS Church had contended its sole focus in California was "specifically same-sex marriage and its consequences." Beyond that, the document clarified that the church did not oppose other rights for gay and lesbian Americans, including issues of hospitalization, medical care, housing, and employment. Shortly before and especially after Prop 8, the LDS Church even advocated for some of these rights and made substantial changes in its own beliefs and practices.

In 2007, Brigham Young University revised its honor code to distinguish between homosexual behavior and sexual orientation. Same-sex physical acts would qualify students for expulsion from the university, but gay students who remained chaste were welcomed as students. "One's sexual orientation is not an Honor Code issue," the new wording read, reflecting mainstream terminology rather than historic Mormon language about homosexuality.[96] Two years later, LDS officials backed two Salt Lake City ordinances extending housing and employment protections to gays and lesbians. Michael Otterson, director of the church's Public Affairs office, explained that the ordinances were consistent with the church's beliefs in human dignity and were "fair and reasonable," but also, importantly, did "not do violence to the institution of marriage."[97] When the US Senate passed the Employment Non-Discrimination Act in 2013, a bill that banned discrimination based on sexual orientation or gender identity in the workplace, five Mormon senators (out of seven) supported the bill.[98] Lay Mormons who wanted to make the church a more welcoming place for their gay and lesbian friends created Mormons Building Bridges and marched in gay pride parades across the country in 2012. LDS officials kept silent about the group and its activities, a significant departure from the retaliatory measures enacted against the organization Mormons for ERA in

---

96. Julia Lyon, "BYU Changes Honor Code Text About Gay Students," *Salt Lake Tribune*, April 17, 2007.

97. Matt Canham, Derek P. Jensen, and Rosemary Winters, "Salt Lake City Adopts Pro-Gay Statues—with LDS Church Support," *Salt Lake Tribune*, November 10, 2009.

98. Matt Canham, "Senate Passes Gay-Rights Bill With Help From Mormon Lawmakers," *Salt Lake Tribune*, November 7, 2013, www.sltrib.com/sltrib/politics/57097466-90/bill-discrimination-exemption-gay.html.csp.

the 1970s.[99] Although the church had supported the Boy Scouts of America's policy of excluding gay scouts and leaders that had been affirmed by the Supreme Court in 2000, Mormon officials declared they were "satisfied" with the BSA's 2013 decision to allow gay scouts in the organization, a move other religious conservatives greeted with denunciations and mass exits.[100] In summer 2015, it briefly appeared that the LDS Church might sever ties with Scouting before it finally offered its continuing endorsement, based on the BSA's exemption for religious organizations to choose their own adult leaders.[101] As some pointed out, the changes in BSA's positions resembled the LDS Church's own increasing inclusiveness toward its gay and lesbian members.[102]

That change reflected not only social change, but also important theological developments for the LDS Church in the early twenty-first century. This evolution further distinguished Mormonism from religious conservative allies in the same-sex marriage fight who maintained a more consistently anti-gay stance. Building on the church's growing compassionate tone from the 1990s, Mormon teachings in the 2000s stressed God's love for those suffering from same-gender attraction rather than his judgment.[103] Instead of a spiritual weakness or an evil desire, same-sex attraction was a "real" condition and something that those who dealt with "may never be free of…in this life."[104] Those who resisted the temptation were held up in church lessons as particularly valiant models of devotion to admire.[105] Departing from Spencer W. Kimball's advice in the 1960s, LDS officials also made it clear that most

---

99. Neil J. Young, "Equal Rights, Gay Rights and the Mormon Church," *New York Times*, June 13, 2012, http://campaignstops.blogs.nytimes.com/2012/06/13/equal-rights-gay-rights-and-the-mormon-church/; Peggy Fletcher Stack, "Years of Tension Yield to Thaw Between Gays, Mormons," *Religion News Service*, January 3, 2013, www.religionnews.com/2013/01/03/years-of-tension-yield-to-thaw-between-gays-mormons/.

100. Peggy Fletcher Stack, "Mormons Say They're OK With Change in Scout's Gay Policy," *Salt Lake Tribune*, April 26, 2013; Daniel Burke, "Baptists Plan Exodus from Boy Scouts," *CNN Belief Blog*, May 31, 2013, http://religion.blogs.cnn.com/2013/05/31/southern-baptists-to-urge-churches-and-members-to-cut-boy-scout-ties.

101. See "Church Re-evaluating Scouting Program," *Mormon Newsroom*, July 27, 2015, www.mormonnewsroom.org/article/church-re-evaluating-scouting-program; "Church to Go Forward with Scouting Program," *Mormon Newsroom*, August 26, 2015, www.mormonnewsroom.org/article/church-to-go-forward-with-scouting-program.

102. Stack, "Mormons Say They're OK With Change in Scout's Gay Policy."

103. *God Loveth His Children*, 2007, www.lds.org/manual/god-loveth-his-children/god-loveth-his-children?lang=eng; "Compassion for Those Who Struggle," *Ensign*, September 2004, www.lds.org/ensign/2004/09/compassion-for-those-who-struggle.

104. Jeffrey R. Holland, "Helping Those Who Struggle with Same-Gender Attraction," *Ensign*, October 2007, 44.

105. "Compassion for Those Who Struggle"; Holland, "Helping Those Who Struggle with Same-Gender Attraction."

same-sex attracted Mormons should not enter into heterosexual marriage to resolve those feelings.[106]

The church also softened its treatment for even those who engaged in homosexual activity. The church's updated 2010 *Handbook of Instructions* indicated chaste gay Mormons could hold temple recommends and serve in leadership positions, but, more notably, it counseled church leaders to work with those engaged in homosexual behavior to "have a clear understanding of faith in Jesus Christ, the process of repentance, and the purpose of life on earth." While those who persisted in homosexual activities were "subject to Church discipline," this still marked a significant change from earlier church handbooks that had called for excommunication for anyone who engaged in a homosexual act.[107] The 1998 *Handbook* had also removed excommunication as the immediate response to homosexual activity, but its policies still treated "homosexual thoughts or feelings" interchangeably with "homosexual behavior" as occasions for repentance and did not sanction celibate gay Mormons for church callings or temple recommends.[108] Even the different section titles between the 1998 and 2010 documents reflected the church's evolving position. While the 1998 *Handbook* addressed "Homosexual Behavior," the 2010 policy guide considered "Homosexual Behavior and Same-Gender Attraction." Mormon teachings regarding homosexuality in the new millennium continually emphasized the meaningful difference between homosexuality and homosexual behavior—a distinction made clear in the 2010 *Handbook*, the revised BYU honor code, and in countless church talks and publications. A church website, mormonsandgays.org, released in 2013, underscored that point saying that homosexuality was not a "sin" or "disease or illness" nor even a choice. Only acting on the temptation of homosexuality was sinful.[109] Finally, the website made prominent in its title and contents the church's new willingness to use the word "gay," a term it had generally avoided in the past.

Given all this, some observers wondered if the LDS Church would also change its position on gay marriage. When the church stayed out of the same-sex marriage issue on four state ballots in 2012, it only heightened those speculations. In all four states—Maine, Maryland, Washington, and

---

106. "Interview with Elder Dallin H. Oaks and Elder Lance B. Wickman: 'Same-Gender Attraction,'" *Mormon Newsroom*, December 12, 2012, www.mormonnewsroom.org/article/interview-oaks-wickman-same-gender-attraction. The interview with Oaks and Wickman was conducted in 2006.

107. "Homosexual Behavior and Same-Gender Attraction," *Handbook 2: Administering the Church*, 2010, section 21.4.6, www.lds.org/handbook/handbook-2-administering-the-church.

108. "Homosexual Behavior," *Church Handbook of Instructions, Book 1: Stake Presidencies and Bishoprics*, 1998, reprinted at www.provocation.net/chi/chi99.htm.

109. "Being True to Religious Belief," located at Mormonsandgays.org.

Minnesota—the anti-same-sex marriage side had suffered defeat, and their leaders cited the absence of the LDS Church and its funds as a critical factor in the losses.[110] Skipping out on 2012 now seemed more in line with the church's overall decision to lay low during an election where one of their own, Mitt Romney, campaigned for the White House; it may have also reflected a politically savvy determination about the limits of the church's influence especially in states where its membership was minimal.

This changed in 2013 when the frequent LDS battleground of Hawaii again considered same-sex marriage.[111] After the Supreme Court overturned DOMA, Hawaii's governor, Neal Abercrombie, called for a special legislative session to consider the Hawaii Marriage Equality Act. In response, Hawaiian LDS officials drafted a letter to be read in church services. "The Church's position in relation to same-sex-marriage is unchanged," the letter announced. Mormons were encouraged to let their representatives "know where you stand."[112] Outside of Hawaii, two talks at that month's General Conference firmly reiterated the church's opposition to same-sex marriage's legalization. As before, that position was justified in terms of Mormon doctrine that heterosexual marriage remained "crucial to God's eternal plan."[113] Apostle Dallin H. Oaks, the church's leading spokesman on same-sex attraction, lamented laws permitting same-sex marriage were "becoming popular in our particular time and place."[114] Despite this, the legislature legalized same-sex marriage in Hawaii.[115]

---

110. Reuters, "Mormon Church Shift on Gay Marriage Brings Momentum to Pro-Equality Camp," *Huffington Post Religion*, March 26, 2013, www.huffingtonpost.com/2013/03/26/conservatives-give-gay-marriage-momentum_n_2958314.html; Stephanie Mencimer, "Mormon Church Abandons Its Crusade Against Gay Marriage," *Mother Jones*, April 12, 2013, www.motherjones.com/politics/2013/04/prop-8-mormons-gay-marriage-shift.

111. Stephanie Mencimer, "Election Over, the Mormon Church Quietly Re-enters the Gay Marriage Fight," *Mother Jones*, October 29, 2013, www.motherjones.com/politics/2013/10/mormon-church-gay-marriage-hawaiii; Trudy Ring, "Mormon Church Back in Marriage Equality Fight in Hawaii," *The Advocate*, October 30, 2013, www.advocate.com/politics/marriage-equality/2013/10/30/mormon-church-back-marriage-equality-fight-hawaii.

112. Letter to Dear Brothers and Sisters, undated, www.hawaiifreepress.com/Portals/0/Article%20Attachments/LDS%20Marriage%20Letter%20Oct%202013.pdf, linked at "Hawaii LDS Churches Release New Letter on Gay Marriage," *Hawai'i Free Press*, October 15, 2013, www.hawaiifreepress.com/ArticlesMain/tabid/56/ID/10828/Hawaii-LDS-Churches-Release-New-Letter-on-Gay-Marriage.aspx.

113. Russell M. Nelson, "Decisions for Eternity," October 2013, www.lds.org/general-conference/2013/10/decisions-for-eternity.

114. Dallin H. Oaks, "No Other Gods," October 2013, www.lds.org/general-conference/2013/10/no-other-gods.

115. Reid Wilson, "Hawaii Senate Approves Same-Sex Marriage Bill," *Washington Post*, November 12, 2013, www.washingtonpost.com/politics/hawaii-poised-to-legalize-same-sex-marriage/2013/11/12/e0ead1ac-4be9-11e3-9890-a1e0997fb0c0_story.html.

In Utah, the LDS Church witnessed the surprising legalization of same-sex marriage in December 2013 when a federal district court overturned a state constitutional amendment defining marriage as between a man and woman. The church quickly objected to the ruling and instructed all LDS leaders in Utah that they were not to administer any same-sex marriages, especially not in Mormon ward buildings or temples.[116] After about one thousand same-sex couples married in Utah, the US Supreme Court issued a stay on further gay marriages while the state appealed the federal district court judge's ruling.[117] The LDS Church again reminded its members of heterosexual marriage's eternal purposes and urged them to study that doctrine as outlined in "The Family: A Proclamation to the World," the document the church had directed its members to during every same-sex marriage skirmish since 1995.[118] Yet polling in Utah indicated that Mormons, despite their church's efforts, were changing their minds about gay marriage. A Brigham Young University study revealed that 54 percent of Mormons now supported civil unions for gay couples with only 38 percent—down from 69 percent in 2004—saying they opposed any legal recognition for same-sex partners.[119]

This represents an important challenge the LDS Church may face if it continues to work against the legalization of gay marriage. While the nation's increasingly favorable political climate for same-sex marriage makes the church's work all the more difficult, the support or even resignation of lay Mormons to the inevitability of legalized gay marriage across the country raises important questions of theology and authority for the LDS Church. Since the Equal Rights Amendment battle, the LDS Church has consistently argued that same-sex marriage contradicted the divine plan for marriage and salvation even as it has evolved its positions on homosexuality and gay rights nearly alongside national trends. "We are pro-marriage, not anti-gay," a Prop 8 training document for Mormon volunteers had explained.[120] The LDS Church had formulated this rationale during their involvement in the state DOMA fights of the 1990s as a

116. "Church Instructs Leaders on Same-Sex Marriage," *Mormon Newsroom*, January 10, 2004, www.mormonnewsroom.org/article/church-instructs-leaders-on-same-sex-marriage.

117. Jack Healy and Adam Liptak, "Justices' Halt to Gay Marriage Leaves Utah Couples in Limbo," *New York Times*, January 6, 2014, www.nytimes.com/2014/01/07/us/justices-block-gay-marriage-in-utah-pending-appeal.html.

118. "Church Instructs Leaders on Same-Sex Marriage."

119. Niraj Chokshi and Carol Morello, "Utah's Battle Over Gay Marriage is a Sign of a Larger Shift," *Washington Post*, December 23, 2013, www.washingtonpost.com/politics/utahs-battle-over-gay-marriage-is-a-sign-of-a-larger-shift/2013/12/23/82d65988-6c00-11e3-a523-fe73foff6b8d_story.html.

120. McKinley and Johnson, "Mormons Tipped Scale in Ban on Gay Marriage."

shrewd political tactic to temper criticism, but that distinction may have become blurrier as the church came to support certain gay rights in the twenty-first century. In explaining their comfort with same-sex marriage, heterosexual Americans have contended that gay unions have no measurable effect on their own marriages. Latter-day Saints appear to be acknowledging the same, but this directly contradicts Mormon arguments against same-sex marriage, weakening the theological contention for the unique and elevated status of heterosexual marriage in the Mormon plan of salvation. As the LDS Church moves forward, it will have to decide whether its theology of marriage warrants ongoing political opposition to same-sex marriage in the face of a dramatically altered cultural and judicial landscape.

PART III

Gender

8

Mahana, You Naked!

MODESTY, SEXUALITY, AND RACE IN
THE MORMON PACIFIC

Amanda Hendrix-Komoto

IN 1969, BRIGHAM Young University produced *Johnny Lingo*, a short film about a young woman from a small island in the South Pacific who is ridiculed for her ugliness and snarled, unkempt hair.[1] I first remember seeing *Johnny Lingo* at a birthday party when I was eight or nine years old. Likely eating too much cake, I watched as middle-aged women congratulated themselves on the number of cows their husbands had offered for their hand in marriage, and wondered why anyone would pay so much for large, chittering women who were far from the ideals of beauty circulating in the United States. At the end of the movie, the willingness of a skilled trader to pay eight cows—an unprecedented amount—for her bride price transforms Mahana into a beautiful woman. As a child, I nodded uncritically at her transformation.

It wasn't until I watched it again with my friends in graduate school that I began to think about its larger cultural and social meanings. What struck me was how *naked* Johnny Lingo was. Since none of the characters was explicitly marked as Mormon, it had never occurred to me to think about the nakedness of their bodies in the film. As a graduate student, however, I realized that it was a Mormon production and found myself fixated on Lingo's shoulders, chest, and waist. Why was Johnny Lingo allowed to be partially naked in a Mormon film? If he had been a white Mormon man, I would have expected him to appear fully clothed. My discomfort was partially the result of my removal from Mormon culture. Although I am not Mormon, I had been immersed in Mormon culture as a child and had never thought critically about Mormon understandings of modesty. The rules that governed Mormon bodies—deciding which parts of the body should be covered and what could be uncovered—seemed natural. The friends that I made as a graduate student in Ann Arbor, however, did not share the Mormon belief that tanned shoulders

---

1. *Johnny Lingo,* directed by Judge Whitaker (1969; Provo: Brigham Young University).

and uncovered knees were immodest. Eventually, however, my experiences at
the University of Michigan helped me realize that Mormon ideas about the
body were embedded in a particular theology and understanding of the world.

Race was also an issue. As a result of graduate school, I had become at-
tuned to the meanings of race in ways that I had not been as a child in southeastern Idaho. I found myself wondering, Why was it okay for Johnny Lingo
to be naked from the waist up but not for white Mormon missionaries? How
did white Mormon men and women understand the bodies and sexuality of
Polynesian members of their church? The answers to these questions lie partially in the unique position that Polynesians occupy within the Church of
Jesus Christ of Latter-day Saints.

Mormon theology creates a sacred genealogy for Polynesians that con-
nects them to the people of Israel. This identification, however, is not un-
ambiguous. In popular Mormon theology, Polynesians are identified as
both Nephites and Lamanites. The former group is portrayed as fair-
skinned and generally more righteous in the Book of Mormon, while God
marked the latter group with dark skin for their transgressions.[2] Mormon
scripture, however, also places the Lamanites at the center of God's re-
demptive plan, promising that they will one day be restored to their place
within God's kingdom. Jared Hickman has argued that the Book of Mormon
can be read as an "Amerindian apocalypse" that deconstructs American
ideas about Manifest Destiny.[3] Native Hawaiian communities decimated by
the effects of American imperialism would find much in Hickman's reading of the Book of Mormon to sympathize with. The identification of
brown-skinned people as Lamanites, however, has also led to casual racism
within the church.

Of course, the Book of Mormon has not been the only source of Mormon
ideas about Polynesia. Mormon images of the Pacific are frequently overlaid
with the sexualized images of Polynesian men and women that have circulated within wider American culture.[4] According to Jane Desmond, these
images create a beguiling, acquiescent vision of Polynesia that belies the existence of American colonialism.[5] They also reduce Pacific Islanders to their

---

2. Hokulani Aikau, *A Chosen People, A Promised Land: Mormonism and Race in Hawai'i*
(Minneapolis: University of Minnesota Press, 2012), 43–44.

3. Jared Hickman, "The Book of Mormon as an Amerindian Apocalypse," *American
Literature* 86 (September 2014): 429–461.

4. Andrew Grainger, "Rugby Island Style: Paradise, Pacific People, and the Racialisation of
Athletic Performance," *Junctures* 9 (June 2009): 46–50.

5. Jane Desmond, *Staging Tourism: Bodies on Display from Waikiki to Sea World* (Chicago:
University of Chicago Press, 1999).

physicality so that they become their bodies, "gleam[ing] like polished bronze," in the words of one 1939 travel book.[6]

This essay explores the tensions that emerged over the portrayal of Polynesians within white Mormon culture in the twentieth century. Native Hawaiian and Polynesian Mormons saw their faith not as a white import but as being firmly grounded in the experiences of their ancestors. In the mid-twentieth century, the emphasis that church leaders like Spencer W. Kimball placed upon the heritage of men and women who could claim to be descended from the people of the Book of Mormon mirrored the understanding that some Native Hawaiians and Polynesians had of their faith. It also connected Polynesians to American Indians and other indigenous Mormons, creating a pan-Lamanite identity. At the same time, however, many white Mormons were uneasy about the possibilities of interracial marriage that this emphasis represented. In Hawai'i, the tensions over the position of Polynesians within the Mormon Church became particularly apparent at the Church College of Hawai'i (renamed Brigham Young University-Hawai'i Campus in 1974) and the Polynesian Cultural Center (PCC). The Church College was opened in 1955 to provide higher education for students throughout the Pacific who had already finished their educations at local institutions.[7] In the mid-twentieth century, however, it became a space where the separation between different races threatened to come undone. Some white Mormons worried about the possibility that young white women who had been unable to find suitable husbands in Utah would marry Polynesian men. Tensions at the Polynesian Cultural Center, on the other hand, centered on the commodification of Polynesian culture and the willingness of the church to display the bodies of Polynesian students to earn money.

In this essay, I argue that tensions at the Polynesian Cultural Center and the Church College of Hawai'i were reflective of a larger ambivalence within Mormon culture about the position of Polynesian men and women that had its roots in the portrayal of the peoples of the Book of Mormon. Hokulani Aikau has argued that white Mormons simultaneously elevate Polynesians as a "chosen people" while discriminating against them within their wards and communities.[8] White Mormons frequently participate in the colonial discourses that have defined the relationship between the Pacific Islands and the

---

6. Joseph Walker McSpadden, *Beautiful Hawaii* (New York: Thomas Y. Crowell, 1939), quoted in Desmond, *Staging Tourism*, 125.

7. Greg A. Prince, *David O. McKay and the Rise of Modern Mormonism* (Salt Lake City: University of Utah Press, 2005), 179–180.

8. Aikau, *A Chosen People, A Promised Land*, ix–xii.

United States as a whole. The portrayal of Polynesian men and women within the church has been inflected with sexuality and the possibility of seduction. The emergence of the Church College of Hawai'i and the PCC in the mid-twentieth century coincided with a growing Native Hawaiian activism that demanded recognition of Hawaiian land claims and openly criticized the racist portrayals of Native Hawaiians in American popular culture. The convergence of the growth of this movement and the growth of BYU-Hawai'i and the PCC meant that the latter became highly politicized spaces in which Polynesian Mormons sought to understand the tensions within their identity. White leaders also sought to control the possibility present at these institutions that differences between racial groups would be erased. Although scholars have focused on the PCC as an "ethnic theme (park)" that commodifies the bodies of Polynesian students that work there, the tensions between modesty, religious faith, and racial identity have a much longer history and reach within Mormon culture.[9]

Sons of Mosiah: Mormon Identity in America and the Pacific

The tensions over religious faith, sexuality, and modesty that became an important part of discussions about the Polynesian Cultural Center did not begin in the 1950s. Indeed, Mormon discussions about Polynesia had coupled concerns about sexuality with recognition of their sacred lineage as early as the nineteenth century. Louisa Barnes Pratt, who served a mission on the island of Tubuai in the mid-nineteenth century with her husband Addison, wrote that "in the principles of chastity," Polynesians "seem[ed] wreckless." Even if a woman was known as "unvirtuous" and "unchaste," she was not "denounced as unworthy of a son or brother in wedlock" as long as she reformed her habits after marriage.[10] In spite of Pratt's concerns about sexual immorality, however, she recognized Polynesians as being descended from the people of the Book of Mormon. When Pratt was asked about the Book of Mormon in the Pacific, she told her listeners that the book was about the Tahitians' "ancient fathers."[11]

The descriptions of Polynesians within Pratt's writing emphasize the tension over the place of Polynesians within Mormon theology. Although Pratt

---

9. Andrew Ross, *The Chicago Gangster Theory of Life: Nature's Debt to Society* (London: Verso Books, 1994), 43.

10. Louisa Barnes Pratt, *The History of Louisa Barnes Pratt: Mormon Missionary Widow and Pioneer*, ed. Donna Toland Smart (Logan: Utah State University Press, 1998), 167.

11. Ibid., 149.

recognized the divine lineage of Polynesians and other indigenous people, she saw them as fundamentally sinful. The Book of Mormon may have provided her with an explanation for this duplicity. In her diary, Louisa wrote that she felt that the Tubuai could have been "a paradise" if "the people [had] one spark of enterprise." Whatever spark they had once had, however, had been "smothered beneath the rain of ages, and swept away with the knowledge their forefathers once possessed."[12]

In spite of the ambiguous portrayal of the purported ancestors of indigenous people within the Book of Mormon, many Polynesians found a positive identity within its stories. The men and women to whom Pratt ministered adopted a refracted version of the language of white missionaries concerning their ancestors. In the twentieth century, many indigenous Mormons continued to find a positive identity within the Mormon church. They were encouraged to do so by a general effort among the LDS Church hierarchy in the mid-twentieth century to reemphasize the importance of the descendants of the people of the Book of Mormon. Early Mormons saw the Book of Mormon as being a history of indigenous people of the Americas. Mormon missionaries saw themselves as calling forth God's chosen people and rekindling the knowledge that American Indians had once had of their glorious past. Before the Second Coming, American Indians and other indigenous people would be redeemed and made "white" and "delightsome."[13] By the twentieth century, however, conflicts between American Indians and white Mormon settlers had led the church to de-emphasize the role that the redemption of the Lamanites played in Mormon theology and culture.

The 1943 ordination of Spencer W. Kimball, a businessman from Thatcher, Arizona, to the church's Quorum of the Twelve Apostles, led to a revival of interest in the fate of the Lamanites. Kimball felt as though he had been specially called to minister to American Indians and to indigenous people as a whole. On April 6, 1954, he publicly denounced Mormon racism, openly condemning a "Mrs. Anonymous" who had sent him an angry letter claiming she had never thought she would see "an Indian buck appointed a bishop—an Indian squaw to talk in the Ogden Tabernacle—[and] Indians to go through the Salt

---

12. Ibid., 167.

13. 2 Nephi 30:6; For early Mormon interest in Native Americans, see Ronald Walker, "Seeking the 'Remnant': The Native American during the Joseph Smith Period," *Journal of Mormon History* 19 (Spring 1993): 1–33; Ron Romig, "The Lamanite Mission," *John Whitmer Historical Association Journal* 14:1 (1994): 25–33; Leland Gentry, "Light on the 'Mission to the Lamanites,'" *BYU Studies* 36:2 (1996–1997): 226–232; and Mark Lyman Staker, *Hearken, O Ye People: The Historical Setting of Joseph Smith's Ohio Revelations* (Salt Lake City: Greg Kofford Books, 2009), 49–69.

Lake Temple." Kimball fired back, reminding her that she was denigrating the descendants of the Israelites.[14] Referencing specific characters from the Book of Mormon—the "sons of Mosiah," "the great Nephi," and "the children of the Ammonites"—he called his listeners' attention to the connections between indigenous people and the heroes of the Book of Mormon.[15] "Do not prate your power of speech or your fearlessness," he cautioned, "unless you too could stand with the Prophet Samuel on the city wall, dodging stones and spears and arrows while trying to preach the gospel of salvation. The very descendants of this great prophet are with us. They may be Navajos or Cherokees."[16]

Kimball's speech had a powerful effect on its listeners. Eugene England, who had just been called with his wife as a missionary to Samoa, believed that the speech redeemed him and his wife of their "liberal condescension" toward Polynesians. They were "open for the first time to go and learn and to be permanently affected" by those they had been called to serve. Kimball's speech also marked the beginning of the revitalization of the church's efforts to transform the lives of American Indians.[17] Kimball supported the development of the Indian Placement Program, which arranged for thousands of Native American children to temporarily leave their families to live with white Mormon foster parents. Kimball served as a Quorum member until 1973, when he became the president of the LDS Church.

Kimball's presidency occurred at the same time as a movement in Hawai'i and the United States to revitalize and preserve indigenous cultures. Clinton Kanahele, an elementary and high school principal who had served in church leadership, worried that future generations would be unable to speak the Native Hawaiian language. To help preserve the language, he interviewed elderly Native Hawaiian men and women in 1970. What emerged out of the interviews was the deep connection that Kanahele and others felt to an Israelite past.[18] In a conversation that he had with one man, Kanahele cited the

---

14. Spencer W. Kimball, "The Evil of Intolerance," *Improvement Era,* June 1954, 423.

15. Ibid., 425–426.

16. Ibid., 426.

17. Eugene England, "A Small and Piercing Voice: The Sermons of Spencer W. Kimball," *BYU Studies* 25 (Fall 1985): 78.

18. There is a fascinating and extensive literature on the acceptance of a Lamanite heritage in the Pacific. Much of it, however, focuses not on Hawai'i but on New Zealand. See R. Lanier Britsch, "Maori Traditions and the Mormon Church," *New Era,* June 1981, 37–46; Peter Lineham, "The Mormon Message in the Context of Maori Culture," *Journal of Mormon History* 17 (January 1991): 62–93; Ian Barber, "Between Biculturalism and Assimilation: The Changing Place of Maori Culture in the Twentieth-Century Mormon Church," *New Zealand Journal of History* 29 (October 1995): 142–169; and Grant Underwood, "Mormonism, the Maori, and Cultural Authenticity," *Journal of Pacific History* 35 (September 2000): 133–146.

wailing that occurred when two women met as evidence that Polynesians were descended from Israel. He recalled the women "weeping" as they remembered the past, "not merely showing grief but crying unashamedly" like "the Israelites of old."[19] In another interview, Kanahele connected the Hawaiian custom of circumcising their children with a piece of bamboo to the Israelites. He believed that Native Hawaiians had continued this practice since their ancestors had landed in the islands.[20]

The Mormonism found within Kanahele's interviews was intimately joined to Native Hawaiian culture. Although white missionaries like Joseph F. Smith and Castle Murphy were important figures within the Mormon community in Hawai'i, the oral interviews emphasized the spiritual power of Native Hawaiians. With one man, Kanahele discussed Jonah Wahinepee, a Native Hawaiian Mormon missionary who was "renowned...[for] administering to the sick."[21] Another woman remembered her aunt as an extremely religious woman: "Hawaiians are accustomed from the time of our forefathers to walk with God. My tutu always walked with God. She was always praying. She did not work otherwise. Everything she seemed to know."[22] Kanahele added in one interview, "We Hawaiians are a God-fearing people; we are God observing people."[23] The descriptions that these men and women offered interwove Christianity with the fabric of life in the Native Hawaiian Mormon community. They saw themselves not as a colonized people who had lost their traditional religious customs but as a people who had reclaimed their ancient religious heritage and who were naturally drawn to God. The world of the past, of the first Native Hawaiian converts to Mormonism, had been one that

------

19. Gus Kaleohano, interview with Clinton Kanahele, June 11, 1970, 19–20, Clinton Kanahele Collection, Brigham Young University, Hawai'i, Digital Collections and Archives, Lā'ie, Hawai'i, https://library.byuh.edu/sites/library.byuh.edu/files/archives/img/Clinton%20Kanahele%20Interview%20PDFs/Gus%20Kaleohano%20Interview.pdf.

20. Rose Manu and Mary Malo, interview with Clinton Kanahele, July 30, 1970, 18-19, Clinton Kanahele Collection, Brigham Young University, Hawai'i, Digital Collections and Archives, Lā'ie, Hawai'i, https://library.byuh.edu/sites/library.byuh.edu/files/archives/img/Clinton%20Kanahele%20Interview%20PDFs/Rose%20Manu%20&%20Mary%20Malo%20Interview.pdf.

21. Paul and Carrie Eli, interview with Clinton Kanahele, June 27, 1970, part 2, pg. 4, Clinton Kanahele Collection, Brigham Young University, Hawai'i, Digital Collections and Archives, Lā'ie, Hawai'i, https://library.byuh.edu/sites/library.byuh.edu/files/archives/img/Clinton%20Kanahele%20Interview%20PDFs/Paul%20&%20Carrie%20Eli%20Interview.pdf.

22. Luka Kinolau, interview with Clinton Kanahele, June 29, 1970, 26, Clinton Kanahele Collection, Brigham Young University, Hawai'i, Digital Collections and Archives, Lā'ie, Hawai'i, https://library.byuh.edu/sites/library.byuh.edu/files/archives/img/Clinton%20Kanahele%20Interview%20PDFs/Luka%20Kinolau%20Interview.pdf.

23. Rose Manu and Mary Malo, interview with Clinton Kanahele, July 30, 1970, 12.

was infused with the divine. Although Kanahele focused on Native Hawaiians, the faith of other Polynesian men and women was just as strong. Emma Lobendahn, a woman who had lived in Samoa, New Zealand, and Fiji, remembered a time when the members of her branch had fasted to heal her body. One afternoon, the elders of her church came to her house. They refused the food her mother offered and instead knelt down to anoint her with oil. That night, her mother "dreamed of a medicine to cure [her]." Emma knew "it wasn't just a dream," and was cured in two weeks.[24]

The claiming of an Israelite identity by Polynesian men and women allowed them to reconcile their Mormonism with their identity as Pacific Islanders. Although Mormon missionaries were often successful in the Pacific, the faith challenged Polynesian ideas about the family and demonized some of their cultural practices. In Tonga, for example, the Mormon emphasis on the nuclear family sat uneasily with Tongan understandings of kinship. The close, intimate relationships that Mormonism demanded between members of the nuclear family violated the expectation in Tonga that brothers and sisters will remain a respectful distance from each other and that individuals ultimately owe their allegiance not to their individual family but to wider kinship groups.[25] According to Niko Besnier, many of the men and women to whom he described seeing a Mormon brother and sister exercising at a local gym reacted with disgust, "comparing the practice to the behavior of animals."[26] In Hawai'i, native converts to Mormonism asked about polygamy and were interested in the ways in which Mormonism mirrored aspects of their faith that had been denigrated by Protestant Christianity. The men and women who joined the LDS Church in the nineteenth and early twentieth centuries, however, were marginalized within the Hawaiian Islands. Harassed by their former co-religionists and alienated from their families, they moved to Lā'ie and Lāna'i to escape the abuse they had endured and to help create a physical Zion in the Pacific.[27] The interviews that Kanahele collected paper

24. Debbie Hippoliteatulai Wright, Rosalind Meno Ram, and Kathleen L. Ward with Rowena L.K. Davis, Jessika Lawyeratulai Tora, and Seini Mu'amoholeva, "'*Olelo*': Women of Faith Speak," in Grant Underwood, ed., *Pioneers in the Pacific: Memory, History, and Cultural Identity among the Latter-day Saints* (Provo: Religious Studies Center, Brigham Young University Press, 2005), 76.

25. Tamar Gordon, *Inventing Mormon Identity in Tonga* (PhD diss., University of California, Berkeley, 1988), 139–163.

26. Niko Besnier, *On the Edge of the Global: Modern Anxieties in a Pacific Island Nation* (Redwood City, CA: Stanford University Press, 2011), 213.

27. R. Lanier Britsch, "The Lanai Colony: A Hawaiian Extension of the Mormon Colonial Idea," *Hawaiian Journal of History* 12:1 (1971): 70–71; R. Lanier Britsch, *Moramona: The Mormons in Hawaii* (Lā'ie: Institute for Polynesian Studies at BYU-Hawai'i, 1989), 37; Matthew Kester, *Remembering Iosepa: History, Place, and Religion in the American West* (New York: Oxford University Press, 2013), 58–67.

over any conflicts between being Mormon *and* Polynesian. Instead, being Mormon becomes integral to their identity as Polynesians. The interviews also attempt to redeem early converts to Mormonism in Polynesia from their marginalized positions, portraying them not as men and women who were forced from their jobs and homes but as people who had the ability to heal the sick and call upon the power of God.

The adoption of a distinctly Mormon identity that denied any conflict between being a member of the LDS Church and cultural authenticity was not unique to Polynesia. Throughout the twentieth century, men and women who had been identified as being descendants of the Book of Mormon claimed that identity as a source of spiritual strength. In the 1930s, Margarito Bautista Valencía used the connection in Mormon theology between Latin America and the Book of Mormon to claim a natural supremacy for indigenous Mexicans. For Bautista, it was Mexican members of the church who represented God's chosen people, not their white co-religionists.[28] Although white members were ambivalent and even dismissive of Bautista's understanding of the Book of Mormon, his understanding of Mormonism as a faith that empowered brown people would have resonated with Polynesian and Native American Mormons who saw in the Book of Mormon a story of their people. Mormonism provided Polynesians, Latinos, and American Indians with a faith that placed their people and their stories at its center. For them, accepting Mormonism was not accepting a white faith; it was accepting a past and history of their people that had been forgotten.

Ultimately, many white Mormons were uncomfortable with constructions of Mormonism that placed "indigeneity" at its center. Unlike Bautista and the men and women that Kanahele interviewed, white Mormons saw the beginnings of their faith in the history of white settlers who colonized Utah and made the desert "blossom as a rose."[29] Although white Mormons intellectually accepted the idea that indigenous people played a prominent role in the Mormon story of ultimate redemption, they were uncomfortable with interracial marriage and shared many of racist assumptions about nonwhite people with other white,

---

28. Thomas W. Murphy, "Imagining Lamanites: Native Americans and the Book of Mormon" (PhD diss., University of Washington, 2003), 146–181; Armand L. Mauss, *All Abraham's Children: Changing Mormon Conceptions of Race and Lineage* (Urbana: University of Illinois, 2003), 147–150; Jason H. Dormady, "'Not Just a Better Mexico:' Intentional Religious Community and the Mexican State, 1940–1964" (PhD diss., University of California, Santa Barbara, 2007), 199–218; Elisa Eastwood Pulido, "The Spiritual Evolution of Margarito Bautista: Mexican Mormon Evangelizer, Polygamist Dissident, and Utopian Founder, 1878–1961" (PhD diss., Claremont Graduate University, 2015).

29. Isaiah 35:1.

middle-class Americans.[30] The conflict between these two visions of Mormonism was particularly apparent at the Church College of Hawai'i, where administrators continually had to navigate between the fears white Americans had about interracial marriage and their responsibility to their Polynesian students.

Race and Sex in the Dorms: Interracial Marriage and the Church College of Hawai'i

The fears that white Mormons had about interracial marriage were part of a larger discourse in American society about the overt sensuality of the Pacific. The image of Pacific Islanders as sexually permissive, always willing, and beguiling had its origin in the eighteenth and nineteenth centuries. In this period, Polynesia became infamous for its uninhibited sexuality as travelers returned from the Pacific with stories of bare-chested women willing to sell their bodies for iron nails.[31] Although European travel literature portrayed Polynesia as a sexual paradise, it was always a place of danger. Its very seductiveness contained the possibility that white men would be overcome by its charms and would choose to live among Pacific Islanders instead of within the white community.[32] Sexuality was not the only way that Polynesian bodies were portrayed as slightly dangerous. Although white sailors frequently tattooed their bodies in the eighteenth and nineteenth centuries, the practice was viewed as askance by white, middle-class respectable society.[33]

---

30. See Jared Farmer, *On Zion's Mount: Mormons, Indians, and the American Landscape* (Cambridge, MA: Harvard University Press, 2008).

31. Michael Sturma, *South Sea Maidens: Western Fantasy and Sexual Politics in the South Pacific* (Westport, CT: Greenwood Press, 2002), 25. For the sexualization of Pacific Islanders in the eighteenth century, see also Anne Salmond, *Aphrodite's Island: The European Discovery of Tahiti* (Berkeley: University of California Press, 2009).

32. Emily Manktelow, "Missionary Families and the Formation of the Missionary Enterprise: The London Missionary Society and the Family, 1795–1875" (PhD diss., King's College, 2010), 34–76; Nicolas Thomas, *Islanders: The Pacific in the Age of Empire* (New Haven, CT: Yale University Press, 2010), 37–40; and Michelle Elleray, "Crossing the Beach: A Victorian Tale Adrift in the Pacific," *Victorian Studies* 47 (Winter 2005): 164–173.

33. There is a large scholarship on the role of tattooing within Polynesian culture. Tattoos, however, were not frequently mentioned in the papers that I examined. This list of books on tattoos is not comprehensive. It is meant to give readers a sense of the wide variety of work on tattooing that is currently being published. See Alfred Gell, *Wrapping in Images: Tattooing in Polynesia* (Oxford: Clarendon Press, 1996); Samuel Otter, *Melville's Anatomies* (Berkeley: University of California Press, 1999), 9–49; Robert D. Craig, *Handbook of Polynesian Mythology* (Santa Barbara: ABC-CLIO, 2004), 244–249; Margo DeMello, *Bodies of Inscription: A Cultural History of the Modern Tattoo* (Durham, NC: Duke University Press, 2000), 45–48; and Kerstin Knopf, "'An Interminable Cretan Labyrinth': Tattoos as Text in Melville's Sea Fiction," in Caroline Rosenthal and Dirk Vanderbeke, eds., *Probing the Skin: Cultural Representations of our Contact Zone* (Newcastle upon Tyne: Cambridge Scholars Publishing, 2015), 122–159.

Mormon theology, in identifying indigenous people as the people of God, offered an alternative understanding of the Pacific. Mormon missionaries were also more willing to live within indigenous communities in the Pacific than Protestant missionaries. Rather than enmeshing themselves in white, middle-class Victorian families that were meant to protect men from the lures of indigenous women, Mormon missionaries lived and ate in indigenous communities.[34] Brigham Young also encouraged several white Mormon men to marry indigenous women in the United States in hopes that the unions would hasten the redemption of the Lamanites.[35] What is interesting about these marriages is not that Mormon men were having sex with indigenous women, but that the white Mormon community was willing to accept them as legitimate marriages.

By the mid-twentieth century, however, white Mormon leaders had rejected interracial marriage as a possibility. In a 1965 address, Spencer W. Kimball warned students that marriage was "a very difficult thing under any circumstances and the difficulty increases in interracial marriages."[36] A 1982 compilation of his earlier teachings included the statement that he had never intended his admonitions to "accept the Indians" to "encourage intermarriage."[37] Instead, he wrote that the church leadership was "unanimous…in feeling and recommending that Indians marry Indians, and Mexicans marry Mexicans; the Chinese marry Chinese and the Japanese marry Japanese; that the Caucasians marry the Caucasians, and the Arabs marry Arabs."[38] This prohibition was echoed in church statements that its support for the black civil rights movement did not extend to interracial marriage. Although this rhetoric mirrored the feelings of many other white Americans toward interracial marriage, many nonwhite members of the church felt betrayed. Chieko Okazaki, who served in the presidency of the Relief Society, remembered being a student in Hawai'i during World War II. In response to hearing an apostle discourage Japanese women and white servicemen from marrying each other, she found herself wondering, "Why is it that the Church doesn't look upon us, who are of a different race, as [being] worthy to marry a white Mormon man?" Although the likely answer to that

---

34. Amanda Hendrix-Komoto, "Imperial Zions: Mormons, Polygamy, and the Politics of Domesticity in the Nineteenth Century" (PhD diss., University of Michigan, 2015), 65–102.

35. John Turner, *Brigham Young: Pioneer Prophet* (Cambridge, MA: Harvard University Press, 2012), 210.

36. "Interracial Marriage Discouraged," *Church News*, June 17, 1978.

37. Spencer W. Kimball, *The Teachings of Spencer W. Kimball*, ed. Edward L. Kimball (Salt Lake City: Bookcraft, 1982), 302.

38. Ibid., 303.

question and the racism that she experienced throughout her life in the church bothered her, she told the historian Greg Prince that she held onto the gospel and the idea "that our Father in Heaven and Jesus Christ would not look at us as any different from white members."[39]

In the mid-twentieth century, Utah was a predominantly white space. According to the 1950 Census, only 1.7 percent of the state's population was nonwhite.[40] Two decades later, the number had only risen to 2.6 percent.[41] Although conversions in Latin America and high membership rates in Polynesia were beginning to change the church as a whole, interracial marriage was still relatively rare. Utah had originally outlawed marriages between white men and women and African Americans. Even in the nineteenth century, however, Utah law had remained silent about the possibility that white men and women might choose to marry Polynesians or Native Americans.[42] White women and men undoubtedly developed forbidden relationships. Those relationships, however, remained illicit. The overturning of anti-miscegenation laws in Utah in the mid-twentieth century opened up the possibility of interracial marriage. As the church leaders' statements against the practice suggest, however, most Mormons continued to imagine Utah as a white space where individuals were protected from the seductive bodies of African Americans, Asians, and other nonwhite people.

This imaginary was not in play in Hawai'i. In the mid-twentieth century, American popular culture depicted Hawai'i as an idyllic space where racial mixing was possible and even beneficial. It was able to do so only by ignoring violence between white soldiers and local communities and the routine sexual harassment of Native Hawaiian women.[43] Jane Desmond has argued that this vision of Hawai'i offered Americans an opportunity to view a racial difference that was exotic, enticing, and far less threatening than the tensions between

---

39. Greg A. Prince, "'There is Always a Struggle': An Interview with Chieko N. Okazaki," *Dialogue: A Journal of Mormon Thought* 45 (Spring 2012): 117.

40. US Census Bureau, "1950 Census of Population," vol. II, part 44, 21, www.census.gov/prod/www/decennial.html.

41. US Census Bureau, "1970 Census of Population," vol. 1, part 46, table 18, 2015, www.census.gov/prod/www/decennial.html.

42. Patrick Q. Mason, "The Prohibition of Interracial Marriage in Utah, 1888–1963," *Utah Historical Quarterly* 76 (Spring 2008): 108–131; Peggy Pascoe, *What Comes Naturally: Miscegenation Law and the Making of Race in America* (New York: Oxford University Press, 2009), 85–93.

43. Christina Klein, *Cold War Orientalism: Asia in the Middlebrow Imagination, 1945–1961* (Berkeley: University of California Press, 2003), 249–257.

white and black Americans.[44] Although many Mormons participated in this image of the Hawaiian Islands, individual church administrators sometimes worried about the effects that interracial marriage would have on church members and counseled against it. Members in Hawai'i would have received similar instructions as those elsewhere.

The Church College of Hawai'i, in particular, became a space where the church sought to prevent racial mixing and where the separation between different races threatened to come undone. The church had initially opened the college in 1955 to serve students in Hawai'i and the South Pacific.[45] White students from the mainland sometimes enrolled and dated nonwhite students. White administrators struggled with the possibility of racial intermixing. Other church leaders had echoed Kimball's statements about interracial marriage. Former college president Owen J. Cook told an interviewer that students who were considering attending Church College were sometimes counseled not to out of fears that they would marry outside of their racial group.[46] Cook was somewhat more willing to tolerate such marriages, but ultimately cautioned against them. He confided to the interviewer that marriage to a Polynesian man could provide white girls "who had no dating [experience] on the mainland, because maybe they [were] too big" an opportunity to fulfill expectations that they marry. They "came out here and … were popular girls."[47] In addition to denying the possibility that women who conformed to white beauty standards would be attracted to Polynesian men, Cook's statement played upon the association of indigenous people with corpulence. As Amy Erdman Farrell has argued, anthropologists, historians, and sociologists have often focused on the acceptance of fatness in nonwhite cultures without examining how fat shaming became enshrined in white, middle-class identity.[48] Although Cook's assertion was meant to be sympathetic, he cast some of the white girls who decided to attend the Church College of Hawai'i as unattractive and aberrant.

Other church leaders were unwilling to even consider interracial marriage. According to Cook, one told him interracial marriage was "a religious

---

44. Desmond, *Staging Tourism*, 68.

45. Prince, *David O. McKay and the Rise of Modern Mormonism*, 179–180.

46. Owen J. Cook, oral history, March 8 and 11, 1980, 32, Polynesian Culture Center, series I, box 2, folder 3, Joseph F. Smith Library Archives and Special Collections, Brigham Young University, Hawai'i, Lā'ie, Hawai'i.

47. Ibid.

48. Amy Erdman Farrell, *Fat Shame: Stigma and the Fat Body in American Culture* (New York: New York University Press, 2011), 59–81.

problem." He paraphrased the man as saying "that if the Lord had wanted that[,] He would have arranged for it from the beginning."[49] Church leaders tried to frame their opposition to interracial marriage broadly, arguing that their concerns grew not out of a need to protect the purity of white girls but out of a desire to minimize cultural conflict in a marriage. Cook noted, however, that concerns about interracial marriage arose only when white girls and boys from Utah and Idaho were involved. "The Brethren were not concerned," he told an interviewer, "if a Tongan married a Maori or a Samoan married a Hawaiian.... Those types of marriage did not concern the Brethren, but the Caucasian did."[50] According to Cook, it was the inclusion of white bodies that ultimately made racial crossings undesirable. Marriages that crossed boundaries only between Asian or Polynesian cultures did not evoke the same response in spite of the church leadership's insistence that any marriage between cultures was undesirable. Mormon theology cast Polynesians as being God's chosen people and suggested that the coming of God's kingdom would ultimately depend on the redemption of nonwhite peoples. The church hierarchy and members of college's administration, however, were uneasy about fully embracing Polynesians and American Indians as their brethren if doing also meant accepting mixed raced marriages. It is important to note that the effects of this racism were long-lasting. Although Okazaki felt that most white Mormons did not openly talk about race by the time she was interviewed in 2005, she was certain that "if they had to make a choice in relation to their child or grandchildren marrying into another race, they'd have hard feelings about it and might try to stop it."[51]

Mahana's Body: Modesty and Sexuality in the Mormon Pacific

Much of the scholarly literature concerning the Mormon presence in Hawai'i has focused on the Polynesian Cultural Center. When the center initially opened in 1963, it boasted six Polynesian villages as well as facilities for tourists to buy souvenirs, eat, and refresh themselves.[52] Scholars have criticized the center for presenting an ahistorical, timeless view of Polynesia that denies

---

49. Owen J. Cook, oral history, March 8 and 11, 1980, 32.

50. Ibid.

51. Prince, "'There is Always a Struggle,'" 116.

52. Vernice Wineera, *Selves and Others: A Study of Reflexivity and the Representation of Culture in Touristic Display at the Polynesian Cultural Center in Lā'ie, Hawai'i* (PhD diss., University of Hawai'i, 2000), 106.

the effects of American colonialism in the Pacific.[53] The continued presence of the United States in the Hawaiian Islands has meant that scholarly work there has political ramifications. Academics such as Haunani-Kay Trask, J. Kēhaulani Kauanui, and Noenoe Silva see themselves as working in a colonial setting in which indigenous peoples are explicitly devalued and sexualized.[54] The popularity of Mormonism within Native Hawaiian and Polynesian communities means that scholars focusing on the religious tradition have had to grapple with its relationship to American colonialism in the Pacific. In many ways, the PCC has become a touchpoint for scholars—a required piece for academics who want to work on Mormonism in the Pacific Islands. While some Mormon scholars have argued that Polynesians occupy a special place within Mormonism, others see the Mormon treatment of Pacific Islanders as racist and paternalistic.

The PCC has always been the center of controversy. In the mid-twentieth century, Charles Barenaba, Lemaefe Galea'i, and other locals worried about the potential effects of the center on the students who would work there and on its ultimate meaning for visitors and students alike. An oral interview with Barenaba highlights the concerns that some in the local community had. Barenaba worried that creating a cultural center where white tourists would watch Polynesian students dance was the equivalent of creating a "human zoo."[55] Although this critique could be leveled at other heritage sites like Colonial Williamsburg or Nauvoo, it was the cultural voyeurism in which white tourists engaged when they visited the PCC that made the accusation particularly salient in Hawai'i. The center's portrayal of Pacific Islanders as carefree papered over the racism, poverty, and sexual harassment that Polynesians routinely encountered in Hawai'i and America's continuing colonial relationship with the region.

---

53. Ross, *The Chicago Gangster Theory of Life: Nature's Debt to Society*, 43–86; Hokulani Aikau, *A Chosen People, A Promised Land: Mormonism and Race in Hawai'i*, 109–128; and Christopher Balme, "Staging the Pacific: Framing Authenticity in Performances for Tourists at the Polynesian Cultural Center," *Theatre Journal* 50 (March 1998): 53–70. For Mormon responses to these critiques, see Wineera, *Selves and Others*; and Max E. Stanton, "The Polynesian Cultural Center: A Multi-Ethnic Model of Seven Pacific Cultures," in Valene Smith, ed., *Hosts and Guests: The Anthropology of Tourism* (Philadelphia: University of Pennsylvania Press, 1989), 247–262.

54. Haunani-Kay Trask, *From a Native Daughter: Colonialism and Sovereignty in Hawai'i* (Honolulu: University of Hawai'i Press, 1993); J. Kēhaulani Kauanui, *Hawaiian Blood: Colonialism and the Politics of Sovereignty and Indigeneity* (Durham, NC: Duke University Press, 2008); and Noenoe Silva, *Aloha Betrayed: Native Hawaiian Resistance to American Colonialism* (Durham, NC: Duke University Press, 2004).

55. Charles Barenaba, oral history interview, 12, Center Series (PCC Series), box 1, folder 3, Joseph F. Smith Library Archives and Special Collections, Brigham Young University-Hawai'i, Lā'ie, Hawai'i.

Instead of portraying a Polynesia in constant contact with the outside world, white tourists paid to see a spectacle in which students performed a "primitive identity" that was increasingly far removed from their actual experiences in Tonga, Samoa, New Zealand, and French Polynesia.

The anthropologist Andrew Ross uses the banter of the Samoan performer Sielu Avea with audiences at the PCC to discuss the types of performance that tourists encounter at the center. Ross describes the act as a kind of "Samoan Borcht Belt shtick" and reproduces part of Avea's monologue. The Samoan man tells visitors that they can use "hammers, knives, screwdrivers, [and] dynamite" to break open a coconut. "A lady from Canada," he laughingly tells the audience, "came here last week and told me that she put a coconut on the ground and ran it over with a lawnmower. A young man from Texas put on his .45 and shot the thing between the eyes, while his mother-in-law was holding the coconut." He then picks up a rock and tells the audience that Samoans use stones to open coconuts. He warns them, however, not to blame him if it doesn't work. He, after all, is "pure Samoan, [and] this is a Hawaiian coconut, made in Taiwan."[56] Ross portrays the PCC as one of the "ethnic theme parks" in which individuals are forced to pretend "to shun money, property, and all of the returns of modernity"—to play the savage—"in exchange for a living wage."[57] As Ross notes, however, Avea's act is not uncomplicated. He plays with the assumptions of his audience. While he encourages tourists to imagine a Pacific where Samoan boys climb coconut trees with their hands and feet, Avea also reveals the way that the image is being manufactured. Guns, factories in Taiwan, and lawnmowers are as much a part of the story he weaves as palm trees and sand.

Of course, the PCC is not the only place where Mormon Polynesian bodies have been displayed. In 1971, Native American students from the Provo campus of BYU began traveling the United States as part of a performance troupe called the Lamanite Generation. It eventually included Polynesians and Latinos as well. The show created an idealized vision of indigenous cultures that mirrored those represented at the PCC.[58] Its elaborate performances in the 1970s occurred at the same time as the members of the American Indian Movement held a protest outside the church's annual conference, demanding that the church donate 1 million dollars a year to Indian social programs for a decade.[59]

---

56. Ross, *The Chicago Gangster Theory of Life*, 48.

57. Ibid, 43.

58. Mauss, *All Abraham's Children*, 92.

59. Ibid., 101; Amanda Hendrix-Komoto, "Boycotting General Conference 40 Years Ago: The Lamanite Generation, the American Indian Movement, and Temple Square," *Juvenile Instructor* blog, April 12, 2013, www.juvenileinstructor.org/boycotting-general-conference-50-years-ago-the-lamanite-generation-the-american-indian-movement-and-temple-square/.

Polynesian men have also become a fixture on the American football field. A child of Samoan heritage is fifty-six times more likely than any other American to join the NFL, leading CBS to dub the archipelago "Football Island."[60] The article's title elides the fact that American Samoa is actually a group of several islands and atolls. The culture of football in Samoa emphasizes the potential it offers for social mobility. Individuals who travel to the United States to play football are able to enroll in American universities that would otherwise be impossible for them to attend.[61] As Fa'anofo Lisaclaire Uperesa has pointed out, however, the opportunities that American football offers are "highly gendered." Football is a "hypermasculine" and "implicitly (hetero)sexualized" game that is "largely limited to biological males." Individuals are encouraged to "[perform] a dominant masculinity and [repress] any indication of nonnormative heterosexuality."[62] The position of football within Samoa then has been ambiguous. While it offers individuals the opportunity to receive a better education than they otherwise might, it also encourages them to embrace an overt masculinity that forecloses opportunities for others.

It is possible to extend this critique to the Polynesian Cultural Center, which has offered students educations that would have been impossible otherwise but also commodified their bodies. On the one hand, students who worked at the center in the mid- to late-twentieth century worked at a facility that was meant to revive and revitalize the cultures of Polynesia. Many of the students had never participated in the folk arts and dances that they were supposed to demonstrate for tourists. The older men and women who performed at the center taught them how to carve wooden figures into meeting houses, how to dance with fire, and how to climb coconut trees. These efforts coincided with the desire of the church to teach Polynesian students living in Hawai'i their native languages and to reinforce the idea that Polynesians were descended from the people of the Book of Mormon.[63] The association of these customs with the culture of the ancient Israelites meant that working at the PCC could become a religious experience. The first brochures that center produced described it as "drawing together of Polynesians in the bond of the

---

60. Scott Pelley, "American Samoa: Football Island," *CBS News*, January 17, 2010, www.cbsnews.com/news/american-samoa-football-island-17-09-2010/. See also Mike Sager, "The Samoan Pipeline," *California Sunday Magazine*, https://story.californiasunday.com/samoan-football-pipeline.

61. Fa'anofo Lisaclaire Uperesa, "Seeking New Fields of Labor: Football and Colonial Political Economies in American Samoa," in Alyosha Goldstein, ed., *Formations of United States Colonialism* (Durham, NC: Duke University Press, 2014), 210–212, 223–224.

62. Ibid., 211.

63. Wineera, *Selves and Others*, 97–98.

spirit."[64] According to the Māori poet and former vice president of the PCC Vernice Wineera, references to "the spirit" at the center can refer religiously to "'the Spirit of God,' 'the Spirit of Christ,' or 'the Spirit of the Gospel,'" or culturally to shared Polynesian values. She argues that often these multiple meanings are combined at the PCC.[65] As a result, work at the PCC is at once meant to deepen a student's appreciation of the gospel and their Mormonness at the same time as it meant to provide them with a deeper access to a Polynesian cultural identity that is seen as endangered and slowly being lost. It can be a place of deep cultural and religious satisfaction.

Critics like Barenaba, however, worried about that students were being asked to commercialize their faith and that the labor they performed had no deeper meaning. In an interview he gave to an oral history researcher interested in the history of the center, Barenaba critiqued the ways in which the center commodified Polynesian culture and engaged students in menial labor. The jobs the center was offering "just didn't seem like [they] would be the kind that would give a fulfilling experience in life. Entertainment six days a week with about the only sane thing going on was church on Sunday and then six more days of entertaining. Whether it's a sive or pese or serving supper, lunch and dinner, frying hamburgers, it's still a catering kind of thing for kupe, (for money) from other strangers."[66] In some ways, the unease that community members felt about the PCC were the result of differing understandings of the meaning of performance. Scholars have argued that Mormons living in the continental United States frequently see performance as a form of missionary work and do not necessarily make the same distinctions between religious faith and entertainment that are evident in some of Barenaba's objections. Rather, entertainment becomes a form of proselytization and a way to participate in the religious life of the community.[67]

This language was present at the PCC, and Barenaba himself hoped that it was reflection of reality. He had doubts, however. Like many Hawaiians, his experience with entertainment probably grew not out of Hill Cumorah Pageant or church performances but out of luaus performed on the Waikiki strip. Church members had long been concerned about the morality of

---

64. Quoted in ibid, 128.

65. Ibid.

66. Barenaba, oral history interview, 13.

67. See Ellen McHale, "'Witnessing for Christ:' The Hill Cumorah Pageant of Palmyra, New York," *Western Folklore* 44 (January 1985), 34–40; Megan Sanborn Jones, "Imaging a Global Religion, American Style: Mormon Pageantry as a Ritual of Community Formation," in Daniel Belnap, ed., *By Our Rites of Worship: Latter-day Saint Views on Ritual in Scripture, History, and Practice* (Provo: Religious Studies Center, 2013), 317–348.

participating in tourist culture. In an oral interview, Verdetta Kekuaokalani described her experience working for a company that provided leis to tourists when they disembarked their aircraft. When she married her husband, however, she no longer worked for the company and maintained her respectability. "I was getting old," she explained to the interviewer, "too old to stand outside on the airport runway and give laies.... My husband was working for Pan American so we both worked at the airport at the time and it wasn't all that terrific, you know, his wife was out there giving laies to strangers, let alone kissing them."[68] Although young Hawaiian women frequently worked within the tourist industry, Kekuaokalani's marriage meant that the propriety of her doing so was suspect. Her attentions were to be focused on her husband, not on white tourists or visiting businessmen. Some Polynesian Mormons worried about the possibility that the PCC would provide students with an entry into the Hawaiian tourist industry. According to Ken Baldridge, a historian and former professor at BYU-Hawai'i, some of the people living in the towns that surrounded the PCC worried about the effect that the center would have on their children. They feared they would "end up in the Waikiki strip." In the same sentence, he admitted, "some of that has happened."[69]

The relative nakedness of bodies at the PCC heightened concerns about the center's propriety. Since the late nineteenth century, Mormons living in Hawai'i had been told about the importance of participating in Mormon temple worship and of wearing sacramental undergarments afterward to remind them of the covenants they had made. The outfits that students were expected to wear at the PCC made it impossible for them to wear garments while they were performing. For critics of the PCC, this was a moral compromise. "We always thought the people had to wear their garments all the way through," Barenaba told an interviewer. "You only took them off when you go to take a bath, then you'd put them back on. There's no time that you separate yourself [from] the garment."[70] When David O. McKay traveled to the Pacific in the mid-1950s, he expressed concerns about the appropriateness of the clothing that Tahitian dancers typically wore for Mormon women. A Tahitian labor missionary at the PCC explained that the girls who danced for McKay had been wearing just a "bra." Instead of watching the performance, McKay averted his eyes and refused to look at the young women. When the

---

68. Verdetta Kekuaokalani, oral history interview, 14, Robin Kay Oral History Collection, L. Tom Perry Special Collections, Harold B. Lee Library, Brigham Young University, Provo, Utah.

69. Ken Baldridge, oral history interview, 13, PCC Series, box 1, folder 2.

70. Charles Barenaba, oral history interview, 14, Center Series (PCC Series), box 1, folder 3.

performance was over, McKay talked to the people assembled about why the dances were inappropriate. The labor missionary's father had initially opposed the dances. As McKay spoke to the congregation, the man's father cried.[71] At the center, Mormon Polynesians who performed this dance covered their stomachs in concession to the faith's ideas about modesty. The increased modesty of the dresses, however, did not completely allay concerns about the displays of women's bodies. Individuals like Barenaba were concerned that the outfits frequently violated the expectations at Church College's expectations for modesty. His concerns were likely deepened by changing understandings of modesty within the Mormon Church itself.

The development of the PCC occurred at the same time as the mid-century tightening of modesty codes in Utah. Mormon ideas about modesty in the twentieth century had initially emphasized speech, self-respect, and conduct in addition to the length of hemlines and the presence of cap sleeves on dresses.[72] In the 1950s, Kimball delivered a speech at BYU admonishing young women for adopting immodest styles to be fashionable.[73] "Unchastity is the great demon of the day!" he announced. The "immodest clothes" that Mormon girls and their mothers had adopted was "contribut[ing] directly and indirectly to the immorality of this age." They wore "short skirts and body-revealing blouses and sweaters," "flaunting [temptation] before young men" and "talk[ing] about sex as freely as they talk about cars."[74] Other church leaders echoed this emphasis on women's clothing. In 1969, Mark E. Petersen cited reports that sex crimes had doubled in Tokyo because of the increase in women wearing miniskirts.[75]

This emphasis upon clothing reduced ideas about modesty and chastity to the types of clothing that women wore and focused the surveillance of the morals of Mormon girls upon their bodies. In the theology that Kimball and others espoused, a girl's respect for her parents and her acceptance of the gospel were visible in the clothes that she chose to wear. A girl who succumbed to fashion and wore tight sweaters and short skirts gave away what was "most

---

71. Wineera, *Selves and Others*, 211–212.

72. Katie Blakesley, "'A Style of Our Own': Modesty and Mormon Women, 1951–2008," *Dialogue: A Journal of Mormon Thought* 42 (Summer 2009): 20.

73. Ibid., 21.

74. I originally encountered Kimball's speech in Blakesley, "'A Style of Our Own,'" 20–21, but also read the original speech from which I drew these quotations. Spencer W. Kimball, "A Style of Our Own: Modesty in Dress and in Relationship to the Church," *An Apostle Speaks to Youth* (Provo: Brigham Young University Press, 1951).

75. Mark E. Petersen, *Way to Peace* (Salt Lake City: Bookcraft, 1969), 249.

dear and precious above all things."[76] This emphasis upon modesty was part of set of larger concerns about the potential influence of the feminist movement and youth counterculture upon Mormon youth.[77] The development of a dress code at BYU and the emphasis of the church hierarchy for women attempted to separate Mormon women from feminists who had adopted a more liberal view of sexuality and women's roles. Requiring Mormon women to wear clothing that covered their shoulders and knees at a time when sleeveless dresses and form-fitting clothing was popular made the differences between Mormon women and other women visible. It inscribed difference upon women's bodies and made modest clothing a requirement of the gospel. After Kimball's speech, young women "kimballized" their dresses, sewing sleeves onto their formal attire and putting away sweaters that were too tight to meet the new requirements.[78]

Although the Hawaiian Islands were physically removed from the Wasatch Front, Mormon women there received many of the same messages about the importance of the family and modesty as women living in Utah. Kapua Sproat had attended Oregon State University before transferring to Church College. She was teaching there when she heard a talk about the importance of women staying within the home. "Although I was only teaching half time," she told the interviewer, "I…realized…they meant me too. And so I stayed home."[79] Sproat's interview also emphasized the importance of women embracing their femininity. She felt that the feminists she met when attending the International Women's Year Conference in Houston were overly "militant" and masculine. "If you closed your eyes," she said, "you wouldn't think they were women."[80] The language that she used demonstrates the degree to which many Mormons living in Hawai'i had internalized the same ideas about femininity as Mormons living in the continental United States. When the Mormons delegates for the International Woman's Year Conference from Hawai'i arrived in Houston, they found that their ideas about the family more

---

76. Spencer W. Kimball, *Teachings of Spencer W. Kimball* (Salt Lake City: Bookcraft, 1982), 265. The scriptural reference for Kimball's quote is Moroni 9:9.

77. Blakesley, "A Style of Our Own,'" 24; Martha Sonntag Bradley, *Pedestals and Podiums: Utah Women, Religious Authority, and Equal Rights* (Salt Lake City: Signature Books, 2005), 69–76, 82–92.

78. Blakesley, "A Style of Our Own,'" 3.

79. Kapua Sproat, oral history interview, 15, Robin Kay Oral History Collection, L. Tom Perry Special Collections, Harold B. Lee Library, Brigham Young University, Provo, Utah.

80. Ibid., 15.

closely aligned them with other Mormons rather than with the other, more liberal women like Patsy Mink who represented the islands.

The reactions of these women to the dress and the behavior of the women around them suggests how thoroughly they had accepted the teachings of the LDS Church surrounding modesty, sexuality, and the roles of women. For some individuals living near the center, the PCC represented a challenge to the ideals that they had adopted as members of the Mormon faith. They objected to some of the practices of the PCC. The outfits that students wore at the PCC were often less modest than the clothing that they were expected to wear at the BYU-Hawai'i or in Sunday meetings in spite of concessions to Mormon ideas about modesty. Through General Conference, church publications, and local leaders, Polynesian students were told that their bodies were to be covered, that they were to wear skirts that came to their knees, that they shouldn't expose their shoulders, or bare their stomachs. At the cultural center, however, Polynesian students were asked to expose their bodies to promote their culture and earn scholarship money. For some community members, the PCC raised questions about how Polynesian bodies were valued. Why was the church willing to ask Polynesian students to display their bodies in ways that would be unacceptable for white students? Other Polynesian Mormons supported the PCC but wondered whether the uncovering of Polynesian bodies as part of a tourist performance was sending the right message about what it meant to be Mormon and Polynesian.

Conclusion

For most of this essay, I have focused on the conflicting visions of modesty that Mormon Polynesians received in the mid-twentieth century. Although LDS Church leaders emphasized the importance of covering the body in conference talks and articles for the *Ensign*, the Church College of Hawai'i and the PCC asked the students who worked there to uncover parts of their bodies in a belief that in doing so they better embodied Polynesian culture. It is important, however, not to end this essay without situating Mormon portrayals of the Pacific within larger conversations about American colonialism. The discomfort that some Polynesians felt with the Polynesian Cultural Center grew partially out of recognition of the congruence between American and Mormon discourses about the Pacific. In the mid-twentieth century, American popular culture depicted Hawai'i as an idyllic space where racial mixing was possible and even beneficial.[81] It was able to do so only by ignoring the routine

---

81. Klein, *Cold War Orientalism*, 249–250; Desmond, *Staging Tourism*, 7.

violence white soldiers inflicted upon local communities. In addition to nuclear testing, Pacific Islanders have also experienced violence focused on the bodies of individual women. Although members of the LDS Church condemned sexualized violence, the images that the PCC promoted of happy, welcoming Polynesian students, untouched by American civilization and existing in some sort of "traditional" state, played into the images of Polynesia so common in American culture. When students performed on stage, they were asked to embody a welcoming, beguiling vision of Polynesia removed from the specifics of time and place.

The congruence between Mormon portrayals of the Pacific and American colonial discourses has meant that the critiques made of the PCC in the mid-twentieth century have remained salient. In 2009, for example, a professor at the University of Hawai'i named Vernadette V. Gonzalez wrote an article accusing the Polynesian Cultural Center of trying to contain the sexuality of Tahitian dancing while simultaneously playing upon it. She describes a young woman beginning to dance in the Tahitian village at the PCC, "shaking her hips slowly at first" and "then speeding up to a hypnotic frenzy."[82] Gonzalez argues that the focus is on the woman's "gendered, native body." "Even as she remains modestly clothed in a strapless form-fitting dress and a grass skirt that further focuses attention on her swiveling hips," she writes, "the sheer physical demands of the dance emphasize her corporeality and the sensual, sexual aspect of the dance."[83]

Mormon scholars such as Gina Colvin have echoed Gonzalez's analysis. Colvin is a Māori woman who identifies as Mormon and has been an important critical voice within the community. In describing her experiences working at the PCC during a Mormon podcast, she claimed that she felt "demeaned" by her experience as a student worker. She portrays the process of getting dressed to work in the Māori village at the PCC as a kind of "strip[ping]" in which she was asked to exchange her long shorts for "stringy…strappy things" that never would have been allowed just a few yards away at BYU-Hawai'i.[84]

Gonzalez and Colvin's critiques resonate with those made earlier. They occur, however, in a very different cultural context. In the mid-twentieth century, the idea that Polynesians, American Indians, and other indigenous people had a special position within the LDS Church as a result of their status

---

82. Vernadette V. Gonzalez, "Consuming 'Polynesia': Visual Spectacles of Native Bodies in Hawaiian Tourism," in Norman K. Denzin, ed., *Studies in Symbolic Interaction*, vol. 33, (United Kingdom (Blingley, UK: Howard House, 2009): 208–209.

83. Ibid., 209.

84. Gina Colvin, 'Anapesi Ka'ili, Luana Uluave, Joanna Brooks, and Dan Witherspoon, *Pacific Island Mormon Identities Podcast 87*, podcast audio, Mormon Matters, April 5, 2012, 2014, http://mormonmatters.org/2012/04/05/87-88-pacific-island-mormon-identities.

as Lamanites was in its ascendancy. In the last third of the twentieth century, that idea underwent a rapid decline. Beginning in the 1970s, the LDS Church began to shift its emphasis away from programs designed to aid American Indians, Polynesians, and other indigenous people toward a more general emphasis on the Book of Mormon. By the late 1980s, an American Indian man who had been ordained to the Quorum of the Seventy found that the church's General Authorities directly challenged his claims that the church should be focused on the descendants of the people of the Book of Mormon.[85]

In recent years, scholars have also begun to question the possibility that Polynesians and American Indians are of Israelite descendant. In a 2002 essay, Thomas Murphy argued that DNA evidence suggested that American Indians originated not in a group of Israelites who escaped the destruction of Jerusalem around 600 BCE, but in northeastern Siberia.[86] Just two years later, Simon Southerton echoed his findings, publicly decrying the suggestion that American Indians and Polynesians were of Israelite origin.[87] The challenges that scholars like Murphy and Southerton have made to claims that Polynesians are descended from the people of the Book of Mormon have made leaders even more unwilling to emphasize the importance of the idea of "the Lamanite" to Mormon theology and culture. The continued salience of the critiques of the PCC suggests the degree to which questions of sexuality and modesty have defined discussions about the position of Polynesians within Mormon popular culture and theology.

Although Spencer W. Kimball's leadership in the mid-twentieth century led to an increased emphasis on the place of indigenous people in Mormon theology, concerns about the intersections of race, sexuality, and modesty persisted in the Pacific. The presence of white students at the Church College of Hawai'i raised concerns about interracial marriage and the possibility that young white women would be attracted to the bodies of Polynesian men. For some Polynesians and nonwhite members of the church, the concerns of white Mormon parents about interracial marriage suggested that they occupied a secondary place within the church that was incommensurate with Mormon theology. The church's administration seemed concerned about protecting the sexuality of white women at the same moment that it was willing to display the bodies of Polynesian students.

---

85. David Grua, "Elder George P. Lee and the New Jerusalem: A Reception History of 3 Nephi 21: 22–23," *Juvenile Instructor* blog, August 27, 2013, www.juvenileinstructor.org/elder-george-p-lee-and-the-reception-history-of-3-nephi-2122-23/.

86. Murphy, "Imagining Lamanites," 230.

87. Simon G. Southerton, *Losing a Lost Tribe: Mormons, DNA, and the Mormon Church* (Salt Lake City: Signature Books, 2004).

In recent years, white Americans have become increasingly accepting of interracial marriage. Concerns about sexuality and modesty, however, have continued to be an important part of discussions about the status of Pacific Islanders within the LDS Church. Although few white parents would be willing to write a letter to college administrators bemoaning the possibility that their daughter would fall in love with a Polynesian man, expectations for white and indigenous bodies have remained incongruous. The association of Polynesian culture with savagery has allowed church officials to display the bodies of Polynesian students in a way that would be impossible if the students were white. It is this incongruity that has inspired Mormon Polynesians to critique the center. Although questions about sexuality, racial identity, and religious faith have long been a part of the Mormon experience in the Pacific, the popularity of the PCC has made it a lightning rod for these discussions.

9

Housework

THE PROBLEM THAT DOES HAVE A NAME

Kate Holbrook

FOLLOWING WORLD WAR II, much of the country linked femininity with housework. When second-wave feminists challenged patterns of female domesticity, they reacted to post-World War II propaganda—a ubiquitous refrain that housework provided women ultimate fulfillment and that women belonged full-time at home. American society after the war "experienced a surge in family life and a reaffirmation of domesticity that rested on distinct roles for women and men."[1] Both men and women married younger, had children earlier, and raised larger families than the previous generation had.[2] Consumerist messages aimed at women promised them fulfillment in housekeeping if they used the right products and took advantage of cutting-edge household technologies like dishwashers and improved refrigerators. Women who became disappointed with these promises looked for alternative solutions, such as more equitable sharing of household tasks.

As women throughout the country proposed different solutions to housework, two strands of thought took shape. Some women sought ways to complete housework that would free them to pursue more fulfilling interests. They thought happiness would result when women made space for their whole selves. Others claimed that female happiness was to be found in securing the contentment of men. Disregarding their own distaste for housework and keeping their homes comfortable for others (and themselves beautiful for others) would make them happy despite the drudgery of housework. While Latter-day Saint voices adopted both of these approaches, most Latter-day Saint women approached housework as an opportunity to nurture family members. Neither approach received full sanction in official LDS circles. However, changes in the Relief Society curriculum during this time show how

---

1. Elaine Tyler May, *Homeward Bound: American Families in the Cold War Era* (New York: Basic Books, 1988), xiv.

2. Ibid., ix.

an ideal that romanticized the nature of women's relationship with house-work gained purchase in official forums.

Second-Wave Feminism and the Problem of Housework

Housework was one reason the civil rights movement gave birth to a woman's movement. As participants in the civil rights movement actively questioned social mores, they also reevaluated assumptions about women and house-work. Women in the movement—working long hours and risking harm, even death, in support of racial equality—applied the analysis and tools for achiev-ing that equality to their experiences as women.[3] Through housework women were both marginalized (housework took time away from more visible move-ment work) and identified as second-class citizens (leaders don't wash dishes). The discord between the rights they were trying to achieve for black Americans and the sexual discrimination their male fellows in organizations such as SNCC and SDS heaped upon them led many women from the cause of civil rights to a new movement for women.[4]

Meanwhile, Betty Friedan, who published her explosive book *The Feminine Mystique* in 1963, spoke in incendiary terms of housework as something to escape: "Women who 'adjust' as housewives, who grow up wanting to be 'just a housewife,' are in as much danger as the millions who walked to their own death in the concentration camps.... They are suffering a slow death of mind and spirit."[5] She described "the problem that has no name," that many women who were living the American dream, with a comfortable home and healthy children, felt something was wrong. This life of tending to house and children did not yield for them the promised satisfactions. On the contrary, some of them became deeply depressed and, recognizing their fortunate circum-stances relative to much of the world, could not understand the reasons for that depression. Friedan insisted homemakers' dissatisfaction was due to

---

3. "Twice in the history of the United States the struggle for racial equality has been mid-wife to a feminist movement. In the abolition movement of the 1830s and 1840s, and again in the civil rights movement of the 1960s, women experiencing the contradictory expecta-tions and stresses of changing roles began to move from individual discontents to a social movement in their own behalf. Working for racial justice, they gained experience in organiz-ing and in collective action, an ideology that described and condemned oppression analo-gous to their own, and a belief in human 'rights' that could justify them in claiming equality for themselves." Sara M. Evans, *Personal Politics: The Roots of Women's Liberation in the Civil Rights Movement and the New Left* (New York: Vintage Books, 1980), 24.

4. Ibid.

5. Friedan herself was Jewish and did not use the concentration camp imagery lightly. Betty Friedan, *The Feminine Mystique* (New York: Norton, 1963).

inadequate opportunities to develop and exercise talent as well as messaging in advertisements and magazine articles that insisted that women were most naturally and fully satisfied by doing housework. She argued that the messaging caused cognitive dissonance as it did not match women's real experiences. In 1966, Friedan collaborated with forty-nine women and men—including church women, academics, politicians, nuns, and labor leaders—to found the National Organization for Women (NOW).[6] Their statement of purpose read, "To take the actions needed to bring women into the mainstream of American society *now*...in fully equal partnership with men."[7]

Many second-wave feminists articulated the problem of housework as an issue of unjust separate spheres and the subordination of women. In their view, separate spheres meant that women ended up doing unpleasant and unappreciated work. No one thought housework was unnecessary, but they tried to imagine new possibilities for managing housework that would improve their family relationships and allow them time to pursue their own intellectual or professional interests. Alix Kates Shulman, for example, consulted with her husband to create a "marriage agreement" that would help them to share housework and childcare responsibilities in a more equitable manner. Shulman wrote:

> After I had been home with the children for six years I began to attend meetings of the newly formed women's liberation movement in New York City. At these meetings I began to see that my situation was not uncommon; other women too felt drained and frustrated as housewives and mothers.... When I added up the chores I was responsible for they amounted to a hectic 6 A.M. to 9 P.M. (often later) job, without salary, breaks or vacation.[8]

While caricatures portray feminists of this era leaving their husbands and children, many activists thought the separate spheres approach they were following was hurting their family life. They sought alternative approaches to managing housework and childcare because they wanted to improve life at home.

Enacting the principles and schedule of their new agreement worked brilliantly for Shulman and her husband. Two years after composing the

---

6. "Honoring Our Founders and Pioneers," *National Organization for Women*, http://now.org/about/history/honoring-our-founders-pioneers/; Ann Braude, "A Religious Feminist—Who Can Find Her? Historiographical Challenges from the National Organization for Women," *The Journal of Religion* 84 (October 2004).

7. Pauli Murray, *Song in a Weary Throat: An American Pilgrimage* (New York: Harper & Row, 1987), 368.

8. Alix Kates Shulman, "A Marriage Agreement," *Up From Under*, September 1970, 7.

agreement, Shulman reported that her new schedule had given her time to write three children's books, a biography, and a novel in addition to producing an edited volume, all of which were slated for publication. She emphasized what enacting the agreement had done for her family life. "We each have less work, more hours together and less resentment.... Perhaps the best testimonial of all to our marriage agreement is the change that has taken place in our family life. One day after it had been in effect for only four months our daughter said to my husband, 'You know Daddy, I used to love Mommy more than you, but now I love you both the same.'"[9]

Shulman's success at home did not rely solely on her ability to craft a sound agreement; it also required a dedicated spouse. Other women, like Pat Mainardi, found that even if their partners initially agreed to share housework, their devotion soon waned once the reality of executing those chores settled in: "The longer my husband contemplated these chores, the more repulsed he became, and so proceeded the change from the normally sweet considerate Dr. Jekyll into the crafty Mr. Hyde who would stop at nothing to avoid the horrors of—*housework*." In analyzing her husband's reaction, Mainardi detected a theme that he not only disliked the work, but thought it beneath him. Mainardi's article was funny at the same time that it inflamed those readers who related to her experience. She had identified a crucial area of resistance shared among feminist compatriots: housework consumed substantial amounts of time, and was sufficiently unpleasant that many men refused outright to do it. Moreover, while refusing it they also devalued it.[10] For men to devalue housework while expecting their wives to complete it damaged family relationships. In cases of divorce, ex-husbands might blame the women's movement for fostering their former wives' discontent, while those former wives blamed their husbands for damaging family relationships by refusing to share the responsibilities of housework.

Overtly religious feminists also looked for means to make housework play a less-consuming role their lives, so they could be more than housekeepers. Just as the tenets of their religious faith drove many women to participate in the movement for civil rights, so many women came to understand feminism as the logical extension of their religious beliefs.[11] Members of Church Women

---

9. Ibid., 5–12.

10. Pat Mainardi, "The Politics of Housework," in Robin Morgan, ed., *Sisterhood Is Powerful: An Anthology of Writings From The Women's Liberation Movement* (New York: Vintage Books, 1970), 447–454. See also Margaret Benston's Marxist analysis of housework as stuck in the premarket stage and therefore not considered real work. Margaret Bentson, "The Political Economy of Women's Liberation," *Monthly Review* 21 (September 1969): 13–25.

11. Evans, *Personal Politics*, 29.

United (CWU), for example, believed that no one should be oppressed and that faith should motivate Christians to liberate the downtrodden. In 1965, CWU member Hannah Bonsey Suthers labeled excessive attention to home life "idolatry." Suthers argued that putting housework in proper perspective would help women to be better Christians and mothers. The mother most able to raise free, independent, and responsible children is one that sees homemaking as an important part of her life instead of the absolute whole of her life. "To achieve the 'glorious freedom of the children of God,'" she argued, "we must labor painfully to heal and restore capacities that have been diseased or atrophied by traditional neglect: the capacities for autonomy, independence, individuality, self-fulfillment, self-realization, the grace to grow from strength to strength."[12] Suthers and her colleagues in the CWU believed that women's stewardship existed within and extended beyond the home, and they "refused to regard the wielding of a vacuum cleaner as a religious experience."[13] Suthers did not argue explicitly in her article that men should share housework; she focused more on children sharing the load for their own good. Neither did she reject the idea of the domestic as rightfully female. What she sought were ways to minimize the energy housework consumed and maximize a life beyond housework.

Housework and the Mormon Woman: Two Competing Views

Like Suthers, Latter-day Saint women envisioned the religious life as requiring more than housework. Since its inception on March 17, 1842, the Relief Society had invited LDS women to extend their spiritual responsibilities beyond the borders of their home. Relief Society members felt called to assist in the temporal and spiritual salvation of others, so they did not have time to make of housework that idol against which Suthers warned. During the mid-twentieth century, Relief Society members participated in organizations such as the International Council of Women, Community Chest, the Red Cross, and local social service organizations. They were also involved in the National Council of Women (NCW), which Relief Society general president Belle

---

12. Hannah Bonsey Suthers, "Religion and the Feminine Mystique," *Christian Century*, July 21, 1965, 911–914.

13. Caryn E. Neumann, "Enabled by the Holy Spirit: Church Women United and the Development of Ecumenical Christian Feminism," in Stephanie Gilmore, ed., *Feminist Coalitions: Historical Perspectives on Second-Wave Feminism in the United States* (Urbana: University of Illinois Press, 2008), 113–114.

Spafford headed from 1968 to 1970.[14] The Relief Society itself raised money through bazaars, ran its own magazine, oversaw and stocked the shelves of the Mormon Handicraft Store, produced temple clothing, and managed its own adoption and foster care programs. Relief Society members actively participated in many of these ventures in addition to serving the members of their own congregations, from feeding the hungry to preparing the dead for burial. Many active Relief Society members found they had to make housework efficient so they had time for all their other religious and community obligations.

LDS homemaking guru Daryl V. Hoole, whose first book came out the year before *The Feminine Mystique,* devoted decades of her life to teaching women how to avoid making an idol of housework, on the one hand, or falling prey to the despair it could cause, on the other. Hoole assumed that instruction in more efficient homemaking would help a depressed homemaker, and that efficient execution of housework would free time for more fulfilling activities. With the 1962 publication of *The Art of Homemaking* and lectures first at Brigham Young University (BYU) and then throughout North America as part of the Know Your Religion speaker circuit, Hoole established herself as the leading authority on keeping an LDS home. Hoole did not agree with the articles and advertisements that portrayed housework as essential to women's lasting fulfillment. She saw housework as a means to an end, and that end was a better, richer family life.

The Art of Homemaking asserted that women could thrive while fulfilling their duties at home. She taught women how to work faster and better, how to involve family members so that they weren't doing it alone, and how to make sure they performed their work in a way that harmonized with their larger goals. "An ideal homemaker," she wrote, "makes the best use of her time and energy by being efficient so that she is able not only to keep up with her housework, but...to be a companion to her husband and a friend and teacher to her children. She is also able to pursue some personal interests which further contribute to her happiness and development."[15] Hoole identified which tasks were essential (the dishes, bed-making, picking up clutter, food preparation) and which might be postponed during times of illness or when life was otherwise particularly busy. She advised readers to perform the essential tasks before starting something new, such as organizing a closet, so

---

14. Jill Mulvay Derr, Janath Russell Cannon, and Maureen Ursenbach Beecher, *Women of Covenant: The Story of Relief Society* (Salt Lake City: Deseret Book Company, 1992), 275–278, 310–311, 313–315, 319–322, 335–338. Jennifer Reeder and Kate Holbrook, eds., *At the Pulpit: Latter-day Saint Women Speak* (Salt Lake City: Church Historian's Press, forthcoming 2017).

15. Daryl V. Hoole, *The Art of Homemaking* (Salt Lake City: Publishers Press, 1962), 3–4.

their families' needs would still be met. And she included illustrations for how to structure the playroom and the laundry, so they would be easy to maintain and so that other family members could help to keep order.

Hoole was a theologian of housework, framing its purpose in terms that gave it religious significance. She recommended praying for help to do it well. "Prayer," she taught, "can lift you when you are discouraged; you can fulfill your responsibilities more effectively if you pray about them; through prayer you can set the noblest of all examples for your children."[16] Hoole also weighed the substance of her ideas and writings against scripture, and she articulated those aspects of LDS belief, such as raising righteous children worthy to accompany their parents through the eternities, that gave housework deeper meaning. For many LDS women, Hoole provided a lifeline of practical information that transformed their experiences of housework and their relationships with their children. Other women found themselves unable to live up to her prescriptions and resented her ideal. Admirers described their gratitude for Hoole's work in letters to her: "My life has been changed." "I owe much to you for my sanity and success as a homemaker." "Prophets have admonished us to make our homes a bit of heaven. Sister Hoole has done more to help women bring this about than anyone else in the Church."[17] A critic, on the other hand, wrote: "Daryl's books provided many great ideas for organization, planning, and cleanliness, but the realities of living with many small children in a small home on a fixed budget with few resources often resulted in frustration.... Dealing with daily challenges of struggling children, learning problems, business challenges, and the normal washing, cleaning, and being where one needed to be on time, with everyone fed and dressed and smiling was a sure ticket to disillusionment."[18]

Hoole strategized to make housework efficient in order to create space for other endeavors. Her LDS contemporary, Helen Andelin, argued that happiness would come when women learned to make the men in their lives content. In her extraordinarily popular 1963 book, *Fascinating Womanhood*, Andelin wrote that unhappy marriage, rather than housework, was at the root of women's dissatisfaction at home. She therefore advised women to perform better in their female roles to create happy marriages. Like Hoole, Andelin assumed that housework was women's responsibility and offered practical suggestions for how to perform it as efficiently and painlessly as possible. For example, she advised those women who did not feel joy in cleaning toilets or

---

16. Ibid.

17. Daryl V. Hoole to Kate Holbrook, October 8, 2015.

18. Anonymous to Kate Holbrook, October 7, 2015.

scrubbing floors to accept the drudgery as an inevitable part of life. She suggested women simplify both by not overscheduling their lives and by getting rid of excess possessions ("In simplifying a household, everything should be either useful or beautiful"), and to organize their work, commitments, and priorities.[19] Both Andelin and Hoole spoke of housework as necessary for happy families, and both drew on the centrality of eternal families in the LDS vision of the good life.

But their visions of a whole woman were not the same. Andelin's goal in writing was to instruct women how to be lovable to the men in their lives. Instead of asking men to share tasks, she suggested women encourage men to perform "masculine" household duties and to exaggerate their own femininity. Andelin told her readers to "let go completely" of masculine tasks (paying bills, keeping books, painting, repairing), to "dispense with any air of masculine strength, ability, competence…and acquire a spirit of sweet submission."[20] If a woman found she had to do a feminine job, she should do it in a feminine (incompetent) manner. "You need not perform masculine tasks with manly efficiency…. Your husband will soon realize you need masculine assistance. If you can work as well as he can, he'll never come to your rescue."[21] Andelin's prioritized list of household tasks also reflected the degree to which housekeeping and man-keeping were intertwined. On her daily to do list, she prioritized "my appearance" first, before cooking, cleaning, doing laundry, or shopping.[22] She taught that the feminine woman "doesn't neglect her hair, face, figure, or clothes. She looks as pretty as she can at all times."[23] Her recommended fashions were those that most accentuated the differences between men and women, such as dresses, gauzy fabrics, and ruffles. "As you acquire a more feminine appearance, he will notice you more, find you more appealing and respect you more," she taught.[24] Where Hoole linked housework with the work of salvation, as a necessary aspect of building and nurturing eternal families, Andelin wrote about performing housework well as a means of keeping a man's love. She placed a great deal of emphasis on female appearance and on molding the female self.

---

19. Helen Andelin, *Fascinating Womanhood* (New York: Bantam Books, 1992), 233.

20. Ibid., 274–275.

21. Ibid., 275.

22. Ibid., 230–234.

23. Ibid., 248.

24. Ibid., 249–251.

Although church leaders repeatedly declined Andelin's invitation to use her book as part of official church curriculum, Relief Societies throughout the country hosted *Fascinating Womanhood* workshops.[25] Many members of Relief Society embraced her message. Other church members, including in particular faculty members of the Family Life Department at BYU, opposed Andelin's message, objecting to the female subordination she taught would improve marriage and home life. Their aversion may have been provoked by some of Andelin's more extreme pronouncements, such as advising women to respond to uncooperative husbands with "childlikeness" or to design their clothing based on little girls' clothing.[26] Because she understood herself as doing God's work, sharing truths that would decrease the divorce rate, Andelin was deeply hurt when church officials distanced themselves and the institution from her work. Her own bishop outlawed *Fascinating Womanhood* classes in the congregation. When they did not embrace her ideas, she labeled Belle Spafford and other female leaders her enemies.[27]

Following the publication of *Fascinating Womanhood*, BYU master's degree student Lois Richins Monroe explored another solution to the problem of housework. In contrast with Andelin's theory that women would find happiness primarily through gratifying their men, Monroe's research suggested that women were happier when they spent fulfilling time outside of their homes. In a research sample of thirty mothers married to BYU students, Monroe found that mothers who worked full time had more positive feelings about the "homemaking role" than those who did not.[28] Women who earned more money also had more positive feelings about their employment. Thus her study suggested that women who spent forty hours a week outside of their homes, earning a fair wage, would have more positive feelings about the work they performed at home. Monroe's work did not imply that housework belonged outside of women's sphere, but that other outside-the-home work belonged in it.

Feminist LDS women rarely and only gently challenged the notion that housework was solely women's domain, but they did insist that women cultivate lives beyond housework. One unnamed contributor to the 1971 "pink" issue of *Dialogue: A Journal of Mormon Thought*, an issue written and edited by

---

25. Helen Andelin, recorded interviews, Pierce City, Missouri, 2002, Andelin Archive, cited in Julie Debra Neuffer, *Helen Andelin and the Fascinating Womanhood Movement* (Salt Lake City: University of Utah Press, 2014), 174.

26. Ibid., 318–345.

27. Neuffer, *Helen Andelin and the Fascinating Womanhood Movement*, 98–110.

28. Lois Richins Monroe, "Attitudes of Employed and Non-Employed Latter-Day Saint Mothers Toward the Homemaking Role and Outside Employment" (master's thesis, Brigham Young University, 1965), 61, Church History Library, Salt Lake City, Utah.

women and about women, asserted, "We are led to believe that proper husband–wife roles are clearly spelled out. It seems to me that an attempt to
follow these behavior molds harms more marriages than it helps. My husband and I work together to keep the house clean." Future Chief Justice of the
Utah Supreme Court Christine Durham also noted in that issue, "The division of labor in most families is made not on the basis of individual talents but
on the basis of sex.... I feel very strongly that husbands and wives should be
able to exercise their free agency in working out their respective social and
family functions."[29] Many LDS women throughout the 1970s would continue
to argue that their sphere extended beyond the walls of their homes without
overtly rejecting housework as an additional necessity.[30]

In contrast to Monroe and the changes advocated by feminism, however,
other women continued to speak (outside the home) and write against wom-
en's work outside the home. By 1973, Andelin's Protestant disciple Marabel
Morgan had become famous in her own right and was raising her voice with
solutions to housework derivative of Andelin's proposals.[31] In *The Total
Woman*, she advised women to establish and complete priorities each day,
putting them down on paper, starting to make dinner after breakfast, and
being flexible.[32] Morgan taught that women would find the energy they needed
to face domestic frustrations by linking with Jesus's light.[33] Much of Morgan's
writing, like Andelin's, focused on treating husbands with particular attention, sublimating women's own desires when necessary to foster a happy marital relationship. She also famously talked at length about sex as key to a happy
home—a development that repulsed Andelin—linking housework with sex

---

29. Shirley Gee, ed., "Dirt: A Compendium of Household Wisdom," *Dialogue: A Journal of Mormon Thought* 6 (Summer 1971): 85; Christine Meaders Durham, "Having One's Cake and Eating It Too," *Dialogue: A Journal of Mormon Thought* 6 (Summer 1971): 38–39.

30. Claudia L. Bushman, *Mormon Sisters: Women in Early Utah* (Cambridge: Emmeline Press, 1976); Vicky Burgess-Olson, *Sister Saints* (Provo: Brigham Young University Press, 1978). Eventually some voices became more directly challenging. The year after her excom-munication, Sonia Johnson described the time she had housekeepers while living in Korea during the early 1970s as having been one of the happiest in her life, "freed from the bondage of housework to be able to have a full life of my own outside the house." Recalling how her mother's life was confined to the domestic sphere, she surmised, "The family is a very narrow sphere. It is cruel to bottle up immense talents there." See Sonia Johnson, *From Housewife to Heretic* (Garden City, NY: Doubleday, 1981), 53, 62.

31. Morgan was teaching Andelin's courses when a publisher approached her about writing her own version of *Fascinating Womanhood*. Andelin encouraged Morgan to write the book, although she asked her to credit her ideas, which Morgan did not do. Neuffer, *Helen Andelin and the Fascinating Womanhood Movement*, 81–82.

32. Marabel Morgan, *The Total Woman* (Old Tappan, NJ: F. H. Revell, 1973), 30–36.

33. Ibid., 171–179.

when she suggested on a talk show that a woman might greet her husband clothed in nothing but that indispensible kitchen tool Saran Wrap.[34] Morgan closed her book with a promise: "Once the inside of your house is decorated; once the outside of your house is painted; once your power source is the Light of the world, you will find yourself in a new and exciting dimension—one where you, too, can become a super wife and a Total Woman."[35]

Changes to the Relief Society Housework Curriculum

While lay voices debated the role housework should play in women's lives, exploring varied but ostensibly family-affirming approaches to housework, the Relief Society instigated several curriculum shifts during the 1960s. When thinkers like Andelin analyzed housework, they tended to romanticize home life. Although Relief Society headquarters never endorsed Andelin's ideas, two major curriculum shifts contributed to a similar romanticizing of home life and even expanded the boundaries of housework to include women's physical presentation.

The first shift was in lesson authorship. In the 1950s, women with careers had written the curriculum on housework and signed their names to the lessons, which gave readers a sense that a working and knowable woman was behind each piece of instruction. By 1970, Relief Society lessons included no byline and thus appeared to come from the church as an institution instead of from a person, providing no individual model of a professional woman for others to know and follow. At the same time that women like Betty Friedan were arguing that the solution for unhappy women was to develop their talents, work outside the home, and free themselves from housework, church lessons on housework decreased the visibility of working women. By the early 1970s, lessons were not written by individual women with professional experience in relevant fields, but by anonymous groups.[36]

This was especially visible in the official curriculum on housekeeping. With a few isolated exceptions, each year from 1915 to 1965, one woman at a time was assigned to write all of the Work Meeting lessons. Many of these authors gave very pragmatic guidance because they themselves were trained

---

34. Margaret D. Kamitsuka, *The Embrace of Eros: Bodies, Desires, and Sexuality in Christianity* (Minneapolis: Fortress Press, 2010), 166–167.

35. Ibid., 188.

36. Elaine Jack was head of the curriculum committees and oversaw this process, not only for homemaking, but for all Relief Society lessons. Elaine L. Jack, interview by Kate Holbrook, November 1, 2013.

in domestic science. In her lessons from 1953 to 1956, for example, Utah Cooperative Extensive Service writer Rhea H. Gardner discussed in the most matter-of-fact terms money management, household equipment, and food preparation and service. Subsequent authors wrote about "household operations," "physical safety," and caring for the sick.

Virginia Cutler, who wrote the lessons from 1962 to 1964, was also a widely known professional. She had earned a master's degree from Stanford in 1937 and a PhD in home economics from Cornell University in 1946. Before writing Relief Society lessons, she worked as a home demonstration agent for the University of California Extension Service then as a professor and the head of the Home Economics Department at the University of Utah, where she established the Family Home Living Center. In 1954, she agreed to be the education advisor for the State Department's International Cooperation Administration, organizing home economics programs in schools and at workshops for two years in Thailand and five years in Indonesia. Cutler was well-prepared to write Work Meeting lessons.

Cutler's lessons approached housework in a professional way that emphasized efficient performance over any romanticized notion that it could provide women's ultimate fulfillment. Her nine lessons for 1962 began with an exam called the Family Values Test, which was intended to help individual women develop relevant goals for the coming months. She referred to women with families as "home managers" and different parts of the kitchen as "work centers," which included the "sink center," the "cooking center," and the "mixing and food preparation center."[37] In one of her articles, she lauded a woman who did research at the library and wrote to her local extension service for information on kitchen planning. She cited recent studies in her lessons, such as one by Marie Geraldine Gage at Cornell regarding savings from "unpaid-for services that replace bought goods and hired help."[38] Cutler's curriculum had the formal, professional feel she brought from her broader work experience.

When women outside the field of home economics began to write the Relief Society curriculum content, however, the tone changed from pragmatic to romantic. Celestia Taylor wrote most of the Homemaking lessons from October 1966 through 1970, when the church's correlation efforts decreed that the *Relief Society Magazine* would cease publication. Like Gardner, Cutler, and others before them, Taylor was a professional woman; she taught English courses at BYU, had a master's degree, and had taken summer courses at the University of California

---

37. Virginia F. Cutler, "The Latter-Day Saint Home Is Well Organized," *Relief Society Magazine*, August 1962, 616–617.

38. Virginia F. Cutler, "The Latter-Day Saint Home Exemplifies Thrift," *Relief Society Magazine*, January 1963, 65.

at Berkeley and Columbia Teachers' College.[39] She had no professional experience in home economics, however, and recalled that when she was first requested to write the lessons, she was "overwhelmed at the assignment" and felt her "complete inadequacy as any kind of an authority on the subjects in this field."[40]

In addition to lesson authorship changing from one professionally trained woman to a committee, a meeting name change represented an increasing romanticization of women and domestic labor. "In harmony with the Correlation Program, the lessons for the coming year are being written so they may be presented in such a way that every sister at Relief Society will become involved in the discussion," the Relief Society announced in 1966. "The titles of the courses, beginning in October 1966, reflect this new concept of involvement. Theology is now called 'Spiritual Living'; Work Meeting— 'Homemaking'; Social Science 'Social Relations'; and Literature has taken on a new depth and becomes 'Cultural Refinement.'"[41]

This announcement suggested that title changes were an effort to harmonize Relief Society curriculum with the larger church-wide efforts of the correlation program.[42] During the mid-1960s, the part of the correlation effort that oversaw the production of church print materials encouraged curriculum writers to produce lessons that involved participation. With this goal in mind, two of the title changes make sense: "Social Science" has the sense of a lecture topic for a person pursuing an advanced degree, whereas "Social Relations" sounds like something the general public could discuss. Likewise, "Theology" has a rarefied air, but most people could contribute to a discussion of "Spiritual Living." "Cultural Refinement" is not substantially more accessible than "Literature," but it does address a broader range of interests. The switch from "Work Meeting" to "Homemaking" stands out from the others. The term "work" already functioned "in such a way that every sister at Relief Society [would] become involved in the discussion." So this title change did not foster an impression of more accessible lessons. Instead, it marked a change in the church's official framing of women's domestic labor, from pragmatic, everyday chores to a portrait that more explicitly recommended housework as a broadly defined and all-consuming feminine pursuit.

---

39. Celestia J. Taylor, *Through A Lifetime* (Provo, UT: self-published, 1977), 45–49.

40. Ibid., 124.

41. "New Titles for Lesson Courses," *Relief Society Magazine*, June 1966, 460.

42. Correlation, an effort to orchestrate the activities of both distinct and overlapping church entities to reduce excess expenditures of money and effort, has occurred several times throughout church history. But the 1960s and 1970s in particular represent an era of Correlation—a time during which successive church presidents David O. McKay, Joseph Fielding Smith, and Harold B. Lee worked to coordinate and refine the running of the church.

The name "Work Meeting" fit what was done at those meetings: learning to work and working. The new title "Homemaking" also came to convey what happened at meetings, discussing in broad terms the efforts women made to transform their houses into homes. Lessons still included practical information and tips. The curriculum also adopted a defensive tone, as if its committee of authors was concerned that women under the influence of second-wave feminism might neglect housework. The title "Homemaking" provided a justification for housework as it made explicit the link between cooking, cleaning, and the development of feminine attributes with nurturing husbands and children. Work was gender-neutral and grounded in practical considerations. Homemaking was romantically feminine.

This solidifying link between gender and homemaking became clear in the final lesson preview ever published in the *Relief Society Magazine*, in June 1970.[43] Whereas the lesson preview in June 1960 described "Caring for the Sick in Your Home," the preview in 1970 was markedly different in its assumption that women needed to be convinced of the importance of housework:

> The woman who devotes her talents to being a creative homemaker and a lovely wife and mother is making an unmatched contribution to society. In a world where young people are confused and uncertain, mothers must set the example of poise, loveliness, level-headedness and stability. In our course of study for this year we will give specific helps in good grooming, modesty in dress, and the importance of daily exercise. We will discuss the blessings that come to a woman and her family by her having right attitudes, improving her mind, watching her speech, and developing a pleasing personality—all factors in molding "A Lovelier You."[44]

The 1960s began with the goal of teaching participants more effectively to care for the sick and ended with "A Lovelier You." "Molding" was an appropriate word choice—these lessons read like materials from a finishing school rather than concrete instruction to sharpen housekeeping skills. They underscored that in a world "where young people are confused and uncertain" (code for challenges raised by second-wave feminism and youth culture) LDS

---

43. After the Relief Society Magazine ceased publication in 1970, all Relief Society curriculum was published annually in separate manuals called *Relief Society Courses of Study*. The new *Ensign* magazine that replaced the *Relief Society Magazine* was written for both women and men and did not include Homemaking lesson plans.

44. "Homemaking Discussions Education for Living: A Lovelier You," *Relief Society Magazine*, June 1970, 468.

women would keep the home fires burning. To achieve this new ideal of poise and loveliness, housework had expanded beyond cooking and cleaning to include grooming, modesty, and exercise. Moreover, lessons in the 1970s also revealed an undercurrent of anxiety that women would neglect their housework, led astray by assertions that men might be responsible for it as well. Whereas earlier lessons assumed women's competence, these lessons expressed worry that women who focused on concerns beyond the home were no longer adequate homemakers. For example, the curriculum fretted "that a surprising number of women, within the Church as well as outside of it, are lacking in the knowledge and the skills that are required to meet the challenges confronting them—particularly in their homes and in the rearing and training of their families." Women, it said, had begun "to underestimate the importance of their role as homemaker or their need to be educated about homemaking skills in order to properly and adequately fulfill this role."[45] Ironically, this admonition came precisely at the same time that the Relief Society was offering less instruction about actual housework skills than it had in the past.

Conclusion

This chapter has analyzed an era sufficiently prosperous for women to entertain such questions as what was wrong in their marriages and home lives, and what was keeping them from the happiness June Cleaver seemed to experience on TV (while the woman portraying her worked outside the home as an actor).[46] American women saw that housework could be a problem. Who should do it, how to do it, and how to feel good about doing it were poignant questions because the answers directly impacted individuals' status and well-being. Housework could breed resentment or it could become spiritual work, calling women to serve, to forgive, to endure, or find satisfaction in its daily performance. Some women devoted the bulk of their lives to discharging housework, while others engaged in rich extra-domestic activity. Far from innocuous, the issue of housework broke up both marriages and social movements. Women's thoughts about housework during this period of rapid social change also flowed through their pens. Two main approaches resulted from these exchanges, the first in which women approached housework as something to manage, part of a larger existence that could be carefully structured to

---

45. 1971–1972 *Relief Society Courses of Study* (Salt Lake City: Relief Society of The Church of Jesus Christ of Latter-day Saints, 1971), 189.

46. *Leave it to Beaver* ran from 1957–1963. See Internet Movie Database, www.imdb.com/title/tt0050032.

allow for the flourishing of a whole woman. The second approach focused on women's happiness being irrevocably tied up with the satisfaction of the men in their lives. Adherents of this school kept house to keep their men, and housekeeping included the careful fashioning of their appearance and comportment.

While a shared commitment to healthy family life undergirded Latter-day Saint thoughts about housework, the different ways in which they approached it reflected the variety of opinion in the broader culture, as did the multiplicity of their ideas about what would help a family to flourish. Individual Mormon women developed philosophies based either on successful homemaking as part of a broad vision of fulfillment or happiness rooted primarily in catering to others. Changes in the Relief Society curriculum suggest an institutional leaning toward the latter philosophy by the early 1970s, which would increasingly make Mormon discourse about women and the home divergent from a broader culture they had largely paralleled only a few years earlier.

10

Saying Goodbye to the Final Say

THE SOFTENING AND REIMAGINING OF MORMON MALE HEADSHIP IDEOLOGIES

Caroline Kline

> *By divine design, **fathers are to preside** over their families in love and righteousness and are responsible to provide the necessities of life and protection for their families. Mothers are primarily responsible for the nurture of their children. In these sacred responsibilities, fathers and mothers are obligated to help one another as **equal partners**.*[1]

THE ABOVE SENTENCES are instantly recognizable to members of the Church of Jesus Christ of Latter-day Saints. Since its publication in 1995 by the First Presidency and Quorum of the Twelve Apostles, "The Family: A Proclamation to the World" has been enthusiastically embraced by LDS members and leaders, with many Mormon homes featuring framed "Proclamations" on their walls. This short statement outlining the LDS Church's views on marriage and gender roles has achieved near-canonical status, as it is quoted frequently in semiannual church-wide conferences, the church's official *Ensign* magazine, and church-produced teaching manuals. The Proclamation stands as a striking example of the dual discourse the contemporary LDS Church employs regarding marital dynamics and gender roles, as it simultaneously embraces both the narrative of male presiding and the narrative of equal partnership within the family.

This contemporary emphasis on both male/female equality and male headship within marriage is a recent development. Traditionally, Mormon teachings about family organization and roles have been unapologetically patriarchal, with LDS Church authorities designating husbands as having the right to make final decisions in the home. Over the past three decades,

---

1. "The Family: A Proclamation to the World," *Ensign*, November 1995, 76, emphasis added.

however, Mormon leaders have softened male headship language. Rather than husbands acting as final decision makers and expecting obedience from wives, husbands are now to preside in the home by offering loving guidance and leadership in religious rituals and training. Simultaneously, Mormon authorities have embraced an egalitarian marital rhetoric as they encourage spouses to support and help one another as equal partners. Thus, contemporary Mormonism occupies a discursive space that paradoxically contains both the narrative of male presiding and the narrative of equal partnership within the family.

This movement toward a softening in Mormon male headship ideology parallels trends in conservative American Protestantism. W. Bradford Wilcox notes that male headship in conservative Protestantism has been redefined since the women's movement in the 1970s. Rather than past understandings of unequivocal male authority within the family, supporters of Protestant male headship now emphasize that "male leadership is oriented toward service—hence, the near universal use of the term *servant-leadership* in conjunction with discussions of male authority."[2] This more recent emphasis on servant-leadership, a corollary to Mormonism's new softer understanding of male presiding, orients men away from domineering activity and toward attending to the spiritual and emotional needs of their family members.[3] In practice, according to Sally Gallagher, servant-leadership advocates are generally partnership-oriented and highly pragmatic, despite their embrace of the principle of male familial leadership.[4] Mormonism's Proclamation emerged at roughly the same time as the 1998 Southern Baptist Convention's resolution that it is the wife's duty "to submit herself graciously to the servant leadership of her husband," even as she stands as an "equal to him."[5] These 1990s statements on the family marked, for both traditions, a simultaneous resistance and accommodation to egalitarian ideals.

This essay examines changing Mormon discourse about familial male headship and equal partnership through both official church statements and through feminist Mormon reflections on the topic. First, I chart significant moments in Mormon leaders' discourse on marriage, as these leaders nuanced

---

2. W. Bradford Wilcox, *Soft Patriarchs, New Men: How Christianity Shapes Fathers and Husbands* (Chicago: University of Chicago Press, 2004), 172.

3. Ibid., 188.

4. Sally K. Gallagher, *Evangelical Identity and Gendered Family Life* (New Brunswick, NJ: Rutgers University Press, 2003), 100.

5. "Comparison of the 1925, 1963, and 2000 Baptist Faith and Message," Southern Baptist Convention, www.sbc.net/bfm2000/bfmcomparison.asp.

and promoted changing conceptions of male presiding and equal partnership. Next, I examine the ways church leaders' evolving discussions of Eve reflected and justified these newer understandings of marital roles and power dynamics. Finally, I examine Mormon feminist participation in the changing discourse about gender roles within the family. This participation ranges from outright rejection of the idea that men can simultaneously preside and act as equal partners to a reenvisioning of an increasingly limited male presiding concept.

Presiding: A History

Official Mormon discourse on male presiding and marital gender roles has shifted perceptibly throughout the LDS Church's 185-year history. Patriarchal thought saturated early Mormon theology and practice. In this, nineteenth-century Mormonism stood with the vast majority of other Christian traditions of the time, which insisted on male headship in home, church, and polis. In nineteenth-century Utah, Brigham Young stood as a particularly vociferous promoter of male headship, stating, "Let our wives be the weaker vessels, and the men be men, and show the women by their superior ability that God gives husbands wisdom and ability to lead their wives into his presence." Young even went so far as to remind women that a husband was to be considered not only her head, but her "God." This patriarchal ideology, B. Carmon Hardy argues, found its most powerful ally in the Mormon doctrine of polygamy, which was seen by several Mormon leaders as a brace for male authority in the home.[6]

Polygamy was one marker of Mormon masculinity in the nineteenth century. Another marker was priesthood, which continues to be essential to the Mormon construction of masculinity.[7] Priesthood, which in the Mormon conception is the power and authority to act in the name of God, is conferred on

---

6. B. Carmon Hardy, "Lords of Creation: Polygamy, the Abrahamic Household, and Mormon Patriarchy," *Journal of Mormon History* 20 (Spring 1994): 128–129. While Brigham Young placed women in a subordinate role in much of his rhetoric, in practice, many Mormon women of nineteenth-century Utah were necessarily independent, since polygamy so often meant male absence from women's lives. Joan Iversen discusses the way Mormon polygamy, despite its patriarchal theological basis, led to women's greater autonomy, self-sufficiency, and close bonds with other women. Joan Iversen, "Feminist Implications of Mormon Polygamy," *Feminist Studies* 10 (Autumn 1984): 505–522.

7. Amy Hoyt and Sara M. Patterson, "Mormon Masculinity: Changing Gender Expectations in the Era of Transition from Polygamy to Monogamy, 1890–1920," *Gender & History* 23 (April 2011): 74.

every worthy Mormon man ages twelve and up, and it now stands as one of the most emphasized justifications for male leadership in the Mormon home.

Nineteenth-century Mormon rhetoric of male leadership stemming from male superiority began to slip away in the twentieth century, replaced by an emphasis on God's desire for order in the home. In 1915, Mormon theologian John Widtsoe, later a member of the Quorum of the Twelve Apostles, justified male headship within marriage in the following way: "The family is the basis of society on earth, and as there must be organization among intelligent beings, someone must be spokesman for the family. In the family, the man is the spokesman and the presiding authority, and therefore, the Priesthood is bestowed upon him."[8] Notably, notions of male superiority and female inferiority are entirely absent from this justification. Also absent are references to New Testament passages which clearly call for female submission. Since the early twentieth century, Mormon leaders like Widtsoe have generally avoided appealing to Pauline statements on female submission in their discussion of gender roles, a rhetorical choice that stands in contrast to conservative Protestant justifications for male familial leadership.[9] Rather, Widtsoe associated male leadership in the home with priesthood and with the need for organization. Mormon authorities in the mid-twentieth century continued to emphasize male authority in the home, though they, like Widtsoe, tended to justify this with discussions of separate gender roles which were largely lacking in discussions of male superiority.

With the rise of the women's movement in the 1970s, the topic of gender roles in marriage garnered increasing attention in church publications.[10] A 1973 *Ensign* article by Brent Barlow emphasized organization in its explanation for male headship, going so far as to equate the leadership of the father in the family with that of a bishop in the ward:

---

8. John A. Widtsoe, *Rational Theology* (Salt Lake City: Signature Books, 1997), 97.

9. There are a number of possible reasons why Mormon leaders, unlike conservative Protestants, have avoided appealing to Paul in their discussion of gender roles, one of which is that Mormons are simply not as tied to the Bible as their evangelical neighbors. As conservative Bible readers, but not literalists, leaders like Widtsoe had the freedom to downplay stark Pauline gender role prescriptions (female submission, women's silence in churches, etc.) in favor of modern prophetic guidance and revelation, which has at various points opened up some space for women's voices in church (see Doctrine and Covenants section 25) and affirmed a more agentive role for women in society and family. See Martha Sonntag Bradley, *Pedestals and Podiums: Utah Women, Religious Authority, and Equal Rights* (Salt Lake City: Signature Books, 2005), 7–24.

10. See Laurence R. Iannaccone and Carrie A. Miles, "Dealing with Social Change: The Mormon Church's Response to Change in Women's Roles," in *Social Forces* 68 (June 1990): 1231–1250.

> A Latter-day Saint husband or father presides over his wife and family in
> much the same way a bishop, stake president, or elders quorum president
> presides over the specific group to which he is called.... Suppose you
> had two stake presidents, two elders quorum presidents, two Sunday
> School presidents, two Primary and Relief Society presidents presiding
> over each of the priesthood quorums, groups, and auxiliaries. How
> would the Church function? Would "law and order" prevail? Similarly,
> should two people preside over each other in a marriage, particularly
> when one holds the priesthood and has been divinely designated
> to preside?[11]

This vision of male headship in the home is expansive in its scope. Since
bishops and stake presidents have unilateral power to override others' objections and to make final decisions, Barlow's vision of male presiding in the
home is starkly patriarchal. The worry about "law and order" disintegrating
without clear male decision-making power hints at his discomfort with the
messiness of compromise and negotiation which would characterize later
church leaders' advice about decision making within marriage. Like many
church authorities, Barlow associated male presiding with male priesthood holding.

Barbara B. Smith, the general president of Relief Society during some of
the most tumultuous years of the women's movement, likewise embraced the
concept of male presiding in both home and church. However, in a 1976 interview published in the *Ensign* magazine, she simultaneously advocated cooperative and nonhierarchal relationships between men and women.
Speaking of her own experiences as general president of the Relief Society
working with male church leaders, she stated:

> And incidentally, isn't it interesting that this same kind of pattern can
> work in the homes between husband and wife. All that the Brethren
> have taught me says that we have a companion relationship—not infe-
> rior or subordinate, but companion, side-by-side. The priesthood pre-
> sides, but each of us contributes a vital part to make the whole complete.
> This isn't my plan. It's the Lord's plan, and leaders who apply it and
> husbands and wives who abide by it know not only that it works, but
> also that it gives each party his or her greatest joy.... If woman has the

---

11. Brent Barlow, "Strengthening the Patriarchal Order of the Home," *Ensign*, February 1973.

role of a true companion and helpmeet to her husband, both are magnified and challenged.[12]

While Smith did not challenge the concept of male presiding, she did layer in notions of cooperative relationships between men and women which are devoid of female subordination. The word that encapsulates her vision of woman's role is "companion." This concept of the female as true companion shifted slightly within church discourse in the coming years into a more explicitly egalitarian concept of female as equal partner. In this way Smith anticipated the dual discourse between male presiding and equal partnership that later came to characterize church leaders' rhetoric on male/female relationships.

The 1980s saw further efforts to temper starkly patriarchal constructions of male presiding. In a 1982 *Ensign* article, Dean L. Larsen, a member of the Church's Presidency of the Seventy, cautioned men to proceed very carefully when in disagreement with their wives:

> In the Lord's system of government, every organizational unit must have a presiding officer. He has decreed that in the family organization the father assumes this role…the wife acts as a loving, knowledgeable counselor, helpmate, and partner.…The husband must assume the role of leadership and see his wife as a knowledgeable counselor and partner in decision-making.…If, ultimately, a husband must propose a course of action in the absence of complete agreement, he must sense the great responsibility in taking this role and should do so with great care.[13]

Once again, Larsen attributed male headship to the need for order, but he was careful to emphasize the need for constructive dialogue and conversation between husband and wife. His statement that the wife acts as both "counselor" and "partner" in decision making even as the husband assumes the role of leader straddled traditional patriarchal and emerging egalitarian discourses about marital dynamics.

Within a few short years, Mormon rhetoric on power dynamics within the home shifted noticeably toward an emphasis on equal partnership in decision making. In 1988, a column in the *Ensign* magazine called "I have a Question" featured a conversation on how men are to preside in their homes.

---

12. Barbara B. Smith, "A Conversation with Sister Barbara B. Smith, Relief Society General President," *Ensign*, March 1976.

13. Dean L. Larsen, "Marriage and the Patriarchal Order," *Ensign*, September 1982.

Rather than conferring ultimate authority to the male priesthood holder, Dennis Lythgoe, whom the article quotes, stated:

> Yet the family needs someone to preside, and the Lord has designated the father to fulfill that role.... Having one person designated as the presiding officer suggests order—not superiority. All important deliberations and decisions within the family should involve the husband and the wife equally.... Insistence on the decision-making right is undesirable for either the man or the woman. The couple should discuss their differences, candidly consider the pros and cons, then make a decision both can live with.[14]

Lythgoe clung to the rhetoric of male presiding, yet he effectively defanged the concept. No longer did it involve male ultimate decision making, or men acting as bishops in their homes, which he designated as "undesirable." Rather, he emphasized dialogue until both are in agreement. We see here the rhetoric of male headship coupled with the practice of egalitarian decision making and partnership most Mormon leaders would take in the years to come.

Notably, Lythgoe also delineated what presiding would increasingly come to mean in the following decades: male participation and leadership in religious training and rituals within the family. Lythgoe explained that men preside in their families by overseeing Family Home Evening, calling on family members to say prayers, giving blessings, and performing priesthood ordinances. *Family Guidebook*, a small booklet first published by the church in 1992 and most recently reissued in 2006, echoed Lythgoe's explanation of how exactly a man is to preside when he is also an equal partner, though it also added a few more duties: providing the necessities of life, planning family outings, and overseeing family history and scripture study.[15] In the whole guidebook, mothers were specifically (not in conjunction with fathers) mentioned four times. This contrasts to fathers who were specifically mentioned (not in conjunction with mothers) at least forty times. Throughout, however, the pamphlet contains a handful of references to equal partnership between husbands and wives. This overwhelming emphasis on male duties in the home indicated a strong push from church authorities to encourage male participation within the family. That this male participation so often took the form of leadership indicated that church leaders saw male leadership as the most effective way to urge fathers to interact with children and participate in

---

14. "I Have a Question," *Ensign*, April 1988.

15. *Family Guidebook* (Salt Lake City: Church of Jesus Christ of Latter-day Saints, 2006).

family rituals and programs. Not only did it discourage men from neglecting family duties and childrearing, but it also gave men specific (and relatively benign) ideas about how exactly to assume presiding leadership in a family. Thus it headed off potentially coercive, abusive, or domineering behaviors that harshly patriarchal cultures might consider acceptable.

In a 1989 *Ensign* article, H. Burke Peterson of the Presiding Bishopric emphasized this new stance that male familial presiding does not mean male decree making. In doing so he articulated the strategy church leaders would increasingly take in shifting the male presiding discourse away from decision making. He stated, "In the order of heaven, the husband has the authority to preside in the home.... The relationship of a man and a woman should be one of partnership. A husband should not make decrees. Rather, he should work with his wife until a joint decision palatable to both is developed."[16] Burke retained the language of male presiding, but firmly shifted the meaning of the term away from ultimate decision making.

The 1990s saw the dual discourses of both equal partnership and male presiding virtually canonized in "The Family: A Proclamation to the World." Since this proclamation was addressed to the world, male presiding in this document was not associated with priesthood holding. Rather, it was located in "divine design," hearkening back to that notion of male headship being linked to order which Widtsoe emphasized in the early part of the century. With its emphasis on eternal gender, the Proclamation also indicated the church staking a position in the culture wars and debates over gender essentialism. By the end of the 1990s, the rhetoric of equal partnership coupled with male presiding was widely and enthusiastically embraced by church leaders. Apostle Boyd K. Packer's 1998 statement about marital power dynamics was emblematic of this now fully emerged discourse: "In the home it is a partnership with husband and wife equally yoked together, sharing in decisions, always working together. While the husband, the father, has responsibility to provide worthy and inspired leadership, his wife is neither behind him nor ahead of him but at his side."[17] Packer firmly uncoupled presiding from decision making, emphasizing instead equal partnership.

A recent contribution to the discussion of male presiding emerged in the June 2012 *Ensign*. The article, given a prominent place on the front cover of the magazine, had an interesting structure in which author Randy Keyes used principles he learned from priesthood councils to inform how couples should counsel together in the home. In this way, he rhetorically linked his ideas not

---

16. H. Burke Peterson, "Unrighteous Dominion," *Ensign*, July 1989.

17. Boyd K. Packer, "The Relief Society," *Ensign*, May 1998.

only to principles that church leaders have espoused in recent decades about marriage, but also to the very structure of the priesthood-led church. He wrote, "The husband's patriarchal duty as one who presides in the home is not to rule over others but to ensure that the marriage and the family prosper.... The husband is accountable for growth and happiness in his marriage, but this accountability does not give him authority over his wife. Both are in charge of the marriage."[18] Keyes effectively neutered male presiding in this definition. He kept the rhetoric of male headship, and even strengthened it with his use of the term "patriarchal," but then defanged it in practice. To preside and live up to a man's patriarchal duty means to ensure that his wife and family are happy. Absent were the usual explanations that presiding means leadership in family religious rituals and training.

While the concept of Mormon male headship has evolved away from decision making in the last several decades, several themes recurred in Church leaders' explanations of this concept. First, in many of these statements, a profound respect for organization and order emerged. Men must preside because chaos would result without a clear family head. Secondly, priesthood was often correlated with men presiding in the home, though the Proclamation indicated that priesthood is not the sole justification for male headship. Third, presiding in recent years has come to be increasingly associated with religious training, religious officiating, and general male participation in the home. This new concept of presiding retained traditional verbiage but shifted the practice away from decision making; in effect, it limited the realm of male authority in the home as it simultaneously opened up new conceptual space for leaders to encourage men to become intimately involved with their families. The shift in meaning of the preside concept also allowed leaders to introduce a simultaneous discourse of marital equal partnership.

Maintaining Plausibility: The Shift Toward an Inspired Eve

Mormon leaders' discourse on marriage illustrates their evolving understanding of the scope and content of male headship. Interestingly, Mormon leaders' discourse on Eve reflects a similar shift. In the twentieth century, reconceptualizations of the role, status, and purpose of Eve became a central theological vehicle for disseminating and reflecting new understandings of marital partnership. By appealing to the figure of Eve, church leaders added scriptural credibility to their evolving conceptions of gender roles and there-

---

18. Randy Keyes, "Counseling Together in Marriage," *Ensign*, June 2012.

fore worked to maintain the plausibility of their shifting pronouncements about male headship.

Although the change in Mormon leaders' conceptions of familial male headship is clear, the cause of it is less clear. Social scientists have connected shifts in gender roles within religious organizations to shifts in gender roles in the larger host society. Laurence Iannaccone and Carrie Miles analyzed articles from the *Ensign* magazine from the 1950s to 1985 and found that the LDS Church, though initially resistant, ultimately accommodated social change in women's roles.[19] They note that successful churches "must engage in a continuing balancing act, trading off between religious traditions and social norms."[20] Armand Mauss developed the similar idea that new religious movements prosper when they maintain a balance between assimilation to the larger society and separateness from it.[21] According to this theory, for the LDS Church to grow and prosper it must constantly renegotiate its relationship with larger social trends, including changing views of gender norms. This line of thought posits external forces as the primary cause for the change in Mormon rhetoric about gender roles, but it does not address how these shifts in rhetoric and definitions are accommodated internally within the church. For the church to maintain viability with its adherents, it must maintain the plausibility of its claims. But how is plausibility maintained if church leaders' definitions and gender role prescriptions change—sometimes rapidly, as we saw in the decade of the 1980s?

I argue that the church's ability to maintain plausibility is due in part to church leaders' reconceptualizations of the status and role of Eve that emerged throughout the twentieth century. Others have discussed the gradual shift in the Mormon conception of the Fall, from it being a necessary sin, to transgression, to benevolent choice. Accompanying the changing conceptions of the Fall were the changing conceptions of Eve, who went from cursed woman to excused actor to inspired equal partner.[22] Church leaders' conceptualizations of Eve are inextricably interconnected with how they conceptualize women, gender roles, and marital power dynamics. As church leaders increasingly

---

19. Iannaccone and Miles, "Dealing with Social Change," 1246.

20. Ibid., 1247.

21. Armand Mauss, *The Angel and the Beehive: The Mormon Struggle with Assimilation* (Urbana: University of Illinois Press, 1994), 5.

22. See Jolene Edmunds Rockwood, "The Redemption of Eve," in Maureen Ursenbach Beecher and Lavina Fielding Anderson, eds., *Sisters in Spirit: Mormon Women in Historical and Cultural Perspective* (Chicago: University of Illinois Press, 1987), 3–36; Boyd Jay Petersen, "'Redeemed from the Curse Placed Upon Her': Dialogic Discourse on Eve in the *Woman's Exponent*," *Journal of Mormon History* 40 (Winter 2014): 135–174. See also Beverly Campbell, *Eve and the Choice Made in Eden* (Salt Lake City: Bookcraft, 2003).

promoted Eve as noble, courageous, and inspired equal partner propelling humankind on its journey toward divinity, they created theological space for justifications for equal partnership marriages, even as they maintained past structures of (a progressively softening) male headship. Thus church leaders' discourse on Eve reflected new understandings of marital partnership as it simultaneously maintained its male headship ideology.

While notions of godly order and priesthood have certainly influenced Mormon conceptions of proper gender hierarchy, women's status and marital power dynamics have also been connected to the status of Eve since the beginnings of Mormonism. This link between Eve and women's status is cemented in Mormonism's temple endowment ceremony, which takes the participants through the Eden story. In this ceremony, Adam and Eve are archetypes for every man and woman. The women embody Eve and make covenants that pertain to Adam and Eve's pre- and post-Fall experience. One of the women's covenants specifically pertains to the "curse" laid upon her after she eats the fruit—that her husband rules over her. Consequently, Mormon women as they embody Eve in temples today covenant to hearken unto their husbands' counsel as their husbands hearken unto God.[23]

Given this ritual association of women's status with Eve that persists even today, it makes sense that early Mormon leaders tended to evoke Eve's subordination to justify female subordination in the home. For example, nineteenth-century apostle and polygamist George Q. Cannon explicitly connected Eve's curse to women's subordination, though he claimed that polygamy could redeem women from the curse that her desire should be to her husband.[24]

Two generations later, J. Rueben Clark also appealed to the example of Eve to discuss women's role and status. He saw Eve as the perfect and noble model of women's purpose in this life, to become mothers of spirits waiting for bodies:

> Eve came to build, to organize, through the power of the Father, the bodies of mortal men....This was her calling; this was her blessing, bestowed by the Priesthood. This is the place of our wives and of our mothers in the Eternal Plan. They are not the bearers of the Priesthood....They are builders and organizers under its power...pos-

---

23. For a brief discussion of this covenant, see David John Buerger, *The Mysteries of Godliness: A History of Mormon Temple Worship* (San Francisco: Smith Research Associates, 1994), 178.

24. George Q. Cannon, "Celestial Marriage," October 9, 1869, *Journal of Discourses* 13: 206–207.

sessing a function as divinely called, as eternally important in its place as Priesthood itself.[25]

Clark's rhetoric on Eve and womankind is positive but circumscribed; he saw Eve's purpose as reproductive, and he consequently saw women's purpose in the same light. These reproductive duties, as noble as they are, were conceptualized as "under its [Priesthood] power," which he associated with Adam and males throughout. In this way, he alluded to female subordination, but chose to focus instead on women's distinct gender role as mothers.

As the women's movement arose in the early 1970s, church leaders gave renewed attention to marital gender roles, once again justifying positions by evoking Adam and Eve. In 1976, LDS Church President Spencer W. Kimball de-emphasized stark male dominance in marriage:

> As He [God] concludes this statement [to Eve] he says, "and thy desire shall be to thy husband, and he shall rule over thee." (Gen. 3:16.) I have a question about the word rule. It gives the wrong impression. I would prefer to use the word preside because that's what he does. A righteous husband presides over his wife and family.

While Kimball here explicitly defined the male role as presider, at other points in his talk he anticipated more egalitarian rhetoric when he repeatedly referred to the marriage relationship as a "partnership." He also viewed "our beloved Mother Eve" as inspired for finding joy in the children she would have and for her willingness to take on the problems of mortality. From this point on, rhetoric on gender hierarchy within marriage would overwhelmingly invoke the softer, more malleable concept of "man presiding," while rhetoric of "man ruling over" began to be abandoned.[26]

In a 2007 *Ensign* article, General Authority Bruce Hafen held up Eve as Adam's equal partner, as he distanced Mormonism from other Christian traditions that blame Eve and punish women with subordination:

> The incorrect idea in Christian history that wives should be dependent began with the false premise that the Fall of Adam and Eve was a tragic mistake and that Eve was the primary culprit. Thus women's traditional submission to men was considered a fair punishment for Eve's sin.

25. J. Rueben Clark, "Our Wives and Our Mothers in the Eternal Plan," *The Relief Society Magazine*, December 1946, 800–801.

26. Spencer W. Kimball, "The Blessings and Responsibilities of Womanhood," *Ensign*, March 1976.

Thankfully, the Restoration clarifies Eve's—and Adam's—choice as essential to the eternal progression of God's children. We honor rather than condemn what they did, and we see Adam and Eve as equal partners.[27]

Here Hafen boldly emphasized equal partnership discourse at the expense of preside/rule-over discourse, even going so far as to interpret "help meet to Adam" as "help equal to Adam." This rhetorical move echoed President Howard W. Hunter, who stated in 1994, "The Lord intended that the wife be a helpmeet for man (meet means equal)—that is, a companion equal and necessary in full partnership."[28] Hafen attempted to fit the Genesis "rule over" pronouncement into his equal partnership framework by first reinterpreting the word rule and secondly changing the pronoun "over" to "with":

Genesis 3:16 states that Adam is to "rule over" Eve, but this doesn't make Adam a dictator. A *ruler* can be a measuring tool that sets standards. Then Adam would live so that others may measure the rightness of their conduct by watching his. Being a ruler is not so much a privilege of power as an obligation to practice what a man preaches. Also, *over* in "rule over" uses the Hebrew *bet*, which means ruling *with*, not ruling *over*. If a man does exercise "dominion…in *any degree* of unrighteousness" (D&C 121:37; emphasis added), God terminates that man's authority.[29]

Male presiding ideology only fit into Hafen's argument because he connected it with male priesthood, which he saw as a necessary counterbalance to women's "innate spiritual instincts." With women's spirituality balancing out men's priesthood, he advocated both men and women acting interdependently and counseling reciprocally with each other. Given the reality of LDS doctrine on male presiding, which is near-canonized in the Proclamation and ritualized in the temple endowment ceremony, Hafen went just about as far as he could in shifting the discourse toward an equal partnership focus.

This brief overview demonstrates how Eve and the curse have been interpreted in different times to inform Mormon gender role ideologies. As contemporary Mormon leaders increasingly viewed Eve as noble and inspired, they chose to use the Eden story to de-emphasize women's submission and

---

27. Bruce C. Hafen, "Crossing Thresholds and Becoming Equal Partners," *Ensign*, August 2007.

28. Howard W. Hunter, "Being a Righteous Husband and Father," *Ensign*, November 1994.

29. Hafen, "Crossing Thresholds and Becoming Equal Partners."

emphasize instead equal partnership. In doing so, they created theological space to employ the newer discourse on marital power dynamics—that of equal partnership, even as they retained the existing but softened patriarchal preside rhetoric. In this way, during decades of major reconceptualizations of power dynamics within marriage, shifts in rhetoric and understanding of male headship were accommodated internally. If Eve was a noble equal partner (if still presided over by her husband), then women were too. Aided by these theological reconceptualizations of Eve, Mormon leaders attempted to maintain the plausibility of their church's shifting claims on gender roles.

Mormon Feminist Participation in Male Headship Discourse

Church leaders' rhetoric on male headship has softened distinctly over the last forty years, at once becoming redefined to mean positive male participation in the home and also mediated by equal partnership language. Increasingly positive pronouncements by church leaders about Eve and thus womankind reflected the changing discourse about marital power dynamics and helped church leaders maintain the plausibility of their claims as their understandings of male presiding shifted. If we accept the social scientific claim that the church must continually adapt to society's changing conception of gender roles in order to maintain an optimal balance between assimilation and separation, it is reasonable to assume that future adaptations might occur in Mormon rhetoric on these issues. Church leaders do not speculate publically about this. However, there is a flourishing of Mormon feminist thought that does speculate, innovate, and critique current Mormon gender role constructions. Examining Mormon feminist participation in this discourse illuminates weaknesses of current Mormon gender role constructions and suggests new possibilities toward framing a more egalitarian ideology.

I have thus far examined church leaders' changing understandings of male headship, yet Mormon discourse is far broader than official pronouncements from church hierarchy. For decades there has been a lively subculture of intellectual and feminist Mormons writing outside of church-sponsored forums. In recent years, Mormon feminists have engaged in spirited conversations, often on blogs, about the dual discourse of male headship and equal partnership. While all these Mormon feminists work to make space for greater egalitarianism within a Mormon framework, their reflections on the topic span the ideological spectrum. On the more conservative end is political scientist Valerie Hudson, who embraces male presiding and equal partnership rhetoric even as she works to balance out power differentials. Like so many other Mormons, Hudson turned to the Eden story to inform her vision of proper gender purpose and roles, interpreting Eve as opening and presiding over the gate to life (represented by the tree of knowledge of good and evil), while Adam opens and presides over the gate to salvation (represented by the tree of life) through his exercising of priesthood ordinances.[30] In an attempt to make reciprocal men and women's obedience obligations, Hudson suggested that men hearken unto their wives in their stewardship of life, just as women hearken unto their husbands in their stewardship of religious ordinances and training. She therefore created a parallel between the separate stewardships, with both partners hearkening unto one another. "We would be remiss if we did not see that there were two hearkenings, two gifts given, two gifts received," she stated. With this balanced parallel, she has room to insist that the LDS Church promotes absolute equality between men and women in marriage and that gender equality is an essential ideal for Mormons. She explained, "Relationships of gender equality are the bricks of Zion, without which you cannot build Zion, because gender equality is how Heavenly Mother and Heavenly Father live."[31]

Of particular interest is the way Hudson worked to limit the realm of men's presiding authority in marriage to male leadership in religious ordinances and training. In doing so, she bravely tackled the fraught hearken temple covenant, asserting that it is not her spiritual obligation to hearken to her husband in any realm other than in his exercising of priesthood ordinances within the family.[32] Ultimately, Hudson's complementarian exegesis of the Adam and Eve story plays into the common Mormon "motherhood/priesthood" corollary, though she innovatively raised up motherhood as a stewardship that men must hearken unto. Also, her absolute insistence on the importance of gender equality and her mention of Heavenly Mother throughout demarcates this scriptural reading as a feminist Mormon project.

While raising up women's presiding stewardship and restricting the male one, Hudson's reading of Adam and Eve and of men's and women's distinct purposes and roles falls somewhat flat for Mormon feminists on the other end of the ideological spectrum, who roundly reject the motherhood/priesthood

---

30. Valerie Hudson, "The Two Trees," *FairMormon*, www.fairlds.org/fair-conferences/2010-fair-conference/2010-the-two-trees.

31. Ibid.

32. Ibid.

corollary.[33] These feminists insist that the true corollary to motherhood is fatherhood, and that the motherhood/priesthood parallel leaves childless women questioning their purpose in life.[34] These more critical feminists point out the contradictions of adopting the equal partnership discourse while simultaneously clinging to a rhetoric and practice of male headship. Kiskilili, a blogger on *Zelophehad's Daughters*, described the church's current stance as "Chicken Patriarchy" and called the church out for the contradictions inherent in its discourse:

> Chicken Patriarchy never allows itself to be pinned down to a single perspective; chameleonlike, it alters its attitude from day to day and sometimes even from sentence to sentence, too chicken to stand up for what it believes. By refusing to settle down in any one place on the map, Chicken Patriarchs can embrace egalitarianism and still continue to uphold time-honored traditions of male authority.[35]

For the church to insist on men and women's equality at the same time it embraces patriarchal structures, language, and ritual is, according to Kiskilili, an attempt to obscure the real power differential between Mormon men and women. This is a danger to Mormon feminists like Kiskilili, who finds nothing salvageable or honorable in the current practice of utilizing both discourses.

Other Mormon feminists are more hopeful about the rise of egalitarian discourse, even if it is still accompanied by patriarchal language. Elsewhere I point out that a gradual shifting of emphases is how change comes about in the LDS Church, and that this newer focus on egalitarian principles might be signaling the possibility for a permanent shifting away from patriarchal family dynamics.[36] While this slow transition toward egalitarian discourse might not satisfy some Mormon feminists, it does indicate the possibility of a gradual trajectory away from male headship discourse within the family, if not the

---

33. Sonja Farnsworth, "Mormonism's Odd Couple: The Motherhood-Priesthood Connection," in Maxine Hanks, ed., *Women and Authority: Re-emerging Mormon Feminism,* (Salt Lake City: Signature Books, 1992), 299–314.

34. Lynnette made these points and more in her thorough critique of Hudson's "Two Trees." Lynnette, "A Critique of 'The Two Trees,'" *Zelophehad's Daughters* blog, November 1, 2011, http://zelophehadsdaughters.com/2011/11/01/the-two-trees/.

35. Kiskilili, "The Trouble with Chicken Patriarchy," *Zelophehad's Daughters* blog, November 30, 2007, http://zelophehadsdaughters.com/2007/11/30/the-trouble-with-chicken-patriarchy/.

36. Caroline Kline, "Chicken Patriarchy," *Feminism and Religion* blog, January 16, 2012, http://feminismandreligion.com/2012/01/16/chicken-patriarchy-by-caroline-kline/.

ecclesiastical structure. When language and conceptions shift, changes in practice and structures become more feasible.

In many Mormon feminist circles, however, the dual discourse has been roundly rejected as disingenuous. One writer articulated the impossibility of having men both preside and act as equal partners: "If one class of people always presides and the other class never has the opportunity to do so, there is an inherent and undeniable inequality in that system."[37] She also articulated a vision of where Mormon discourse on gender must go in the future, if the church truly does want to foster relationships of equal partnership:

> The only way...to truly foster the kind of equal partnership the church allegedly endorses, is to jettison all discussion of patriarchy and of roles universally delineated along the lines of sex. We cannot prescribe as universally applicable men's role as provider/protector and women's role as nurturer if we genuinely want to foster equality between men and women inside of marriage.[38]

This statement exemplifies a common trend in Mormon feminist circles: to advocate and embody a fluid approach to gender roles, based on individual inclination and circumstance. Given this flexible approach to gender roles, many of these more critical Mormon feminists are wary of gender complementarianism—the theological view upheld by most Mormons that men and women have different but complementary roles in the home and society. They see complementarian ideas being used to box men and women into universally applicable gender identities and roles. Many of these Mormon feminists would agree with Christian feminist theologian Rosemary Radford Ruether, who stated, "Whatever nuances of difference in style may exist through biology and socialization, men and women each possess the full range of all human capacities."[39] In other words, many of these Mormon feminists would not deny that there may be differences between women and men, but they

---

37. Amelia, "On the Sexist Nature of Benevolent Patriarchy," *The Exponent* blog, August 21, 2011, www.the-exponent.com/on-the-sexist-nature-of-benevolent-patriarchy-2. One should note, however, that there have been recent isolated efforts by church leaders to include women in some sort of presiding role within the family. L. Tom Perry said in 2004, "There is not a president and vice president in a family. We have co-presidents working together eternally for the good of their family." L. Tom Perry, "Fatherhood—An Eternal Calling," Church News, April 10, 2004, 15. Such language including women in a presiding role within the family remains very rare.

38. Amelia, "On the Sexist Nature of Benevolent Patriarchy."

39. Rosemary Radford Ruether, "Reimagining Families," excerpt in Samuel Wells, ed., *Christian Ethics: An Introductory Reader* (Malden, MA: Blackwell Publishing Ltd., 2010), 253.

would deny that such differences should determine every man and every woman's role in the home and in the community. They do not object to individual men and women choosing to inhabit different roles in their individual families, but they do strongly oppose the prescriptive nature of universally applicable and externally enforced gender roles.

Taylor Petrey expanded the progressive and feminist conversation on Mormon gender role conceptions by examining the ways this discourse is employed to lift up heteronormativity and deny the legitimacy of same-sex relationships. After quoting the lines from the Family Proclamation about men presiding and women nurturing, he wrote, "This notion of 'gender' as roles operates as a critique of homosexual relationships because at least one 'confused' partner fails to conform to his or her 'proper' gendered identity as masculine or feminine....This view may be used to object to homosexual relationships because such relationships may include one or both same-sex parents as subverting the role assigned to their 'gender.'"[40] Petrey noted that the Proclamation does go on to minimize differences between the sexes through its mention of equal partnership, but he argued that ultimately the prescription for men to preside serves to delegitimize same-sex relationships: "The retention of earlier language about 'presiding' along side more modern emphasis on 'equal partnership' reveals the necessity of hierarchical views of males and females in marriage as a necessary aspect of marking same-sex relationships as illegitimate."[41] Previous feminist critiques of marital Mormon gender role prescriptions primarily focused on the way these prescriptions constricted and suppressed heterosexual women, but Petrey's work importantly illuminates the way that hierarchical gender role prescriptions, even when accompanied by egalitarian phrasing, marginalize a whole other group of people who do not fit the heteronormative and gender role-laden paradigm outlined in the Proclamation.

The link between gender roles and the Eden story in past and current official rhetoric suggests another possible dimension of future change. For most of the twentieth century, women in the temple covenanted to "obey" their husbands. Reflecting the changing rhetorical trends away from stark male dominance, in 1990 the language of this covenant was changed to having women covenant to "hearken" unto their husbands in righteousness.[42] These

---

40. Taylor G. Petrey, "Toward a Post-Heterosexual Mormon Theology," *Dialogue: A Journal of Mormon Thought* 44 (Winter 2011): 125.

41. Ibid., 126.

42. Buerger, *Mysteries of Godliness*, 170. No official explanation was given for the altered language.

liturgical changes retained the concept of male headship, but softened it. Given the current rhetorical movement toward emphasizing equal partnership, it is possible that continued external and internal forces might lead to further changes in this covenant, as it becomes increasingly dissonant for Mormon women to engage in ritual submission to their husbands. For example, having the women covenant to hearken *with* rather than *to* their husbands would, with the change of one preposition, be a change toward a more consistent message about equal partnership. Such an alteration could pave the way for further shifts away from male familial headship ideology, perhaps ultimately resulting in a ritual change which removes gendered covenants altogether. Such changes would be welcomed by many Mormon feminists.

Mormon feminists present different visions for the future of male headship ideology. On one end, there is a movement toward creating more balance in power between husbands and wives, as each hearken to the other and preside over the other in their separate stewardships. On the other end are feminists who reject the dual discourse, advocate a complete end to male headship and universally prescribed gender roles, and envision space for same-sex relationships within a Mormon religious framework. Somewhere between the two are feminists who are optimistic that the rise in egalitarian discourse might slowly lead to a further de-emphasis of male headship and perhaps even future changes in temple liturgy. Although different in approach and vision, these Mormon feminist reflections are all evidence that there is a segment of Mormons who desire a discourse on marriage that better fits the new egalitarian behavior patterns and ideals espoused by church leaders. Practical egalitarianism coupled with largely theoretical or ceremonial male presiding is ultimately unsatisfying to many Mormon feminists.

Within the space of four decades Mormon conceptions of male presiding have been noticeably curtailed, with Mormon leaders ultimately rejecting male familial decision making in favor of productive dialogue and compromise. Simultaneously, church leaders' increasingly enthusiastic embrace of Eve as a wise and noble archetype for Mormon women reflected and added theological credibility to new ideas about women as equal partners in marriage. Not fully satisfied with church leaders' coupling of male headship and egalitarian rhetoric, Mormon feminists have actively participated in discourse regarding Mormon gender roles, offering various strategies and reimaginings to deal with this tension.

While the rhetorical trend toward embracing women as equal partners has no doubt contributed toward altering power dynamics within contemporary Mormon marriages, one of the most significant outcomes of the rhetorical shifts of the last several decades may be the increase of male participation in the home. This new understanding of male headship—that of proactive, helpful male participation and child nurturing in the home—blurs gender roles that had been established in traditionalist marriages from previous generations. No longer are men's most important roles in life that of breadwinner and server in the church. Now presiding in the home through nurturing children, overseeing religious training, and strengthening marriages is equally (if not more) important and stressed by church leaders. This experience of active nurturing fatherhood, combined with the socioeconomic reality of more families reliant on two incomes, may in turn be a significant shaper of future trends, as a new generation of Mormon men increasingly participates in a lived theology closer to equal partnership.

11

Blogging the Boundaries

MORMON MOMMY BLOGS AND THE
CONSTRUCTION OF MORMON IDENTITY

Kristine Haglund

AN ANTHROPOLOGIST TRYING to make sense of Mormonism from media coverage during the "Mormon Moment" inaugurated by Mitt Romney's 2012 presidential campaign might have concluded that most Mormon women were feminists. A perfunctory sampling of headlines yields dozens of articles with titles like "Mormon Feminists' Roaring Comeback,"[1] "The Rise of Mormon Feminist Bloggers,"[2] "Mormon Feminists Don't Like Romney,"[3] and "Mormon Feminists? Yes, They Exist, and They're for Obama."[4] The story of feisty descendants of polygamist pioneers standing up to patriarchal oppression seemed irresistible to journalists who wanted to give more dimension to an American faith that is both familiar and exotic—embodied by the square-jawed, perfectly handsome Mitt Romney, whose perfect Americanness made him seem somehow alien. Mormon feminists standing up to patriarchy revived the familiar 1960s narrative of resistance to The Man.

It is possible to read Mormon women's history as a tale of oppression and subservience, punctuated here and there by heroic bursts of feminist progress. At the same time, historians have frequently read Mormon women's publications as proto-feminist loci of self-expression, and official resistance to or co-opting of these publications as a sort of backlash against women's

---

1. Taylor Petrey, "Mormon Feminists Roaring Comeback," *Real Clear Religion*, January 9, 2013, www.realclearreligion.org/2013/01/09/mormon_feminists_roaring_comeback_251934.html.

2. Frieda Klotz, "The Rise of Mormon Feminist Bloggers," *The Guardian*, March 19, 2012, www.theguardian.com/lifeandstyle/2012/mar/19/rise-of-mormon-feminist-bloggers.

3. Erika Eichelberger, "Mormon Feminists Don't Like Romney," *Mother Jones*, October 19, 2012, www.motherjones.com/mojo/2012/10/mormon-feminists-romney-women.

4. Peter Henderson, "Mormon Feminists? Yes They Exist, and They're for Obama," *Chicago Tribune*, October 18, 2012, http://articles.chicagotribune.com/2012-10-18/news/sns-rt-us-usa-campaign-mormonwomenbre89i052-20121018_1_mormon-feminists-exponent-ii-mitt-romney.

assertion of independence from patriarchal control.[5] But the story has always been more complicated than that. Mormon women were ardent suffragists *and* defenders of polygamy; they were cheerful, creative homemakers *and* defenders of women's right to paid employment and nondiscrimination; they were reluctant to give up their magazine publishing *and* eager to contribute to the work of the LDS Church's expansion by supporting correlation; they were both supporters *and* opponents of the ERA. Whether progressive or more conservative voices, Latter-day Saint women have been believers in and practitioners of a patriarchal religion. The independence that contemporary scholars have celebrated in these publications was very rarely a protest against patriarchy in principle, even when it was a site of resistance to particular elements of the culture underwritten by patriarchal Mormonism.

Similarly, the burgeoning narrative of a resurgent Mormon feminism via social media misses the concurrent development of conservative voices among Mormon women and the proliferation of explicitly anti-feminist writings and Internet groups. Mormon women's blogs, completely independent of centralized control, now clearly demonstrate the ideological diversity that has always characterized Mormon women's personal writings, and they ought to complicate our narratives of Mormon women's agency. As Saba Mahmood has poignantly demonstrated in her work on women in the Muslim piety movement, "agentival capacity is entailed not only in those acts which resist norms, but also in the many ways one *inhabits* norms."[6] Mormon women who have inhabited Mormon norms, rather than resisting them, have too often been perceived and portrayed as one-dimensional props in a patriarchal order, while women who have, in one way or another, resisted this order have been taken as worthy subjects of scholarly work.

Privileging the work of recognizably "feminist" Mormon women as actors, in opposition to traditionalist Mormon women who are presumed to be passive objects of patriarchal control, reproduces the marginalization of their voices. We ought to take note of the ways in which even women who might self-identify as feminists also defend Mormonism, and we certainly need to examine the cultural production of Mormon women who either do not identify as feminists or who express explicitly anti-feminist views. The brief but already complex history of Mormon women's participation in online publishing and social media illuminates women's roles in Mormonism's negotiation with

---

5. See Maxine Hanks, *Women and Authority: Re-Emerging Mormon Feminism* (Salt Lake City: Signature Books, 1992) and Claudia L. Bushman, *Mormon Sisters: Women in Early Utah* (Logan: Utah State University Press, 1997).

6. Saba Mahmood, *The Politics of Piety: The Islamic Revival and the Feminist Subject* (Princeton, NJ: Princeton University Press, 2012).

modernity, and exposes ideological divisions that have, in the past, been muted by shared participation in religious rituals and a strong sense of community in lived Mormonism. In this essay, I trace the development of nonsponsored, uncorrelated sites of expression for women who consider themselves "mainstream," "orthodox," or "conservative"[7]—that is, women who want, above all, to demonstrate their obedience and submission to patriarchal dictates through their independent writing and publishing—from performing a stereotypical conception of Mormon femininity, to applying Mormon cultural and doctrinal concepts to contemporary political issues, and even articulating innovative interpretations of Mormon doctrine.

The Rise and Fall of LDS Women's Publishing

Mormon women's publishing began early in the life of the LDS Church. Several early Mormon women leaders—notably Eliza R. Snow, who had published poetry beginning at the age of fourteen, as well as Emmeline Wells, Louisa Greene Richards, and others—had literary ambitions. The frontier territory in which the Saints settled was also a wide-open cultural frontier, where fledgling musical groups, dramatic productions, and literary and political publishing enterprises flourished in the rich soil of a religion determined to "seek wisdom from the best books" and gather all truth from whatever source. Early Mormon women's publications embodied this adventuresome truth-seeking ethos with spiritual exhortation, political agitation, literary endeavors, and practical household tips sharing space in the pages of the *Woman's Exponent*, the *Young Women's Journal*, and various curricular materials circulated for the LDS Church's organizations for women (Relief Society), teenage girls (Young Women's), and children (Primary). Eventually, the more polished *Relief Society Magazine* took the place of these first publishing endeavors, and more official oversight from the general presidencies of these auxiliaries narrowed the range of content somewhat. Still, for the first two-thirds of the twentieth century, multiple perspectives and distinctive voices coexisted comfortably between the covers of the magazine.

---

7. I have generally used the term "orthodox" in this article, although I recognize that it is far from a perfect shorthand. "Conservative" carries too much political freight, and "mainstream" involves a normative judgment about the parameters of Mormonism that I am neither able nor willing to make. By orthodox, I want to suggest women who both participate in the practices of Mormonism and also assert a wish to think and believe what the leaders of the Church tell them to believe. The women I am here calling orthodox are resistant to arguments made by feminist or progressive (again, imperfect shorthand!) Mormons that practicing Mormons are allowed a wider latitude of belief and some degree of disagreement with Church hierarchs over political or theological issues.

Church-sponsored organizations like Sunday School, the youth auxiliaries, and the Relief Society had been organized somewhat spontaneously, and all of them had published their own curricula, newspapers, and other materials without much direction or coordination with the governing bodies of the church. By the first decade of the twentieth century, there was an impressive amount of publishing going on in Salt Lake City: the *Young Women's Journal*, the *Improvement Era*, the *Juvenile Instructor*, the *Woman's Exponent*, the *Children's Friend*, and the *Elder's Journal* were all being published at least monthly. Except for the *Elder's Journal*, all of these publications were vehicles for women's writing and editorial expression. Although they were given tacit approval as official organs of the church, there was little supervision of their content or production. By midcentury, LDS Church leaders had become concerned with the cost and inefficiency of these multitudinous publication efforts, as well as with the sprawling curriculum production of the various auxiliaries. The bureaucratic initiative of the 1960s and 1970s that came to be known simply as "correlation" aimed to streamline the content, tone, and perspective of all LDS Church publications.

While this centralized control of messaging served an expanding worldwide church well, committee work tended to blunt individual expression, and an unintended side effect was the marginalization of women's distinct voices.[8] The relative independence of the women's, children's, and youth auxiliary organizations had provided important opportunities for women to direct their own activity and expression, even in a patriarchally organized Church. As the centralized patriarchal governance became more bureaucratically entrenched by correlation, women's activities became subject to more review and control by (male) priesthood authority, and their publications were either subsumed into general church publications or came under the control of committees headed by men. The loss of the *Relief Society Magazine* was especially keenly felt. In a letter to a friend, General Relief Society President Belle Spafford noted, "Everywhere I go the women seem to be grieving over the loss of the Magazine."[9]

Simultaneously with the official correlation movement, the church-owned publishing arm Deseret Book Company was consolidating its hold on Mormon-themed offerings for a small but growing number of book-buying Latter-day Saints. While there was no doctrinal mandate for Deseret Book's monopoly, church ownership granted an unofficial but powerfully perceived *nihil obstat* to its offerings. The (probably unintended) cultural

---

8. See Tina Hatch, "'Changing Times Bring Changing Conditions': Relief Society, 1960 to the Present," *Dialogue: A Journal of Mormon Thought* 37, no. 3 (2004): 65–98.

9. Ibid., 78.

effect of correlation was to powerfully inculcate among orthodox Mormons the notion that information and ideas ought to flow from a single, officially approved source.

Nonetheless, in the decade following the announcement of the correlation program, a few independent publications sought to recreate and expand the diversity of expression that had flourished in earlier decades. The quarterly *Dialogue: A Journal of Mormon Thought*, debuted in 1966; a magazine called *Sunstone* began publication in 1975. In 1974, a group of Mormon women in Cambridge, Massachusetts, inspired by their discovery of copies of the original Woman's Exponent in Harvard's Widener Library, began publishing a newspaper devoted to Mormon women's personal writing, called *Exponent II*. The paper's editors described it as "poised on the dual platforms of Mormonism and Feminism," and aimed to show "by [their] pages and [their] lives" that the two were not inconsistent.[10] However, by the time that *Exponent II* was launched, LDS Church members' increased reliance on officially approved content made independently published writing by Mormon women vaguely suspect, even without the further provocation of feminist subject matter. Fifteen years later, LDS apostle Dallin H. Oaks denounced "alternate voices" in a sermon at the church's general conference, formalizing official disapproval and laying the groundwork for the eventual excommunication of six prominent Mormon intellectuals, including several feminists, who had published in independent journals and magazines.[11] The message was clear: only officially church-published materials were safe for orthodox members. Subscriptions to all of the independent publications dropped precipitously, and the possibilities for Mormon women's self-expression in print narrowed almost to the vanishing point.

Performing Religious Commitment Online

The advent of online publishing platforms in the early years of the twenty-first century changed the landscape for Mormon women's publishing as dramatically as it did for the rest of the world of letters and journalism. Not surprisingly, given the history sketched above, the first women's voices to enter the wild new cyberterritory were those of women less constrained by the perceived strictures of orthodoxy. The first blog by Mormon women to gain significant

---

10. Claudia Bushman, "A Wider Sisterhood," *Dialogue: A Journal of Mormon Thought* 11, no. 1 (1978): 97.

11. Dallin H. Oaks, "Alternate Voices," April 1989, www.lds.org/general-conference/1989/04/alternate-voices?lang=eng.

readership and national attention was Feminist Mormon Housewives,[12] started by Lisa Butterworth in 2005 as a place for her to work through the conflicts with Mormon culture she experienced during her personal feminist awakening and to talk to other women who shared her frustrations.[13] *Exponent II* started its own blog in 2006 and began publishing the magazine online in 2007.

For all their popularity, however, these feminist sites represented only a fraction of Mormon women's participation in the blogosphere. Elsewhere, Mormon women were becoming important participants in the phenomenon of "Mommy blogging." A 2011 article in *Salon* pointed out the ubiquity of Mormon women in this part of the blogosphere:

> At first glance, Naomi and Stacie and Stephanie and Liz appear to be members of the species known as the "Hipster Mommy Blogger," though perhaps a bit more cheerful and wholesome than most. They have bangs like Zooey Deschanel and closets full of cool vintage dresses. Their houses look like Anthropologie catalogs. Their kids look like Baby Gap models. Their husbands look like young graphic designers, all cute lumberjack shirts and square-framed glasses. They spend their days doing fun craft projects [and] their weekends throwing big, whimsical dinner parties for their friends, all of whom have equally adorable kids and husbands.
>
> But as you page through their blog archives, you notice certain "tells." They're super-young (like, four-kids-at-29 young). They mention relatives in Utah. They drink a suspicious amount of hot chocolate. Finally, you see it: a subtly placed widget with a picture of a temple, or a hyperlink on the word "faith" or "belief." You click the link and up pops the official website of the Church of Jesus Christ of Latter-day Saints.[14]

Although this *Salon* writer did not recognize these mommy blogs as overtly religious, they were, in fact, thoroughly Mormon. The online performance of wholesome Mormon family living, while never explicitly anti-feminist, provided an implicit counterpoint to women questioning this model.

---

12. Debra Nussbaum Cohen, "Faithful Track Questions, Answers and Minutiae on Blogs," *New York Times*, March 5, 2005, www.nytimes.com/2005/03/05/national/05religion.html?_r=0; Peggy Fletcher Stack, "LDS Web Site Offers 'A Safe Place to Be Feminist and Faithful,'" *Salt Lake Tribune*, October 5, 2007, www.sltrib.com/lds/ci_7098023.

13. Emily W. Jensen, "Mormon Women Speak Online," *Deseret News*, November 10, 2010, www.deseretnews.com/article/705362483/Mormon-women-speak-online.html?pg=all.

14. Emily Matchar, "Why I Can't Stop Reading Mormon Housewife Blogs," *Salon*, January 15, 2011, www.salon.com/2011/01/15/feminist_obsessed_with_mormon_blogs.

While engaged in what might in other cases be understood as feminist activism—making the real lives of women visible and worthy of attention—some Mormon mommy bloggers might have seen their project as actively rejecting feminist goals.[15] Making their lives and their families' lives visible and public was an expression of their belief in the doctrine of a patriarchal church. Even those who were not explicitly anti-feminist were able to gain ready popularity among Mormon women because they celebrated women's activities in the domestic sphere, which Mormon culture has traditionally defined as women's proper domain.

In this uneasy and selective embrace of contemporary social mores, mommy bloggers were performing an important part in Mormonism's awkward dance with its host culture. Twentieth-century American Mormonism has generally embraced the technologies and economies of its host society. However, Mormon commitment to strictly gendered family roles has been an important boundary marker for Mormons in the decades since the second wave of American feminism. Unlike some Christians who are overtly and articulately resisting certain modalities of modernity in their gendered familial practices, Mormon women have had no strong doctrinal rationale for their choices. They are encouraged to be educated and, in most ways, to participate in contemporary economies and social structures. Contemporary Mormonism does not have a robust commitment to the notion of male headship—at least not within the family. Passages from the New Testament that are adduced in some Christian contexts to justify women's submissive roles are rarely cited in Mormon services (or on orthodox blogs).[16] The 1995 quasi-canonical statement of Mormon ideals about the family, titled "The Family: A Proclamation to the World," asserts that "by divine design, fathers are to preside over their families in love and righteousness and are responsible to provide the necessities of life and protection for their families. Mothers are primarily responsible for the nurture of their children." However, these prescriptive statements, already moderated by the insertion of "primarily," are immediately followed by the caveat, "In these sacred responsibilities, fathers and mothers are obligated to help one another as equal partners." Although the *form* of family life privileged by American Mormon culture is similar to that enjoined by those who embrace religiously informed family values, the underlying rationale for this

---

15. Ironically, several Mormon mommy/design bloggers have been successful enough at monetizing their blogs that they now support their families with this income.

16. A subgenre of mommy blogs devoted to "godly femininity," "godly submission," "biblical womanhood," etc. articulate a model of marriage in which wives are explicitly submissive to their husbands. On the changing Mormon discourse of male headship, see Caroline Kline's chapter in this volume.

family form is moderate and gestures toward an egalitarian ideal that would be at home in most progressive American households.

Thus, while Mormon mommy bloggers may regard their blogs as part of the performance of a religious commitment, what they display is sometimes hardly distinguishable from an embrace of American consumer culture and commitment to self-expression. Mormonism is a part of these bloggers' personal brands, to the extent that their chosen lifestyles mirror the post-1970s LDS commitment to a particular family form. But, as the author of *Salon* excerpt article noted, information about Mormonism is included in hyperlinks and other subtle ways; for the most part, these blogs host little explicitly religious discussion or commentary. Although these mommy blogs marked the first significant participation of Mormon women in Internet publishing, it is difficult to locate an orthodox Mormon voice in their performance of prescribed Mormon femininity.

Seek-Out-Pretty

This ideological flexibility is, in some ways, one of the features of Mormonism that has helped it to thrive. Mormonism has maintained geographically bounded communities even as almost all other American denominations have sorted themselves by doctrinal emphasis and commitment. Mormonism has been able to maintain what sociologist Armand Mauss has called "optimal tension" with its American host society by subtly shifting emphases on different facets of Mormon doctrine, without creating stark divisions of the sort that lead to denominational switching among other Christians.[17] At the beginning of the twenty-first century, however, as the "nones"—those with no denominational affiliation—have claimed the title of the fastest-growing religious group,[18] Mormons seem to be struggling to find an "other" against which to define themselves. The same flexibility that has allowed Mormons of various political affiliations to comfortably worship together sometimes also makes it possible for them to invest their political ideals and lifestyle choices with religious significance.

One of the first Mormon bloggers to gain a wide following, Stephanie Nielson, provides an example of this seamlessly integrated religious, cultural, and political outlook in a post that is simply a list of things about which she

17. Armand L. Mauss, *The Angel and the Beehive: The Mormon Struggle with Assimilation* (Champaign: University of Illinois Press, 1994).

18. Pew Research Religion and Public Life Project, "'Nones' on the Rise," *Pew Research Center*, October 9, 2012, www.pewforum.org/2012/10/09/nones-on-the-rise.

feels proud: that she married soon after high school, that she is a Mormon from a large family in Utah with pioneer heritage, that she has "lots of scrapbook albums," that she was a ski instructor, had three children before age twenty-three and breastfed them, that she doesn't drink alcohol or watch R-rated movies, and that her father is a state legislator who "fights for values."[19]

Here Mormon cultural behavior is comingled with conservative American political convictions and even with breastfeeding and ski instruction. Mormonism is fully incorporated into Stephanie's blog as part of her identity and her family's life. During Mitt Romney's run for the presidency, posts about Nielson's political activity were mixed in with family photos, pitches for items from blog sponsors, and descriptions of weekend plans.[20] Of course, associating political convictions and religious ones is not uniquely Mormon. But the degree to which Mormonism is adduced as a motivating and unifying element for lives that seem otherwise similar to non-Mormon lives is striking, as is the impulse to articulate the doctrinal connections to their quotidian pursuits. Sydney Poulton, who blogs at the design and fashion blog *The Day Book*, wrote a post explaining the relationship of Mormonism to her interest in design. She cited one of Mormonism's thirteen Articles of Faith, which reads, in part, "If there is anything virtuous, lovely, or of good report or praiseworthy, we seek after these things,"[21] as a motivation for her pursuit of aesthetic ideals:

> So much of modern day media, world views and culture can be used to tear down and distract from the lovely things in life like family and relationships, or in my case, creating {or trying!} something beautiful through design, style, etc. But the encouragement from LDS church leaders to engage ourselves in ways that enlarge our capacity for happiness {and seek out those things that are "virtuous and lovely"}, has I'm sure, inherently influenced my decisions when it comes to becoming involved in the world of design and style.[22]

---

19. Stephanie Nielson, "Nie Nie: On Being Proud," *NieNie Dialogues* blog, September 15, 2005, http://nieniedialogues.blogspot.com/2005/09/nie-nie-on-being-proud.html.

20. For example, see Stephanie Nielson, "Smooching Mama," *NieNie Dialogues* blog, November 15, 2011, http://nieniedialogues.blogspot.com/2011/11/smooching-mama.html.

21. See number 13 of the Articles of Faith of the Church of Jesus Christ of Latter-day Saints, in *The Pearl of Great Price* (Salt Lake City: The Church of Jesus Christ of Latter-day Saints, 2013).

22. Sydney Liann, "Why Are Mormons So Cool?," *The daybook* blog, September 14, www.thedaybookblog.com/2011/09/why-are-mormons-so-cool.html.

Gabrielle Blair, at Design Mom, offered a few more possible explanations, including creativity borne of growing up in large families with fewer resources, confidence in personal writing from being encouraged to keep journals, time to pursue creative interests when full-time mothering becomes less than all-consuming, and education in the excellent design department at BYU. She also mentions the same Article of Faith as Poulton, concluding:

> In the case of Design Mom, I never had the 13th Article of Faith in mind, but I have tried to create a space where I could share every lovely and praiseworthy thing I come across. I wonder if everyone raised as a Mormon has this admonition to seek-out-pretty stamped on our brains. An admonishment to keep an eye out for beauty is a lovely sentiment to be raised with, and easily adopted by anyone—religious or not.... My religion is far from perfect—there are aspects of it that drive me bonkers. But I particularly love this part of it.[23]

Blair's pithy paraphrase, turning "if there is anything virtuous, lovely, or of good report or praiseworthy, we seek after these things" to "seek-out-pretty" is representative of the kind of applied theology that animates many Mormon mommy blogs. Mormon ideas of continuing revelation, an open canon, and the possibility of revelation to individual believers make space for this sort of theological play, and for the potential sacralization of the material world and quotidian life. Inhabiting, rather than resisting, these Mormon ideas lends spiritual expansiveness to the stuff of domesticity and also seems to provide religious justification for transgressing cultural norms about women's employment and public activity.

A commenter on Blair's blog named Katrina Crane added another credible Mormon explanation for the popularity of home and design blogs among Mormon women:

> Mormon women grow up learning to give talks to the congregation, share talents and quazi-talents [*sic*], like play the piano EVEN IF YOU REALLY ONLY KNOW HOW TO PLAY THE VIOLIN! *points to self.* You are part of enrichment committees, primary programs, blue and gold banquets and young women projects. Once a month you talk to people that you might not stop on the street otherwise. Where else can you have 7 girls and be asked to serve as the cub scout leader?

---

23. Gabrielle Blair, "What's Up with Mormons and Design Blogs?," *Design Mom* blog, May 6, 2011, www.designmom.com/2011/05/whats-up-with-mormons-and-design-blogs/.

Crane's comment underscores the importance of praxis in Mormonism. A Mormon life is pragmatic, active, and often improvised. Doctrinal explication is largely incidental to the duties of membership and is performed not by trained theologians but by laypeople who give sermons in Sunday worship services, teach Sunday School classes, and supervise youth groups. Mormon traditionalists' confident, articulate advocacy for their points of view, like Mormon feminists' vocal self-expression, are products of this Mormon socialization and training. Mommy blogs embodied the integration of diffuse and inchoate Mormon ideas into a particular kind of life. Eventually, though, the verbal imperatives of the blogging medium, as well as encouragement from Mormon leaders, led Mormon women to begin articulating arguments and justifications for different political views or lifestyle choices in a new context where verbal expression of religious ideas was divorced from the ways Mormons usually enact their beliefs.

Finding Voice in Sharing the Gospel Online

Despite the potential for conflict and after some initial hesitation, in the 2000s Mormon leaders embraced the opportunities of Internet communication as a means of sharing Mormon ideas and values with a wider audience.[24] In 2008, LDS apostle M. Russell Ballard gave a commencement address exhorting the graduates of BYU-Hawaii to use the Internet, which he said was a divinely inspired tool, "to share the gospel and to explain in simple and clear terms the message of the Restoration."[25]

Orthodox Mormon women responded enthusiastically, if at first somewhat awkwardly, to this directive. Decades of correlation-induced suspicion of materials lacking official imprimatur and the liberal slant of the earliest Mormon discussions online made many orthodox women uneasy about speaking in their own words online. One of the earliest Mormon blogs run by a woman was simply a collection of quotations from the LDS Church's

---

24. For instance, in 1999, L. Tom Perry cautioned: "The Internet is a new source of information that offers tremendous opportunities as well as another potential—becoming addicted. Unfortunately, with the blessings of the new information age also come challenges, as evil influences have a new medium of transmission and new ways of infiltrating our minds. Worldly influences enter our homes in new shapes and forms to challenge our resolve to use our time wisely and for the Lord's purposes." See L. Tom Perry, "A Year of Jubilee," October 1999, www.lds.org/general-conference/1999/10/a-year-of-jubilee.

25. M. Russell Ballard, "Sharing the Gospel Using the Internet," *Ensign*, July 2008, www.lds.org/ensign/2008/07/sharing-the-gospel-using-the-internet?lang=eng.

general authorities.[26] Mormon women are heavily socialized to avoid "contention," and the most orthodox women also frequently employ the most oblique communication style—disagreements are expressed subtly and the mere tolerance of open contradiction frequently drives conservative Mormon women away from heated discussions of feminist issues on blogs or Facebook. For instance, much of the discussion about women's issues in the so-called Mormon bloggernacle has been centered around the blog Feminist Mormon Housewives (fMh). It is unusual, however, to find conservative LDS women debating in the comment sections. They more frequently post responses to feminist ideas they may have encountered at fMh on their own blogs, where commenters are more like-minded. When there is open confrontation between liberals and conservatives, it is far more likely to be between conservative men and liberal women than among women with opposite views.[27]

The discomforts of online communication for women who have been socialized to be deferential to authority and solicitous of others is evident in this post from Kathryn Skaggs, whose blog is called "A Well-Behaved Mormon Woman."[28] Skaggs describes an interaction with another LDS woman who seemed to think that Skaggs "was completely out of control in…writing about Mormonism in such an open way," and wondered how Skaggs "could…possibly think that [she] had a right to teach about the LDS Church, while [she] had absolutely no authority?" Despite Skaggs having hyperlinked both Elder Ballard's encouragement to blog and several references to the official church website, her correspondent was bothered by any nonauthoritative expression related to her faith. Skaggs expressed her own personal discomfort at "finding myself on opposite sides of thought with another member of the Church, let alone a woman or sister in 'Christ'!" "Her main issue was not really the topic at hand," Skaggs reported, but rather that "I should not be

---

26. Perhaps this is why Pinterest is a favorite among Mormon women, who have created a cottage industry in producing thousands and thousands of quotations from General Conference sermons in fancy fonts on frilly backgrounds. This way of appropriating male-centric, male-generated discourse for a feminine space is probably more comfortable for many orthodox and culturally conservative Mormon women. It is a way of making an assertion without being personally assertive.

27. One result of this discomfort is that there are relatively few conservative Mormon women's blogs that directly engage doctrinal questions or so-called women's issues; the blogs mentioned below, while not an exhaustive catalog, do represent a substantial fraction of conservative Mormon women's blogs that have more than a few dozen followers and offer substantive discussions of overtly religious topics.

28. It is difficult to read this title as other than a passive-aggressive jab at another Mormon woman, Laurel Ulrich, who coined the phrase "Well-behaved women seldom make history," but Skaggs has never made any such intent explicit.

writing about the LDS Church online and purporting to have authority in some way to do so—which I don't."[29] Skaggs thus used her public online platform to engender the ideal of harmony and disclaim any distinctive authority for her own voice. Elder Ballard's commencement address and subsequent, similar injunctions to "use the Internet and the social media to reach out and share…religious beliefs" placed women whose primary motivation for talking about Mormonism online was sharing authoritative teachings in the paradoxical position of having to articulate those teachings in their own independent, unauthorized voices.[30] Where "following the Brethren" often had meant that women had learned *not* to express their personal interpretations of Mormon teaching, they were now being asked to do precisely that. As Skaggs's anecdote makes clear, both speaking out and finding themselves in disagreement with other Latter-day Saint women were new and uncomfortable experiences.

While largely presenting themselves as simply stating what "the Brethren" have said, orthodox Mormon women are often theologically innovative, as in this post on a blog called "My Soul Delighteth in the Scriptures":

> The prophets have said, "Gender is an essential characteristic of individual premortal, mortal, and eternal identity and purpose" and that "Mothers are primarily responsible for the nurture of their children." But…it doesn't really come right out and say what it means to be a woman, although I think the implication is maybe there.
>
> As I have been studying and praying and asking Heavenly Father for more wisdom and understanding, I think I can say (with at least *some* conviction) that *being a woman means being a mother*.[31]

From this identification of women with mothers, the writer draws several conclusions about women's nature: that they are to be "intelligent and educated," "strong, steadfast, and immovable" leaders in their homes and in the world, invested with the power of the priesthood—though not ordained to priesthood office in the Church—and creators of life. Although none of these conclusions is particularly novel (indeed, each is supported by an authoritative

---

29. Kathryn Skaggs, "Blogging for the Lord, Or at Least I Thought I Was," *A Well-Behaved Mormon Woman* blog, April 22, 2008, http://wellbehavedmormonwoman.blogspot.com/2008/04/blogging-for-lord-or-at-least-i-thought.html#.VDVv7ed8EI0.

30. L. Tom Perry, "Perfect Love Casteth out Fear," October 2011, www.lds.org/general-conference/2011/10/perfect-love-casteth-out-fear.

31. Becca, "Mother in Danger," *My Soul Delighteth* blog, June 7, 2012, http://delightinscripture.blogspot.com/2012/06/mother-in-danger.html, emphasis in original.

quotation), the amalgamation of these ideas as a way to explicate a passage from "The Family: A Proclamation to the World" that the writer found unclear is original. Because Mormonism has no professional theologians or ministers, this kind of theological exploration is not only licit, but encouraged and validated.

Another notable feature of this post that distinguishes it from official church discourse is that it addresses the kinds of concerns about the equation of motherhood and womanhood that might be raised by more progressive or feminist-leaning Mormon women:

> As I have studied gender identity and womanhood, I kept resisting this notion, that being a woman means being a mother. I felt that it wasn't a fair explanation. That by linking the two we leave out millions of women who will never be "mothers."...
>
> [But] in God's plan, the imperfections of this world do not matter...all the imperfections of this world will never change eternal truth. And I feel like the eternal truth is that women are to be mothers.[32]

Such posts thus frequently display awareness of progressive critiques of their position, and even express some sympathy for the core sentiment underlying the criticisms, but ultimately dismiss them as misguided and unfaithful.

Even on blogs that are not exclusively "mommy blogs," devoted to children and homemaking, Mormon women overwhelmingly approach theology through the lens of their choices about family life. "The Family: A Proclamation to the World," though not officially canonized, is cited far more often than other scriptures and is almost invariably the authoritative warrant cited for non- or anti-feminist sentiments. This is not particularly surprising, given the emphasis on the proclamation in official church publications and curricula in the last several years. The other frequently cited warrant is the Mormon temple liturgy, which is usually discussed in oblique terms or referenced vaguely. This liturgy ritually enacts what Mormons call "The Plan of Salvation," beginning with the creation of Adam and Eve and ending with the faithful being ushered into heaven. The fact that these are the sources on which Mormon women call when articulating their belief—rather than, for instance, the biblical verses frequently cited by evangelical women—suggests again the importance of performance, of praxis, in the personal formation and group affirmation of Mormon identity. *Doing* Mormonism is as important for these

---

32. Ibid.

women as believing it. Moreover, the focus on family and motherhood allows for a rhetoric that, while resisting feminism, is gentle and apolitical, and focused on performance—on narrating stories of Mormon women's experience that implicitly oppose feminist ideologies. "The personal is political" is a truism that transcends ideological boundaries.

Articulating Anti-Feminist Orthodoxy

It seems possible that Mormon feminists and orthodox Mormon women might have kept to their separate cyberniches sharing theology, recipes, and stories indefinitely if Internet discussions hadn't started to infiltrate "real-life" Mormonism. As Neylan McBaine has documented, the Internet began to be used within Mormonism as a tool for crowd-sourced action around 2012, when bloggers at Feminist Mormon Housewives undertook a telephone survey of LDS temple practices around allowing menstruating girls and women to participate in baptismal ordinances.[33] They discovered that the policies were inconsistent, with no clear rationale. In response, LDS Church spokesman Scott Trotter clarified that official policy was to allow full participation of girls and women.[34] Later that year, a group of LDS women organized, via social media, the collective wearing of pants (rather than traditional dresses or skirts) to church meetings on a particular Sunday as a way of demonstrating that "there is more than one way to be a good Mormon woman."[35] In early 2013, an Internet-organized letter-writing campaign drew attention to the fact that women had not yet been invited to offer prayers in sessions of the LDS Church's semiannual general conference, and requested that the privilege be extended to them. Also in 2013, a group called Ordain Women launched a website with profiles of Latter-day Saints who believe that women should be ordained to priesthood in the LDS Church and requested admission to the (traditionally male-only) priesthood session of general conference.[36] Their requests were denied, both in October 2013 and April 2014, and one of the founders of the group, Kate Kelly, was excommunicated in June

---

33. Neylan McBaine, *Women at Church: Magnifying LDS Women's Local Impact* (Salt Lake City: Greg Kofford Books, 2014), 13.

34. Peggy Fletcher Stack, "Menstruating Mormons Barred from Temple Proxy Baptisms?" *Salt Lake Tribune*, March 5, 2012, www.sltrib.com/sltrib/blogsfaithblog/53650972-180/temple-women-baptisms-mormon.html.csp.

35. "Our Mission," *Pants to Church*, http://pantstochurch.com/home.

36. "Ordain Women: Women Seeking Equality and Ordination to the Priesthood," *Ordain Women*, http://ordainwomen.org.

2014.[37] The church did, however, make the priesthood session available via online streaming, thus opening it to any women who cared to watch at home.

The "Wear Pants to Church" event evoked furious reactions from men and women alike. The organizers of the event received threatening messages dire enough to warrant official investigation—one commenter on the Facebook event page suggested that women who showed up in pants should be shot.[38] Many of the more articulate critics based their objections on the idea that a "demonstration" in sacrament meeting was an inappropriate disruption of a worship service. Others suggested that women who feel marginalized or oppressed at church just don't understand the gospel, while still others focused on the idea that any sort of agitation over women's issues was the beginning of a slippery slope toward demanding women's ordination and effacing all differences between men and women. One blog comment vividly captured several of these objections. She asserted her own understanding and acceptance of the basic principle of equality before dismissing as "ridiculous" any public demand for it: "I get it that men and women should be equal. That we should all be treated with the same respect. I really do. BUT this whole pants to church business is ridiculous. What is that going to prove?" Then she invoked the slippery slope argument, suggesting that women adopting cultural expressions of masculinity would lead to the physical acquisition of secondary male sexual characteristics and finally the spiritual appropriation of male priesthood privilege: "And when is it going to stop? Next it's going to be women cutting their hair in a 'missionary style' hair cut, or trying to grow facial hair, or demanding that females get the priesthood." Finally, this commenter turned to the proclamation on the family and her own personal experience to insist on what is perhaps the crux of all of these discussions—the apparently irreducible assertion that equality does not require sameness:

> In the Proclamation it clearly states that we each have our own divine roles.... We are DIFFERENT! That's how God created us. Yes, we can be equal, but men and women are NOT the same, and then never will be. I feel VERY blessed to be a woman in this church. I was lucky enough to grow up never feeling degraded. I've always been proud of who I am, and I've always been taught that I am special and have a beautiful divine nature given to me by a loving Heavenly Father. I LOVE being female.... I

---

37. Neylan McBaine, *Women at Church: Magnifying LDS Women's Local Impact*, 13.

38. Timothy Pratt, "Mormon Women Set Out to Take a Stand, in Pants," *New York Times*, December 19, 2012, www.nytimes.com/2012/12/20/us/19mormon.html?_r=0.

love that we can wear dresses and heels and makeup and look beautiful and elegant. . . . Especially to church, where we are supposed to dress our best and come for worship.[39]

Another common focus of criticism directed toward feminist Internet-based crowd-sourced action was the triviality of the stated problems. Many people asserted that being judged for not fitting in is not a significant problem in Mormon congregations, accusing the participants of "whining" or making a mountain out of a molehill. This same critique was leveled when the exclusion of women from saying prayers in general conference was pointed out. For instance, a woman named Andrea Peterson Boardman posted on the Let Women Pray in General Conference Facebook page: "Wow this page is ridiculous! I'm sorry you feel the need to waste your time. It's sad you have such low self esteem in who you are that you blame something irrational and pretend it has something to do with inequality."[40] The critique that women's concerns were trivial was leveled again when activists began speaking about ordination. A commenter named Heidi Jansson wrote on an early post on Ordain Women's Facebook page, "I am dying laughing because I totally thought this was a joke. Why in the world would you want more responsibility than you already have?? . . . I'm sorry but this is ridiculous!"[41]

However, not all of the responses were so dismissive. The controversy surrounding Ordain Women was notable as a moment in which conservative Mormon women in substantial numbers took to the Internet not only to showcase their performance of Mormon values about home and family, but to forcefully articulate an anti-feminist orthodoxy. The dominant argument that these women make against women's ordination is that women's capacity to be mothers is in some way equivalent to men's right to hold priesthood office. The complementarian arguments that were frequently adduced in opposition to marriage equality are reiterated as support for the idea that men and women are so essentially different that they need not perform the same roles to be

---

39. C. Jane, "The Worst Thing Is Pants," *C. Jane Kendrick* blog, December 12, 2012, www.cjanekendrick.com/2012/12/the-worst-thing-is-pants.html?showComment=1355338473583-c80290875766628265427.

40. Andrea Peterson Boardman, Facebook post, January 12, 2013, 11:51 pm, www.Facebook.com/LetWomenPray/photos/a.469938633043804.91889..469339066437094/469956319708702.

41. Heidi Jansson, Facebook post, April 6, 2013, 1:34 am, www.Facebook.com/events/314421635351211/permalink/314421638684544/?comment_id=317261585067216&offset=0&total_comments=157.

"equal" to men in the church. On the blog of Mormon Women Stand, Laurie White writes:

> The world would have us believe that motherhood is somehow demeaning, or at least not worthy of attention. . . . It is one thing for women to stand up for our equality, and quite another to be ungrateful for our very womanhood. The fight for equality has turned into a bashing of our eternal counterparts. That is not in conformity with God's laws. . . . Submitting to the Father's will not only brings joy, but spreads joy.
>
> It is my prayer that we all find nobility in motherhood and joy in womanhood. I cherish my femininity.[42]

White's reference to "submission" is unusual in a Mormon context, and it is worth noting that it is submission to God the Father that she enjoins, not submission to a husband. Mormon women almost never cite biblical injunctions that buttress other Christian notions of male headship. Even here, where submission is praised, there is allowance for "stand[ing] up for equality."

In this paradoxical commitment to both equality and submission, these bloggers frequently cite "The Family: A Proclamation to the World," with its injunction that fathers are to preside and also be "equal partners" with their wives in order to derive a theory of church governance in which men preside but women are somehow equal. One post by Rebecca Andrews simply rewrote the language of the proclamation to apply to the church as well as the family, for instance: "By divine design, [the brethren] are to preside over [the Church] in love and righteousness and are responsible to provide the necessities of life and protection for [the Church]. [The sisters of the Church] are primarily responsible for the nurture of [the members of the Church]. In these sacred responsibilities, [brethren and sisters] are obligated to help one another as equal partners." She then concluded, "So here we have it—men have different roles in the Church than women do." The idea that the patriarchy governing the church is similar to patriarchy in the family is a common assertion. What is novel here is taking the Family

---

42. Mormon Women Stand is a group that formed on Facebook and other social media outlets in March 2014. They describe themselves as "LDS Women who, without hesitation, sustain the Lord's Prophet, the Family Proclamation as doctrine and our divine role as covenant women for Christ." The founders of the group claim that they did not form in opposition to Ordain Women, but the coincidental timing and subject matter suggest some correlation. See Tad Walch, "New LDS Women's Group Quickly Gains Steam on Facebook," *Deseret News*, April 3, 2014, www.deseretnews.com/article/865600201/New-LDS-womens-group-quickly-gains-steam-on-Facebook.html?pg=all.

Proclamation and extrapolating from it a theory about church governance, rather than, for instance, using Christ's ordination of men to the apostleship as warrant for all-male priesthood and extending that model into the home.[43]

Many criticisms of Ordain Women were procedural. A surprising number of these critiques included statements such as "I don't really care whether women are ever ordained," always followed by "but" and a critique of Ordain Women's tactics. Some objected simply to the disruption of sacred space (as they had with Wear Pants to Church), and others were more concerned with inviting media attention to conflict in the church and the potential "embarrassment" for the institution. At the root of these criticisms, though, was the sense that what members of Ordain Women were doing just isn't the right way to do Mormonism. Mormons are not supposed to petition (or, pejoratively, "lobby") or speak in the language of "rights." Mormons are not supposed to care about "worldly" notions of power. Mormons are supposed to trust their leaders to receive revelation "in the Lord's time."

It is in these procedural criticisms that the deep struggle between Mormon ways of knowing and being and contemporary liberal ideals is manifest. The frequent recurrence of the word "worldly," as a critique of both feminist theory and Mormon feminists' methods, is an important tell. In fact, Mormon feminists are able to articulate a very Mormon rationale for their actions, and they can draw on the history of their staunchly pro-suffrage Mormon foremothers for a model of assimilating progressive ideas from "the world" with full approval of Mormon authorities. Mormon belief in continuing revelation makes it fundamentally innovative; and the active, pragmatic nature of lived Mormonism not only makes it necessary for individual members to do some of this innovation, but also, to a large degree, gives them license to do so. On the other hand, the heavily centralized structure of the LDS Church, and the authority invested in contemporary statements from church hierarchs, gives warrant to church members who distrust their coreligionists' interpretations. The conflict is, to be sure, a smaller one than the conflict Mahmood describes between pious Islamic women and similar forces of modernity, but "liberal" and "orthodox" Mormons trying to communicate with each other over how much modernity Mormonism can assimilate face similar chasms between their fundamental understandings of God, prophetic authority, and human agency.

---

43. Becca, "Women and the Priesthood," *My Soul Delighteth* blog, May 21, 2012, http://delightinscripture.blogspot.com/2012/05/women-and-priesthood.html.

Conclusion: Different Trajectories

Mormonism's short history has required varying styles of accommodation; Armand Mauss describes this work in terms of a pendulum swinging between assimilation and retrenchment.[44] The Internet destabilizes the central fulcrum of that pendulum, as authority is rendered diffuse and official statements no longer speak for the whole. Members of the LDS Church who wish to be obedient to the exhortation to share Mormonism in their online communications are faced with the necessity of articulating their own version of Mormonism, doing the work of assimilation that used to be authoritatively directed and collectively performed. The anonymity and remoteness of online communication disrupts the shared social and spiritual practices of Mormon congregations that traditionally papered over differences in belief. It is hard to really hate someone who has visited you monthly to talk about spiritual topics, or brought you dinner when you were ill, or worked alongside you at the welfare farm, or taught your children in Sunday School, even if their politics or their interpretation of scripture are vastly different than one's own. It is far easier to hate someone you have never seen who expresses those variant views as a comment on your blog post. The latter half of the twentieth century saw Mormonism successfully transcend the geographic proximity and kinship networks that had bound Mormons to one another; it remains to be seen whether Mormonism as a set of shared practices can survive the disembodied articulation of its motley doctrine on the Internet.

The difficulty of this evolution is poignantly illustrated in the blogs of Stephanie Clark Nielson (mentioned above) and her sister, Courtney Clark Kendrick. Both of them started blogs very early in the mommy blogging era. Courtney wrote humorously about the trials of infertility and her life as a Mormon woman who was not yet a mother, while Stephanie wrote about making a beautiful and happy home for her growing brood. Both blogs gained large followings after Stephanie was injured in a near-fatal plane crash and Courtney blogged about her sister's survival and recovery. After her injury, Stephanie resumed her very traditional, very orthodox Mormon mommy blog. Courtney became a mother, a newspaper columnist, an outspoken nonfeminist, and then, to everyone's surprise, a feminist after all. She described her dawning realization that she was not entirely happy with the traditional roles she had previously defended. It was a realization that involved restructuring her partnership with her husband and thinking in new ways about both motherhood and fatherhood:

---

44. See Mauss, *The Angel and the Beehive*, x.

After a few years of trying to figure things out, we finally decided a new approach. We were both unhappy with our situation—he was never home and I never left home. He would quit his job and we would utilize a "farm mentality" where we would each put in 100% of all the work. This meant there were no roles, we both worked, we both parented, we both cleaned the house and took responsibility for the totality of our lives. When I worked writing and blogging, he cleaned and took care of the children, when he produced or acted in film I was at home.... Showing our children respect and cooperation at home is our hope. This idea of having equal voices and opportunities has challenged us to explore the way we live in almost all aspects of our lives—childbirth, parenting, teaching our children the gospel.

Responses to this revelation on Courtney's blog were mostly, but not uniformly, positive. Critics frequently referred to the Family Proclamation and argued that complementary roles, like priesthood and motherhood, could be equal despite not being the same. One commenter cited 1 Corinthians—*"neither is the* man without the woman, *neither* the *woman without the man"*—but most relied on the proclamation and on their personal feelings of being respected and treated as equals by their husbands and other Mormon men.

Several months later, Courtney declared that she was a supporter of Ordain Women. She wrote (and posted on her blog) a letter to her three daughters:

I want you to know that through the same channels that I felt I should go on a mission, or marry your dad, I also felt like I should pray and hope for women's ordination. I don't believe God doesn't intend for women to be ordained. There is no scriptural or doctrinal declaration proof of this concept. And certainly there is no harm in asking and praying for what is in your heart. After all, this is what led to the beginnings of our church—and a pattern we often repeat—ask God for what you desire. Ask, knock, ponder, pray, have faith, have hope.

Mormonism is our heritage—it's in our bedtime stories and our daily rituals. It's in the way we worship and the way we hope.... And I believe we're still shaping our doctrine.[45]

---

45. C. Jane, "To My Mormon Daughters," *C. Jane Kendrick* blog, May 21, 2012, 2014, www. cjanekendrick.com/2014/07/to-my-mormon-daughters_15.html.

The criticisms of this post were more vehement than those responding to her earlier post about being a feminist. Some declared Courtney an "apostate." However, only a few referred to the Family Proclamation or to the arguments about complementarity that were adduced in objection to the earlier post on feminism. Instead, they appealed to the authority of the prophet to set direction for the church or to the unchanging nature of Mormon doctrine.

The fact that traditionalists appeal to completely different doctrinal arguments in response to what might, at first glance, seem like a difference in the degree of feminist identification rather than a wholly different phenomenon, suggests that these defenders of the status quo with regard to Mormon gender roles are no less sophisticated in their grasp of the issues at stake than those whose articulation of their position relies on language and arguments more familiar to academics inclined to interpret them through the lens of liberal notions of progress. They are engaged in projects of theological innovation, doctrinal interpretation, and cultural resistance (in this case to the dominant liberal culture of non-Mormon America) that are complex and interesting on their own terms.

A few days after Courtney published her letter to her daughters, Stephanie offered a response on her blog. In her typically telescopic and center-justified prose, she echoed the theme of prophetic authority and the limits of acceptable personal adaptation that had characterized the most critical comments on Courtney's blog:

> I think its most wise to align myself and my actions with what the prophets
> are teaching and if they don't align, I am off—not them, not ever....
> I feel I need to stress again the fact that I love my all of my Mormon
> sisters—I respect them because they are good mothers, daughters,
> friends, providers, and because they genuinely want to be good....
> But in that same breath, I also fear for them because Mormon women
> are also covenant keeping women,
> and when they break or forget those covenants they have made with God,
> they cannot be protected, prepared, trusted, or empowered.
> And that is what I have to say about that.[46]

One hopes that there is, in fact, much more to say. While coming to conclusions wholly at odds with their feminist sisters' interpretations, traditionalist Mormon women are engaged in a fundamentally similar project of engaging

---

46. Stephanie Neilson, "A Mormon Woman," *NieNie Dialogues* blog, July 18, 2014, http://nieniedialogues.blogspot.com/2014/07/a-mormon-woman.html.

and articulating a Mormon understanding of the world in the twenty-first century. Failing to register their voices by paying attention only to those who resist Mormon norms and not to their sisters who, in Mahmood's language, devoutly and creatively inhabit those norms, is to miss much of the nuance and subtlety of modern Mormon theological and cultural negotiation.

PART IV

Religious Culture

12

The Evangelical Countercult Movement and Mormon Conservatism

Matthew Bowman

IN RECENT YEARS Robert Wuthnow and many other sociologists have observed that American religion since the middle of the twentieth century has divided itself not primarily along lines of theology and denomination, but rather by competing worldviews that bisected denominations and in practice looked much like the political camps calling themselves conservative and liberal. James Davison Hunter calls these sides "orthodox" and "liberal," the difference between them being allegiance to external, transcendent sources of authority and subjective loyalty to individual experience. In practice, Hunter's orthodox and liberal camps resemble Wuthnow's conservatives and liberals, defined by degree of attachment to tradition and participation in social and political action. Both authors place Mormons in the "orthodox" wing of the spectrum.[1] Since the 1960s, Mormons have taken socially conservative positions on a range of issues, including abortion, women's rights, and same-sex marriage. Perhaps most compellingly, non-Mormon social conservatives have recognized Mormons as an ally; more evangelicals, proportionately, voted for the Mormon presidential candidate Mitt Romney in 2012 than they had for John McCain in 2008.[2]

And yet at the same midcentury moment that Mormonism began to join this conservative coalition, those evangelicals who formed its core began to

---

1. Robert Wuthnow, *The Restructuring of American Religion* (Princeton, NJ: Princeton University Press, 1988); James Davison Hunter, *Culture Wars: The Struggle to Define America* (New York: Basic Books, 1991).

2. Pew Forum on Religion and American Life, "White Evangelicals and Support for Romney," *Pew Research Center*, last modified December 7, 2012, www.pewforum. org/2012/12/07/election-2012-post-mortem-white-evangelicals-and-support-for-romney/. On modern Mormon social activism, see Claudia Bushman, *Contemporary Mormonism: Latter-day Saints in Modern America* (Westport, CT: Praeger, 2006), 112–120; J. B. Haws, *The Mormon Image in the American Mind: Fifty Years of Public Perception* (New York: Oxford University Press, 2013), 74–99.

sharpen their criticism of the LDS Church. A parallel chronology is telling. In 1953 the Mormon apostle Ezra Taft Benson joined Dwight Eisenhower's cabinet and began a political career as a vociferous anti-communist. Later that same year an evangelical named John L. Smith founded Utah Ministries, a mission specifically targeted to Mormons in Salt Lake City that has spurred dozens of imitators. In 1958, the midlevel Mormon leader Bruce R. McConkie published a book called *Mormon Doctrine*, which denounced evolution, embraced a theology of scripture near to biblical inerrancy, and darkly warned the social decay prophesied in the book of Revelation was upon us. Only a few years earlier, a Baptist minister named Walter Martin wrote a bestselling book called *The Rise of the Cults*, which warned that Mormonism "rivals anything pagan mythology ever produced" and castigated the Mormons for their lack of respect for the Bible.[3] In 1982, in part as a result of aggressive Mormon political action, the Equal Right Amendment went down to defeat. The same year, a film titled *The God Makers*, designed by evangelical ex-Mormon filmmakers to debunk Mormonism, premiered in California and has been shown to hundreds of thousands of evangelicals over the past several decades. In other words, it is a historical oddity that at the same time that Mormons were joining a coalition of social and theological conservatives, conservative evangelicals intensified their theological attacks on Mormonism.

There are several possible reasons for this. Certainly, evangelicals were alarmed at the rapid growth of Mormonism in the mid-twentieth century; during the presidency of David O. McKay alone, from 1951 to 1970, the church tripled in size, from 1 million to 3 million. As Walter Martin warned, "The Mormons are moving ahead in their battle to out evangelize evangelical Christianity."[4] Along with Mormonism's rapid growth came its increased social acceptability within American culture broadly defined. Armand Mauss and Jan Shipps are only the most prominent authors to call this midcentury accommodation between Mormons and American culture in general a sign of assimilation. They point at the growing popularity of the Mormon Tabernacle Choir, the appointment of Benson to Eisenhower's cabinet, and other such

---

3. Bruce R. McConkie, *Mormon Doctrine* (Salt Lake City: Bookcraft, 1958); Walter Martin, *Kingdom of the Cults* (Grand Rapids, MI: Zondervan, 1954), 183.

4. Martin, *Kingdom of the Cults*, 148. On evangelical fear of Mormon growth see "And the Saints Go Marching On: The New Mormon Challenge for World Missions," in Francis Beckwith, Carl Mosser, and Paul Owen, eds., *The New Mormon Challenge* (Grand Rapids, MI: Zondervan, 2002), 59–90; Philip Jenkins, *Mystics and Messiahs: Cults and New Religions in American History* (New York: Oxford University Press, 2000), 172–176.

symbols to demonstrate that Mormonism had, by 1960, become fully conversant in the mores of American culture.[5]

Indeed, only a few decades before, the Mormon apostle James Talmage had explained to an audience of non-Mormons that Mormons were in fact on the cutting edge of American life. "Every studious reader of recent commentaries on the Holy Scriptures, and of theological treatises in general, is aware of a surprising progressiveness in modern views of things spiritual," he said. "In the new theology 'Mormonism' has pioneered the way." By way of example he offered Mormonism's rejection of the "unscriptural and repellent dogma of inherent degeneracy and the contaminating effect of original sin." He stated that Mormonism "proclaims the possibility of eternal advancement," urging human beings to seek constant progress. According to Talmage, these twin doctrines made Mormons the world's foremost seekers of knowledge and education, and he insisted that this practice made of Mormonism "a coherent and mutually helpful body, in which the ties and prejudices of diverse nationality and of varied tradition are swallowed up."[6] In short, for Talmage, Mormonism exemplified the achievements that many of the nation's reformers were seeking: confidence in human accomplishment, interest in science and philosophy, and an eagerness to reconcile the particularities of its faith with the values of American elites in the academy and in culture. Talmage and other Mormon thinkers regularly cited the work of liberal Protestant thinkers such as the scientist James Dana, the influential sociologist Herbert Spencer, and the philosopher John Fiske. An observer at Brigham Young University noted that higher criticism of the Bible was accepted and taught in its classrooms. A Sunday School committee of the church in 1949 recommended that its teachers study the work of John Dewey and Ernest Chave, two leading lights of liberal Protestantism and the progressive education movement.[7] In all these

---

5. Jan Shipps, "From Satyr to Saint: American Perceptions of the Mormons, 1860–1960," in *Sojourner in the Promised Land: Forty Years among the Mormons* (Urbana: University of Illinois Press, 2000), 51–97; Dennis Lythgoe, "The Changing Image of Mormonism," *Dialogue: A Journal of Mormon Thought* 3 (Winter 1968): 45–58; Armand Mauss, *The Angel and the Beehive: The Mormon Struggle with Assimilation* (Urbana: University of Illinois Press, 1994), 60–77; Chiung Hwang Chen and Ethan Yorgason, "Those Amazing Mormons: The Media Construction of the Latter-day Saints as a Model Minority," *Dialogue: A Journal of Mormon Thought* 32 (August 1999): 107–128.

6. James E. Talmage, *The Vitality of Mormonism* (Salt Lake City: Deseret News, 1917), 6, 11, 15.

7. For references to progressive Protestants, see John A. Widtsoe, *Joseph Smith as Scientist* (Salt Lake City: Young Men's Mutual Improvement Association, 1908), 112, 115; James E. Talmage to F.C. Williamson, April 22, 1933, James E. Talmage Papers, L. Tom Perry Special Collections, Brigham Young University, Provo, UT. "Report to Church Board of Education: Observations at BYU, November 28–December 10, 21 January 1911," Church History Library, Salt Lake City, Utah. *Seminary Handbook* (Salt Lake City: LDS Department of Education, 1949), 23.

ways, Mormons embraced the confidence and reforming ethos of America's moderate-to-liberal Protestants.

For many liberal Protestants, agreement about the desirable qualities of human character overshadowed divergences of speculative theology, precisely because liberal Protestantism was coming to value behavior more than belief. In 1911, a Methodist minister named Frederick Fisher published an article called "A Methodist Minister's View of Mormonism." Therein, Fisher defended Mormonism for many of the same reasons Talmage had. "Some of their young men lead the world in scholarship," he declared. "Mormonism eagerly welcomes the best ideas and aids which the age can furnish to uplift humanity." He went so far as to say "Mormonism is a deeply religious body—an evangelical Protestant church," and expressed a desire "not for a chasm between Gentile and Mormon, but a union." He expressed confidence that Mormons "will some day come to see as we see—that the bond of the future Christianity will not be a Church, but Christ." Fisher met with a good deal of criticism for his favorable assessment of the Mormons. A Methodist conference in Colorado passed a resolution condemning the article, and the Methodist journal *Zion's Herald* accused Fisher of naiveté. Nonetheless, in a later editorial the *Outlook* defended its correspondent, agreeing that "Mr. Fisher may be too sanguine…but what Utah needs today is not bitterness, but brotherhood."[8]

Fisher praised the Latter-day Saints as "a half million, praying, Bible reading, law abiding, thrifty God fearing men and women." He admired those Mormon traits that most resembled his own liberal Protestantism: a love for education and a forward-looking evangelism that conflated conversion to Christianity with respectable civilization. When his adversaries denounced his praise, they did so by complaining that Fisher had overlooked those features of Mormonism that seemed most alien. *Zion's Herald* challenged the complacency behind Fisher's blunt, brief assertion that "Polygamy is dead." The Presbyterian General Assembly declared that Mormonism's doctrine of the nature of God seemed less Christian than Muslim, calling it "more abhorrent to pure Christianity than to Islam."[9]

---

8. Frederick Vining Fisher, "A Methodist Minister's View of Mormonism," *Outlook*, July 29, 1911, 727–728. On Fisher see Janice Dawson, "Frederick Vining Fisher: Methodist Apologist for Mormonism," *Utah Historical Quarterly* 55 (Fall 1987): 359–369.

9. "A Methodist Minister's Defense of Mormonism," *Current Opinion* 51 (November 1911): 536–537. See also Kathleen Flake, *Politics of American Religious Identity* (Chapel Hill: University of North Carolina Press, 2004), and J. Spencer Fluhman, *"A Peculiar People": Mormonism and the Making of Religion in America* (Chapel Hill: University of North Carolina Press, 2012).

Yet over the next several decades, Fisher's points won more and more converts among American Protestants. In 1930, Arthur Hansen published an article in the *Christian Century* titled "Our Neighbors the Mormons." The magazine was the unofficial national organ of what was called after World War II the American Protestant "mainline." Hansen, a Baptist minister who lived within what he called "the orbit of the Mormon empire," dismissed the questions that had so vexed Fisher's critics as such, and even suggested that Mormonism was a form of Christianity "in some degree," and that "its Christian factor has constantly been raised to a higher degree." Fisher also praised Mormon civic-mindedness and generosity. "We hobnob with the Mormons in our clubs and never know the difference, or we mix in a friendly game of volleyball," he wrote. "It is not unusual for a funeral to be conducted jointly by a Protestant clergyman and a Mormon bishop. Each offers the best consolation of which he is capable and the bond of sympathy is strengthened." Hansen optimistically concluded that their "progressive spirit encourages the hope that the Mormons will yet build a true church of Jesus Christ for the present age."[10]

Twenty years later, Frank Morley, a native Scotsman and the pastor of Grace Presbyterian Church, published a sermon of his own, going even further than Hansen and Fisher. Titled "What We Can Learn from the Church of Jesus Christ of Latter-day Saints," Morley followed Hansen in dismissing potential doctrinal disputes. He allowed that Mormons "believe in things that we would find a little peculiar, perhaps, like eternal progression, revelation taking place today—prophetic revelation—and eternal marriage. They don't believe that death makes any divorce. But is this faith bad?" His answer was no, and his evidence was the Mormon lifestyle: "Idleness, laziness, living off the government—these things to them are evil.... No tea, no coffee, no liquor, and no tobacco (which will immediately rule out a good many of us). You have to be morally clean, you have to pay a tithe, and you have to be an active worker in the church.... It's a family centered religion." Finally Morley warned, "Unless we can revive the laymen of the Presbyterian Church, of the Protestant church, I don't believe the Protestant church has any great future." Mormonism, to his mind, was a model for how to do it.[11] This was a far cry from the criticisms of Mormonism that Fisher dealt with four decades earlier.

---

10. Arthur Hansen, "Our Neighbors the Mormons," *Christian Century*, May 28, 1930, 687.

11. Frank Morley, *What We Can Learn from the Church of Jesus Christ of Latter-day Saints* (Calgary: Grace Presbyterian Church, 1954), 2–3.

At the same time, the trauma of the Second World War and Cold War had driven many American religionists together in a quest for common ground and what were coming to be called "Judeo-Christian values," that were, happily, consonant with American patriotism and capitalist democracy.[12] The Mormons— well-scrubbed teetotalers—were well equipped to participate in that conversation, and ecumenical, mainline Protestants were settling into a comfortable willingness to give Mormons the benefit of the doubt, because they were comfortable with downplaying doctrine in favor of ethical behavior to begin with. Over and over again the *Christian Century* and other mainline commentators acknowledged but excused Mormon doctrinal oddness in order to praise Mormon virtue. In 1962 the *Christian Century* captured the nuance almost perfectly. The journal editorialized that "the Mormon past includes a number of historical and dogmatic positions not generally accepted by the American mainstream," but also argued that Mormon doctrine was less relevant to George Romney's campaign for governor of Michigan than the candidate's political positions and moral behavior. "Must candidates for high office in the US be secularists?" the author rhetorically asked those who mined Mormon theology in order to critique Romney. "Would this whole matter go unnoticed except for the potential for exploitation?"[13] As J. B. Haws notes, the question of whether Mormons were Christian seemed to be a nonissue in the 1950s and 1960s among mainline Christians. The *Century*, at least, called the LDS Church "a Christian" body.[14]

But at the same time, as the qualified praise of Morley and Hansen demonstrates Mormon assimilation was never quite complete, because even to mainline Protestants, doctrine continued to matter. For many mainline Protestants, the doctrine that seemed the most troubling was Mormonism's position on race. Until 1978, the LDS Church refused to ordain black men to the priesthood and denied black men and women access to temple worship, where the most important Mormon sacraments are administered. This position was justified with a constellation of teachings that asserted African spiritual inferiority often via a presumed lineage to the biblical figures of Cain and Ham.[15] This racial doctrine troubled many mainline Protestants precisely

---

12. On Judeo-Christianity see Kevin Schultz, *Tri-Faith America: How Jews and Catholics Held America to its Protestant Promise* (New York: Oxford University Press, 2011), 48–68; Mark Silk, "Notes on the Judeo-Christian Tradition in America," *American Quarterly* 36 (Spring 1984): 65–85.

13. "The Book of Mormon Enters Politics," *Christian Century*, March 28, 1962, 382.

14. Haws, *The Mormon Image in the American Mind*, 34–35.

15. Lester Bush, "Mormonism's Negro Doctrine," *Dialogue: A Journal of Mormon Thought* 8 (Spring 1973): 11–68. W. Paul Reeve, *Religion of a Different Color: Race and the Mormon Struggle for Whiteness* (New York: Oxford University Press, 2015), especially 106–140.

because it contradicted Mormonism's seeming good citizenship in other areas, and the *Christian Century* reported on it frequently in the 1960s and 1970s. The tone that most of the writers in the *Century* took when confronting these restrictions was bemusement. Mormons seemed so well-attuned to other aspects of American life that this policy seemed an aberration crying for reform or elimination with continued upward progress. As one 1966 article title asked, "Is Mormonism Reformable on Race?" The answer seemed a qualified yes: the author hoped that George Romney's national profile would awaken the Mormons to the civic demands of modern American life. Likewise, in 1970 the *Christian Century* editorial page called the restriction "incredibly primitive," but also noted that "Mormon liberals, including educators and students, have been trying to rectify the matter." The journal invited some such liberals, like the sociologist Lowry Nelson, to make such reformist statements in its pages.[16]

The *Christian Century's* efforts were an attempt to draw Mormonism into the ecumenical consensus that the *Century* had taken as its mission to build for the previous fifty years of its history. Given that, the theories of Hunter, Wuthnow, and the rest seem to hold up: liberal Protestants, attracted by Mormon virtues, saw the opportunity for consensus building, only to be occasionally stymied by Mormonism's socially backward policies.[17]

But parallel to such seeming rapprochement, the three decades from the 1940s to the 1960s saw the emergence of conservative factions in both traditions. While mainline Protestants could celebrate Mormonism's apparent commitment to civic-minded and disciplined behavior, to more conservative evangelicals that was simply a façade. Their critique of Mormonism and other movements they deemed un-Christian ran deeper than simple doctrinal dispute. Evangelical reengagement with American politics and culture in the decades after World War II was mobilized in part by the conviction that incorrect theology led to pathological social organization; in other words, heretical movements like Mormonism were dangerous. Francis Schaeffer, the iconoclastic evangelical intellectual, drew on Dutch Reformed Calvinism to argue that theology was important, because the "worldview" that theology created shaped not simply belief, but behavior, values, and political positions—the

---

16. "Pigskin Justice and Mormon Theology," *Christian Century*, January 21, 1970, 67; Lowry Nelson, "Mormons and Blacks," *Christian Century*, October 16, 1974, 949–950.

17. On the Century's mission, see Elesha Coffman, The Christian Century *and the Rise of the Protestant Mainline* (New York: Oxford University Press, 2013).

totality of one's function in society.[18] Mormonism's apparent assimilation, then, could simply not be trusted. Likewise, while James Talmage had once heralded Mormonism's commitment to self-improvement as the foundation for its compatibility with American culture, following World War II Mormon leaders more skeptical of American life and particularly of the growing Protestant presence therein began to levy similar accusations at evangelicals, finding in evangelical claims to authority signs of Protestant degeneration.

In 1942, a set of prominent fundamentalist Protestants founded the National Association of Evangelicals. Over the next decade and a half, a series of para-church organizations mobilized around the evangelistic work of Billy Graham. With that, many fundamentalists vaulted back into the public view rebranded as "neoevangelicals" or simply "evangelicals." Of course, not all fundamentalists embraced Graham and the NAE. The hothead Carl McIntire held to the term fundamentalist, blasted the National Association of Evangelicals (NAE) as "Protestants Imitating Rome," and warned that "God's people cannot join in the communion with unbelief and apostasy!"[19] Some indeed preferred greater separatism than Graham practiced, but, generally, neoevangelicals shared with their fundamentalist counterparts a suspicion of mainline Protestantism's ecumenism and weak adherence to what they believed Christian orthodoxy to be, warning that its laxity led to cultural decay. The NAE indeed distanced itself from the term "fundamentalist," but its flagship institution, Fuller Theological Seminary, required faculty and students to affirm biblical inerrancy, and the NAE rejected any denominations and organizations that affiliated with the National Council of Churches, the organization of the mainline. *Christianity Today*, an evangelical counterpoint to the liberal *Christianity Century*, affirmed that it was abandoning the term fundamentalist "not because of any inclination to disavow traditional fundamentals of the Christian faith," but because the word lacked "scriptural content." Instead, neoevangelicals embraced the concept of "worldview."[20]

---

18. On Schaeffer and worldview, see Jack Rogers, *Claiming the Center: Churches and Conflicting Worldviews* (Louisville, KY: Westminster John Knox Press, 1995), 1–23; David Naugle, *Worldview: The History of a Concept* (Grand Rapids, MI: Wm. B. Eerdmans Publishing Co., 2002), 5–31; Barry Hankins, *Francis Schaeffer and the Shaping of Evangelical America* (Grand Rapids, MI: Wm. B. Eerdmans Publishing Co., 2008), 81–92.

19. Carl McIntire, *Christian Beacon*, May 10, 1951, 8; Carl McIntire, *Christian Beacon*, June 21, 1951, 2, 5, cited in George Marsden, *Reforming Fundamentalism: Fuller Seminary and the New Evangelicalism* (New York: Oxford University Press, 1991), 135.

20. Cited in Axel Schafer, *Countercultural Conservatives: American Evangelicalism from the Postwar Revival to the New Christian Right* (Madison: University of Wisconsin Press, 2011), 43-44. On neoevangelicalism, see Matthew Avery Sutton, *American Apocalypse: A History of Modern Evangelicalism* (Cambridge, MA: Harvard University Press, 2014), 263–293. On neoevangelicals and worldview, see Molly Worthen, *Apostles of Reason: The Crisis of Authority in American Evangelicalism* (New York: Oxford University Press, 2014), 15–17, 23–31.

As the idea of worldview was coming to prominence among evangelicals, so too did the category of cults. Evangelical leaders defined them as small religious movements that not only offered wrong theology but in consequence also a destructive worldview. *The Fundamentals,* a series of books published from 1909 to 1917, included entries on a variety of such movements that carefully documented their theological failures, but it was not until midcentury that the category became a determinative whole.[21] Jan van Baalan's 1938 book *The Chaos of the Cults* was the first to use the term, but as he revised it four times over the next two decades, other writers like J. Oswald Sanders, Julius Bodensieck, and Anthony Hoekema also contributed to a popularization of the term. Though John Morehead and other scholars have observed that the actual countercult movement has never consisted of more than a few hundred people, its influence among evangelical Christians has been disproportionately large. In 1985 *Newsweek* called Walter Martin's breakthrough 1965 book *The Kingdom of the Cults* one of the ten bestselling books on a spiritual topic in American history. The 1982 film *The God Makers* gained an even wider showing; the film's producers claimed that it was being shown to about a thousand evangelical church groups a month in 1983.[22]

Attention to the notion of worldview helps make clear why evangelicals began to talk about cults in the postwar period, and particularly why they so often used the relatively new language of pop psychology to explain its dangers. Though many remained wary of it, in the 1950s some evangelicals like Hildreth Cross and Clyde Narramore sought to use psychology to better explain evangelicalism, positing the existence of a "Christian personality" made healthier and more complete through conversion.[23] Evangelicals seized upon this language, arguing that cults not only warped Christian doctrine but enabled dysfunctional personality types. This, then, made the opening of an offensive against the cults a matter not merely of obscure doctrine, but of the

---

21. Volume 5 of *The Fundamentals* included a chapter on Mormonism, written by R.G. McNiece, a Presbyterian minister living in Salt Lake City. McNiece claimed that it was an "anti-American" and "anti-Christian" system, "intended to deceive the ignorant." R. G. McNiece, *The Fundamentals,* 12 vols. (Chicago: Testimony Publishing Company, 1909–1917), 5:112–113. Another early work is 1917's Wiliam Irvine, *Heresies exposed,* 10th ed. (New York: Loizeaux Bros, 1964), 1, 8, which does not use the word "cult" but argues that a variety of "heresies" were deceived by the myth of "progress," and as such erected "a veil between needy man and a waiting God."

22. John Morehead, "From Cults to Cultures: Bridges as a Case Study in a New Evangelical Paradigm on New Religions," paper presented at Center for the Study of New Religions Conference, Salt Lake City, Utah, June 11, 2009; Douglas Cowan, *Bearing False Witness: An Introduction to the Christian Countercult* (Westport, CT: Praeger, 2003), 72; Haws, *The Mormon Image in the American Mind,* 115.

23. See David Watt, *A Transforming Faith: Explorations of Twentieth Century Evangelicalism* (Philadelphia: Temple University Press, 1991), 137–155.

stability of American society. In *The Kingdom of the Cults*, Walter Martin cited the work of the psychologist Milton Rokeach to diagnose what he called the "psychological substructure of cultism," concluding that cultists of all kinds "manifest a type of institutional dogmatism" and "invest with the authority of the supernatural" whatever "pronouncements are deemed necessary "in order to compensate for the psychological inadequacies that they were undoubtedly suffering. Cults were not merely theologically flawed religions—they also promoted a dysfunctional "cult personality," which posed a threat to social stability and American virtue.[24] Thus by the 1950s, the countercult movement was fully underway, targeting Mormonism not simply as a theological error, but as a threat to American life.[25]

The primary problem for the countercult movement as it began was that Mormons in the mid-twentieth century hardly seemed to be suffering from the sort of social failures that countercult ideology seemed to dictate. In 1959 *Time* magazine celebrated the soon-to-be governor of Michigan, the wealthy Mormon auto executive George Romney, who publically credited his personal and professional success to his religion.[26] Walter Martin conceded that "the average Mormon is usually marked by many sound moral traits. He is generally amiable, almost always hospitable, and extremely devoted to his family." But he and other countercultists warned that the Mormons' seeming normality was in fact a thin veneer hiding social decay. Martin saw in it conspiracy, warning that "the Mormon hierarchy would have the Christian public and the public in general to believe that Mormonism has never been any different than it now is on the surface.... But in reality, almost all contemporary non-Mormon writers concur in their classification of Mormonism historically as a polygamous, not-Christian cult."[27] Wesley Walters, a Presbyterian minister who spent vast amounts of time researching the youth of Joseph Smith, wrote in *Christianity Today* that Mormons "boast an extraordinarily well organized welfare system and a love for culture and the good things of life," but

---

24. Martin, *Kingdom of the Cults*, 25–26.

25. Scholars have distinguished between "countercult" and "anti-cult" activities; the second term is usually applied to secular critics of new religious movements, who assail them for restricting civil liberties, "brainwashing," and so on. The countercult movement, on the other hand, is normally identified with Protestant Christianity and its distinctively religious critique of many of the same groups. While the anti-cult movement arose in the 1970s, the countercult movement (though not the phrase) is far older. See Cowan, *Bearing False Witness*, 15–20; George Chryssides, *Exploring New Religions* (London: Cassell, 1999).

26. "The Dinosaur Hunter," *Time*, April 6, 1959, 84.

27. Walter Martin, *The Maze of Mormonism* (Santa Ana, CA: Vision House, 1978), 7.

at the same time, they were "enmeshed in a religion so materialistic in emphasis and so lacking in reverence."[28]

All cults, Martin was convinced, were simply manifestations of the great spiritual failure of the twentieth century, the worldview called "modernism," which the fundamentalist *Sunday School Times* defined as "primarily, and in its worst form, the worship or deification of man." Modernism was responsible for higher criticism of the Bible and evolution, which the *Times* located at the root of Nazism in Germany, and which other evangelicals later summoned to castigate abortion and the women's movement in the 1960s and 1970s.[29] Anthony Hoekema linked cults to modernism when he warned that that "humility goes against the grain of human nature. Man wants to be his own lord and master," and that "the most basic characteristic of the cult" was its indulgence of this flaw. Cults in his telling embraced a "tendency to perfectionism. There is among the members of the cult a feeling of superior holiness."[30] That sense of superiority hid for cultists their own flaws, thus rendering them dysfunctional individuals unfit for democracy.

Oddly enough, the late 1960s Mormon theology was in many ways drifting as close to evangelical pessimism about human morality as it ever had. This can be seen especially through the lens of two Mormon leaders in particular whose voluminous writings gained them the midcentury reputation of Mormonism's leading theologians (though neither had formal theological training). In 1951 Joseph Fielding Smith, great-grandnephew of Joseph Smith, became the president of the Quorum of the Twelve Apostles, first in line to the presidency of the LDS Church. He was already in his seventies and had a reputation as an intellectual, but over the next decade, by virtue of a regular column in a church periodical and authorship of several books, his star ascended even higher. He was followed by his son-in-law, Bruce R. McConkie, a midlevel church leader who in 1958 published a book with the audacious title of *Mormon Doctrine: A Compendium of the Gospel* that proved wildly popular and propelled him in 1972 to the Quorum of the Twelve Apostles. Both Smith and McConkie embraced conservative theological language about the nature of scripture and other topics, and yet were thoroughly willing to lob rhetorical

---

28. Wesley P. Walters, "Mormonism," *Christianity Today*, December 19, 1960, 228, 230.

29. *Sunday School Times*, December 12, 1939, 914. On modernism and the crises of the 1960s, see Sutton, *American Apocalypse*, 354–359.

30. Anthony Hoekema, *The Four Major Cults* (Grand Rapids, MI: Wm. B. Eerdmans Publishing Co., 1963), 373.

salvos back and forth with the theologically conservative evangelical counter-cult movement.[31]

The hermeneutical theory of anthropologist Brian Malley helps to illumi-nate the difference between these groups. Malley has observed that conserva-tive evangelicals' arguments about biblical inerrancy in practice work as a system of authority and applicability rather than as an actual hermeneutical strategy. The purpose of asserting that the Bible has a plain meaning perceiv-able because of some form of divine inspiration, according to Malley, "is not so much to establish the meaning of the text as to establish transitivity be-tween the text and beliefs." That is, "evangelicals use literal interpretation to mean 'normal' interpretation, in contrast to special figurative or rhetorical hermeneutics." Thus they can assert the interpretations they call "normal" have greater biblical warrant, and hence theological authority, than other in-terpretations.[32] Insofar as conservative Mormons accepted evangelical lan-guage about the provenance of scripture, they were actually accepting a certain style of rhetoric about authority. The two groups, in Malley's terms, possessed different "normal" interpretations of the Bible, and it was precisely that gap between the similarity of their hermeneutical method and the differences be-tween their conclusions that infuriated the countercult movement and sparked the conservative Mormon response: to starkly emphasize the gap be-tween their own claims to truth and the apostasy of the rest of the world.

The countercult movement was quite aware of the gap between themselves and Mormons, and diagnosed it as a sign of social and psychological dysfunc-tion. For instance, in *The Kingdom of the Cults*, Walter Martin blasted McConkie's writings as a collection of "theological double-talk."[33] Martin ac-knowledged that "Mormons are generally considered by many to be funda-mentalists, and sad to say zealous Mormon missionaries quote the Bible far more freely than many true Christians."[34] But he also warned that "it is simple for a cultist to spiritualize and redefine the clear meaning of biblical text and

---

31. For the careers of these men, Gregory Prince and William Robert Wright, *David O. McKay and the Rise of Modern Mormonism* (Salt Lake City: University of Utah Press, 2005), 45–53.

32. Brian Malley, *How the Bible Works* (Walnut Creek: Altamira Press, 2005), 73, 98. See also Christian Smith, *The Bible Made Impossible: Why Biblicism is not a Truly Evangelical Reading of Scripture* (Grand Rapids, MI: Brazos Press, 2012); Amy Johnson Frykholm, *Rapture Culture: Left Behind in Evangelical America* (New York: Oxford University Press, 2007); Susan Friend Harding, *The Book of Jerry Falwell: Evangelical Language and Politics* (Princeton, NJ: Princeton University Press, 2001).

33. Martin, *Kingdom of the Cults*, 164–165.

34. Walter Martin, *Rise of the Cults* (Santa Ana, CA: Vision House, 1977), 51.

teaching so as to be in apparent harmony with the historic Christian faith."[35] Ed Decker, one of the founders of the countercult organization Ex-Mormons for Jesus, warned that "although it uses Christian language to disguise its paganism," Mormonism was in fact a conflation of Hinduism and occultism, an odd combination that Decker concocted to explain Mormon teachings about the relationship between God and humanity.[36] This issue of language was of great importance to Martin and other countercultists; as evangelicals, they believed that the Word of God had power, and cultist manipulation of it was in part what made them so dangerous. Mormons were not simply flat out wrong, but threatening because they parodied true Christianity.

Martin and his fellow countercultists were right, in a sense. In the 1950s and 1960s, Mormon theology entered a period some scholars call "Mormon neoorthodoxy" or "retrenchment Mormonism"; the first term emphasizes its similarities to contemporary Protestantism (neoorthodoxy's emphasis on sin and the transcendence of God), and the second emphasizes its particularities (a concurrent emphasis on Mormon exclusivism and priesthood authority).[37] The two interpretations are not contradictory. Despite its growing affinity for aspects of conservative evangelical theology, Mormons were in fact using the language they borrowed from evangelical writers not to draw Mormonism closer to Protestantism, but to reemphasize its own uniqueness and authority. Armand Mauss has observed that midcentury Mormons emphasized a high view of scripture as a means to emphasize their own unique prophetic authority.[38] McConkie and his neoorthodox colleagues emphasized the direct inspiration of the Bible in order to establish a model by which to understand themselves, just as Susan Friend Harding describes Jerry Falwell using biblical stories to describe his own ministry.[39] Thus, claiming divine inspiration for the Bible was the equivalent of claiming divine inspiration for those men the Mormons venerated as contemporary prophets.

Smith and McConkie indeed spoke about scripture in language that echoed evangelical biblical inerrantists. As McConkie wrote, "All scripture is true.... Scriptural utterances are given to man by revelation from the Holy

---

35. Martin, *Kingdom of the Cults*, 19–21.

36. Ed Decker and Dave Hunt, *The God Makers: The Shocking Truth About What Mormons Really Believe* (Irvine, CA: Harvest House, 1996), 68.

37. The first phrase is in O. Kendall White, *Mormon Neo-Orthodoxy: A Crisis Theology* (Salt Lake City: Signature Books, 1987); the second in Armand L. Mauss, in *The Angel and the Beehive: The Mormon Struggle with Assimilation* (Urbana: University of Illinois Press, 1994).

38. Mauss, *Angel and the Beehive*, 157–177.

39. Harding, *The Book of Jerry Falwell*, 85–105.

Ghost. These statements, made by the power of the Holy Spirit, consist of the identical words which the Lord himself would speak under the same circumstances."[40] Compare this to Harold Lindsell, a near-exact contemporary of McConkie, whose 1976 book *Battle for the Bible* was the most popular expression of the theory conservative Protestants call plenary inspiration: "Inspiration may be defined as the inward work of the Holy Spirit in the hearts and minds of chosen men who then wrote the Scriptures so that God got written what he wanted. The Bible in all of its parts constitutes the written Word of God to man. The Word is free from all error in its original autographs.... It is wholly trustworthy in matters of history and doctrine."[41] At the same time, Mormons frequently claimed that the Bible was understood best when interpreted through the lens of modern Mormon scripture. Mark Petersen, a Mormon apostle and theological ally of McConkie and Smith, declared that "there can be no question of the fact that Latter-day Saints accept the Bible as it stands probably more fully and literally than any other group." Yet Petersen clarified, "When augmented by modern scripture as the Book of Mormon indicates would be the case it can direct us into the paths of eternal salvation."[42] The Bible should be interpreted through the ministry of modern Mormon theology: it was properly understood not in its own right, but in subordination to Mormonism's prophets and additional scripture.

McConkie illustrated the method Petersen described when he claimed that the biblical patriarchs Abraham, Isaac, and Jacob "knew about Christ, baptism, salvation, and temple ordinances, and had the holy priesthood and all the rest.... There will surely be a day when we will have the Old Testament in its original form, so it will demonstrate that fact."[43] Similarly, Joseph Fielding Smith attempted to link Paul's teachings to Mormon practice of genealogy and ordinance work for the dead, musing, "perhaps we do not have the full texts of Paul's instruction to Timothy and Titus. We may be sure, however that he would not take a stand in opposition to the teachings of the prophets who went before him. Genealogical research must have been done in the days of

40. Bruce R McConkie, *Doctrinal New Testament Commentary* (Salt Lake City: Bookcraft, 1966), 1:55.

41. Harold Lindsell, *The Battle for the Bible* (Grand Rapids, MI: Zondervan, 1976), 30.

42. Mark E. Petersen, *As Translated Correctly* (Salt Lake City: Deseret Book Company, 1966), 6, 17. Harding, *The Book of Jerry Falwell*, 50–55.

43. Bruce R. McConkie, "The Doctrinal Restoration," in Monte S. Nyman and Robert L. Millet, eds., *The Joseph Smith Translation: The Restoration of Plain and Precious Things* (Provo: Religious Studies Center, 1985), 22.

Paul which he did not condemn."[44] The Mormons expected scripture to conform to the teachings of prophetic leadership, but, following Malley, they also leaned upon scripture itself to provide legitimation for that leadership. Thus, the various revisions of Hebrew Bible narratives Joseph Smith produced featured prominent biblical figures—Adam, Eve, Moses—receiving Christian baptism, testifying of Jesus, and so on. A 1949 manual for Mormon missionaries instructed its students to teach their converts that "the true Church of Christ cannot exist without continual revelation from God; the true church is not founded upon scripture." But at the same time, it also instructed missionaries that "the effectiveness of your mission will depend upon how thoroughly you are willing to memorize scripture—the convincing missionary has paid the price of hard mental labor." Memorization would allow the missionaries to master practice speeches the manual offered, like this:

> Peter, speaking to Cornelius in Acts 10:34–5 says this, Of a truth I perceive that God is not respecter of persons, but in every nation he that feareth him and worketh righteousness is accepted with him. Now Peter states, in every nation! In light of this, Mrs. Jones, is it just as logical to you that God would send prophets to the American side of the world, as to the Eastern continent, where the Bible was written?[45]

The manual's simultaneous assertion and qualification of scriptural authority illustrated Joseph Fielding Smith's arguments about right and wrong ways to interpret scripture: "One proclaimed by the great mother church is that there is a sure way of interpretation and this is the power vested in the pope who is infallible in such interpretation. The other view is that man must depend upon his own reason for his scriptural understanding." The first he ascribed to Roman Catholics, the second to individualistic Protestants. Unfortunately, Smith argued, both of these interpretations were faulty, for "it is only natural when the heavens are closed and men are left to grope and find their way without divine aid there will be confusion."[46] What was needed consistently to interpret scripture was more scripture: the inspired revelations of Mormon

---

44. Joseph Fielding Smith, *Answers to Gospel Questions* (Salt Lake City: Deseret Book Company, 1957), 1:216.

45. Richard Lloyd Anderson, "A Plan for Effective Missionary Work: Northwestern States Mission," 1949, 8, 17, 2, Church History Library, Salt Lake City, Utah.

46. Joseph Fielding Smith, *The Restoration of All Things* (Salt Lake City: Deseret Book Company, 1965), 66, 69.

leaders. As Smith argued, "Guided by the Book of Mormon, Doctrine and Covenants, and the Spirit of the Lord it is not difficult for one to discern the errors in the Bible.... The Doctrine and Covenants contains the word of God to those who dwell here now. It is our book."[47]

Evangelicals consistently dismissed this way of interpreting scripture as subjective, dependent upon the changeable state of Mormon leaders. Carl Henry, the greatest neoevangelical theologian, worried that Mormons subscribed to the "functionalist approach" to religion, which emphasized a religion's capacity to make one feel good about life over its objective truth claims, and argued that such functionalism offered "no objective criterion for distinguishing Jehovah's Witnesses, Swedenborgians, Mormons or so called Christian Buddhists from the New Testament church."[48] That is, Mormons were emotionally needy, wanting emotional reassurance in the face of threatening fact, which is why Lindsell labeled Mormonism "fideism," a faith based upon choice rather than evidence. Hoekema argued that this was derived from anxiety. "Apparently the Mormons wish to be wiser than Christ himself," he marveled, shaking his head at what he deemed the unbiblical Mormon doctrine of universal salvation. He tried to deduce some understanding of why individual Mormons would embrace nonbiblical doctrines, and concluded that "people find in the cult a warm and brotherly fellowship which they have failed to find in a church.... Other factors often weigh more heavily than the rational."[49] All such criticisms laid a foundation for Walter Martin's definition of a cult: "a group of people gathered around a specific person's interpretation of the Bible." It is here that pathology again entered into the ways countercultists interpreted Mormonism: in their reading, those who joined cults succumbed to the subjective proof of emotion and personal appeal and rejected the objective evidence evangelicals saw in the Bible.[50]

Ultimately, then, to the countercultists, Mormonism was thoroughly modernistic, which is to say it was a creature of the worst excesses they saw in the postwar age: materialism, self-aggrandizement, and resting comfortably in a corrupt American society. In the *Moody Monthly*, a conservative evangelical journal, the pastor Gordon Fraser noted that Mormon "teachings have special appeal to any one who likes the idea of lots of religion with a minimum

---

47. Joseph Fielding Smith, *Doctrines of Salvation* (Salt Lake City: Bookcraft, 1975), 1:191, 3:199.

48. Carl Henry, *God, Revelation, and Authority* (Grand Rapids, MI: Zondervan, 1965), 138.

49. Harold Lindsell, *The Bible in the Balance* (Grand Rapids, MI: Zondervan, 1979), 363; Hoekema, *Four Major Cults*, 23, 407–408.

50. Martin, *Kingdom of the Cults*, 11.

separation from worldliness."[51] According to this interpretation, Mormonism required a curious blend of wishy-washiness and comfortable self-regard: a personality needy enough for the easy answers Mormonism offered combined with the sort of credulity that allowed one to believe they might become a god. Martin wrote, "To board the Mormon train one needs a strong imagination [and] a supreme ego."[52] According to Anthony Hoekema, "we hear a prominent Mormon author say that in order to receive the highest grade of celestial exaltation one must keep the commandments of the Lord in all things—implying that this can be done and is done by many Mormons."[53] Hoekema claimed that Mormonism, like other cults, offered "definite convictions," "zeal," and a "strong sense of urgency," and preyed upon those who were uncertain about themselves, those who "fall for everything" by offering them such an exalted view of their potential.[54]

Ironically, however, as evangelicals were assailing Mormonism for its seeming comfort in a worldly American society, Smith and McConkie were leveling a like critique, convicting evangelicals' own doctrine by salvation by grace alone as the product of flaws in personality. McConkie labeled salvation by grace by the God of the classic trinity the "chief heresy of a new fallen and decadent Christianity." He warned that "the protestant churches [are] the harlot daughters which broke off from the great and abominable church." Further, McConkie followed the countercult movement itself, extrapolating from what he considered inadequate theology to the psychological disorder which inevitably underlay it. He mused that "anytime men can devise a system of worship that will let them live after the manner of the world, to live in their carnal and fallen state, and at the same time one which will satisfy their innate and instinctive desires to worship, such to them is a marvelous achievement."[55] This psychological diagnosis of evangelicals paralleled evangelicals' diagnosis of Mormonism: each religion found in the other a cover for lax morality, a secret desire to sin, and an attachment to worldly decadence. The similarity of polemic is striking, as is the language of psychology that informed it.

After George Romney's son, Mitt, announced a bit for the presidency in 2008, the editors of the *Christian Century* revealed that not much had changed

---

51. Gordon Fraser, "Mormonism," *Moody Monthly*, June 1959, 16.

52. Martin, *Rise of the Cults*, 55.

53. Harold Lindsell, *The Bible in the Balance* (Grand Rapids, MI: Zondervan, 1979), 363. Hoekema, *Four Major Cults*, 53, 376.

54. Ibid., 3–4.

55. McConkie, "What Think Ye of Salvation By Grace," Church History Library, Salt Lake City, Utah; McConkie, *Mormon Doctrine*, 317–318.

for mainline Protestants since the journal covered his father. "If indeed Romney were elected and proved to be a president who pursued peace, served justice and remembered the poor, and if his presidency thereby lent prestige to Mormonism, we would have to say that the boost was in some sense deserved," the editors wrote, revealing that they still believed Romney's ethics outweighed his heterodoxy.[56] Five years later, writing in *Christianity Today*, the evangelical Stephen Mansfield worried about the question. "There will be a price to voting for Romney, of course," he wrote, warning that Mormonism would "enjoy heightened visibility and influence" should Romney win. After reviewing traditional countercult arguments about Mormon theology, he concluded that "it is a legitimate question, then, whether anything about Mitt Romney's Mormon identity should concern us as we decide how to vote."[57]

And yet, Mansfield's wrestle with the question revealed how difficult it was becoming to sustain the conviction that their religion's status as a cult disqualified Mormons from participation in public life. The more successful Mormons were, and the more thoroughly Mormons like Romney seemed to embrace the indictment that evangelicals levied upon a corrupt American culture, the harder it became to insist their religion made them full participants in that corruption. The 2012 Romney campaign was a case in point. Though Mansfield agonized over the question, he ultimately concluded that, in fact, the mainline position on Mormonism was correct. "Voting for Mitt Romney—yes, a Mormon former bishop—is certainly a moral option for followers of Jesus Christ. For those who want a pro-life, pro-free market, pro-business, pro-defense, and America first champion, Mitt Romney is their man. It is no sin or dishonor of God to vote for him, even though his Latter-day Saint religion is far from orthodox Christianity," Mansfield declared.[58] Mormonism might be a cult, but this did not bar Mormons from righteousness. Inadvertently, it seemed, Mansfield had stumbled into the same position of Arthur Hansen and the rest of the midcentury mainline. Mitt Romney himself had shown the way. In 2007 he argued, "It is important to recognize that while differences in theology exist between the churches in America, we share a common creed of moral convictions," and went on to praise the moral virtues of a variety of American religions.[59]

---

56. "A Mormon President?" *Christian Century*, January 15, 2008, 14.

57. Stephen Mansfield, "No Perfect Options," *Christianity Today*, August 31, 2012, 74–75.

58. Ibid., 74.

59. Mitt Romney, "Faith in America," *National Public Radio*, last updated December 7, 2007, www.npr.org/templates/story/story.php?storyId=16969460.

What had changed? The evangelical convictions that drove the countercult movement remained largely the same: Mansfield decried Mormon heresy. Rather, despite the movement's best efforts, Mormonism's success at integrating itself into American culture, and particularly into the conservative coalition that evangelical Protestants had spearheaded, forced evangelicals like Mansfield to find a way to resolve the divergent mandates they felt pressed upon them. On the one hand, they wanted to defend theological orthodoxy; on the other, they hoped to advocate for conservative politics. Mansfield's approach to Mormonism was an attempt to have it both ways. Their political activism had forced Romney and Mansfield into the sort of practical pluralism the midcentury mainline was also attempting to create: a community where differences of theology did not preclude civic cooperation. The countercult movement had always insisted that theological heterodoxy posed a danger to political stability. Changing political circumstances, however, made it difficult for evangelicals to maintain their once-stalwart defense of orthodoxy.

13

Holding on to the "Chosen Generation"

THE MORMON BATTLE FOR YOUTH IN THE LATE
1960S AND EARLY 1970S

Rebecca de Schweinitz

AT THE OCTOBER 1969 LDS General Conference, Church President David O. McKay exulted in the progress of modern America—a country that had just put a man on the moon. He also expressed dismay at the turmoil and moral decay of the nation. Pointing to Gallup polls that suggested young Americans held increasingly lax moral standards, often rejected home and family life, consumed alcohol and illicit drugs at alarming rates, and seemed more prone to crime and delinquency than earlier generations, McKay focused his remarks on Mormon youth, calling on them to champion traditional values and commit to self-mastery. At the same conference, Apostle Boyd K. Packer charged that militant student protests and events like Woodstock stood as evidence that young people were "frantically" "clinging" to political and social issues in misguided attempts to satisfy deeper spiritual needs. He encouraged young Mormons not to cut their traditional "moorings," and to look to parents and the church rather than to peers and "causes" to find meaning in life.[1]

LDS Church leaders had reason for alarm. The emergence of a "world community," and the escalation of technological, economic, and social change, had ushered in what social scientists like Margaret Mead called "a new phase of cultural evolution." In the Age of Aquarius it was no longer certain that society's elders could effectively prepare the young for what lay ahead. Youth increasingly questioned traditional institutions and authority, rejecting as "archaic" passive socialization models that promoted "submission to authority, hard work, social conformity, and orderliness." Young people expected to be heard and to make their own path to the future. For America's traditional

---

1. David O. McKay, *Conference Report*, October 1969, 5–9; Boyd K. Packer, *Conference Report*, October 1969, 36–38.

religions, this meant a notable exodus of youth from the pews. Internal studies suggested a similar decline in religious activity rates among Mormon youth.[2]

To combat this trend, in the late 1960s and early 1970s Mormon leaders introduced "preventative measures to hold all youth close to the church."[3] Paradoxically—and perhaps out of necessity—those measures reflected the very attitudes about idealism and agency that underpinned the countercultural movement that threatened to lead Mormon youth astray. LDS leaders validated youth values and young people's desires to shape their own lives and improve the world. Giving them opportunities for service and voice within the organizational framework of the church, leaders celebrated youth agency and empowered young people at the same time that they reinforced social cohesion, the religion's principles, and its membership rolls. Leaders also drew on distinct Mormon theological ideas about freedom, choice, and authenticity to challenge popular interpretations of those terms. Appropriating certain values of modern youth culture, LDS leaders created a meaningful yet bounded place for agency-conscious young people within the faith. In their efforts to strengthen the commitment of Mormon youth to their religious heritage, leaders employed a variety of strategies, from pep talks and praise, to expanded forums for youth voice and new methods of religious education. LDS cultural productions also played a role in the development of church messages for youth, teaching young people—and giving them a chance to act out—their parts as members of a "chosen generation" of Latter-day "warriors."

Not a Gap

Notwithstanding their concerns, leaders often chose to minimize the idea of youth dissent within the church. Expressing primarily hopeful views about LDS youth, they insisted that young Mormons "take their faith seriously" and that "a generation bond, not a gap, between students and the priesthood exists." Church authorities like Marion D. Hanks, Gordon B. Hinckley, and Presiding Bishop John H. Vandenberg argued that the "minority" of youth who "get so much press attention" did not represent the "solid majority of our young people

2. Margaret Mead, *Culture and Commitment: A Study of the Generation Gap* (New York: Doubleday & Company, Inc., 1970), 54, 51; Henry Malcolm, *Generation of Narcissus* (New York: Little, Brown, 1971), 18, 155, 239; BYU Department of Youth Leadership, "Young Adult Male Attitudes and Interests of the Church of Jesus Christ of Latter-day Saints: A Research Report," July 1970. In *Youth and the Church* (Salt Lake City: Deseret Book Company, 1970), 10–11, The Church of Jesus Christ of Latter-day Saints Church History Library, Salt Lake City, Utah (hereafter CHL), for example, early 1970s Church President Harold B. Lee described (and decried) the societal changes outlined here.

3. Delbert L. Stapley, "MIA Conference talk," 1969, CHL.

who want to do well" and who "desire guidance in reaching success." In fact, leaders suggested that the church's youth were more not less committed to societal and religious ideals than the older generation, describing them as "patriotic, purposeful, current, sensitive, concerned, thoughtful, involved, full of faith, anxious to serve." Young Men's President Robert Backman explained: "Our young men and women have a deep sense of purpose and a keen appreciation for our social needs.... They want to make this a better world in which to live." And President David O. McKay affirmed: "We may expect in our students more idealism ... more wholesome courage and faith."[4]

Such sentiments echoed those of contemporary politicians, civil rights organizations, and labor and education leaders who lauded the "ethical, idealistic sprit" of youth and pointed out there were more young people saying, "build man, build, [than] burn, baby, burn." Some secular leaders and groups challenged negative stereotypes of youth in hopes of convincing the political establishment and adult citizens to extend voting rights to eighteen-year-olds. Others aimed to convince idealistic youth themselves to keep their faith in the social order. Like these contemporaries, Mormon leaders seemed especially concerned with endorsing youth values and signaling to young people that they need not rebel against traditional institutions in order to realize their aims.[5]

Expressing sympathy with youth perspectives, LDS leaders placed young people's noble desire "to restore innocence and purity to the world"—their "deep and consistent concern for things spiritual and eternal"—at the center of their "current unrest." Mormon youth's increasing tendency to "go astray" could be explained by an understandable "loss of faith in the ruling generation." Casting youth as "bewildered and emotionally upset" victims, confused by adults who "present a blurred image of American ideals and values to the

---

4. Marion D. Hanks, "On These Principles," *Improvement Era*, November 1969, 45; Marion D. Hanks, *Conference Report*, October 1967, 57–58; Howard W. Hunter, "We Are a People of Destiny," Vault Talks, folder 76, CHL; Lewis S. Feuer, *The Conflict of Generations: The Character and Significance of Student Movements* (New York: Basic Books, 1969), 3; Millard Dale Baughman, *What Do Students Really Want* (Bloomington, IN: Phi Delta Kappa Educational Foundation, 1972), 43; Marion D. Hanks, "Tell and Show," *The Improvement Era*, November 1969, 5; Robert Backman, "Youth's Opportunity to Serve," *Ensign*, July 1973, www.lds.org/ensign/1973/07/youths-opportunity-to-serve; David O. McKay, *Conference Report*, April 1968, 70. For a broad look at the LDS response to the youth problem see the November 1969 issue of *The Improvement Era*.

5. Henry Malcolm, *Generation of Narcissus*, 20; Senate Judiciary Committee, *Hearings Before the Subcommittee on Constitutional Amendments of the Committee on the Judiciary on S.J. Res. 14, and S.J. Res 78 Relating to Lowering the Voting Age to 18*, 90th Cong., 2d sess., May 14–16, 1968, 43. See Rebecca de Schweinitz, "'The Proper Age for Suffrage': Vote 18 and the Politics of Age From World War II to the Age of Aquarius," in Corinne T. Field and Nick L. Syrett, eds., *Age in America: Colonial Era to the Present* (New York: New York University Press, 2015), 209–236.

youth of today," Mormon authorities diagnosed the "youth problem" as an *adult* problem. "The young are sensitive; they see the gap that exists between our stated convictions and our conduct," former educator Marion D. Hanks explained.[6] According to such leaders, the seeming rebelliousness of young people did not stem from a disturbing and insurmountable generation gap, or from cynicism and impiety on the part of youth. Rather, rebellion originated in a lack of well-defined guidelines and with grown-ups who failed to meet their family responsibilities and live their professed values. The remedy for such a problem was clear.

Other Christian groups in the United States responded to waning youth religiosity in this period by softening or de-emphasizing doctrine and religious study, and by moving toward youth programs centered on entertainment, self-fulfillment, and collaboration with external entities on social justice issues. Catholic religious training, for instance, became less authoritarian and distinctive and more "secular and generic." Methodist youth organizations steered away from "clearly articulated core beliefs" and lifestyle demands and increasingly worked with "secular institutions to improve and serve society," while evangelicals aggressively "retooled their youth environments" to create a "hip Christian youth culture" that reflected the styles of the period and the "pleasurable," emotionally satisfying side of spiritual life.[7] LDS leaders like Packer considered such accommodations to be "signs of apostasy." Instead of "comprising," in an effort not to "lose youth," the church resolved to be an "ensign." Viewing young people as fundamentally "confused…about life and its purposes," and in search of "identification, security, and standards and values in which they can place their trust," Mormon leaders reiterated the importance of core religious beliefs. Rather than relax their rhetoric and lower their expectations for youth, church leaders emphasized stark distinctions between right and wrong, offered harsh condemnations of shifting moral and social values (and cultural manifestations of those values, like rock music, short skirts, and beards), and recommitted the church to religious education through Sunday Schools for all ages and expanded high school "Seminary" and college-age "Institute" scripture study programs. Between 1965 and 1971

---

6. Marion D. Hanks, *Conference Report*, October, 1969, 102; Albert L. Payne, "Religious Concerns of Our Youth," *Improvement Era*, January 1970, 23; Dr. G. Homer Durham, "These Times: Student Unrest," *Improvement Era*, May 1969, 107; Delbert L. Stapley, "The Challenge of Effective Youth Leadership, Our Responsibility to the Youth of the Church," M.I.A. Conference Talk, June 1968, CHL; Garth Allred, "A Study of Expressed Attitudes of Selected LDS Youth Regarding Selected Social Trends" (master's thesis, Brigham Young University, 1971), 29–31; Hanks, *Conference Report*, October, 1967, 58.

7. Thomas E. Bergler, *The Juvenilization of American Christianity* (Grand Rapids, MI: Wm. B. Eerdmans Publishing Co., 2012), 148, 150, 184–190, 199–201.

the number of young people enrolled in Seminary classes increased from 103,500 to 141,514 and the number of Institute programs increased from 166 to 326. Additionally, the church expanded these programs internationally and added home study options for many LDS youth.[8]

The LDS Church also counseled adult members to live their religion and dedicate themselves to family life. Identifying a "need for exemplary parents," leaders encouraged women to be "keepers of the home" instead of wage earners, and warned fathers that to put work, civic affairs, status, and their own needs above home life—or to manifest double standards—would result in dire consequences for their children. Youth "want people to be really real," they said, and cautioned: "the reason that many children go astray is because parents need to be better examples." Repeating the arguments of prominent social scientists, leaders warned that "when adult authority ceases to function effectively, the young are victimized by each other." Furthermore, the church specifically linked "hypocrisy in the lives of adults" with young people's drug use.[9]

In 1969, the church presented its understanding of and prescription for youth and their parents in the film *That Which Was Lost*. The production's main character, Rick Baldwin, is a "thoughtful troubled teenager caught in a war of values." Searching for authenticity, he rejects the phoniness of his father, whose schedule book and image in the community appear to mean more to him than his children. Rick would rather be like Turtle, the head of a drug-using hippy clan, who might be "far out" in some ways, but to the seventeen-year-old, "a lot more honest than most people"—as well as more attentive and accepting. Larry, Rick's intrepid priests quorum (sixteen- to eighteen-year-old male youth group) advisor, ultimately saves both the boy and his father by convincing Mr. Baldwin to get his priorities back on track

---

8. Bruce M. Lake, "The Organization and Function of the Latter-Day Saint Student Association" (PhD diss., University of Southern California, 1968), 4; Boyd K. Packer, *Conference Report*, October, 1973, 22; Allred, "A Study of Expressed Attitudes of Selected LDS Youth Regarding Selected Social Trends," 75; William E. Berrett, *A Miracle in Weekday Religious Education* (Salt Lake City: Salt Lake Printing Center, 1988), 92, 147; On trends among other Christian churches see Bergler, *Juvenilization*; Jon Pahl, *Youth Ministry in America: 1930 to the Present* (Peabody, MA.: Hendrickson Publishers, Inc., 2000); John Turner, *Bill Bright and the Campus Crusade for Christ* (Chapel Hill: University of North Carolina Press, 2008).

9. Victor L. Brown, "Wanted: Parents with Courage," *Improvement Era*, May 1970, 46; Vandenberg, *Conference Report*, October 1967, 78. LDS leaders buttressed their arguments by calling on public experts like Yale theologian Liston Pope. See Pope, "Traditional Values in Transition," in Eli Ginzberg, ed., *Values and Ideals of American Youth* (New York: Columbia University Press, 1961) 229–230; Kenneth Godfrey, "A Growing Generation," *The Improvement Era*, November 1969, 8; Hanks, *Conference Report*, October 1969, 99; Allred, "A Study of Expressed Attitudes of Selected LDS Youth Regarding Selected Social Trends," 35; N. Eldon Tanner, *Conference Report*, October 1970, 51.

and by helping Rick to understand that while the church has "nothing new," neither is there "anything new in the new morality." "The same old laws still apply."[10]

Affirming to youth the "need for order" found in the "eternal truths" taught by the church, and to adults, the need to take responsibility for young people and accept them "without reservation," *That Which Was Lost* deromanticized the supposed generation crisis captured and represented by J. D. Salinger's *Catcher in the Rye.* University of Chicago theologian Joseph Sittler, whose interpretations of the youth problem were presented at campuses across the country and repeated by many other commentators, including Mormon leaders, explained the plight of Holden Caulfield (and Rick Baldwin), and nonfictional youth like them. Young people, he said, are "sardonic, not because [they are] tough but precisely because [they are] tender." They may be "flip, contemptuous and bitter not because [they] despise values or ideals—but because [they] see these verbally celebrated by [their] elders, and regularly betrayed." As Mr. Baldwin explains his falling out with Rick: "He said he wouldn't go to college [or church] and end up a hypocrite like me."[11]

The script also reflected the church's often gendered construction of the youth problem and its solutions. Male characters and their actions dominate the storyline—from Rick, whose struggle lies at the center of the narrative; Larry, for whom the popular dictum "do my own thing" comes to mean watching out for the wayward youth; Mr. Baldwin, who, at the film's climax chooses his son over his appointment book and public standing; and Turtle, who talks about "brotherhood" but decides to "cut out" rather than help a follower "freaking out" on drugs. While Rick's mother is absent from the plot, Bishop Tyler, a fifty-ish "efficient executive man" with "insight and compassion," also appears as an important actor, advising and directing Larry's efforts through the appropriate hierarchical line of priesthood authority.

The only notable female role is Lily. "Always a mess," the "frail, nondescript girl with quiet almost expressionless manner" encourages Rick to leave Turtle's group while he still can. It's too late for her. The narrative strips Lily of

---

10. BYU Department of Motion Picture Production, *That Which Was Lost*, video cassette (Salt Lake City: The Church of Jesus Christ of Latter-day Saints, 1969), CHL.

11. Ibid; Joseph Sittler, "The Interior Aspects of Change," in Ginzberg, ed., *Values and Ideals of American Youth*, 294. Methodists also explicitly recognized youth rebellion as an expression of positive values. But, as Thomas Bergler, explains, Methodist youth leaders tended to channel idealistic young people into secular social service work at the cost of preserving the church, and to (inadvertently) make "normal" church structures seem "all but useless" to a meaningful, socially engaged life. See Bergler, *Juvenilization*, 184–187.

any agency, explaining that "a groovy guy" tricked her into taking LSD (she thought it was candy) at age fourteen. The Mutual Improvement Association (MIA) Parent and Youth Night program that year even more directly downplayed female self-determination. In *A Blue Ribbon Affair* Jennie explains, "I'm glad I'm a girl. Boys have to make so many decisions." Another young woman retorts, "but girls have to live with the decision that boys make." A young man then explains his plight (and that of all young men) quite differently: "I've got all these things inside, pulling me." In both *That Which was Lost* and *A Blue Ribbon Affair* only male characters consciously wrestle with competing choices.[12]

Just as leaders focused on young men, understood to be "more independent in their thinking and less conforming," they emphasized the role of fathers and male priesthood authority in solving the youth problem. Leaders believed that women did not need as much convincing. Although anxious about the influence of a growing feminist movement, they saw women as "naturally" family-centered and religiously oriented. Nonetheless, they exhorted all parents to protect the idealism of youth so that they would not "sour into cynicism." All adults were to make concerted attempts to be available, to listen, and to respect young people's individuality. Don't "turn off teens" by judging young people or comparing their choices to those of past generations, authorities advised. Avoid criticism. Find "common ground." "Learn and practice the skills of communication...even though it may sometimes be a difficult process."[13] Rather than silence youth, leaders adopted the youth values of the time; they made a determined effort to validate youth voice and to create a culture of greater equality between the generations.

LDS congregations across America acted out the church's advice in the MIA's 1968–1969 Parent and Youth Night musical, *Make Mine Happy*. Built on a series of vignettes that demonstrate "a happy family needs to include everyone,"

---

12. Irwin Phelps, "A Blue Ribbon Affair," *MIA Youth Parent Night Program*, 1969–1970, CHL.

13. Allred, "A Study of Expressed Attitudes of Selected LDS Youth Regarding Selected Social Trends," 150; George W. Hubbard and his Daughter Elizabeth, "Turning Off Teens," *Improvement Era*, July 1970, 36; John H. Vandenberg, "The Presiding Bishop Talks to Parents About Communication," *Improvement Era*, May 1970, 5. On leaders' views of women, see, for example, Harold B. Lee, "President Harold B. Lee's General Priesthood Address," October 1973, www.lds.org/general-conference/print/1973/10/president-harold-b-lees-general-priesthood-address?lang=eng. The May 1969 issue of *The Improvement Era* offers a range of articles that reflect how church leaders thought about women. Other Christian churches in the period similarly moved toward a focus on listening to youth, favoring, for instance, programs and teaching methods that emphasized open-ended discussion rather than indoctrination. See Bergler, *Juvenilization*, 194, 204.

the program in some ways trivialized the generational divide. It coached parents, prone to complain about popular TV shows, celebrities, and "savage" music and dance styles, to try out their children's "noise," "groovy" new moves, and other interests. Why not "learn to like" them? And instead of groaning about their son's grades or daughter's failure to appreciate the "advantages" the younger more economically secure generation enjoyed (such as ballet classes, piano lessons, and charm school), the program counseled fathers and mothers to stop forcing young people "to be something they don't want to be." In making clear that including everyone meant listening to and valuing youth as autonomous individuals, the program reflected the church's participation in a larger western cultural shift away from caretaking philosophies of youth toward a consideration of youth as independent social and political agents. "I'm not a reflection of you. I'm a person, too," the script's young characters, in an assertion of agency, sing to their parents. "I take you as you are. Why can't you take me as I am?"[14]

As LDS leaders called mothers and fathers home, and committed them to authentic and egalitarian living and listening, so as "to merit the gratitude of a grateful teenager," they put institutional structures to work to support family life. They reinvigorated, for instance, the Family Home Evening (FHE) program by introducing lesson manuals in 1965, by setting aside Monday as a church-wide family night in 1970, and by highlighting FHE as an opportunity "for each member of the family to express himself" and for youth to "direct" family meetings and discussions. Leaders also drew attention to genealogy work and made efforts to engage youth in that work. With young people "looking for a community to which they can belong," the church imagined ancestor research for LDS temple rites as a way to give young people a positive sense of identity and direction rooted in religion and family (instead of in peer cultures). They hoped that "the generation gap so much spoken about today [could] be prevented through implementing [in a concrete way] the concept of the eternal family."[15]

---

14. "Make Mine Happy," *MIA Parent Youth Program,* 1968–1969, CHL. On shifting philosophies of youth see Michael Grossberg, "Liberation and Caretaking: Fighting Over Children's Rights in Postwar America," in Paula S. Fass and Michael Grossberg, eds., *Reinventing Childhood After World War II* (Philadelphia: University of Pennsylvania Press, 2012), 19–37.

15. Marvin J. Ashton, "Courage," *Improvement Era,* June 1970, 41–42; Ernest L. Eberhard Jr. "Questions and Answers," *New Era,* July 1971, www.lds.org/new-era/1971/07/qa-questions-and-answers?lang=eng; "Family Home Evening," *The Improvement Era,* November 1969, 73; Dr. W. Dean Belnap, "Involving Youth in Genealogy," *Improvement Era,* July 1969: 64. For a contemporary analysis of youth and the FHE program, which includes recommendations to further involve youth and see that their interests are addressed, see Don Leroy Miller, "A Study of Factors Which May Influence Attitudes of LDS Teen-agers Toward Family Home Evening," (master's thesis, Brigham Young University, 1969). The LDS Church's focus on families in this period contrasts with the efforts of other Christian youth organizations that tended to emphasize peer-group programs.

Gospel Activists

LDS leaders also addressed the youth problem of the period by embracing and channeling youth activism. Articulating a generally positive sense of youth ethics, and an awareness that young people were searching for ways to express their values (and might easily be misled in that search), leaders worked to convince young people that if they wanted to give themselves "to great causes," they need look no further than the church and its programs. University administrator and General Authority G. Homer Durham explained that though "a conservative institution" that teaches people to "hold fast to that which is good," the LDS Church also "stands for…change," for "overcoming evil with good." If some youth countercultures characterized institutional religion as archaic and, therefore, dead authority, LDS leaders spoke of faith as "a living, vital force," and the church as "a great pulsating organization." Appropriating the impulses of contemporary youth culture, leaders encouraged young Mormons who might be attracted to powerful images of young people changing the world by fighting for racial and gender equality, and against poverty and the war in Vietnam, "to become gospel activists" and to "get involved on the side of righteousness." Using the "tools" of their religion, and following its "formula for success," young people, they insisted, would find "meaning and adventure." Apostle Neil A. Maxwell explained that youth who sought "lofty goals…[and] real exhilaration," who wanted to reform and change society, could find essential "preventative medicine" in the church. "This is not a gospel of not doing," leaders insisted. Following and spreading LDS teachings, they promised, could be an effective and personally meaningful way to "alleviate [the] social ills" they cared about. More than that, "great youth and outstanding leaders [could] work together within the framework of the restored Gospel" to "bring about that Zion for which we long."[16]

Leaders also linked the origins of the church to modern youth values. LDS publications suggested that just as today's high school and college youth express "their concern…for the future of the world around them,"

---

16. George Romney, "Youth Holds the Key," in Marion D. Hanks, Elaine Cannon, and Doyle L. Green, eds., *How Glorious is Youth* (Salt Lake City: Deseret Book Company, 1968), 110–111; "Q and A: Questions and Answers," *New Era*, May 1971, www.lds.org/new-era/1971/05/qa-questions-and-answers?lang=eng; Gordon B. Hinckley, *From My Generation to Yours… With Love* (Salt Lake City: Deseret Book Company, 1973), 31, 71, 76; Thane Packer, *Applying Gospel Principles Through Church Youth Programs*, 2nd ed. (Provo: BYU Press, 1975), i; Richard L. Evans, *Conference Report*, October 1968, 43–44; Neil A. Maxwell, "Goals Unlimited," in Hanks, Cannon, and Green *How Glorious is Youth*, 25; "Q and A: Questions and Answers," *New Era*, February 1971, www.lds.org/new-era/1971/02/qa-questions-and-answers?lang=eng; Godfrey, "A Growing Generation," 9.

so, too, had the young Joseph Smith thought hard and deep about the complex problems of his time. "Six founders of the Church," they pointed out, "were thirty years old or younger...four of the original apostles [of the Restoration] were twenty-three years old." (Like the counterculture of the 1960s, Mormonism had begun as a youth movement—a religious counterculture that incorporated the ideals of freedom and democracy into its theology and organizational structure.) Further connecting the progressive qualities of youth with religious belief, and affirming contemporary young people's sense of self-importance, leaders highlighted the relatively young ages at which a number of biblical and Book of Mormon figures took up God's work, emphasizing that "God has been very generous in calling on youth when revealing his truths."[17]

The youth activism of the period had developed to challenge traditional institutions and authority. LDS leaders, however, utilized the rhetoric of youth idealism and activism to support the church and its mission, maintaining that the "only clear solution to our problems is to make our professed Christianity real." LDS leaders clearly responded to young people's own desires—their zeal and longing for "a piece of the action"—but did so by providing service opportunities through the church.[18] As Vandenberg explained: "Youth are idealistic and impressionable and need to have opportunities for service in the framework of the priesthood and auxiliaries." In 1971, the church introduced one such opportunity through the M-Men and Gleaners program (for unmarried high school graduates through age twenty-five). The new "meaningful Christianity" component involved youth-designed and directed projects that sometimes mimicked secular programs like Big Brother, Big Sister.[19] Such specific programmatic adaptations, as well as an overall "new emphasis on involvement of youth in service projects," addressed what Maxwell called "the

---

17. Jay M. Todd, "The New Era," *New Era*, January 1971, www.lds.org/new-era/1971/01/the-new-era?lang=eng; John Vandenberg, "In Search of Truth," *Improvement Era*, June 1970, 58–59.

18. Tanner, *Conference Report*, October 1968, 47; Hanks, *Conference Report*, October 1969, 102.

19. John Vandenberg, "The Presiding Bishop Discusses How Church Helps Youth Meet the Problems of Today," *Improvement Era*, September 1970, 72–73; "News of the Church," *New Era*, September 1971, www.lds.org/new-era/1971/09/news-of-the-church?lang=eng; Elaine Cannon, "Their Book of Acts," *New Era*, February 1971, www.lds.org/new-era/1971/02/their-book-of-acts?lang=eng. The LDS Church's inclusion of single young men and women up to age 25 fit with how "youth" had been defined in American society since the 1930s. On this see Rebecca de Schweinitz, *If We Could Change the World: Young People and America's Long Struggle for Racial Equality* (Chapel Hill: University of North Carolina Press, 2009), 29–32.

major concerns of the young…to make sure that the institution of the Church is relevant and responsive."[20]

Describing sample youth service initiatives in the *New Era* (the church's newly renamed, designed, and centrally controlled magazine for youth), editor and future LDS Young Women's President Elaine Cannon lauded Mormon youth while disparaging the counterculture. For Cannon, whether engaged in church-planned civic activities such as community tutoring and carpool programs, free music lessons for underprivileged youth, recreational therapy for hospitalized children, or in church-related service like fundraising for LDS temple-building projects, LDS youth's actions proved that "Young Mormons are different":

> They aren't protesters or dissidents, though they have a cause to champion, and they get as upright about social issues as anybody else these days. They clamor for involvement to make life meaningful, too. Their difference lies in what they do about what everyone is talking about. While their counterparts are backing shouts of peace and equality with rocks and fists, Mormon students are quietly chronicling a book of *acts* worthy of publication.[21]

As Cannon's comment suggests, LDS leaders affirmed that young people "shouldn't be sideline sitters." While contrasting "the world's" version of youth activism with the equally vigorous but "constructive voluntary action" available through church-sponsored programs and institutions, church leaders proscriptively juxtaposed the positive acts and approach of Mormon youth who worked to improve society through "appropriate" channels with the "useless" riots and violent protests of "restless, unchallenged young people."[22]

Mormons were not alone in appropriating youth values for institutional ends. For instance, politicians and groups like the National Education Association that were trying to lower the national voting age from twenty-one to eighteen also hoped to convince "restive, concerned, earnest and informed" young people to

---

20. Kent C. Wilson, *LDS Youth Programs 1970–1977*, 1977, 11, CHL; Jim Jardine and Rich Boyer, "Interview with Neal A. Maxwell," *Improvement Era*, September 1970, 47–49. Significantly, LDS efforts in this period specifically linked the church with youth values and social-service opportunities while other Christian groups (especially Methodists) often located such opportunities outside of church structures, and sometimes in opposition to the institutional church and its programs. See Bergler, *Juvenilization*, 184–187.

21. Cannon, "Their Book of Acts," *New Era*, February 1971.

22. Richard L. Evans, *Conference Report*, October 1968, 44; Boyd K. Packer, *Conference Report*, April 1968, 33.

replace "nihilistic attacks on the establishment" with "constructive youth activity." And both groups aimed to provide youth with "wholesome" "tools of expression" for shaping "the future course of the society in which they live," whether through the "pressure valve of the franchise" or through internally generated "outlets" and "ports of opportunity" for "strength and service." Mormons were also not alone among American Christian churches in drawing on youth idealism and activism. But while other groups, notably Methodists and Catholics, often encouraged young people to pursue social service opportunities outside church structures, and to develop an externally, socially (rather than primarily religiously) oriented identity, the LDS Church—perhaps feeling its own minority status—channeled youth efforts internally, that is, into strengthening the LDS community as an institution and as the chief source of young people's identity.[23]

Nonetheless, Mormon-sponsored youth projects reflected the broader sociopolitical American context, and at times even closely resembled events in centers of secular student activism like Berkeley. The *New Era* drew on the language of militant activism to describe one such case, reporting that "an army of protesting Brigham Young University students" had "invaded" a deteriorating rural Utah community. Protesting "against those who riot," these young people painted old homes, created new parks (complete with tennis courts, picnic tables, and barbeque facilities), installed sprinklers, tore down dilapidated buildings, planted flowers, cleared vacant lots, and cleaned streets. "The student power" on display in Santaquin, the LDS magazine reported, "demonstrated that students can change things within the system and at the same time make the world a much better place for others." More pointedly, the project (and Mormon media coverage of it) demonstrated the church's efforts to appeal to youth values and to provide "opportunities for action... *in the*

---

23. "Excerpts from the Testimony of Monroe Sweetland to the California Assembly Hearings on Lowering the Voting Age," April 9, 1970, National Education Association Papers, folder 9, box 2699, Estelle and Melvin Gelman Library, George Washington University, Washington, DC; Senate Judiciary Committee, *Hearings*, May 14–16, 1968, 2, 43–45; Project 18, "Fact Sheet," National Education Association Papers, folder 9, box 2705 Estelle and Melvin Gelman Library, George Washington University, Washington, DC; James Brown, "Report to National Convention," 1968, NAACP Western Region Papers, folder 6, box 5, Bancroft Library Special Collections and Archives, University of California at Berkeley; Gloster Current, "Excerpts of the 1966 Annual Report of the Director of Branches and Field Administration,1966," NAACP Papers (microfilm), frames 2–7, reel 6, part 29; *To Establish Justice, To Insure Domestic Tranquility: The Final Report of the National Commission on the Causes and Prevention of Violence* (New York: Bantam Books, 1970), 189; Brian Kelly, "Student Power at Santaquin," *New Era*, January 1971, www.lds.org/new-era/1971/01/student-power-at-santaquin?lang=eng; Evans, *Conference Report*, October 1968, 43–44; L. Tom Perry, "Sessions Outline Priesthood MIA," *Church News*, June 23, 1973, 5. On Methodist and other religion's youth programs see Bergler, *Juvenilization*.

Church." At least one participant thought the institution succeeded in offering an acceptable substitute form of engagement, describing the Santaquin project as "an out-of-sight…kind of peaceful protest." It was a protest that mirrored the 1969 creation of People's Park in Berkeley, where University of California students worked against the establishment to turn a planned housing lot into a space of beauty for the local community—and to promote a new social order. In Santaquin, on the other hand, youth worked *with* church and local authorities toward shared, community-building goals. As one student remarked: "I've seen activity on this scale in the Bay area—but then, the riots weren't exactly approved."[24]

Student Voice in the LDS Church

At the same time the church offered alternative avenues of activism, it followed national trends in making youth leadership and input central components of its youth programs. Closing the generation gap required two-way communication in the church as well as in families. Mormon leaders noted: "the student voice is a common phrase these days. We're all aware young people want to speak and be heard. Our young people have the same temperament and desire and that voice is saying some interesting things." A survey by the Presiding Bishopric confirmed that more than 75 percent of the youth questioned wanted to be "more involved in the planning of their own activities." The church obliged, ending "all-Church" and regionally based cultural and sports programs in favor of activities focused on local youth interests, and creating new congregation-level organizational structures that incorporated young voices and fostered "peer leadership."[25] In 1969, for instance, the church replaced the adult-heavy Priesthood-Youth Activity Committee with

---

24. Kelly, "Student Power at Santaquin," *New Era*, January 1971; Evans, *Conference Report*, October 1968, 43 (emphasis mine). Evangelicals in this period similarly sought to create events that reflected countercultural youth values, although their events, as John Turner notes, embraced "the activism of the student left" while rejecting its sociopolitical agenda. In short, evangelicals believed in overcoming the problems of the world through conversion, while Mormons also recognized the value of social service work. See Turner, *Bill Bright and the Campus Crusade for Christ*, 132.

25. Brigham Young University Motion Picture Production Department, *Latter-day Saint Students Association*, video cassette (The Church of Jesus Christ of Latter-day Saints, 1971), CHL; John H. Vandenberg, *Conference Report*, October 1968, 32; Victor Brown, "The Aaronic Priesthood MIA," *Ensign*, July 1973, www.lds.org/ensign/1973/07/the-aaronic-priesthood-mia?lang=eng&query=the+aaronic+priesthood+mia. Such changes also represented the growing international character of the church. Notably, despite growing diversity, the institution clearly understood the "youth problem" primarily in terms of white, middle-class American youth.

the Bishop's Youth Council (BYC). Composed primarily of youth leaders, the BYC invited feedback from adult advisors "when needed," but adults were to offer mostly "silent support" and "never to dominate." Authorities explained that the councils allowed youth to "be totally involved in selecting their activities and tested and taught great leadership principles without being smothered by too many adult leaders." Grown-ups might still need to "temper [youth's] unbridled enthusiasm and zeal with their experience and practicality," but the new structure aimed to provide young people with "safe" opportunities "for self-discovery and self-direction," increasing their commitment to the church in the process.[26]

A 1971 *New Era* article contrasted the church's new youth-directed model (and its effects) with previous, more custodial approaches to youth programs. The article depicts one group of adult leaders spending considerable time and money planning an elaborate youth activity that few young people actually attend. The adults wonder: "What's Wrong with Youth?" When *youth* from another ward plan a low-budget event that attracts high numbers of youth, including young people from his own congregation, the bishop of the first group recognizes his faulty thinking, and observes: "The only thing that's wrong with youth is not letting them control their own activities. When you do, there is no youth problem."[27]

Among college-age youth, the church similarly fostered appropriate "student expression" and the development of church leadership and an expressly Mormon identity through the Latter-day Saint Student Association (LDSSA). Piloted in 1965 in Utah and California as a way to keep track of and coordinate and promote the religious activities and orientation of student-age members not attending LDS schools, by 1969 the church boasted nearly three hundred LDSSA units across the United States and Canada. Observers at the time noted that the new youth-centered organizational structure reflected the church's concern about "religious dropout" rates and a growing cultural "emphasis on education as a process" in which "people mature best by doing." It also respected young members' own expressed "wish to be deeply involved." "Rather than being imposed by a higher authority," youth themselves, through student-led councils (primarily male, and chosen by regional adult male authorities), shaped and carried out a "meaningful student program...based on the needs of students." Among other activities, LDSSA youth planned

---

26. Stephen W. Gibson, "New Bishop's Youth Council," *Deseret News*, May 2, 1969, 52; Backman, "Youth's Opportunity to Serve"; "Some Challenges for Leaders of Young Men," *Improvement Era*, June 1970, 68.

27. "What's Wrong with Youth?," *New* Era, 1971.

firesides, ping pong tournaments, campus lunch programs, tutoring services, and Christmas parties; acted as liaisons with university clubs; wrote informative and inspiring newsletters; advised Institute directors and teachers on curricula; and helped coordinate activities among campus and Mormon student programs. Although internal reports indicated that young people were substantially less interested in the "correlated" hierarchical priesthood line of authority under which the LDSSA functioned than were church leaders, student feedback and increased MIA and Institute attendance rates suggest that the LDSSA indeed helped many young people find "balance" in their academic pursuits and spiritual lives, or at least encouraged them to "upgrade their devotion and increase their loyalty" to the church during "this vital time."[28]

Expanding on what Boyd K. Packer and others identified as a revelatory "pattern of programming" that allowed young people, from age twelve to twenty-five, to be "more dominant" and to assume greater "responsibility for applying gospel principles," the church also began to give young people more control over their religious classes. For instance, in the early 1970s, young men and young women class presidents started selecting their own counselors. Presiding Bishop Victor Brown described this opportunity for expanded participation in church governance as a "motivating force" for young male and female members who would "realize the tie they have with the priesthood" as they prayerfully considered who to ask to serve with them in youth leadership positions.[29]

Internal studies on LDS youth demonstrated two important findings: first, that Mormon youth harbored an "extreme dislike" for religious education programs; and second, that Seminary and Institute attendance positively correlated with LDS temple marriage and lifelong church activity. Influenced by this research and by a general sense of the "[generation] gap widening more quickly in our time," leaders attempted to reconnect youth to the church by repackaging these programs. Soliciting advice from college-age youth, they established new religious courses, such as one taught at San Francisco Bay Area Institutes titled "Your Religious Problems." They also redesigned other youth classes and achievement programs to be more self-directed and to allow for greater individual choice. Moreover, authorities encouraged all youth religious teachers to employ interactive learning techniques, such as role-play. Leaders

---

28. Lake, "Organization," 42–43, 51, 55, 57; The Church of Jesus Christ of Latter-day Saints Students Association, "pamphlets," CHL; "Interim Report Effects of LDSSA," typescript, CHL; BYU Motion Picture Production Department, *Latter-day Saint Students Association*. See also various LDSSA newsletters in the CHL.

29. Boyd K. Packer, *Conference Report*, October 1973, 23; Brown, "The Aaronic Priesthood MIA"; John H. Vandenberg, "The Bishop's Youth Council," *Improvement* Era, December 1969, 116–117.

cautioned: "We cannot be lulled into believing that the Sunday school is providing gospel solutions for large portions of our young people." Suggesting that teachers could only "help us fulfill our religious objectives" if they changed their "role from being the sole dispenser of knowledge to that of a resource person, a manager of learning," leaders charged religious instructors to "get into a new line of thinking. You can't keep operating as you have before…young people will not stand for it!" Only by carefully working to "close the gap between watching and participating," through the use of collaborative, "sharp [teaching] tools," could religious educators hope to "help youth internalize" Mormon beliefs.[30]

Other Christian organizations in the late 1960s and early 1970s likewise moved to incorporate youth voice and greater youth participation in their programs. Catholics, Evangelicals, and Methodists alike moved away from "indoctrination" techniques and toward youth-led, open-ended discussions and "informal environments designed to give teenagers a sense of personal attention" and involvement.[31] And it was hardly coincidental that a movement to lower the voting age to eighteen gained considerable traction in this same period, partly by proposing that bringing youth directly into the political process would help restore young people's faith in democracy and steer their activism toward legitimate and manageable forms. Like other contemporary religious and secular leaders who recognized the growing need to positively encourage rather than control youth, the LDS Church similarly, and explicitly, hoped to keep youth from feeling "estranged from a [church organizational] system that has little room" for them, and to inspire youth to be "anxiously engaged in a good cause, doing many things of their own free will." To this end, LDS authorities emphasized a "two-way street" between youth and their

---

30. BYU Motion Picture Production Department, *Latter-day Saint Students Association*; Berkeley LDSSA, "The Insti-tutor," March 1969, CHL; "The New Priesthood Personal Achievement Program," *Improvement Era*, August 1970, 28–29; Eleanor Knowles, "New Directions in MIA," *Improvement Era*, August 1970, 30–31; BYU Department of Youth Leadership, "Young Adult Male Attitudes and Interests of the Church of Jesus Christ of Latter-day Saints: A Research Report," 85, 63, 23; William E. Berrett, "The Generation Gap" (Summer School Address to Seminaries and Institutes of Religion personnel, 1968): 1, CHL; Roy E. Welty, "The Development of Structured Situations for Role Playing the LDS Department of Seminaries and Institutes of Religion" (master's thesis, Brigham Young University, 1971), 22–23; Albert L. Payne, "How to Get Student Involvement," *Improvement Era*, May 1970, 68–69; Allred, "Study," 2. Contemporary studies also showed that young men disliked the Boy Scout program. Again, rather than abandon the program, which leaders believed taught important values and provided essential guidance to male youth on the path to manhood, the church determined that calling better, more dynamic, responsive scout leaders would help youth feel more invested in the program.

31. See Bergler, *Juvenilization*, 204, 207.

parents and leaders, made adults into "shadow leaders," and rendered young people cocreators of their own programs.

But while most "Vote 18" supporters anticipated that idealistic and open-minded youth would positively alter American democracy, and some American religious groups were more concerned with improving society and encouraging youth activism than with self-preservation, LDS leaders at the time, however well-meaning, and despite their rhetorical and theoretical commitment to youth agency, clearly aimed to influence youth, not to be influenced by them. Listening to young people would help parents and leaders "get into their lives"—youth who felt respected would develop "more confidence in their church leaders" and be more likely to "rely on counsel and advice from those in high places." Although intended to positively highlight the prominent role of youth in LDS programs, the church's adoption in the 1970s of the term "shadow leaders" to describe adult advisors also betrays a hidden, more coercive objective of the shift to "youth leadership." Pointed reminders from church authorities that youth ideas required clearance from empathetic (and wiser) adults who retained ultimate veto power over youth decisions, as well as repeated references to the "correlated," priesthood organization of redesigned youth programs, likewise reveal the church's discomfort with actually empowering youth to "do their own thing." They also signal leaders' primary aim: that such programs would provide youth in this "crazy mixed-up world" with the "shepherding influence of the priesthood," and in so doing, bring them into "the main stream of the church." Recognizing that "the more a student is involved in developing institutional goals, the more likely he is to become closely identified with the program and what the [institution] is undertaking to do," LDS leaders maintained a vital sense of agency among youth, even as they channeled young people, via service and "training" opportunities within existing institutional structures, toward predetermined "responsible adult roles" and ways of, as Neal A. Maxwell put it, "succeeding spiritually."[32]

---

32. Hanks, *Conference Report*, October 1969, 101–102; Stapley, "Effective Youth Leadership"; Backman, "Youth's Opportunity to Serve," *Ensign*, July 1973; Thane Packer, *Applying Gospel Principles Through Church Youth Programs*, 10; McKay, *Conference Report*, October 1968, 8; Robert L. Simpson, "Questions from Youth," *Conference Report*, October 1970, 99; Vandenberg, "The Bishop's Youth Council," 116–117; "Interim Report Effects of LDSSA," 9; Harold B. Lee, "Follow the Leadership of the Church," *Ensign*, July 1973, 99; Perry, "Sessions Outline Priesthood MIA," 5; "Talcott Parsons, A Sociologist's View," in Ginzberg, 276; Neil A. Maxwell, *Conference Report*, October 1970, 96. On the obscuring of youth socialization see James Block, *The Crucible of Consent: American Childrearing and the Forging of Liberal Society* (Cambridge, MA: Harvard University Press, 2012). On Vote 18 see de Schweinitz, "'The Proper Age for Suffrage': Vote 18 and the Politics of Age From World War II to the Age of Aquarius." On other Christian organizations see, for instance, Bergler, *Juvenilization*, 186, 190, 198.

Inculcating Soul Freedom

In addition to giving young people a voice in their families and in the religious organization to which they were voluntarily offering up their free will, church leaders confronted the "challenge of youth" by emphasizing LDS theological ideas about freedom. To be sure, the theme of freedom did not arise wholly in response to the youth problem; Cold War American exceptionalism and anti-communism also inspired Mormonism's freedom discourse. But as they spoke to youth, church leaders regularly used this favorite theme of the counterculture to challenge the counterculture itself.

Affirming the importance of freedom while upending popular conceptions of the term, church leaders insisted that this "word of noble tradition, is a favorite confuser." Mormon leaders encouraged youth to reject the "delusional" freedom espoused by cultural rebels who, they said, sought freedom in "feeling good" or "freedom from moral restraint." True "soul freedom," they argued, could not be found in the absence of "traditions or church restrictions"; "kicking the establishment"; experimentation with drugs, alcohol, and sex; or independence from parents and other authority figures. It could "only be found by accepting the Divine Plan and keeping the commandments." Quoting LDS scripture they encouraged youth to "abide...in the liberty wherein ye are made free; entangle not yourselves in sin." Freedom was the result of making right choices, of escaping "the bondage of sin."[33]

Church talks and articles directed to youth frequently included stories that demonstrated the "illusory freedom" espoused by popular culture. In these narratives, "ex hippies" and other errant youth who do not want to "be bound" by convention pursue rebellious paths, invariably to discover that "instead of being free, [they are] a slave." These "liberated" young people find themselves spending their "creativity, ingenuity, thought, energy, and resources in obtaining and using" the drugs upon which they have become dependent, or in caring for a child on limited means as a young parent who has narrowed their other opportunities in life. The once-defiant characters in these stories repeatedly confirm "the rewards of conformance": "I should have listened to my parents' advice about dating"; "I used to think my parents were forcing me and taking away my free agency"; "I tried that way of life for a time thinking I

---

33. Ezra Taft Benson, *Conference Report*, October 1971, 26; Hinckley, *From My Generation*, 2; Victor Cline, "The Four Supreme Tests of Youth," *Improvement Era*, August 1970, 41–42; David O. McKay, *My Young Friends: President McKay Speaks to Youth*, compiled by Llewelyn R. McKay (Salt Lake City: Bookcraft, 1973): 29; James A. Cullimore, *Conference Report*, October 1967, 47; Tanner, *Conference Report*, April 1968, 109; Victor Brown, *Conference Report*, Oct. 1971, 94; *The Doctrine and Covenants of the Church of Jesus Christ of Latter-day Saints* 88:86 (Salt Lake City: Church of Jesus Christ of Latter-day Saints, 1989).

would find happiness. Instead I found sickness, filth, sorrow, and misery. Thank God in time I repented, and now I'm back on the pathway to happiness...obtained by clean, wholesome living the gospel."[34]

Leaders' counsel to youth highlighted the "power of choices," describing free agency as a sacred gift and validating young people's freedom to make choices. At the same time, leaders warned that choices counter to gospel teachings would "abridge" agency and create "cages." Church authorities encouraged young Mormons to not become "captivated by the temptations of this world." "When one makes a choice," they cautioned, "he irrevocably binds himself to accept the consequences of that choice." Some leaders also drew on unique Mormon beliefs to suggest that in making wrong choices, rebellious youth effectively surrendered their agency and allowed evil spirits who had followed Satan in a premortal war in heaven (and gave up the chance for corporal life) to "take refuge in their bodies." Others turned to Book of Mormon theology to describe young people as engaged in a battle with themselves to become fully free by subduing "the natural man." Using free agency to go against their faith's instructions represented a victory for their base, mortal instincts; to choose to abide by church guidance signified youth's freedom from temporal desires and the realization of a higher, more godlike—more authentic—self. Only "orthodoxy," "doing the right things," "conscious self-mastery," "conformance to law," could "guarantee freedom" and "increase happiness." As a Berkeley LDSSA newsletter article relayed the church's philosophy about freedom, a disciplined life "sets [one] free to fly."[35]

---

34. Cline, "The Four Supreme Tests of Youth," 42; Tanner, *Conference Report*, April 1968, 109; Richard Salazar, "Drugs, Personality & Youth," *Improvement Era*, July 1970, 41; Robert Simpson, *Conference Report*, October 1968, 98; Howard W. Hunter, "Too Much, Too Soon," Vault Talks, folder 75, CHL; Robert Brailsford, Burbank Region LDSSA, "Prepare Today for Future Happiness," *The Trump*, May–June, 1969, CHL. Church leaders repeatedly simplified and trivialized youth who rejected the church and its teachings. For instance, one article described contemporary youth rebellion as "so conformist and stereotyped that" even church leaders "who may never have met [them] can say how it manifests itself." See "Keep Cool: An Open Letter to Anguished Parents," *Improvement Era*, August 1969, 20.

35. Bernard Brockbank, *Conference Report*, October 1969, 71; Marion G. Romney, *Conference Report*, October 1968, 65–67; Lowell Bennion, *Conference Report*, April 1968, 96; Hanks, "Let's Talk About Youth," *Conference Report*, October 1969, 98; Don J. Black, *This, That and Everything: A Book for Young People* (Provo: BYU Press, 1973), 160; Richard S. Tanner, *We Focus on Youth and Youth Focuses on a Star* (Salt Lake City: Church of Jesus-Christ of Latter-day Saints, n.d.) CHL; McKay, *My Young Friends*, 29; Cullimore, *Conference Report*, October 1967, 47; Robert Simpson, *Conference Report*, October 1968, 98; Neal A. Maxwell, *Conference Report*, Oct. 1970, 97; Berkeley LDSSA, "The Institutor," October 23, 1968, CHL. In contrast to the LDS Church, both Catholic and Methodist churches in this period were reluctant to impose lifestyle demands on youth or to emphasize distinct theological beliefs. And while Evangelicals emphasized a strict moral purity and the importance of conversion, their innovative approaches to attracting and retaining youth members focused on culture rather than theology. See Bergler, *Juvenilization*.

LDS teachings about freedom turned the exercise of agency into a project of self-regulation, one that honored young people's quest for freedom and authenticity at the same time it channeled their behavior into a predetermined field of acceptable social conduct. The 1970–1971 MIA youth musical *Rx* captured this paradigm as it provided a "prescription" for young people who might be struggling over how to best understand and use their freedom. Inverting assumptions about liberation and choice, and disallowing for the possibility that youth who step outside acceptable boundaries might do so for substantive or positive reasons, the production described youth who rebel against parents and the church as giving in to peer pressure. Bud, Cathy, and other youthful characters sing, "We're free...Our right to choose must be allowed," as they experiment with new hairstyles, short skirts, and other popular youth consumer items, as well as make decisions about attending parties and trying drugs. But the script makes clear that the main characters' choices (which notably exclude any that connote deep or sincere spiritual or philosophical struggles) are based on what "everybody else" is doing, not an expression of independent will. Indeed, the youth admit their fears about "fitting in," and repeatedly sing the paradoxical refrain: "We're free. A crowd makes us feel free." A wise pharmacist who has witnessed the young people's activities helps Bud and Cathy recognize that their choices to go against parents and church standards have not been their own. The two youth eventually refuse to take drugs with their friends, not because their parents have warned against it, but because they decide to "think for themselves." In a forceful display of youth agency Bud asserts: "I'm not gonna ask mother or father...I'm gonna think for myself, I can, and I'm going to...*I* think it's wrong." (Cathy makes the same independent choice as her brother.) The last line of the program further underscores the church's agency-validating, self-monitoring message for youth as the pharmacist explains: "In their moment of decision—what friends, mother, father, teacher, and the TV thought didn't make the big difference...The most important person is the person himself. People are what they make of themselves...Your decision is more important by far, than what anything or anybody else can do. What you are is mostly up to you."[36]

Church initiatives—both programs and teachings—from the period, signaled a growing appreciation of youth as autonomous agents, creating an expanded space for the voices, values, and actions of young people within Mormonism, a space that would widen in unexpected and less controllable ways in the decades to come. Yet in the late 1960s and early 1970s, institutional changes that allowed for "the individual initiative" of youth—that

---

36. "*Rx*: Take Though the Following," *MIA Parent Youth Night Script*, 1970–1971, CHL.

stressed young people's agency and participation—made less visible a level of social conditioning that was otherwise becoming untenable among young people in western society. Freedom-conscious youth had rejected traditional, overt attempts at socialization. Church leaders recognized that religious values and development in the faith had to be deeply internalized and naturalized, emanating from young people themselves. The key to "holding on to [Mormon] youth" in the Age of Aquarius was to make adult leadership "more subtle," to get young people dedicated to the church not "because they feel obligated," but, as contemporary research on LDS youth suggested, because they "freely choose to do so."[37]

A Chosen Generation

The LDS Church's efforts in the late 1960s and early 1970s to create a workable model of agency for contemporary youth, one that supported the principles of freedom and choice at the same time it narrowly defined that freedom and discreetly directed young people's decisions and activities into orthodox patterns, were perhaps best signified by the emergence of the theological concept of the "chosen generation." The idea of a chosen generation had periodically appeared in Mormon sermonizing, with one midcentury speaker, for instance, using it to refer to early Mormon pioneers. But beginning in the late 1960s, church leaders began to consistently speak of current LDS youth as a "royal" or "chosen" generation, predestined, because of their superior righteousness, to come to earth during the present time of wickedness and temptation, a time often stated or implied to be the last age of struggle before the Savior's return.[38] At a 1968 General Conference, for example, future general authority and then Bonneville Utah Stake President Russell M. Nelson suggested: "The youth of this generation are the choicest souls, reserved for these latter days." In 1969, *The Improvement Era* labeled Mormon youth "a choice generation," and in 1970, Church President Joseph Fielding Smith, in an oft-quoted passage, declared:

---

37. BYU Department of Leadership, "Young Adult Male Attitudes and Interests of the Church of Jesus Christ of Latter-day Saints: A Research Report," 63, 81. My thinking about youth socialization here is shaped by James Block, *The Crucible of Consent: American Childrearing and the Forging of Liberal Society*.

38. While my research on this term is limited to the 1960s and 1970s, Geoffrey S. Nelson has traced the use of this phrase in Mormon history. See "Chosen Generation," *My Random Thoughts* blog, September 24, 2011, http://geoffsn.blogspot.com/2011_09_01_archive.html.

We have confidence in the young and rising generation in the Church and plead with them not to follow the fashions and customs of the world, not to partake of a spirit of rebellion, not to forsake the paths of truth and virtue. We believe in their fundamental goodness.... Our young people are among the most blessed and favored of our Father's children. They are the nobility of heaven, a choice and chosen generation who have a divine destiny. Their spirits have been reserved to come forth in this day when the Gospel is on earth, and when the Lord needs valiant servants to carry on His great latter-day work.[39]

Smith's successor, Harold B. Lee, similarly preached: "Our youth of today are among the most illustrious spirits to be born into mortality in any age of the world." Apostle David B. Haight used "a chosen generation" as "a wonderful declaration of identity for our youth," and suggested "our youth...are very special." "The Lord," he said, "is counting on them that the prophecies might be fulfilled." Other Mormon authorities likewise expressed confidence in the "great young generation," which would meet "the challenges of [its] time," and fulfill its "destiny."[40]

The "chosen generation" theme appeared in LDS cultural forms as well, most famously (and influentially) in *Saturday's Warrior*. Written in 1973 and performed widely both on stage and in LDS homes (as young Mormons sang along to the LP record), the Douglas Stewart-Lex de Azevedo musical centers on a troubled (not coincidentally) male Mormon youth. Enticed by the ideas of youth countercultures, including concerns about population growth and hopes to build a "world with no more fences," young Jimmy Flinders undergoes a crisis of identity and faith. Notably, two of Jimmy's sisters—one a twin confined to a wheelchair (her physical immobility perhaps symbolic of an idealized immoveable female faith), and the other a yet-unborn spirit (whose future life is somehow dependent on Jimmy's views about abortion)—encourage him to return to his family and beliefs. The musical's title song added a militaristic, apocalyptic undertone to the "chosen generation" concept, describing modern Mormon youth

---

39. Russell M. Nelson, *Conference Report*, October 1968, 90; Elaine Cannon, "A Generation to Hang Your Hopes On," *The Improvement Era*, November 1969, 81; Joseph Fielding Smith, *Conference Report*, April 1970, 5–6; Smith's quote was widely repeated, including in Hanks's "Let's Talk About Youth."

40. Lee, *Youth and the Church*, 176. First published in 1945, this book was expanded and reprinted in 1970, and this idea from it referenced repeatedly from the late 1960s through the 1970s. See also Harold B. Lee, *Conference* Report, October 1973, 7.; David B. Haight, *Conference Report*, October 1973, 42; Marion D. Hanks, *Conference Report*, October 1971, 118; Gordon B. Hinckley, "Watch the Switches in Your Life," October 1972, www.lds.org/general-conference/print/1972/10/watch-the-switches-in-your-life?lang=eng; Backman, "Youth's Opportunity to Serve."

as "strong," fiery-sword-wielding "warriors saved for Saturday...the last days of the world." But before they can make "the darkness fall" and realize their "endless promise," they must first win the even more important "battle raging in the hearts of man." "They must learn," as goes the song's refrain, "why they're here and who they really are." For Jimmy and others of the chosen generation, discovering an authentic identity entails conquering personal "doubts and fears," and aligning thought and action with inherited religious values.[41]

In the late 1960s and early 1970s, many outside the church argued that young people's "ethical, idealistic spirit," and willingness to act on ideals, could help regenerate democracy and usher in a more responsive and moral phase of American life and politics. The church's new construction of the "chosen generation" represented a highly prescriptive theological expression of this view. To be a member of the chosen generation was to be a hero in a grand narrative of eternal consequence. This modern LDS iteration of premillenialism imbued young people's choices with meaning and urgency. The stakes for nonconformity were high, and retaining religious values in the modern era difficult. "Never," after all, had "Satan been more active in influencing the lives of our people." Through the idea of the chosen generation, LDS leaders celebrated young people as eternity's most vital actors at the same time they directed their choices. Youth could remain faithful to the church and in so doing be true to themselves as they fulfilled a great, world-saving mission for which they had been foreordained. Or they could deny their divine destiny and allow themselves to be misled and controlled by the Devil.[42]

Holding on to Youth

In a late 1960s *Improvement Era* article, Marion D. Hanks suggested that "the real 'battle of the century'" was over youth. And the battle to "work out" youth's "destiny...amid the tumult and uncertainty of [the] age" was one to which the Mormon faith committed "vast resources of people, principles, and programs." Mormon leaders in the Age of Aquarius were not the first to encourage youth to internalize beliefs and behavioral patterns. As James Block explains in *The Crucible of Consent: American Child Rearing and the Forging of Liberal Society*, childhood and youth had long been the setting in which consent within and for American society was formed. Needing stability and order, as well as a vol-

---

41. Doug Stewart and Lex de Azevedo, *Saturday's Warrior* (1973). Observations about the widespread reenactment of this musical in LDS homes is based on the author's own experiences.

42. Feuer, *The Conflict of Generations*, 3; Brown, "The Aaronic Priesthood MIA," *Ensign*, July 1973.

untary and free society (or a seemingly voluntary and free society), those shaping nationhood turned to the country's youngest citizens to realize their aims. As the country grew, it instituted childrearing models, schools, and other youth socialization structures that were designed to produce self-disciplined individuals invisibly conditioned to regard social values as expressions of their own nature. Of course, there was always the threat that young people might refuse to voluntarily surrender their will. And indeed, in the 1960s, many young people rejected the illusion of the free society and the idea that their elders could properly guide them into the future. Mass youth protests against traditional authority and a widespread movement to enfranchise young people were two manifestations of these changes.[43]

In a 1969 reflection on youth, Neal A. Maxwell noted that both democracy and religion required "immense self-discipline and 'obedience to the unenforceable.'" Among religious groups, as contemporary observers and later scholars have noted, the LDS Church's efforts to "hold onto their young people" proved uniquely successful. In the "battle" to "hold onto…young people" in the late 1960s and early 1970s, Mormon leaders drew on preexisting doctrinal principles (about human society, freedom, and identity) that corresponded with contemporary youth values, and successfully appropriated some of the rhetoric and spirit of the sixties to revitalize the church's messages, structures, and programs. Young people's desires to improve the world, for instance, fit neatly with Mormonism's "dream of Zion." Church teachings about free agency provided a basis for leaders to recognize youth as independent actors and to recast the meaning and significance of freedom and choice. And Mormon beliefs about eternal life further enabled the church to challenge the counterculture on its own terms. Honoring the fundamental values and agency of youth, they argued that authenticity required being true to the premortal disposition of the soul. Rebellious youth might believe they were in touch with an authentic self, but in truth they had forgotten their interminable identity as members of a chosen generation. When Maxwell and other LDS leaders of the time asked, "Can the tradition and the demands [of youth] be reconciled?" the answer was "yes."[44]

---

43. Hanks, "On These Principles," 45; Godfrey, "A Growing Generation," 9; Block, *Crucible of Consent.* Bergler notes that some other Christian groups in this period, especially Catholics, invested fewer adult and monetary resources in their youth programs than in previous decades. See Bergler, *Juvenilization,* 197.

44. Neal A. Maxwell, "A Good Look at Youth," *Improvement Era,* November 1969, 6; Louis Cassels, *The Mormons Hold Onto Their Young People* (Salt Lake City: Church of Jesus Christ of Latter-day Saints, 1968) (the Mormon Church reprinted and distributed this article, originally published by United Press International, in at least seven different languages in the late 1960s and early 1970s); Bergler, *Juvenilization;* Hanks, "Tell and Show," *The Improvement Era,* November 1969, 5.

14

Everyone Can Be a Pioneer

THE SESQUICENTENNIAL CELEBRATIONS OF MORMON
ARRIVAL IN THE SALT LAKE VALLEY

Sara M. Patterson

IN 1831, JOSEPH Smith dictated a revelation in which his church was told that it must come "out of obscurity and out of darkness."[1] In the late twentieth and early twenty-first centuries, Mormon leaders suggested that various moments in Latter-day Saint history marked the church's progression from an unseen and misunderstood institution to a publicly recognized and respected religion. During the presidency of Gordon B. Hinckley (1995–2008), a prophet well-versed in public and media relations, the church entered a new era of visibility in the United States and abroad. In 1997, Latter-day Saints celebrated the sesquicentennial of the Mormon pioneers' 1847 entrance into the Salt Lake Valley. M. Russell Ballard, a member of the Quorum of the Twelve Apostles and the chairperson of the church's sesquicentennial events, declared that the sesquicentennial was the time for the church to make its history and its identity clear to the rest of the world. "In 1997, the Church received more national and international media coverage than all the other years in Church history combined," noted Ballard.[2] He asserted that "the Church's sesquicentennial celebrations were the most significant thrust in bringing the Church out of obscurity in its history."[3]

At the same time that the sesquicentennial marked a moment of transition in the LDS Church's relations with outsiders, it highlighted several internal changes as well. Within an increasingly globalized church, a church no longer bound together by the ties of spatial proximity, Mormons were coming to understand several concepts in new ways. Gathering, Zion, pioneer identity, and the American West, ideas central to Latter-day Saint theology, were reimagined

---

1. Doctrine and Covenants 1:30.

2. "The Year in Review," *Church News*, December 27, 1997.

3. Sarah Jane Weaver, "In Hallmark Year, Sesquicentennial Touches the World," *Church News*, August 30, 1997. See Brian J. Hill and Michael N. Landon, "The Pioneer Sesquicentennial Celebration," in Susan Easton Black, ed., *Out of Obscurity: The LDS Church in the Twentieth Century* (Salt Lake City: Deseret Book Company, 2000).

to speak to church members in a new global context. No longer rooted in literalism, now unmoored from place, the concepts took on new spiritual meanings. Though these redeployments were not inaugurated in the sesquicentennial events, they came to full fruition there as the church sought to make the journey of a small band of nineteenth-century pioneers meaningful in a new era. The sesquicentennial events celebrated the church's claims about Mormon identity: that Mormons exemplify core "frontier values" associated with being American—industry, hard work, and perseverance. The ritual activities of the sesquicentennial also confirmed for believers that the landscape was evidence of the prophetic office at the core of Mormons' understanding of themselves as a chosen people.

Sesquicentennial Events

Working with Utah's government officials, Mormon leaders planned several events celebrating the pioneers' 1847 entry into the Salt Lake Valley. After all, the sesquicentennial was both a state and a religious celebration. Plans for the entire year included all sorts of activities: the Mormon Tabernacle Choir went on a tour; the church held a Faith in Every Footstep Sesquicentennial Concert in Temple Square; the Museum of Church History and Art hosted an international art competition; Promised Valley Productions put on a play especially written and produced for the sesquicentennial; Brigham Young University set up a Sesquicentennial Spectacular (with all sorts of family frontier activities and fireworks); and the church sponsored a trek that followed the pioneers' footsteps across the western landscape. Latter-day Saints also proposed celebrating the sesquicentennial through service projects. Church leaders suggested that the pioneers had committed their lives to service and that part of church members' expression of their pioneer heritage ought to take the form of providing service to their communities. July 19, 1997 was designated Worldwide Pioneer Heritage Service Day, and about 20,000 church groups dedicated that day (and therefore about 3 million hours) to some form of service in their local communities.[4]

It wasn't just the church, though, that recognized the significance of these events. The New York City Historical Society and the National Museum of American History also sponsored exhibits commemorating the sesquicentennial.[5] For many Latter-day Saints, the acknowledgment of the significance of

---

4. Hill and Landon, "The Pioneer Sesquicentennial Celebration," 164.

5. *Pioneer Sesquicentennial Celebration* (Salt Lake City: The Church of Jesus Christ of Latter-day Saints, 1997), L. Tom Perry Special Collections, Brigham Young University, Provo, Utah.

the Mormon exodus and pioneer trek by national, public institutions was evidence that their church had finally come of age within American culture.

We must also remember that the sesquicentennial was a state affair and the Utah Pioneer Sesquicentennial Celebration Coordinating Council was designed to make sure of that. In the first group newsletter of *The Sesquicentennial Star*, the council noted, "During 1996 we celebrate the 100th birthday of statehood for Utah. The State, in reality, had its birth when the Utah Pioneers made the trek from Nauvoo to Salt Lake Valley in 1847."[6] The council dated Utah origins to the arrival of the Mormon pioneers to their promised land and emphasized 1847 over and above the date of Utah statehood. First, the newsletter declared, "We know there were Native Americans, trappers, and explorers who visited these valleys before the Utah Pioneers came. But we must never forget the purpose of the original trek. It has been referred to as a 'Glorious emergency.' The pioneers came 'because they were compelled to—because they were driven.' They were determined to preserve a heritage for their children through fostering faith in God, devotion to family, loyalty to country, freedom of conscience, commitment to work, service to others, courage in adversity, personal integrity, and unyielding determination."[7] These claims reveal much about the council's understanding of Utah history. The values that were tied to Utahan identity were drawn not from statehood or even from the first inhabitants of and visitors to the state, but instead from the Mormon pioneers. The group readily embraced a narrative that rooted state values in one religious group and saw the Mormon pioneers as the progenitors of Utahan identity.

Sesquicentennial celebrations in Utah encompassed all sorts of artistic commemorations. Church celebrations often included a new hymn written for the events titled "Faith in Every Footstep." The hymn recalls the pioneers as people "Who gave all their heart, mind, and strength to the Lord with wisdom and virtue so clear." The hymn also taught that late-twentieth-century Latter-day Saints were themselves called to the work of building up Zion. While the pioneers remained "examples of virtue and faith," later generations of church members should "assist in this work and thrust in [their] sickle with might."

A musical titled *Barefoot to Zion* was written and performed in honor of the sesquicentennial. The musical portrays a group of English converts to Mormonism on a journey toward faith and toward Utah. The notes accompanying the play's script made several things explicit to would-be directors. First, directors were told that the musical was to communicate and honor the spirit

---

6. *The Sesquicentennial Star* 1, no.1 (November 1995), University of Utah Archives, Salt Lake City, Utah.

7. Ibid.

of gathering, a concept that Mormons in the nineteenth century understood literally as a call to gather together and build Zion in the Great Basin. However, the play notes made a distinction between 1847 and 1997: "The foundation laid by the pioneers is still strong, but the spirit of gathering in the Church is different now. Church members are taught to remain in their homelands, to build up the Church wherever they live. When the characters in *Barefoot to Zion* talk with fervor about the need to go to America to build up Zion, they are being obedient to the Lord's instructions in their day. It is the faithfulness and courage of the pioneers, not the destination of their journey that Church members should emulate."[8] The notes taught a metaphorical and spiritualized notion of gathering. The journey of faith, not the geographic destination, was paramount.

Also, the notes to potential directors of *Barefoot to Zion* emphasized that persons of all backgrounds should envision themselves as pioneers. The instructions explained that "race should not be a factor in casting.... The skin color or ancestral homeland of the actors should have no importance in casting this play. Characters may be played by persons of any ancestry, and no attempt should be made to use makeup to change an actor's skin color. Nor should there be any explanation to the audience if persons of different races play members of the same family."[9] Here we see members of the church trying to reconcile the increasingly diverse nature of the contemporary community with the primarily white ancestry of their nineteenth-century predecessors. In attempting to allay racial explanations and to allow for a multiracial cast, the church navigated a narrow path. The church wanted to celebrate its historical roots while also ensuring that contemporary audiences saw themselves as descendants of those pioneers. Eric Eliason has called this phenomenon the "pioneerification" of new Mormon converts and suggests that the process is a redeployment of what was a powerful symbol within the LDS community in a way that speaks to current situations.[10]

In order to pioneerify the modern Mormon community, church leaders often repeated the claim that all church members were inheritors of the pioneer history. Materials produced by the state of Utah for the sesquicentennial made the same claim for all Utahans. The Utah Pioneer Sesquicentennial Celebration Coordinating Council published a handbook of "97 ways in '97 to Celebrate the

---

8. Promised Valley Productions, *Barefoot to Zion* (Salt Lake City: The Church of Jesus Christ of Latter-day Saints, 1997), Church History Library, Salt Lake City, Utah.

9. Ibid.

10. Eric Alden Eliason, "Celebrating Zion: Pioneers in Mormon Popular Historical Expression" (PhD diss., University of Texas at Austin, 1998), 96–109.

Sesquicentennial" for classrooms throughout Utah. In that handbook, teachers were instructed that "Everyone can be a 'pioneer.'" Alongside activities that served to teach children about the Utah pioneers was material encouraging children to learn about "modern pioneers" and to celebrate their stories as well.[11] Thus both non-Mormon and Mormon Utahans were encouraged to view the Mormon exodus as their shared heritage.

The sense that pioneer identity had expanded was accompanied by a message that it was the values of the West that present Latter-day Saints should share with their ancestors. In this way, church members celebrated the European-American narrative of western progress—they viewed the West as a place that defined individuals and made them Americans. The western narrative embraced here was a simple, nationalist narrative of the West as the space that made Europeans Americans and made Americans unique. Freedom, independence, hope, and courage were celebrated as values that were and are part of *both* Latter-day Saint and American character.

Church-created sesquicentennial publications offered an oft-repeated version of Mormons' nineteenth-century past. The narrative began in Nauvoo "once home and haven but now menacing and unsafe."[12] The pioneers were portrayed as innocents driven out of their homeland and searching for refuge and the freedom to practice their religion. They had been "expatriated from their town (Nauvoo), from their state (Illinois) and from their country (the United States), after suffering physical and emotional harassment and the loss of their property."[13] Persecuted and without a place, the pioneers began their journey.

That narrative then turned from oppression to a celebration of the pioneers' character: "They came because they believed that people could create Zion on earth where pure hearts could find rest and happiness." Over the prairies and western landscapes the people came, "but thousands would die before their journey's end," explain the storytellers.[14] Nonetheless, the pioneers persevered in the face of great odds. Listeners and readers were told to "imagine facing this ridge in a wagon. Then imagine pulling a handcart." Encouraged to step into the narrative told about the pioneers, readers and listeners were taught

---

11. *Utah Pioneer Sesquicentennial Education Handbook* (Utah Pioneer Sesquicentennial Celebration Coordinating Council, 1997), Church History Library, Salt Lake City, Utah.

12. *Pioneer Sesquicentennial Celebration: Drama and Musical Presentations* (Salt Lake City: The Church of Jesus Christ of Latter-day Saints, 1996), L. Tom Perry Special Collections, Provo, Utah.

13. *Pioneer Sesquicentennial* (Deseret Management Corporation, 1997), University of Utah Archives, Salt Lake City, Utah.

14. *Pioneer Sesquicentennial Celebration.*

that they ought to imagine the hardships the pioneers had faced in order to symbolically retrace those footsteps in their own life journeys. "In the heroic effort of the pioneers we learn an eternal truth," Gordon B. Hinckley declared in a sesquicentennial film, "We all must pass through a refiner's fire."[15]

Virtually every sesquicentennial historical narrative of the nineteenth century concluded with a lesson for Mormons today: "We are all pioneers still. With those who have gone before, we journey together, step by faithful step, to arrive at a promised valley and find 'it is the right place.'"[16]

Creating Trekkers

Since 1849, Latter-day Saints have celebrated July 24 as Pioneer Day in remembrance of the day on which Brigham Young saw the valley and declared that it was the "right place." These celebrations of the Saints' movement into the West quickly became elaborate festivals and parades. During the Jubilee celebration in 1897, a four-day event honored the surviving pioneers, fêted as state-makers, faith founders, and people of character. Utahans tended to view pioneer life stories as the stories of a state's citizens and of a chosen people. That 1897 celebration of the pioneers helped mark July 24, 1847, as *the* significant day in Utah's founding rather than its 1896 statehood (which represented, in part, all that the Latter-day Saints had had to give up in order to achieve reconciliation with the US government).[17]

The 1947 centennial celebration was a particularly intriguing attempt to reenact the pioneers' entry into the valley. Put on by the Sons of the Utah Pioneers, a group that frequently funded a number of the memorials and monuments throughout the state of Utah, the main centennial events were also made exclusive by that same group. In order to be as "authentic" as possible, the group chose only descendants of Utah pioneers as the central participants. At that time, both the Sons and Daughters of the Utah Pioneers defined "pioneer" as someone "who came to the geographic area covered by the State of Deseret/Utah Territory; died crossing the plains; or was born in the Utah Territory/State of Deseret before May 19, 1869, the coming of the railroad."[18] Interestingly, the definition of pioneer provided in 1947 was not the first one offered by the Daughters of the Utah Pioneers. At its founding in

---

15. *Faith in Every Footstep*, videocassette, The Church of Jesus Christ of Latter-day Saints, 1997, L. Tom Perry Special Collections, Provo, Utah.

16. *Pioneer Sesquicentennial Celebration.*

17. Daughters of the Utah Pioneers, www.dupinternational.org/.

18. Ibid.

1903, the group defined pioneer as anyone who came to Utah before January 1850. Not too long after that, the DUP extended the time frame for the pioneers to 1853. It was in 1910 that it finally decided upon May 10, 1869, as the final date for the pioneer era, choosing the day that the transcontinental railroads met in Promontory, Utah.[19]

During the 1947 trek, the choice of including only pioneer descendants demonstrated a significant social distinction within the LDS community. Those who were descendants of the pioneers claimed a special, privileged status (often accompanied by socioeconomic status) in Utah, much like the descendants of those who came to America on the Mayflower or those who fought in the American Revolution have claimed a privileged, special status in the nation as a whole. The commemorative program for the event listed all of the participants and every way that they were related to nineteenth-century pioneers. Their ancestry celebrated, the participants were described as "unusual" people who "had to have a vision. Without it, [they] couldn't have understood the grand purpose of the reenactment. [They] had to have a love of heritage, a respect for those who had given so much so that others would be happier."[20]

Continuing their claims to authenticity, the centennial reenactors traveled in seventy-two automobiles in order to represent the seventy-two covered wagons that had traveled with Brigham Young. Those cars were decked out with covered wagon tops, and participants dressed in pioneer clothes and camped out "frontier-style" at night.[21] "Simulated oxen," apparently crafted out of plywood, also accompanied the 143 men, three women and two boys "representing President Young's first company."[22] These 1947 trekkers arrived in the valley in time to participate in a parade down Main Street that ended with ceremonies at Temple Square's Brigham Young Monument. That the procession used simulated oxen pasted to cars points to the ritualization of an imagined western landscape. In an era when Utah still had a strong agricultural and farming economy, it would have been easy enough to use real oxen for the

---

19. *The First Twenty-Five Years* (Daughters of the Utah Pioneers, 1986), Church History Library, Salt Lake City, Utah.

20. D. James Cannon, ed., *Centennial Caravan: Story of the 1947 Centennial Reenactment of the Original Mormon Trek* (Salt Lake City: Sons of the Utah Pioneers, 1948).

21. Itinerary for Utah Centennial Pioneer Trek sponsored by the Sons of Utah Pioneers, July 14–22, 1947, Church History Library, Salt Lake City, Utah.

22. *Souvenir Program and Guide for the Utah Centennial Trek, following along the Old Mormon Pioneer Trail, Sponsored by The Sons of the Utah Pioneers,* 1947 (Salt Lake City: Wendell J. Ashton for The Sons of Utah Pioneers, Inc., 1947), Church History Library, Salt Lake City, Utah.

event. Yet the ritual's pilgrims chose to reenact with cars and fake oxen, demonstrating the celebration of their western past *and* the celebration of how far they had come in "civilizing" that western landscape.

Fifty years later, the 1997 sesquicentennial celebration also attempted to ritualize and reenact the 1847 trek. This time, however, the attempts to achieve authenticity looked different. In 1997, authenticity meant that those journeying on the trail would actually walk, push handcarts, or ride in covered wagons. Some trekkers wore pioneer clothes all the time, some just for the cameras, and some wore their modern-day clothing and attempted authenticity in other ways. While only a select number of church members participated in the trek, church leaders encouraged all Latter-day Saints to visit the trail: "There is no equivalent to experiencing firsthand the Mormon Pioneer Trail." However, they counseled that church members did not need to "retrace the entire trek from Nauvoo to Salt Lake City to experience the spirit of being on the trail." Rather they should "do only that which is most meaningful to you."[23] Here we see an impulse that would rise again and again as the ritual of the trek developed and became popularized in the Latter-day Saint community. Church authorities asserted that the experience of the trail could be distilled into particularly significant moments and that Mormons need not undertake the entire journey in order to learn what the Spirit had to teach them.

The planners for the church-run trek ensured that portable toilets and water trucks followed the participants along the way. Even so, some of the leaders of the trek did not like being called reenactors because they were "dealing with many of the same trials and hardships of the original pioneers."[24] Part of the 1997 trek was called the "authentic camp." Even though participants in this camp lived in dwellings designed after nineteenth-century tents, often wore pioneer-style clothing, and ate food that the pioneers ate, they had access to water and toilets and could walk into towns and enjoy treats at a local restaurant. One authentic camper described the space as looking "like a small community...or a small village. The kitchen is the center area....This is where all of the action takes place. Not only does all of the cooking (a wonderful major part) but the washing of dishes, clothes and all sorts of things. We mend our clothes most of the time near this wondrous place."[25] The 1997

---

23. *The Mormon Pioneer Trail: Church Pioneer Sesquicentennial (150th) Celebration. A Highway and Trail Etiquette Guide* (Salt Lake City: The Church of Jesus Christ of Latter-day Saints, n.d.), University of Utah Archives, Salt Lake City, Utah.

24. Duane S. Carling Reminiscence (b. 1943–), MS16320, Church History Library, Salt Lake City, Utah.

25. Wendy Westergard Journal, July 17, 1997, http://heritage.uen.org/journals/Wc9140ad7519ad.shtml.

trek began on April 19. Over ten thousand people participated in the trek at one point or another; some church members committed to the entire trek, while others walked for a day or a weekend.[26] During the trek, the website following the trekkers received 300,000 hits each week, and trek leaders claimed that about 300 million people had seen a story about the trek in the media.[27]

During the sesquicentennial, some trekkers walked and some rode in wagons. Handcarts, though, have become *the* symbol of Mormon trekking. Why? After all, handcarts were not the only or even the most common mode of transportation for Mormons journeying west in the nineteenth century. Perhaps the handcart as a symbol has become so popular because handcarts can be claimed as a distinctively Mormon symbol while covered wagons have come to symbolize westward movement more generally. No doubt handcarts represent precisely what believers wish to emphasize as they trek: the values of industry, commitment, and faith. The physical labor that accompanies pushing and pulling handcarts allows believers to access those traits in ways that riding in a covered wagon cannot. Handcarts symbolize the values Mormons wish to claim as they reenact the journey west.

The trekkers weren't the only ones on this journey. Together, the press, news crews, and movie companies comprised a significant element of the movement. They followed the trekkers throughout the journey, often asking them to reenact particular moments for news or film footage. One trekker recalled a particular day when "Much of our day was dictated by the CBS news crew. They wanted pretty pictures of us pulling our handcarts over some steep sandhills.... We followed the original wagon ruts and it was really hard pulling in some places. But we were not just there for our own enjoyment—the TV cameras would film us as we went a few hundred yards, then we would have to stop in our tracks while they repositioned the cameras. So, a distance that would normally only take 15 minutes to cross took us almost 45 minutes."[28] That press coverage helped bring the church into the national spotlight in a positive way. And so, trek reenactors were reminded that they had multiple audiences observing their journey. There were fellow Mormons who saw the trek as an opportunity for vicarious pilgrimage, participating through online coverage and through the journals kept by trek participants. Yet trekkers were

---

26. Richard O. Cowan, *The Latter-day Saint Century* (Salt Lake City: Bookcraft, 1999), 282–283.

27. Brian Hill and Karen Hill, *Angels Among Us: Stories from the Sesquicentennial Wagon Train*, audiocassette, Covenant Communications, Inc., 1997, AC 5027, L. Tom Perry Special Collections, Provo, Utah.

28. Brent C. Moore Journal, May 21, 1997, http://heritage.uen.org/journals/ Wc5031413dc6d8.shtml.

also being tracked by outsiders and, in this instance, the trekkers had much control over the narrative being told about them and their religious community. News media outlets writing about the events associated Mormons with the hard work and stick-to-itiveness of the American West. The sesquicentennial trek was a public relations boon for the church, as non-Mormons celebrated the Latter-day Saints as the epitome of American values.

Fifty years after an exclusive centennial celebration that had included only individuals with pioneer ancestors, the definition of a "pioneer" had changed and expanded. That change reflected church leaders' awareness and celebration of Mormonism's growing geographic diffusion and diversity. The 1997 sesquicentennial trek was open to anyone, and believers were taught that they were "pioneers in many ways today in the things we learn and how we conduct our lives."[29] One member of the Quorum of the Twelve Apostles gave a fireside talk that articulated the church's attempt to expand the definition of "pioneer" for those celebrating the sesquicentennial: "When we speak of the great events of our collective past, it is all *our* history. Occasionally I have heard a new convert and someone in another land say, 'My ancestors did not cross the plains or settle Utah.... I do not feel part of that great legacy of the Church.' ... No matter how new you may be to the Church, this is our collective past—we are adopted into all of this history and heritage, if you will, and we have equal claim upon all of its blessings and promises."[30] Church leaders emphasized a spiritual inheritance, a collective identity, and a past to which any Mormon could lay claim. In a similar vein, Gordon B. Hinckley said in a sesquicentennial interview that all members of the church could "draw strength from our pioneer forebears and meet the challenges of today in the same way.... Every member of this Church, whether of pioneer ancestry or baptized yesterday, has a great legacy for which to be thankful. We're all beneficiaries of that tremendous legacy—the faith, the integrity and the vision of our pioneer forebears. They laid the foundations of this community."[31]

By creating a class for LDS seminaries and Institutes of Religion called "Faith in Every Footstep," the institutional church promoted the idea that *every* church member, no matter where he or she lived, had something to learn from the pioneers—that they were church heroes even on the cusp of the twenty-first century. That the material was standardized, meaning it was taught to every teenaged or college-aged believer, meant that the church saw

---

29. Margaret Clark Journals, http://heritage.uen.org/journals/Wcf13741d1f82d.shtml.

30. Jeffrey Holland, "What Mean These Stones?," Ogden Pioneer Days Fireside, July 23, 1995, Church History Library, Salt Lake City, Utah.

31. *Pioneer Sesquicentennial.*

the pioneers as symbols for all and felt a particular need to teach that message to its younger members, who might not see themselves as connected to the pioneers. The material was designed to encourage students to understand the pioneers as spiritual kin and to "see the pioneers and themselves as important participants in the gathering of Israel and the establishment of Zion."[32] At the end of the twentieth and beginning of the twenty-first centuries, that message was taught to an increasingly place-less set of church members.

By creating a sense of community, the trek tied contemporary believers to one another. One 1997 trekker even felt resentment toward folks just stopping by: "Have had several visitors the past two days. It is good to see them and nice of them to drop by, but actually I would prefer not seeing any of them until after we reach the Salt Lake Valley. Not a nice comment to make. The reality is, however, that I just want to enjoy the company of the folks on the Wagon Train until it is over."[33] Here we see the power of the ritual reenactment: a member of the trek saw friends and family members as outsiders, feeling that even familiar faces would be an intrusion on his trek experience and preferring the company of the stranger-trekkers who had been with him over the previous weeks. In that moment, his identity as trekker became his primary social identity and the one to which he clung.

The trekkers experienced a sense of community through shared experiences. During the trek, three couples got engaged and a baby was born. Along the way, the group visited the grave of a Mormon child and dedicated it. "It reminded us of all the children.... who died and were buried...and it became so much more real," recalled one trekker. "I think that was one of the spiritual moments for us. To really feel, at least partially, what it would be like to lose someone."[34]

Trekker Ted Moore vowed to walk from Nauvoo all the way to Salt Lake City. Along the way, one of the friends he had made became sick and had to spend a few days in the hospital. Ted stayed with his friend while he was in the hospital, but in order not to miss the trail, "He went back to the point at which he had left off and then he went back to where he stopped...and walked 40 miles a day...until he caught up." When his friend returned to the trek, Ted pushed him in a handcart until he was able to walk for himself.[35]

---

32. Church Educational System, *Faith in Every Footstep: Instructor's Guide,* 1847–1997 (Salt Lake City: The Church of Jesus Christ of Latter-day Saints, 1996), Church History Library, Salt Lake City, Utah.

33. John Lodefink Journal, MS 15583, Church History Library, Salt Lake City, Utah.

34. Hill and Hill, *Angels Among Us: Stories from the Sesquicentennial Wagon Train.*

35. Ibid.

In later interviews and reminiscences, many 1997 trekkers suggested that the trek strengthened and concretized their faith in God. Several saw a divine plan at work in their participation. As trekker Wendy Westergard put it, "To think that we were adding our own legacy of faith to the trail made us speechless.... It only made everything worth every moment. I know I was born at the right time at the right place. I used to not believe that, but now I have a surety of being born at the right time."[36] Many other trekkers echoed this idea, that God actively intervened in the world to fulfill his plans for individuals and for his church. As Brian Hill recalled, "God was watching over us.... It was as if we were under a protecting blanket." For many trekkers, their reenactment of the pioneers' journey reaffirmed their sense of God's providence. God did indeed work in the world as they had believed.

Many trekkers also repeated the claim that the "veil" between this world and the spirit world was thin—that they could feel the original pioneers traversing the territory with them. They imagined both God and the nineteenth-century pioneers pulling for them, sometimes sensing that they were not the only ones moving their handcarts through particularly difficult stretches of terrain.[37] When the trekkers reached Martin's Cove, they decided to have a testimony meeting. One woman named Jane recounted that as she was walking, she "felt a presence" and eventually said "Grandmother, is that you?" and felt a conviction that it was, in fact, her grandmother, who had laughed at Jane when she converted to Mormonism.[38] For her, the experience affirmed the presence of those who had died, as part of the community. Later, a trekker named Margaret talked about how she felt that "the spirit...moves with the wagon train" when she recalled hearing a voice that told her to go purchase candy bars and find the handcart companies. Margaret "just knew" that the companies were in trouble and traveled to find them and provide them with the sustenance they needed to arrive at the next campsite.[39]

The 1997 trekkers' accounts suggest that they came to know theological and religious claims in a more experiential way than they had previously in their lives. In fact, one of the trek leaders took umbrage at the accusation that the 1997 experience wasn't "authentic." He recounted that the weather was

---

36. Wendy Westergard Journal, May 21, 1997.

37. See, for example, Duane S. Carling Reminiscence (b. 1943–), MS16320, MS19168; Sons of Utah Pioneers, "Angels Are Near Us Monument Dedication," July 2000, Church History Library, Salt Lake City, Utah.

38. Hill and Hill, *Angels Among Us.*

39. Ibid.

similar, that at times they had a hard time getting fed, and that they had to deal with sick animals. "The trail conditions were more real than you imagine," Brian Hill recalled, "so we knew something of suffering." In his account of the trek, Hill went on to say about the pioneers: "In a sense I've read their journals better than the way they could write it."[40] Here Hill claimed an experiential authority to speak about the pioneers. He drew that authority from his trek. He knew them, he said, because he had walked in their footsteps.

Wendy Westergard noted that she and her fellow trekkers created a "moving community." That movement—through time, but also through space—is significant to modern-day interpretations of what is taking place. She imagined that as the pioneers moved forward "the West was opened," and she celebrated the understanding that God manifested promises in a spatial way. Westergard commented that her dream for the trek was one of "doing 'the west,'" which meant, for her, traveling some of the time in a covered wagon.[41] At this time, Mormons were encouraged to see the landscape itself as sacred but also as untouched, emphasizing its significance to the modern gaze. Visitors were told that much of the trail was "pristine" and that they could view the trail and surrounding landscape as "almost unchanged from that viewed by the Mormon pioneers 150 years ago."[42]

"People want to gather," remembered trek leader Brian Hill as he tried to answer the question of why the wagon train was so popular. He wondered why until he *experienced* the trek. He then believed that he "understood that gathering to Zion…is not something that people do just because it is an idle thought or because they are commanded. It is because of the feeling that Zion has." He recalled that it was "like a magnet," not something that participants willed, but that they felt. It was a bond that he considered akin to familial ties and to a truer sense of community than he had felt elsewhere. Zion was a place where "you provide for [people's] needs."[43]

Perhaps one 1997 trekker's phrase best describes what Latter-day Saints imagine happening as they trek, if only for a few hours and if only over a local hill; she described the trek community as a "traveling Zion." She declared that she would "always treasure my small glimpse of an understanding of what Zion is all about." For this trekker, and for many others, the destination Zion—a physical, geographical space that one could locate on a map—was not as important

40. Ibid.

41. Wendy Westergard Journal, May 21, 1997.

42. *The Mormon Pioneer Trail: Church Pioneer Sesquicentennial (150th) Celebration. A Highway and Trail Etiquette Guide.*

43. Hill and Hill, *Angels Among Us.*

as the traveling Zion that developed as people physically labored to push and pull handcarts and moved through space together. Recall the director's notes for the 1997 *Barefoot to Zion* musical: "It is the faithfulness and courage of the pioneers, not the destination of their journey, that Church members should emulate." So it seems that as the notion of the gathering was spiritualized, so, too, were the concepts of Zion and the West. Western geography, particularly in Utah, served as evidence of a divine plan, but Zion was no longer tied to the Salt Lake Valley in the same ways.

The Trail's End

When the 1997 trekkers completed their journey, they did so next to a gift from Utahans of 1947. The 1997 trek ended in This Is the Place (TITP) Park, next to the This Is the Place monument, sculpted by Mahonri M. Young, Brigham Young's grandson. Over 51,000 people greeted the trekkers at the end of their journey, and much pomp surrounded the event. Greeters stood on the two sides of the final mile of the trek, clapping and cheering for the trekkers. As they entered the park, the trekkers passed by several handcarts that had been painted white and a group of people dressed in white standing silently and waving white handkerchiefs. These individuals represented the pioneers who had died during the 1847 journey, and for some, seeing these representatives was "a very spiritual moment. The spirits of those earlier handcart pioneers were definitely present."[44] Their loved ones, as well as many others who had followed their journey online, greeted the trekkers. Experiencing the end of the journey was a coming home of sorts. One of the most well-known trekkers, Larry "Turbo" Stewart, was baptized when the train reached This Is the Place Park, a sign that the trek had, for him, made the spiritual beliefs professed by Mormons seem really real.

After many joyful reunions, everyone gathered around the 1947 monument at the center of the park. Rather than in the Salt Lake Valley itself, the 1997 trek ended when believers reached the point where many believe Brigham Young, their Moses, looked out over that valley and knew that it was their promised land. Why?

In contemporary Mormonism, it is the site of prophetic vision that remains most significant. For Latter-day Saints, the belief that Brigham Young stood in this spot and proclaimed that the Salt Lake Valley would be the church's place of refuge and new place of gathering marks the spot as sacred. In an age in which Latter-day Saints still affirm ongoing revelation but official revelations

---

44. John Lodefink Journal, July 22, 1997.

are fewer and farther between, the site itself confirms church members' sense of prophetic vision. Visitors to the site can look out over the Salt Lake Valley and the landscape itself—including the neatly defined roads, the Great Salt Lake, and the buildings of Temple Square marking the skyline as a Mormon skyline—to confirm the truthfulness of Brigham Young's vision. As trekker Brian Hill remembered, he initially wondered what it would be like to see the valley, but when he arrived at TITP Park, he realized what the pioneers must have felt: "I was overcome...and the emotion that I felt as I stood there and cried was gratitude...I was grateful to God."[45]

As modern trekkers along with their welcomers gathered around the monument, a choir encouraged participants to sing "High on a Mountaintop." Soon thereafter, President Gordon B. Hinckley got up and remarked that the trekkers had done something extraordinary and had caught the imagination of everyone. Hinckley argued that the trekkers in 1997 were more authentic than their 1947 counterparts who rode in cars, and he congratulated them on reaching "the end of the trail." Hinckley also made an interesting set of connections in this space: First, he declared that the "desert has truly blossomed," calling to mind the fulfillment of the prophetic vision that Brigham Young had of the valley. He noted that Young had "recognized the reality of prophetic vision when he declared 'This is the right place.'" And Hinckley declared that Young had known it was the same place that Joseph Smith had also seen in a vision. In so doing, Hinckley connected the western landscape with the prophetic visions of Joseph Smith, suggesting that all that happened to the Church from 1830 onward was part of a divine plan for the Latter-day Saints. Trekkers and their welcomers were invited to *see* the space as confirmation of the truthfulness of it all.

About halfway down the walkway from This Is the Place Monument stands another monument built to memorialize the 1997 reenactment. Titled *Angels Are Near Us*, its bronze bas relief depicts wagons moving across the land, silhouetted against the western sky. The majority of the monument is covered in text, stating that "the trek was a commemoration of sacrifices, joys and was a testament to the honor and greatness of those who went before." It recounts an apostolic blessing that was made before the journey began and describes how the people on the trek in 1997 felt a "spiritual kinship with those who made the trek 150 years ago."

It may seem odd to memorialize a fairly recent reenactment as a significant historical event in its own right, yet the connections to sacred space help us make sense of it. The memorial represents both place and movement.

---

45. Hill and Hill, *Angels Among Us*.

Trekkers had reached the end of the trail—they could look out over the valley just as Brigham Young had 150 years earlier. They could see the geography and city that served as evidence of his prophetic vision.

At the same time, the monument declares that the trail never ends and that the values and the movements of the West will continue even as the people are scattered. The final text of the monument declares that the trekkers' "spirits transcended time and beckoned us to trace their journey for the trail never ends." Indeed, since 1997 trek reenactments have continued to gain in popularity. As of 2004, reservations for the three hundred church-supplied handcarts at the Mormon Handcart Historic Sites in Wyoming were being taken three years in advance.[46] More than sixty missionary couples help manage the throngs of people coming to reenact treks during the summer months.[47]

By 1997, most Latter-day Saints lived outside the United States and most American Mormons lived outside Utah. Only a small minority were descended from the mid-nineteenth-century Mormon pioneers. Nevertheless, the church's collective memory of the experiences of exodus and gathering retained their importance. In 1997, the church found that its pioneer roots helped cast contemporary Mormonism in the positive glow of shared American values. Efforts toward commemoration and reenactment, moreover, attempted to connect contemporary Latter-day Saints to each other and to a common landscape even as church members were increasingly scattered around the globe.

---

46. Rone Tempest, "A Rocky Path for Pilgrims" *Los Angeles Times*, September 6, 2004.

47. Laura Sietz, "Participants Know Popular Treks Are a Far Cry from the Handcart Pioneers' Suffserings" *Deseret News*, July 23, 2010.

15

*"All the Truth Does Not Always
Need to Be Told"*

THE LDS CHURCH, MORMON HISTORY,
AND RELIGIOUS AUTHORITY

John G. Turner

IN 2014, THE Church of Jesus Christ of Latter-day Saints released three
essays providing detailed interpretations of its polygamous past. The essays
describe plural marriage as a divine commandment given to Joseph Smith by
God in 1831 for unclear reasons. When he later hesitated, an angel purportedly
threatened him with a sword, leaving Smith little choice but to obey. The
essays allow that Smith's plural marriages fomented discord with his first wife
Emma Hale, and they reveal that the prophet sometimes moved ahead without
her knowledge or consent. Also, the essays suggest that Smith's marriage to
fourteen-year-old Helen Kimball and his marriages to already married women
were "for eternity alone," though they note the paucity of documentary evidence. The essay on Mormon polygamy in early Utah notes that "plural marriage was a significant sacrifice" for many Latter-day Saints, who embraced the
principle out of obedience rather than enthusiasm. On balance, however, the
essays insist that polygamy need not interfere with either faith or ancestral
pride: "Plural marriage did result in the birth of large numbers of children
within faithful Latter-day Saint homes. It also shaped 19th-century Mormon
society in many ways: marriage became available to virtually all who desired it;
per-capita inequality of wealth was diminished as economically disadvantaged
women married into more financially stable households; and ethnic intermar-
riages were increased, which helped to unite a diverse immigrant population.
Plural marriage also helped create and strengthen a sense of cohesion and
group identification among Latter-day Saints."[1] Just as nineteenth-century
Latter-day Saints faithfully lived out the principle, implied the essays, so should

---

1. "Plural Marriage in the Church of Jesus Christ of Latter-day Saints," *LDS.org*, www.lds.
org/topics/plural-marriage-in-the-church-of-jesus-christ-of-latter-day-saints.

twenty-first-century Mormons accept that God had temporarily instituted plural marriage for the benefit of his restored church. In so doing, they would honor their ancestors.

Major media outlets in the United States and around the world reported on the essays. Although the church had put forth a measured but firm defense of its polygamous past, journalists focused first and foremost on two related topics: 1) the most shocking aspects of Joseph Smith's many marriages; and 2) the church's alleged effort to suppress information about those aspects. "It's Official," informed the *New York Times* front-page headline, "Mormon Founder Had Up to 40 Wives."[2] The Gray Lady was not alone. Print and online news sources across the United States and beyond trumpeted the fact that the Church of Jesus Christ of Latter-day Saints had finally fessed up to its scandalous early history. "The Mormon founder Joseph Smith married as many as 40 women, including a 14-year-old girl," informed London's *Daily Telegraph*. The paper claimed that Smith's polygamy was something that "church leaders have acknowledged for the first time," and *The Telegraph* added that "the disclosure shocked many Mormons."[3]

Contrary to the reporting of the *Times* and the *Telegraph*, Mormon leaders had in earlier times not only acknowledged Joseph Smith's plural marriages but had actively collected and publicized evidence of them. In the late 1800s, the Reorganized Church of Jesus Christ of Latter Day Saints (RLDS, renamed the Community of Christ in 2001), led by Smith's son Joseph Smith III, had vigorously denied that the founding Mormon prophet had married anyone other than Emma Hale. RLDS leaders blamed Brigham Young for the introduction of polygamy and the corruption of the true restoration. In response, Mormon leaders collected and published affidavits from Smith's plural wives, a few of which asserted or implied that the marriages in question were consummated.[4] Smith's polygamy, one would think, was old news.

The church's changing approach to its past, however, was newsworthy. Church leaders had abandoned their vigorous and informative defenses of plural marriage after the tentative and then final abandonment of "the principle" in 1890 and 1904, respectively. Joseph Smith's revelation on celestial

---

2. Laurie Goodstein, "It's Official: Mormon Founder Had Up to 40 Wives," *New York Times*, November 10, 2014, A1.

3. Philip Sherwell, "Mormon Church Finally Admits Founder Joseph Smith was Polygamist with 40 Wives," *Daily Telegraph*, November 12, 2014.

4. See "Plural Marriage," *The Historical Record*, May 1887, 219–234. In one published affidavit (dated March 4, 1870), Benjamin F. Johnson asserted that Joseph Smith had been sealed to Johnson's sister Almera and had then lodged "at my house with my sister as man and wife (and to my certain knowledge he occupied the same bed with her)."

(and plural) marriage remained scripture for Latter-day Saints, and many church publications after 1906 at least referenced his multiple marriages. At the same time decades, however, the church preferred to romanticize Smith's marriage with Emma, and by the early twenty-first century many Latter-day Saints possessed only a dim awareness of Smith's marital practices. Thus, the detail in the November 2014 essays—Smith married women already married to other men; Smith's youngest wife was only fourteen years of age, the daughter of another high-ranking leader; church leaders tacitly sanctioned some polygamous unions after publicly abandoning the practice—surprised church members, non-Mormons, and journalists alike.

The essays on polygamy were part of a larger effort on the part of the church to bring recent, faithful scholarship to bear on the thorniest subjects within its history, in an attempt to alleviate the doubts of members related to such topics. Whether they will succeed in that respect remains unclear. What is clear is that history remains a live, contentious issue for the LDS Church in a manner foreign to the present experience of most other American Christians. Presbyterians are not bothered by John Calvin's role in the burning of Michael Servetus at the stake. American Catholics are largely unconcerned about the past actions of popes, especially of those before their lifetimes. For Latter-day Saints, especially for those who live in the United States, history is very much a present concern. Mormons revere nineteenth-century pioneers, ancestral converts within their own family lines, and their past prophets. For Mormons, the events of the nineteenth century are sacred history, the inauguration of the "dispensation of the fulness of times," years filled with sacred heroes whose actions and words still shape the contemporary church.

All religious movements face crises of authority. These may come when a society or religious group experiences intercultural exchange, periods of adversity, or leadership transitions. Does a prophet truly speak for God? Do clerics possess the proper authority to conduct rituals? Are scriptures a reliable source for knowledge and wisdom? Some traditions face such crises periodically, some rarely, and some with great regularity. In the years following the Second World War, many Christian movements have faced crises of authority, often brought about through encounters with pluralism and the continued ascent of secular and Enlightenment-based assumptions as the standard for public discourse. Issues as diverse as higher criticism of the Bible, evolution, and changing standards of sexuality led to what evangelical author and editor Harold Lindsell called a "battle for the Bible" within Protestant ranks. Mainline Protestants, moreover, found themselves bitterly divided over how to respond to changing cultural standards regarding gender roles and homosexuality.

The LDS Church faced no parallel crisis, largely because Mormonism lacked the liberal theological wing necessary to spark true internecine conflict over these and related issues.

Instead of facing a crisis of biblical authority or cultural authority, the LDS Church regularly encounters the question of prophetic authority through the filter of its history. As Richard Bushman has observed, the "core of Mormon belief [is] a conviction about actual events."[5] Along with most other Christians, Latter-day Saints believe in the historical authenticity of biblical events such as the resurrection of Jesus Christ. For Mormons, however, it is also important to affirm that Joseph Smith received a visit from the God the Father and Jesus Christ, that he translated an ancient record contained on gold plates, and that John the Baptist and three of Jesus's apostles conferred priesthood authority on Smith and Oliver Cowdery. As Jan Shipps once observed, Mormonism offers "faith cast in the form of history," history that unlike that of New Testament Christianity can be readily examined through a host of contemporary sources.[6] Precisely because of that history's centrality, LDS leaders have evidenced fear that exposure to the details of debates over the coming forth of the Book of Mormon and Book of Abraham, the extent of Joseph Smith's polygamy, or the hardnosed leadership of Brigham Young would destroy the testimonies of believing Mormons.

This chapter compares the LDS Church's changing approaches to its history with evangelical conflicts over biblical authority. One might also fruitfully analyze the changing way that the Reorganized Church of Jesus Christ of Latter Day Saints (now the Community of Christ) understood its past, as the RLDS Church's sense of its history and its self-identity moved in very different directions during the second half of the twentieth century. Here, however, the focus is on the larger and more visible Utah-based church. Over the past seventy years, Latter-day Saint scholars and ecclesiastical leaders have offered divergent views on the proper approach to their history. Institutional policies have oscillated between openness and retrenchment, as illustrated in the content of church-sanctioned publications and by the amount of access the church has granted scholars to its archives. Despite a recent trend toward great openness, the issue remains unresolved. Indeed, just a conservative Protestants face ongoing conflicts over biblical authority, it seems likely that Latter-day Saints will endure uncertainty and angst over their history as long

---

5. Richard L. Bushman, *Joseph Smith and the Beginnings of Mormonism* (Urbana: University of Illinois Press, 1984), 188.

6. Jan Shipps, *Sojourner in the Promised Land: Forty Years among the Mormons* (Urbana: University of Illinois Press, 2000), 165.

as their faith centers upon "a conviction about actual events" that are also sub-ject to historical study and analysis.

"Behold, there shall be a record kept among you," begins a revelation dic-tated by Joseph Smith Jr. on the day he and a small number of followers estab-lished what in April 1830 they simply called the Church of Christ.[7] One year later, another revelation called John Whitmer to "write and keep a regular history."[8] Very much in keeping with the Book of Mormon's emphasis on re-cord-keeping and remembrance, these early revelations led to the accumula-tion of a vast array of letters, diaries, minutes, and other documents, preserved despite the frequent tumult of the church's nineteenth-century history. The Church Historian's Office used its rich archival holdings to produce official histories of the church, such as the serially published "History of Joseph Smith," later reworked and republished by B.H. Roberts as *History of the Church of Jesus Christ of Latter-day Saints* (1902–1932). Almost from the start, detractors also wrote historical accounts—usually in the form of exposés—about Joseph Smith's background and about the coming forth of the Book of Mormon. Typically, such authors relied on published sources, testimony from former church members, rumors, and guesswork.

The church occasionally made its historical resources available to church members, who might receive access to the writings and patriarchal blessings of their ancestors. Also, the non-Mormon historian Hubert Howe Bancroft gained access to church records (including community histories, journals, au-tobiographies, periodicals, and newspapers) for his *History of Utah*, which he promised to allow church officials examine prior to publication.[9] Bancroft was an exception, owing to his prominence and apparent willingness to treat the church favorably. Most scholars encountered hesitation or resistance if not outright rejection. Utah historian Dale Morgan abandoned a book titled *The Mormons* because, according to Richard Saunders, the "Church Historian's Office had formally declined his request for access to its manuscript collection."[10] There were several reasons for such reluctance. The Church Historian's Office was understaffed, leaving the tremendous volume of mate-rial in various states of disorganization. Also, the Church Historian's Office worried that scholars would use its materials to embarrass the church.

---

7. Joseph Smith revelation of April 6, 1830, Doctrine and Covenants 21:1.

8. Joseph Smith revelation of ca. March 8, 1831, Doctrine and Covenants 47:1.

9. George Ellsworth, "Hubert Howe Bancroft and the History of Utah," *Utah Historical Quarterly* 22 (April 1954): 99–124.

10. Richard L. Saunders, ed., *Dale Morgan on the Mormons: Collected Works, Part 2, 1949–1970* (Norman: University of Oklahoma Press, 2013), 250.

Indeed, on several occasions, the church found itself embarrassed by scholarly examinations of its past. Fawn Brodie, niece of David O. McKay (then a counselor in the church's First Presidency, and a future church president), used her relation to McKay to talk her way into church's archives as she worked on a biography of Joseph Smith. Brodie, who had already lost her faith in the church, published *No Man Knows My History* (1945), which presented Joseph Smith as a treasure-hunter who created the Book of Mormon to improve his family's dim financial prospects.[11] The church publicly rebutted Brodie's contentions and excommunicated her in 1946. Several years later, active church member Juanita Brooks published the first serious monograph on the 1857 Mountain Meadows Massacre, in which she detailed the extent of Mormon participation in the massacre and arraigned Brigham Young as an "accessory after the fact."[12] During her research, Brooks did not receive access to most church-held records that she requested, and church leaders discouraged her investigation. "All the truth does not always need to be told," Apostle LeGrand Richards counseled her sharply a few years later.[13] Despite her trepidation, the publication of *The Mountain Meadows Massacre* did not lead to ecclesiastical discipline. Even so, in the sharp condemnations of Brodie's biography and in the obvious discomfort with Brooks's findings, church leaders demonstrated that they perceived historical scholarship as a threat to the church because it exposed the human shortcomings of its prophetic leaders.

Of course, the fact that the church itself published such sanitized, providential versions of its history during these years meant that any credible scholar would have quickly uncovered information that the church had decided not to reveal to its general membership. For example, Church Historian Joseph Fielding Smith's *Essentials in Church History* (1922) was designed for church educational use and "for general reading." Smith, the grand-nephew of Joseph Smith and son of early twentieth-century church president Joseph F. Smith, had come of age after the church publicly abandoned the practice of polygamy. Very much a work of providential history, *Essentials* begins with "the antiquity of the Gospel," discusses the "apostasy" of the church after Christ's earthly ministry, and presents the Protestant Reformation and the American Revolution as

---

11. Fawn Brodie, *No Man Knows My History: The Life of Joseph Smith* (New York: Knopf, 1945).

12. Juanita Brooks, *Mountain Meadows Massacre* (Redwood City, CA: Stanford University Press, 1950), 161.

13. LeGrand Richards to Juanita Brooks, November 30, 1955, in Levi S. Peterson, *Juanita Brooks: Mormon Woman Historian* (Salt Lake City: University of Utah Press, 1988), 245. See Newell Bringhurst, *Fawn McKay Brodie: A Biographer's Life* (Norman: University of Oklahoma Press, 1999), chapters 3 and 4.

preparatory works for the restoration of Christ's true church. In its account of the early years of the LDS Church, *Essentials* discusses his great-uncle's 1843 revelation on "eternal marriage" and observes that it included "the doctrine of plural wives." While the book quotes the broader revelation, it ignores the portions of what is now Section 132 of the Doctrine and Covenants that legitimate polygamy. Indeed, Joseph Fielding Smith only obliquely hints that his great-uncle did "act" on the commandment and does not mention any of his many plural wives. By contrast, *Essentials* provides copious coverage of the US government's decades-long anti-polygamy campaign. Similarly, the book describes the Mountain Meadows Massacre as "the deed of enraged Indians aided by a number of white men, who took vengeance into their hands for wrongs committed by a few of the emigrants who were pronounced enemies of both whites and Indians." *Essentials* considers the massacre "unfortunate" in its timing for its stain upon the church's reputation, in that it led to other false accusations against church authorities.[14] Juanita Brooks excoriated Joseph Fielding Smith's conclusions in her *The Mountain Meadows Massacre*.[15] As the decades passed, other scholars as well as some church educators recognized the limitations of *Essentials*. Leonard Arrington termed it a "polemical...morality play."[16] Still, Latter-day Saints were far more likely to read *Essentials* than the histories of Mormonism produced by either believing or non-Mormon scholars. *Essentials* became required reading for many LDS missionaries; especially through the 1970s, many church members gained their understanding of church history from Joseph Fielding Smith's interpretation.[17]

Despite the church hierarchy's rather uneasy relationship with its history, historians—LDS, RLDS, and otherwise—undertook important initiatives in the 1960s to promote academic scholarship on the Mormon past. Leonard Arrington, author of a magisterial economic history of the nineteenth-century church (*Great Basin Kingdom* [1958]), was the prime mover in the establishment of the Mormon History Association in 1965. The following year a group of Mormon scholars founded *Dialogue*, a periodical that in its many articles about Mormonism's history did not shy away from controversial topics. For example, Lester Bush and Armand Mauss both published essays on the

---

14. Joseph Fielding Smith, *Essentials in Church History* (Salt Lake City: Deseret News Press, 1922), preface, 341, 511.

15. See Brooks, *Mountain Meadows Massacre*, 160; Peterson, *Juanita Brooks: Mormon Woman Historian*, 207–208.

16. Leonard J. Arrington, *Adventures of a Church Historian* (Urbana: University of Illinois Press, 1998), 140.

17. Edward Leo Lyman, "The Evolution of Treatment of the Latter-day Saint Past," *Mormon Historical Studies* 11 (Spring 2010): 69.

church's policy banning black men from ordination to the priesthood and all black members from performing the temple ordinances required for eternal exaltation.[18] During these years, peer-reviewed scholarship about the Latter-day Saints and other Mormon groups proliferated, published by faithful Latter-day Saints (such as Arrington, Eugene Campbell, and Thomas Alexander), members of the RLDS Church (such as Robert Flanders), and non-Mormons (including Jan Shipps, Mario DePillis, and Lawrence Foster). Collectively, this wave of scholarship became known as the "New Mormon History," described by Moses Rischin as history "at home among the *avant garde* Gentiles."[19] The avant-garde descriptor was an overstatement, but by focusing on the human experience of the Latter-day Saints as evidenced in the historical record, these historians hoped to transcend the polemical Mormon/anti-Mormon divide that marked earlier eras. In *Great Basin Kingdom*, Arrington defended his "naturalistic treatment" as "a perfectly valid aspect of religious history."[20] The LDS members of this historiographical movement, though, took pains to emphasize that their scholarship in no way threatened the church or the faith of its members. "My own impression," wrote Arrington in 1968, "is that an intensive study of church history, while it will dispel certain myths…will build testimonies rather than weaken them."[21] Arrington hoped that even "naturalistic treatment[s]" of the past would strengthen the faith of those church members who encountered the New Mormon History.

According to Arrington, there was "a remarkable relaxing of the old policies" toward the end of Joseph Fielding Smith's long tenure as Church Historian.[22] Both Mormon and non-Mormon scholars benefited from greater access to the church archives. This relaxing accelerated after Arrington was called as Church Historian in early 1972, a departure from a then-longstanding tradition of appointing General Authorities to that position. (More colloquially

---

18. See Lester Bush Jr., "Mormonism's Negro Doctrine: An Historical Overview," *Dialogue* 8 (Spring 1973): 11–68; Armand Mauss, "Mormonism and the Negro: Faith, Folklore, and Civil Rights," *Dialogue* 2 (Winter 1967): 19–39.

19. Moses Rischin, "The New Mormon History," *American West* 6 (March 1969): 49.

20. Leonard J. Arrington, *Great Basin Kingdom: An Economic History of the Latter-day Saints, 1830–1900*, 2nd ed. (Urbana: University of Illinois Press, 2005), xxvii.

21. Leonard J. Arrington, "The Search for Truth and Meaning in Mormon History," *Dialogue: A Journal of Mormon Thought* 3 (1968): 61. On the "New Mormon History," see Jan Shipps, "Richard Lyman Bushman, the Story of Joseph Smith, and the New Mormon History," *Journal of American History* 94 (September 2007): 498–516; Ronald W. Walker, David J. Whittaker, and James B. Allen, eds., *Mormon History* (Urbana: University of Illinois Press, 2001), chapter 3.

22. Leonard J. Arrington, "Joseph Fielding Smith: Faithful Historian," *Dialogue* 7 (Spring 1972): 23.

known as "the Brethren," General Authorities, including members of the Quorum of the Twelve Apostles, preside over the church as a whole, rather than over specific geographic regions.) The Church Historian's Office was renamed the Historical Department, and following his appointment Arrington oversaw its History Division (a separate Archives Division was also created). Following this reorganization, a broader array of scholars obtained much wider access to the church's holdings. Jan Shipps and Lawrence Foster were among the non-Mormon scholars to benefit from the changed policies.

At the same time as scholars gained greater access to archival holdings, Arrington made plans for a series of sixteen volumes about the church's history, to be published by church-owned Deseret Book beginning with the church's sesquicentennial in 1980. They also envisioned two separate one-volume accounts of church history, a narrative history for church members and a more analytical, topically organized book for interested outsiders. James Allen and Glen Leonard wrote the former, published by Deseret Book in July 1976 as *The Story of the Latter-day Saints*. Allen and Leonard introduced the Latter-day Saints as "basically a religious people" for whom secular affairs were "secondary to a quest for salvation in the restored kingdom of God." According to a foreword penned by Arrington, it appeared "with the approval of the First Presidency." Arrington praised Allen and Leonard for portraying "the exciting, often controversial history of the Saints as fairly and dispassionately as possible" while noting the authors' "orientation as devout believers in the restored gospel of Jesus Christ."[23]

Despite those reassurances, Arrington was nervous about the book's publication. He knew that some church leaders warily eyed his department's projects. In 1974, apostle Boyd K. Packer had warned the church's First Presidency that the department's publications "may have a negative effect upon many," especially on "*our youngsters.*" Packer worried that some Mormon historians had adopted the "principles of their own profession" to the point of judging the church's past by scholarly standards.[24] Packer at this point shared his concerns privately, but other high-ranking leaders publicly sounded the alarm. While Deseret Book was preparing *The Story of the Latter-day Saints* for publication, LDS apostle Ezra Taft Benson delivered an address at Brigham Young University in which he complained that "there have been and continue to be attempts made to bring this [secular] philosophy into our own Church history."

23. James B. Allen and Glen M. Leonard, *The Story of the Latter-day Saints* (Salt Lake City: Deseret Book Company, 1976), vii–viii, ix.

24. Boyd K. Packer to First Presidency, October 24, 1974, excerpted in Lucile C. Tate, *Boyd K. Packer: A Watchman on the Tower* (Salt Lake City: Bookcraft, 1995), 244–245. Emphasis in original.

In particular, historians infatuated with naturalistic explanations for church history "underplay revelation and God's intervention" and "inordinately humanize the prophets of God so that their human frailties become more apparent than their spiritual qualities." Benson alluded to Juanita Brooks's accusation that Brigham Young was an "accessory after the fact" to the Mountain Meadows Massacre, and he complained about scholars who questioned the literal reality of Joseph Smith's first theophany. Benson insisted he loved history, but only a particular sort. "I love history books," he explained, "that tell history as it was—as the Book of Mormon tells it—with God in the picture, guiding and directing the affairs of the righteous." Much was at stake, according to Benson. Naturalistic accounts of church history, he asserted, implied that "the Church has not been telling the truth." In other words, the struggle over history was a matter of ecclesiastical and prophetic authority.[25]

The Story of the Latter-day Saints certainly did not label Brigham Young an "accessory after the fact" to the massacre. While the book mentioned the multiple accounts of Smith's First Vision, it did not suggest that the prophet only *thought* he saw God the Father and Jesus Christ. It did, however, more forthrightly if briefly discuss "controversial doctrines" such as plural marriage and "man's potential for becoming like God." On the former topic, Allen and Leonard observed that Smith "may have begun taking wives as early as 1835," though they demurred on the question of whether or not Smith consummated the marriages. They defended the prophet both from allegations of adultery and from dishonesty. In their account of Joseph Smith's martyrdom, they quoted approvingly from John Taylor's tribute, now included in the LDS Church's Doctrine and Covenants: "Joseph Smith, the Prophet and Seer of the Lord, has done more, save Jesus only, for the salvation of men in this world, than any other man that ever lived in it." It was a book in many ways designed not to offend the church hierarchy and to promote the faith of church members.[26]

Despite the measured approach of *The Story of the Latter-day Saints*, some members of the Quorum of the Twelve Apostles took issue with the book's alleged "absence of inspiration." Ezra Taft Benson asked an assistant, William Nelson, to review the book; the latter concluded that the book was too secular. In September, Benson in a speech to Latter-day Saint educators took issue with historians who presented the Word of Wisdom as "an outgrowth of the temperance movement in America" or who lumped Joseph Smith "among so-called

----

25. Ezra Taft Benson, "God's Hand in Our Nation's History," March 28, 1976, https://speeches.byu.edu/talks/ezra-taft-benson_gods-hand-nations-history/.

26. Allen and Leonard, *The Story of the Latter-day Saints*, 170–171, 198.

'primitivists.'"[27] Allen and Leonard had discussed "primitivism" as an "impulse common to many of the new movements" in early nineteenth-century America, including Mormonism.[28] For Benson, it was important that church leaders and believing historians distinguished Mormonism from its nineteenth-century antecedents. The restoration was a clean break from apostasy, not a refinement or reorganization of existing cultural elements and practices.

Also that September, church president Spencer W. Kimball called Arrington to a meeting of the First Presidency and members of the Twelve. Benson, who along with Mark Petersen was the book's strongest critic, revealed that an LDS institute teacher (for college-age church members) had complained that *The Story of the Latter-day Saints* would cause young people to lose their faith. Arrington respectfully but firmly rebutted the criticism. President Kimball, it turned out, liked the book. It was clear to Arrington, however, that a significant minority of high-ranking church leaders opposed his attempt to produce in-house works of history that would satisfy—or at least come closer to satisfying—the standards of professional history.[29]

Arrington and like-minded colleagues pressed on. He and coauthor Davis Bitton wrote *The Mormon Experience* with non-Mormon readers in mind. Perhaps because of the different intended audience, it generated less resistance from the church leaders who had objected to *The Story of the Latter-day Saints*. Arrington made plans to publish a biography of Brigham Young. Bitton and Arrington publicly insisted that no conflict existed between faith and historical research and writing. "I have never felt any conflict between maintaining my faith and writing historical truth," commented Arrington in a 1979 interview. "If one sticks to historical truth that shouldn't damage his faith in any way. The Lord doesn't require us to believe anything that's untrue." Arrington observed that his decades of interest in Mormon history had "only served to build my testimony of the gospel." Bitton agreed, and he suggested that false conceptions of Latter-day Saint history posed the true threat to the Mormon faith. In other words, church members or converts might have unrealistic expectations of their former leaders or the former beliefs and actions of church members. "One moves into the land of history," Bitton explained, "and finds shattering incongruities which can be devastating to faith. But the problem is with the expectation, not with the history." Bitton added that his own "faith has changed and deepened and become richer and more

---

27. Ezra Taft Benson, "The Gospel Teacher and His Message," September 17, 1976, typescript in author's possession.

28. Allen and Leonard, *The Story of the Latter-day Saints*, 12ff.

29. Arrington, *Adventures of a Church Historian*, chapter 9.

consistent with the complexities of human experience."[30] Ultimately, Arrington and Bitton insisted that rigorous, fair-minded, and sensitive historical research and writing would help produce testimonies able to withstand an honest encounter with the complexities of the past. "I don't have a testimony of the history of the church," Bitton stated many years later, insisting at the same time that *competent historians who have devoted many years of study to the issues have not felt compelled to abandon their faith in the restored gospel.*"[31] For Bitton, a Latter-day Saint's testimony affirmed the truth of the "restored gospel," not any particular account of the church's past.

As was already evident from the response to *The Story of the Latter-day Saints*, however, some church leaders deeply feared exactly the sort of history that Bitton and Arrington advocated. In 1981, Boyd Packer addressed an annual gathering of Latter-day Saint educators (primarily teachers at LDS seminaries and institutes, which provide religious education for Mormon high school and college students) at Brigham Young University, warning them against an excessively academic approach to their church's past. "This problem," Packer explained, "has affected some of those who have taught and have written about the history of the Church." Few of the LDS historians trained at secular institutions would have objected to Packer's insistence that an objective history of the church was impossible "without consideration of the spiritual powers that attend this work." However, Packer also warned about the inclusion of information "whether it is worthy or faith promoting or not." "Some things that are true," he warned, "are not very useful." In particular, he suggested that a focus on the human frailties of past church presidents threatened the testimonies of believing students. Faithful historians, he suggested, should focus on demonstrating the prophetic mantle of past presidents, not their humanity. In short, historians who proceed according to the standards and expectations of their discipline "destroy faith."[32] Richards in 1955, Benson in 1976, and Packer in 1981 had expressed similar concerns. The humanization of Mormon prophets and the contextualization of church history threatened faith, and believing historians did not serve the church by publishing all that they knew.

Despite Kimball's approval of *The Story of the Latter-day Saints*, members of the Quorum of the Twelve maneuvered to chill what Dean May later called the

---

30. "An Interview with Leonard Arrington and Davis Bitton," *Sunstone*, July/August 1979, 38–41.

31. Davis Bitton, "I Don't Have a Testimony of the History of the Church," *FARMS Review* 16 (2004): 339, emphasis in original.

32. Boyd K. Packer, "'The Mantle Is Far, Far Greater Than the Intellect,'" *BYU Studies* 21 (1981): 259–278.

"Arrington Spring."[33] A newly appointed managing director of the Church Historical Department, G. Homer Durham, informed Arrington that he would carefully review all of the division's publications, talks, and proposed writing projects. Per Arrington, Durham reported that some of the Brethren had expressed "suspicion and displeasure" over the "opening of the archives." In response, Durham asked Arrington to omit the fact that documents came from the church's archives when citing them in publications. Scholars, whether members of the church or not, found their ability to conduct archival research greatly constrained. Also, Arrington's critics persuaded Deseret Book to cancel the planned sixteen-volume series on the church's history. Some volumes appeared under other auspices, such as Richard Bushman's *Joseph Smith and the Beginnings of Mormonism.*[34] Quietly, but significantly, Arrington found that he was no longer Church Historian. Arrington's assistants either left or found themselves relocated to the newly created Joseph Fielding Smith Institute for Church History at Brigham Young University. It was clear that at least some high-ranking church officials did not want church employees writing accounts of the Latter-day Saint past according to the standards of academia, at least not under the direct auspices of the church. The Latter-day Saints placed a deep value on their history, but they disagreed about what to do with it.

The intra-Mormon conflicts over Latter-day Saint history resembled the responses of Protestant fundamentalists and evangelicals (as most fundamentalists came to call themselves in the years after 1945) to historical-critical scholarship on the Bible, scholarship that largely originated in Germany and then reached North America in the eighteenth and nineteenth centuries. American Protestants inherited from the sixteenth-century reformers a firm belief in *sola scriptura*, in the Bible as the supreme guide on matters of doctrine and practice. Many Protestant Americans found new scholarly theories unsettling, especially those that disputed the traditional authorship of the Pentateuch, prophets, and gospels. Other critics suggested that ancient Israelites or later editors incorporated Mesopotamian accounts of creation or of a great flood. Still other scholars placed biblical writings in their cultural and literary contexts, for example by examining books such as Daniel and Revelation in the broader context of apocalyptic literature, Jewish and otherwise. Some biblical scholars evidenced great pleasure in debunking sacred texts, in bringing heavenly revelation down to earth, in treating the Bible just like any other book. Many Protestants, however, found even more cautious scholarship threatening simply because it contextualized scripture and humanized biblical authors. For

---

33. Dean L. May, *Utah: A People's History* (Salt Lake City: University of Utah Press, 1987), v.

34. Bushman, *Joseph Smith and the Beginnings of Mormonism.*

Protestant defenders of the Bible, the historical-critical method both offended their sense of the Bible as God's Word and threatened to undermine the faith of ordinary believers.

When first confronted with critical biblical scholarship, "orthodox" Protestant ministers and theologians in the United States sharply defended the historicity, accuracy, and reliability of the Bible. By marshaling their own empirical evidence to defend the Bible, however, they inadvertently made the Bible more vulnerable to further scholarly criticism. If the Bible's authority hinged on its historicity, accuracy, or originality, scholarly criticisms of scripture necessarily undermined that authority.[35] Moreover, because most conservative Protestants acknowledged no extrabiblical authority to shape their interpretations of scripture, conflicts over biblical criticism assumed critical importance. For many conservative Protestants, contests over biblical scholarship became a zero-sum game, in which divine inspiration and human agency competed with each other instead of finding a way to coexist.

In an essay 1894 titled "The Divine and Human in the Bible," Presbyterian theologian B. B. Warfield warned against seeing the divine and human aspects of scripture as "as factors in inspiration that strive against and exclude each other so that where one enters the other is pushed out." That line of reasoning, Warfield observed, leads to the false conclusion "that every discovery of a human trait in Scripture is a disproving of the divinity of Scripture." In other words, by fighting the Bible's critics on those critics' own turf, conservative Protestants—most of whom ignored Warfield's advice—ultimately subverted what they intended to defend.[36]

By the late 1800s and early 1900s, growing numbers of modernist Protestants accepted the findings of historical criticism, and in response their more conservative counterparts repeatedly sought to plug leaks in the biblical dike.[37] Numerous essays in the twelve-volume *The Fundamentals* (which led to the moniker "fundamentalists") sharply rejected the "higher criticism" of the Bible. For fundamentalists and their evangelical descendants

---

35. See Michael J. Lee, *The Erosion of Biblical Certainty: Battles over Authority and Interpretation in America* (New York: Palgrave Macmillan, 2013).

36. B. B. Warfield, "The Divine and Human in the Bible," in Mark A. Noll and David A. Livingstone, eds., *Evolution, Science, and Scripture: Selected Writings of B.B. Warfield* (Grand Rapids, MI: Baker, 2000), 51–58; Mark A. Noll, *Jesus Christ and the Life of the Mind* (Grand Rapids, MI: Wm. B. Eerdmans Publishing Co., 2011), 130–132.

37. On this conflict, see George M. Marsden, *Fundamentalism and American Culture: The Shaping of Twentieth-Century Evangelicalism, 1870–1925*, 2nd ed. (New York: Oxford University Press, 2006). On the development of Protestant modernism, see William R. Hutchison, *The Modernist Impulse in American Protestantism* (Cambridge, MA: Harvard University Press, 1976).

(many fundamentalists embraced anew the term "evangelical" after the Second World War), the matter was never settled, however. Some evangelical theologians carefully embraced certain conclusions of critical scholars and backed away from theories of biblical inerrancy, while other evangelical scholars held their ground. Denominations, churches, seminaries, and a host of other evangelical institutions regularly debated the nature of biblical authority, often producing infighting and schisms. Was the Bible inerrant, not only on matters of faith, but also in the realms of history and science? Or did the Bible express human limitations in its discussion of history and cosmology while still being an infallible guide to matters of faith? Tone and substance both mattered in intraevangelical debates. It was one thing to observe that Genesis apparently contains two accounts of creation. It was another matter to conclude that an editor had spliced together narratives from other Mesopotamian cultures that cast doubt on the historicity of Adam, the flood, or other events in either the primordial history of humanity or the history of ancient Israel.

Evangelicals largely abandoned older institutions such as Princeton Theological Seminary in favor of newly founded bastions of biblical orthodoxy such as Westminster Theological Seminary and Fuller Theological Seminary. However, as Christopher Hays explains, in the ensuing decades "the schools founded by proto-evangelicals came to produce first-rate students, who, in varying degrees, reappropriated the tools, the literature and the assumptions of the biblical academy."[38] By the early 1970s, for example, Fuller Seminary no longer required its faculty to affirm biblical "inerrancy," thereby creating space for a broader range of hermeneutical approaches to scripture but in the process alarming their more conservative counterparts.[39]

In 1976 Harold Lindsell, editor of the flagship evangelical *Christianity Today*, publicly called on conservative evangelicals to defend their churches and institutions from those who would abandon inerrancy. Just as Ezra Taft Benson warned that new approaches to history would undermine testimonies, so Lindsell argued in *The Battle for the Bible* that "a doctrine of an errant Scripture...will result in the loss of missionary outreach; it will quench missionary passion; it will lull congregations to sleep and undermine their belief in the full-orbed truth of the Bible; it will produce spiritual sloth and decay; and it will finally lead to apostasy." In particular, Lindsell worried that without

---

38. Christopher M. Hays, "Towards a Faithful Criticism," in Christopher M. Hays and Christopher B. Ansberry, eds., *Evangelical Faith and the Challenge of Historical Criticism* (Grand Rapids, MI: Baker Academic, 2013), 2.

39. See George Marsden, *Reforming Fundamentalism: Fuller Seminary and the New Evangelicalism* (Grand Rapids, MI: Wm. B. Eerdmans Publishing Co., 1987).

inerrancy evangelicals would not pass on a vibrant faith to their children. Evangelical churches and organizations would sink or swim based on their willingness to defend an inerrant Bible. "Whether it takes five or fifty years," he warned, "any denomination or parachurch group that forsakes inerrancy will end up shipwrecked."[40] Lindsell's book publicly revealed the deep fissues within evangelical ranks on the subject of biblical authority.

Many evangelicals sided with Lindsell. In 1978, leading conservative evangelical defenders of biblical authority gathered together in Chicago and signed a statement defending the concept of inerrancy. "Being wholly and verbally God-given," the resulting statement proclaimed, "Scripture is without error or fault in all its teaching, no less in what it states about God's acts in creation, about the events of world history, and about its own literary origins under God, than in its witness to God's saving grace in individual lives." The evangelical signers rejected the "legitimacy of any treatment of the text or quest for sources lying behind it that leads to relativizing, dehistoricizing, or discounting its teaching, or rejecting its claims to authorship."[41] Underneath the slogan of inerrancy, many fundamentalists recognized a host of possible contradictions or errors in the Bible, attributed most often to errors of transmission or translation, or to lacunae in human understanding. Still, even with such caveats, the 1978 Chicago Statement and ongoing intraevangelical conflicts illustrated that conservative Protestants were no closer to settling the question of biblical authority, even for themselves. Indeed, *sola scriptura* was anything but a stable source of doctrine or practice.

Akin to the signers of the Chicago Statement, Latter-day Saints such as Benson and Packer similarly tended to view the intersection of history and faith as a zero-sum game. If church members or prospective converts learned that Joseph Smith resembled other "primitivists" bent on restoring New Testament Christianity, that the Word of Wisdom resembled other contemporary nutrition movements, or that the early Mormon "law of consecration" had counterparts in communitarian movements, then—Benson and Packer feared—they might find it more difficult to understand the Latter-day Saint restoration as divine (and as a definitive break with forms of Christian apostasy). A fuller understanding of Joseph Smith's humanity might exclude or at least minimize the divinity of his prophetic call. And perhaps more simply, that humanity might conflict with contemporary church members' understanding of prophethood. Tone also mattered a great deal in the context of

---

40. Harold Lindsell, *The Battle for the Bible* (Grand Rapids, MI: Zondervan, 1976), 25, 142.

41. In Barry Hankins, ed., *Fundamentalism and Evangelicalism: A Documentary Reader* (New York: New York University Press, 2008), 24.

Mormon history. Did scholars treat past leaders with reverence, or did they revel in their foibles? Scholars with similar substantive conclusions could sometimes spark very different responses from church leaders.

By the 1970s, intraevangelical debates on the Bible largely recycled and repeated past conflicts. The Latter-day Saints, by contrast, were latecomers to what Protestant church historian Martin E. Marty termed "the challenge of modern historical consciousness and criticism." Christians of all sorts, Marty explained, have found their faith tested once they allowed that biblical events (and presumably texts) have been "shaped by historical forces." Catholic theologians had to grapple with the fact that Catholic teachings and dogma were similarly shaped through the complexities of history rather than simply being delivered in final form by God to ecclesiarchs. Although the issue of evolution and the possible existence of "pre-Adamites" had produced some intra-Mormon conflict in the early twentieth century, the Latter-day Saints by and large sidestepped the Protestant firestorms over higher criticism. Among the Latter-day Saints, the crisis of historical consciousness only arose in earnest during the 1970s, when church members themselves began to publish fuller and more complex accounts of Mormon history. Marty suggested that in the case of Latter-day Saint history, only the First Vision and Book of Mormon truly mattered in the final analysis: "If the beginning of the promenade of Mormon history, the First Vision and the Book of Mormon, can survive the crisis, then the rest of the promenade follows that nothing that happens in it can really detract from the miracle of the whole." Debates over the authenticity of the First Vision and the Book of Mormon matter a great deal, but Marty sidestepped the fact that a host of other issues troubled both church leaders and church members. Thus, the crisis of historical consciousness would prove no less troubling to Latter-day Saints than it had to other Christian groups. Indeed, in some ways, the issue of history for Latter-day Saints was of far more widespread concern for Mormons than biblical criticism was to evangelicals. The finer points of biblical criticism, after all, are more arcane than are questions about Joseph Smith's polygamy or the Mountain Meadows Massacre.[42]

By the mid-1980s, the vision articulated by Leonard Arrington and others had foundered and polemical conflict over the Mormon past reached unprecedented intensity. Protestant opponents of the church, including former church members Jerald and Sandra Tanner as well as Presbyterian minister

---

42. Martin E. Marty, "Two Integrities: An Address to the Crisis of Mormon Historiography," *Journal of Mormon History* 10 (1983): 3–19. On Mormon responses to Darwinian evolution, see Richard Sherlock, "A Turbulent Spectrum: Mormon Reactions to the Darwinist Legacy," *Journal of Mormon History* 5 (1978): 33–59.

Wesley Walters, published articles and books designed to undermine the LDS Church's appeal. Beginning in the 1960s, the Tanners had released materials otherwise inaccessible to most church members, such as the various accounts of Joseph Smith's First Vision and the manuscripts related to the Book of Abraham, a work of scripture published by Joseph Smith in 1842. Sandra Tanner explained that Latter-day Saints only continue to believe because their leaders shield them from historical truth. "Mormon leaders," she stated, "are deliberately keeping from [LDS missionaries] the true history of their religion because they know [Mormons] will have a hard time believing it's from God if [they] saw how it really was all put together."[43] Like Packer and Benson, the Tanners tended to see the Mormon past through the same zero-sum analysis, suggesting that the more individuals learned about the human foibles, weaknesses, and moral lapses of Joseph Smith and other church leaders, the less likely they would be to retain their faith in the church.

It was a 1985 double murder, however, that brought about an unprecedented national focus on the church's approach to its past. In early 1984, Mark Hofmann, a dealer in historical documents, produced a letter purportedly from Smith's early supporter and scribe Martin Harris to then-newspaper editor W. W. Phelps. In the letter, Harris stated that a creature like a salamander—rather than an angel named Moroni—had told Joseph Smith about the golden plates and had then assumed human form. The church acquired the letter through a businessman who purchased it from Hofmann. In 1985, faced with mounting debts and the collapse of his scheme, Hofmann murdered two individuals. Although it quickly became clear that Hofmann's alleged discoveries were artful forgeries, journalists nevertheless framed the story as evidence of a church determined to suppress its embarrassing history.[44]

By the mid-1980s, the church had further restricted access to its archives and subjected the publications and talks of Latter-day Saint intellectuals to high levels of scrutiny. Some scholars reported that archives officials interviewed prospective researchers and forced them to sign an agreement submitting quotes in their context to the church's Copyrights and Permissions Office.[45] Church leaders spoke with some frequency about the dangers of intellectual criticism and warned church members against supporting

---

43. Sandra Tanner quoted in J. B. Haws, *The Mormon Image in the American Mind: Fifty Years of Public Perception* (New York: Oxford University Press, 2014), 120.

44. See Richard E. Turley Jr., *Victims: The LDS Church and the Mark Hofmann Case* (Urbana: University of Illinois Press, 1992). See also Haws, *The Mormon Image in the American Mind*, 137–153.

45. "Church Archives Announces New Access Policies," *Sunstone*, August 1986, 43.

publications such as *Sunstone* and *Dialogue*. According to Lavina Anderson, several scholars found themselves banned from speaking to church audiences and even lost their temple recommends, required for admission to Latter-day Saint temples. For example, in 1985 church headquarters instructed local bishoprics not to extend invitations to Linda King Newell and Valeen Tippetts Avery, who had coauthored an award-winning biography of Emma Hale Smith, Joseph Smith's first wife.[46] A few scholars found themselves quickly moving toward an open clash with church authorities. D. Michael Quinn, a former employee of the Church History Department and then member of the Brigham Young University History Department, published works in 1985 and 1987 detailing—respectively—the church authorization of plural marriages after the 1890 Manifesto and the connections between early Mormonism and magic. According to Quinn, by the fall of 1986, the university had denied him research and travel funding. In early 1988, he resigned his professorship.[47]

The firestorm over the issue of intellectual criticism within the church crested with the September 1993 disciplining of six members, including Michael Quinn. History was not the only source of contention. Indeed, feminism and the Mormon concept of a Mother in Heaven were points of conflict in several cases. Since the late 1970s, however, conflicts over church history had roiled the church, from the reorganization of the Church History Department to the Hofmann case to the publications of Quinn. The New Mormon History, at least as practiced by church members since the 1960s, appeared very much in jeopardy. This impulse toward academic work according to professional standards had produced a raft of high-quality publications and had brought to light countless documents and episodes in the LDS past. Indeed, a few Mormon historians wrote works that satisfied professional standards without attracting noteworthy criticism from church authorities. Richard Bushman's *Joseph Smith and the Beginnings of Mormonism* discussed the Smith family's deep involvement in folk magic and presented it as a prologue of sorts to Joseph Smith's subsequent emergence as a seer and translator. In his telling, Smith eventually left behind his youthful treasure quests when an angel led him to an actual treasure of far greater worth. Whether the topic was Smith's visions or theological claims, Bushman thoroughly contextualized the Mormon prophet within his early nineteenth-century cultural

---

46. See Lavina Fielding Anderson, "The LDS Intellectual Community and Church Leadership: A Contemporary Chronology," *Dialogue* 26 (Spring 1993): 25.

47. D. Michael Quinn, "On Being a Mormon Historian (and Its Aftermath)," in George D. Smith, ed., *Faithful History: Essays on Writing Mormon History* (Salt Lake City: Signature Books, 1992), 92–94.

landscape.[48] At the same time, Bushman explicitly rejected the presuppositions that troubled Benson and Packer. Bushman, indeed, had once called upon Mormon historians to "replace our conventional, secular American presuppositions with more of the penetrating insights of our faith."[49] The positive reaction to *Joseph Smith and the Beginnings of Mormonism* within the academy and the church was a respite from intense conflicts over the Mormon past.

For both evangelicals and Mormons, the respective internecine conflicts over biblical authority and history waned somewhat by the end of the twentieth century. While most evangelicals retained at least a formal belief in the Bible as the supreme source for church teachings, many subtly appealed to emotion, experience, and sentimentality as grounds for knowledge and action.[50] The diffuse structure of evangelical networks and institutions, moreover, necessarily created space for a broad range of opinions. Evangelicals whose understanding of biblical authority shifted might find a home at another church, college or seminary, or parachurch organization. Unlike Latter-day Saints, they had many options.

Still, the Bible always lurked as a source of potential controversy for evangelicals. In 2008, for example, Westminster Theological Seminary suspended biblical scholar Peter Enns for his book *Inspiration and Incarnation* (2005), in which he analyzed similarities between Old Testament and other ancient literatures and also placed the New Testament interpretation of the Hebrew scriptures in its cultural context.[51] If some evangelical organizations have found ways to leave behind past battles over inerrancy, the question of biblical authority remains unsettled. Moreover, during these decades evangelicals found themselves divided on host of matters, many of them clustered around matters of gender and sexuality, including the role of women within churches and families, the appropriate response to divorce, and their positions on homosexuality and same-sex marriage. These disputes were complex, but most evangelicals who embraced conservative positions on such matters understood themselves as defending biblical authority. Contemporary evangelical disagreements over biblical authority, however, are not quite as pervasive and contentious as they were when Lindsell published *The Battle for the Bible* four decades ago.

---

48. Bushman, *Joseph Smith and the Beginnings of Mormonism*.

49. Richard L. Bushman, "Faithful History," *Dialogue* 4 (Winter 1969): 16.

50. See Todd R. Brenneman, *Homespun Gospel: The Triumph of Sentimentality in Contemporary American Evangelicalism* (New York: Oxford University Press, 2014).

51. Sarah Pulliam, "Westminster Theological Suspension," *Christianity Today*, April 1, 2008, www.christianitytoday.com/ct/2008/aprilweb-only/114-24.0.html.

Likewise, the world of Mormon history fifteen years into the twenty-first century is almost unrecognizable from that of the mid-1980s. The Joseph Smith Papers project, launched in 2001, eventually brought many professional researchers back to the Church History Department. In 2008 the church published the first of roughly two dozen volumes of Smith's journals, letters, church minutes, revelation books, sermon transcripts, and other documents. The project has described the Book of Mormon as the "most prominent among Joseph Smith's revelatory dictations" (a recognition that Smith did not "translate" the text in any conventional sense), discussed the fact that Smith was sealed to a number of already married women, and with great detail placed early Mormonism in its nineteenth-century American context.[52]

There were many other signs of change as well. In 2002, the Church History Department released reams of archival documents a large DVD set. Although some material was obscured by redactions, the documents, including most of Brigham Young's outgoing correspondence and a large set of church minutes, brought to light much previously unknown information about the early Utah period of church history. In 2008 Oxford University Press released Ronald Walker, Richard Turley, and Glen Leonard's *Massacre at Mountain Meadows*, a comprehensive account of the massacre published under church auspices. The next year, a new Church History Library opened across from the north side of Temple Square, an imposing, state-of-the art edifice that symbolized the importance the church places on its history. Without fanfare, the church again began opening its archives more fully to a wide array of researchers (including this author).

Finally, the church began more forthrightly instructing its members that its past leaders made human mistakes and did not always live in accordance with either cultural standards of morality or church teachings. At the church's October 2013 general conference, Dieter Uchtdorf, a German-born Latter-day Saint apostle and member of his church's First Presidency, delivered an address that surprised and pleased many church members. To the assembled faithful, Uchtdorf acknowledged that some men and women have left the church or lost their faith because of "things that have been done or said in the past." Uchtdorf did not specify what those things were, and he was quick to note the broad sweep of church history consists of "an uninterrupted line of inspired, honorable, and divine events." Still, he stated, "there have times when members of leaders in the Church have simply made mistakes" and

---

52. Michael Hubbard MacKay, Gerrit J. Dirkmaat, Grant Underwood, Robert J. Woodford, and William G. Hartley, eds. *The Joseph Smith Papers, Documents Volume 1: July 1828–June 1831* (Salt Lake City: The Church Historian's Press, 2013), xxviii.

have done or said things "that were not in harmony with our values, principles, or doctrine." Uchtdorf calmly insisted that despite human imperfections, "God will not allow His Church to drift from its appointed course or fail to fulfill its divine destiny." Uchtdorf's comments came in the context of a speech in which he urged church members to treat those who doubt or even leave the church with greater tenderness, and he gently encouraged those who have left to return to the fold.[53]

It is rather difficult to trace the precise reasons for this deténte between church leaders and an examination of the church's past according to professional, academic standards. One explanation simply has to do with individual leaders. During the time of conflict over Arrington's leadership of the History Division, Boyd Packer and Ezra Taft Benson vigorously opposed the writing of church history according to secular, professional standards. More recently, Richard Turley, Gordon B. Hinckley (church president from 1995 until his 2008 death), and Marlin K. Jensen (Church Historian and Recorder from 2005 until 2012) have reoriented the church's own approach to its past. Other reasons are more diffuse. In recent years, church leaders, including Jensen, have spoken openly about the difficulties posed when church members encounter troubling material about past church leaders, such as Joseph Smith's practice of polygamy, on the Internet. Jensen once observed that his own daughter asked him why he had not informed her of Joseph Smith's polygamy. "Everything's out there for them to consume if they want to Google it," Jensen commented of younger members.[54] Also, since the events of the 1980s and early 1990s, journalists and scholars frequently criticized church leaders as fearing an open examination of the Mormon past. The recent changes certainly suggest church leaders' desire to alter that narrative.

Still, neither evangelicals nor Mormons have left behind their crises of historical consciousness. Evangelicals reared on Bible stories often must reckon as adults with questions of authenticity and historicity. Latter-day Saints, regardless of when they learn of topics such as Joseph Smith's polygamy, compare their founding prophet's behavior with their own understanding of marriage and sexuality. Questions of faith and history remain relevant and controversial for Mormons. In 2013, Swedish Latter-day Saint Hans Mattsson, a former "area authority" with responsibility for the church throughout Europe, publicly aired his doubts about elements of LDS history. Mattsson's

---

53. Deiter F. Uchtdorf, "Come, Join with Us," *Ensign*, November 2013, 21–24.

54. Marlin K. Jensen quoted in Peter Henderson and Kristina Cooke, "Special Report: Mormonism Besieged by the Modern Age," *Reuters*, January 31, 2013, www.reuters.com/article/2012/01/31/us-mormonchurch-idUSTRE80T1CM20120131.

struggles began when members shared information they had encountered on the Internet. Did Joseph Smith really marry additional wives? Did he do so over the opposition of his first wife, Emma Hale? Mattsson found Joseph Smith's practice of polygamy "kind of shocking." He also found troubling information about the Book of Mormon's translation, the Book of Abraham, and the past restrictions on church members of African descent.[55] Mattsson was not alone. Latter-day Saint scholar Terryl Givens portrayed the loss of young members in particular to such doubts an "epidemic."[56] "Maybe since Kirtland [Ohio]," then-Church Historian Marlin Jensen told a class of students in Utah, "we've never had a period of—I'll call it apostasy, like we're having now."[57] Jensen clarified elsewhere that to "say we are experiencing some Titanic-like wave of apostasy is inaccurate."[58]

The ongoing evangelical collision with biblical scholarship suggests that the LDS Church will not find a simple solution or conclusion to questions about its own history. Archives have been more open or more closed at various points. The church has planned, scuttled, and resuscitated historical publications. Various high-ranking church leaders have articulated different approaches to church history. Even so, the "crisis of historical consciousness" identified by Martin Marty is an ongoing. For the foreseeable future, it will remain so, as new generations of Latter-day Saints encounter issues such as Joseph Smith's polygamy or their past leaders' statements on race, women, and homosexuals. The LDS Church does not intend to follow the example of the Community of Christ in reducing its emphasis on the historical and miraculous events of its founding years. Protestants who grant the Bible unrivaled authority condemn themselves, for better and worse, to endless debates about its meaning and reliability. For Latter-day Saints, matters of faith and prophetic authority remain inextricably bound to nineteenth-century historical events, thus always creating space for members and critics alike to question the meaning of those events and the character of those leaders.

---

55. Laurie Goodstein, "Some Mormons Search the Web and Find Doubt," *New York Times*, July 20, 2013.

56. Terryl Givens quoted in Peggy Fletcher Stack, "Mormons Tackling Tough Questions in Their History," *Salt Lake Tribune*, February 3, 2012, www.sltrib.com/sltrib/news/53408134-78/church-lds-mormon-faith.html.csp.

57. Henderson and Cooke, "Special Report: Mormonism Besieged by the Modern Age."

58. Stack, "Mormons Tackling Tough Questions in Their History."

Index